FASCISM

An Anthology

FASCISM
An Anthology

EDITED BY

NATHANAEL GREENE
Wesleyan University

Harlan Davidson Inc.
Arlington Heights, Illinois 60004

ISBN: 0-88295-736-8
(Formerly 0-690-32017-5)

Library of Congress Card Number: 67-30582

PRINTED IN THE UNITED STATES OF AMERICA

81 82 83 84 85CB15 14 13 12 11

Preface

"Fascism," wrote the socialist Angelo Tasca, "is like a completely successful operation: the patient dies and all his illusions are removed." Time has neither softened the severity of his verdict nor blurred our equation of fascism with unprincipled use of power and with the most atrocious acts committed by modern man. The term itself has entered freely into our everyday vocabulary, frequently to be employed indiscriminately in describing dictators, military régimes, even conservatives and the police, anyone, in fact, who incurs the displeasure of the hurler of the epithet. Is it possible to offer a comprehensive description of what it is we mean by "fascism?" We are concerned in this volume with fascism in European history, and the term is employed here to denote fundamentally similar movements and doctrines in Italy, Germany, France, and Spain between the two world wars. Doubtless this fascism was woven from qualities of malice by men of few, if any, scruples. Yet many of its creators and followers were men of generous idealism and lofty aspiration for whom violence was limited to displays of verbal flamboyance. But, once unleashed to topple an allegedly decadent society, violence came to acquire a life and a rationale of its own.

It would be an error to deny Stanley Payne's affirmation that European fascist movements were "not cut of the whole cloth," but it seems self-evident that they were more alike than different, ideological kin springing from similar sources and bearing similar messages to the world. Indeed, these movements were multi-faceted and contained the paradoxes which were the stuff of fascism: order and disorder, appeal to the masses and a conscious élitism, action and stagnation, heroism and corruption, revolution and preservation of the existing social order, purposefulness and ambiguity. In short, fascism was a volatile blend of illusion and reality, the twin qualities being helplessly intertwined, largely incapable either of separation or of identification. These fascist movements shared a common reservoir of frustrations and hatreds, not the least of which was scorn for the values of their civilization. All of them were easily recognizable as products of a world in crisis,—itself the product of war and its legacy

—of political upheaval, and of social and economic dislocation. Crisis was the handmaiden of fascism, without which fascism could not have developed and without the deliberate perpetuation of which it could not have lived—although it was also firmly rooted in fertile historical subsoil.

Not all fascist movements captured state power, and for some the taste for power demanded jettisoning of ideological baggage, while for another, as we know too well, the acquisition of power signaled the eventual fulfillment of the doctrines of its principal creator. European fascism, then, was born of conflict and may have perished inevitably in the new conflict that it sought to create; but it also may have been, as Mussolini boasted, the "characteristic doctrine" of its era.

The nature of these fascist movements and their ideology comprise the subject of the substantial excerpts assembled in this volume. The readings have been chosen with no concern for obvious clashes of opinion, and are intended to serve as introductions to significant interpretative studies of the fascist phenomenon. Emphasis falls mainly upon the substance and meaning of fascist doctrines and upon the roles played by key personalities in the several movements, although an understanding of the conditions that fostered the emergence of fascism in each nation considered should follow easily from the readings. Attention has been given to fascism's exercise of power in Italy and Germany, but not in France or Spain simply because the Vichy and Franco régimes bore only slight resemblance to earlier fascist movements in those countries. Some will protest that the excerpts are too brief: so much the better, since one purpose is to stimulate further investigation. Others will protest that certain works do not figure among the selections: the brief bibliography at the conclusion may be partial compensation for such omissions.

N. G.

Middletown, Conn.

Contents

FASCISM
An Anthology

I. Origins and Definitions of Fascism

The following readings by George L. Mosse and Ernst Nolte deal essentially with the single most perplexing challenge to the historian of modern Europe: why, after a century that had advertised progress and emancipation as its dominant themes, did basically similar movements—avowedly hostile to their world and fearful of the future—arise throughout Europe at almost precisely the same historical moment? For too long, argue both authors, scholarship has been inclined to treat each movement within its national framework and has concentrated excessively upon fascism's most wicked manifestation, Nazism. By avoiding a concept of fascism and by pointing up obvious differences among the several movements rather than searching for their uniformities, it may have escaped us that fascism was not a historical fluke or simply the creation of Mussolini or Hitler, but was the embodiment of the dominant motives of the interwar years. War, revolution, revulsion from modernity, thirst for action, dynamism, participation in collective adventure—these, and many more, were the raw materials of fascism; their presence was felt and exploited everywhere in Europe. Was fascism then primarily an irrational outburst, an exaggerated response to the force of historical change, or was its lame revolution an expression of a desire for reaction with safety? Both authors are wary of categorical judgments, but are persuaded that

1

fascism was grounded as much in reality as in fantasy and fear. Both seek, in slightly differing ways, to account for fascism's explosive appearance and to define its complex nature.

George L. Mosse, professor of history at the University of Wisconsin, is author of several studies in European history and is co-editor of *The Journal of Contemporary History,* from which this article is reprinted. Professor Mosse's recent inquiry into the intellectual antecedents of Nazism, *The Crisis of German Ideology,* has demonstrated the continuing appeal of *volkish* thought from Bismarck's empire through the Weimar Republic. Saturated with contempt for modernity by exposure to *volkish* writings and by membership in organizations heavily impregnated with *volkish* ideas, a significant segment of German society, argues Mosse, was totally unprepared for an experiment in liberal democracy but quite ready to accept the Hitlerian version of the *volkish* message. The article that follows expands upon several of the themes of that book and shows that the *volkish* watchwords of "rootedness," "hierarchy," and "order" were to find their echoes in every fascist movement. Mosse views fascism as an assault upon modernity in all of its aspects, a battle engaged against the very promise of the twentieth century. Like Nolte, he stresses the crucial importance to the manufacture of fascism of the multi-crisis generated by war and revolution and by a climate of insecurity and fear. He also emphasizes that fascism was a movement and an ideology of youth, if only in the sense that its image of dynamism and action was deliberately geared to youthful impatience and imagination. He makes it clear that the success of the fascist leaders was due in large measure to the careful channeling of these longings into their own service.

Ernst Nolte is professor of European history at Marburg University in Germany. His challenging book *Three Faces of Fascism,* from which the following excerpt is drawn, attempts to establish the kinship of three movements—the Action Française, Italian fascism, and German National Socialism—and, by so doing, to demonstrate that fascism was hardly a "foreign element" in its time. We will have an opportunity to examine Nolte's inquiry into the nature of Nazism at another point in this volume. This excerpt parallels, complements, and extends beyond the concerns of Mosse's article. Nolte concurs with Mosse's interpretation of fascism as essentially a reaction against the modern world, but he identifies the modern world as the epoch since 1789, since the French Revolution began the unfolding of a universal "emancipatory process." Nolte diagnoses the fragility of the liberal synthesis after World War I and notes the disintegrating impact of the war upon traditional structures of belief, but he considers the Bolshevik Revolution in 1917 to have been a decisive factor in the creation of fascism—"without Marxism there is no fascism." In his search for "a suitable criterion for the concept of fascism," Nolte has found that antiparliamentarism, or anti-semitism, or the systematic adulation of violence, will not do. Marxism and Bolshevik success, he argues, by apparently representing the ultimate threat to anti-emancipatory elements, led to the emergence of radical resistance in the form of fascism. But there was a double paradox in this fascism. The revolution against which it marshaled its troops could not possibly succeed, and, while fascism adopted an ideological stance "radically opposed and yet related" to that of its enemy, it eagerly emulated many of the enemy's methods. Nolte concerns himself here primarily with the ideology of fascism, and, as readers will discover, he writes to achieve understanding rather than to offer description.

1. The Genesis of Fascism

GEORGE L. MOSSE

In our century two revolutionary movements have made their mark upon Europe: that originally springing from Marxism, and fascist revolution. The various Marxisms have occupied historians and political scientists for many decades, but fascism has been a neglected movement. The reason for this seems plain: the war and the pre-eminent position of Germany within this revolution have obscured its European-wide importance. . . . For by the 1930s there was no nation without a native fascist party, and by 1936 a fascist Europe seemed within the realms of possibility—this even before Germany came to exercise

Source: *The Journal of Contemporary History,* No. 1, *International Fascism, 1920–1945,* pp. 14–65. Copyright © 1966 The Institute for Advanced Studies in Contemporary History, with permission of Harper and Row, Publishers.

its dominance over the movement. To be sure, Italy provided an important model and even tried (if unsuccessfully) to form a fascist international, but the national fascist parties had their own élan and their own problems to deal with. Yet if we want to get closer to the essence of the fascist revolution we must analyse it on a European–wide scale, taking into account important variations, but first trying to establish what these movements had in common. Fascism lacked a common founder, but all over Europe it sprang out of a common set of problems and proposed a common solution to them.

Fascism (although of course the word was not used at the time) originated in the attack on positivism and liberalism at the end of the nineteenth century. This was a general European phenomenon, and examples readily spring to mind. In Italy, for example, D'Annunzio praised man's instincts: 'never had the world been so ferocious'.

The writings of these men reflect the same basic paradox of industrial society: man seems on the one hand robbed of his individuality but on the other it is precisely this individuality which he wants to assert once more. The phenomena of mass man were accompanied by a feeling that the bourgeois age had culminated in conformity while those personal relationships upon which bourgeois morality and security were built had dissolved into nothingness. The tone among many intellectuals and among the young was one of revolt, of a desire to break out of the fetters of a system which had led to such an impasse. Much has been written about the aspect of this revolt which found its clearest reflection in expressionism; it is not often realized that fascism had its origins in the same spirit of rebellion.

Indeed, the idea of both fascism and expressionism share the urge to recapture the 'whole man' who seemed atomized and alienated by society, and both attempt to reassert individuality by looking inwards, towards instinct or the soul, rather than outwards to a solution in those positivist, pragmatic terms which bourgeois society prized. There is nothing surprising in the fact that fascism felt an affinity with expressionist art and literature, and that even a not wholly unimportant segment of national–socialism tried to embrace them.

The key to fascism is not only the revolt but also its taming. For the problem before the fascist leaders was how to make this attitude towards society effective, and to counter the chaos which it might produce. How could the 'constant feeding of one's own exaltation' which D'Annunzio advocated, or the instinctualism of Nietzsche be captured and redirected into politically effective channels? That fascism could find an answer to this dilemma, play the cowboy to this widespread *fin de siècle* mood, explains much of its later success.

Both George Sorel and Gustave Le Bon had suggested answers, for they had shown concern for precisely this problem in the 1890s. A political movement must be based upon the instincts of men and these instincts harnessed to a dedicated leadership. Sorel's myth was the overt rationalization of the deepest feeling of the group. For Le Bon politics had to be based upon the fact of mass man and his irrationality. These two Frenchmen accepted as 'given' the view of human nature which the revolt of the *fin de siècle* had posited and proceeded from there. Fascism shared the ground Sorel and Le Bon had prepared not only by accepting their view of human nature, but also by following out the content they gave to it and the prescription they made for it. Gustave Le Bon believed in the conservatism of crowds clinging tenaciously to traditional ideas. The appeal must be made to this irrational conservatism and it must be combined with the 'magic' influence of mass suggestion through a leader. In this way mass man can be harnessed to a political mass movement, his tendency towards chaos can be curbed, and he can be redirected into positive action.

Le Bon describes admirably how to tame the revolt. The conservatism of crowds was reborn in fascism itself as the instinct for national traditions and for the restoration of personal bonds, like the family, which seemed fragmented in modern society. This conservatism was closely connected with the longing for an end to alienation, for belonging to a definite group. But the group had to be a traditional one, and it had to represent the restoration of the traditional morality. Hitler, for example, believed mass movements necessary because they enabled man to step out of his workshop, where he feels small, and to be surrounded by 'thousands and thousands of people with like convictions'. Alienation was to be exorcized, but on the basis of accepting a view of man as both irrational and conservative. Similarly in Italy an historically centred nationalism was to provide the 'national consensus'.

But the taming was always combined with activism, and this kind of conservatism inevitably went hand in hand with revolution. Both Hitler and Mussolini disliked drawing up party programmes, for this smacked of 'dogmatism'. Fascism stressed 'movement'—Hitler called his party a 'Bewegung', and Mussolini for a time favoured Marinetti's futurism as an artistic and literary form which stressed both movement and struggle. All European fascisms gave the impression that the movement was open-ended, a continuous Nietzschean ecstasy. But in reality definite limits were provided to this activism by the emphasis upon nationalism, racism, and the longing for a restoration of traditional morality. The only variety of fascism of which this is not wholly true we find in France. There a man like Drieu La Rochelle exalted the 'provisional', the idea that all existing reality can be destroyed in one moment. But elsewhere that reality was 'eternal', and the activism was directed into destroying the existing order so that the eternal verity of *Volk* or nation could triumph, and with it the restoration of traditional morality.

The impact of the first world war shows this rhythm of fascism, just as it gave the movement a mass base. The *élan* of the battlefield was transformed into activism at home. The *fasci,* the German storm troopers, and the Iron Guard in Rumania all regarded their post-war world as an enemy which as shock troops they must destroy. Indeed, the leaders of these formations were in large part former front-line officers: Roehm, the head of the SA; Codreanu, founder of the Iron Guard; De Bono in Italy and Szalasi in Hungary—to give only a few examples. But this activism was tamed by the 'magic' of the leadership of which Le Bon had written so much earlier. Among the returned veterans it was tamed all the more easily, for they sought comradeship and leadership with some desperation. Not only because of the war experience, but also because of their sense of isolation within a nation which had not lived up to their expectations.

The 'cult element' was central to the taming process; it focused attention upon the eternal verities which must never be forgotten. The setting was a vital part: the balcony of the Palazzo Venezia, the Casa Rossa, the window of Hitler's new Chancellery. Activism there must be, enthusiasm is essential, but it must focus upon the leader who will direct it into the proper 'eternal' channels.

The liturgical element must be mentioned here, for the 'eternal verities' were purveyed and reinforced through the endless repetition of slogans, choruses, and symbols. These are the techniques which went into the taming of the revolution and which made fascism, even that which leaned on a Christian tradition, a new religion with rites long familiar in traditional religious observance. Fascist mass meetings seemed something new, but in reality contained predominantly traditional elements in technique as well as in the ideology.

To be sure, this taming did not always work. The youthful enthusiasm which presided at the beginning of the movement was apt to be disappointed with its course. Italy, where fascism lasted longest, provides the best example, for the danger point came with the second

fascist generation. There the young men of the 'class of 35' wanted
to return to the beginnings of the movement, to its activism and its
war on alienation—in short, to construct the fascist utopia. By 1936
such youths had formed a resistance movement within Italian fascism
which stressed that 'open-endedness' the revolution had seemed to
promise: to go to 'the limits of fascism where all possibilities are
open'. They would have felt at home in the French fascism of Drieu
La Rochelle and Robert Brasillach, but they were not pleased with the
fascism in power. We can discern similar signs as Nazism developed,
but here the SS managed to capture the activist spirit. Had it not been
for the war, Hitler might well have had difficulty with the SS, which
prized ideology less than power of the will as expressed in naked and
brutal action. But then fascism never had a chance to grow old, except
in Italy: given the ingredients which went into the revolution, old age
might have presented the movement with a severe crisis.

Fascism was a movement of youth, not only in the sense that it covered a short span of time, but also in its membership. The revolt of the
fin de siècle had been a revolt of the young against society, but also
against parents and school. They longed for a new sense of community, not for a 'chaos of the soul'. They were of bourgeois background,
and their dominant concern for several generations had been with national unity and not with social and economic change—something for
which they felt little need. Thus they were quite prepared to have their
urge to revolt directed into national channels, on behalf of a community which seemed to them one of the 'soul' and not an artificial creation. Such were the young who streamed not only into the German
youth movement, but also into the *fasci* and the SA, and made up the
cadres of the Iron Guard as well as the Belgian Rexists. Returned from
the war, they wanted to prolong the camaraderie they had experienced
in the trenches. Fascism offered it to them. It is well to note in this
connection that fascists were a new grouping, not yet bureaucratized,
and the supposed open-endedness made them more dynamic than the
other and rival political parties. The fascist leaders too were young:
Mussolini was 39 when he became Prime Minister, Hitler 44 on at-
taining the Chancellorship, Léon Degrelle was in his early thirties, and
Primo de Rivera as well as Codreanu were in their late twenties.

Youth symbolized vigour and action: ideology was joined to fact.
Fascist heroes and martyrs died at an early age in order to enter the
pantheon, and symbolic representations of youth expressed the ideal
type in artistic form. Hitler liked speed and was a motorcar and air-

plane enthusiast; Mussolini loved his motor bicycle, but when it came to directing their movements, both stressed the rootedness of the true community. Indeed, when they inveighed against the bourgeoisie they meant merely the older generation which could never understand a movement of youth.

The traditionalism of the fascist movement coincided with the most basic of bourgeois prejudices. When Hans Naumann spoke at the Nazi book-burning in 1933 he praised action; the more books burned the better. But he ended his speech by exalting the traditional bonds of family and *Volk*. Such a traditionalism was in the mind of Giuseppe Bottai when he called for a 'spiritual renewal', or when the leading Rexist, Jean Denis, held that without a moral revolution there can be no revolution at all. Some fascisms defined the moral revolution within the context of a traditional Christianity: this is true of the Belgian Rexist movement, for example, as well as of the Rumanian Iron Guard. The Nazis substituted racism for religion, but, once more, the morality was that shared with the rest of the bourgeoisie.

The revolution of youth, of a virile activism, ends up as a revolution of the 'spirit', asserting the primacy of ideology. It is the shared world-view which binds the Nation together and it is this which must be realized. The world-view restores the dignity of the individual because it unites him with those of his fellow men whose souls function in a similar manner, and they do so because all are part of the *Volk,* the race, or the nation.

This is an organic view of the world. It is supposed to take in the whole man and thus end his alienation. A fundamental redefinition of politics is involved in such a view of man and his place in the world. 'Politics', the Italian fascist Bottai wrote, 'is an attitude towards life itself' and this phrase can be repeated word for word from national-socialist literature. The leader of the Iron Guard, Horia Sima, summed it up: 'We must cease to separate the spiritual man from the political man. All history is a commentary upon the life of the spirit.' Such an emphasis meant that cultural expressions of the true community moved to the forefront as symbols of the new society. The national-socialist emphasis upon art and literature did not stand alone; for the leader of Flemish fascism, Joris van Severen, culture was the principle of unity and coordination. He added, typically enough, that culture presupposes a tradition.

The emphasis upon the organic, the creative national community, was supposed to overcome not only political but also class divisions. Georges Valois, the founder of French fascism, made the point when, before the first world war, he described the differences between his beliefs and Marxism. Marxism stressed one class, but he wanted to harness the energy even of the bourgeoisie to the new society. Valois' statement was prophetic, for fascism not only harnessed the energy of the bourgeois class but indeed became a movement whose spiritual revolution, the quest for organic, rooted man, coincided with bourgeois longings, at least in most of the West. It is significant that the classless society was always supposed to be a hierarchical one as well.

Fascism believed in hierarchy, not in terms of class but in terms of service to the *Volk* or nation as exemplified by the leader. In Western, but not German, fascism, the ideal of a corporate state was adopted; a state operating not through parliamentary representation (with its divisive political parties) but through workers and managers sitting together. However they did not sit together as equals; the manager was the 'leader'. Though there exists a considerable fascist literature about such a shaping of the state, in the last resort it was secondary. For if all members of *Volk* and nation shared a common myth, a common soul, then their participation in government need only be symbolized by the leader who has activated their shared human natures through his own activism, his 'heroic will'.

Fascism did stress the aim of social justice, but it would bring this about through the nation, the *Volk,* and not through the imposition of equality. The political and social hierarchies were to be open to all who served. This meant opposition to the old ruling circles, whether bourgeois or noble, and the substitution of new men for the old. Economic hierarchy was also preserved but within this framework a note of social justice was struck: Mussolini had his Charter of Labour and other fascisms drew up similar documents. Once again, fascism offered the best of all possible worlds: order and hierarchy would be maintained, private property would not be expropriated, but social justice would be done nevertheless. Once more this meant the primacy of ideology, ending spiritual alienation as a prerequisite for improving economic conditions.

Lest we brush this aside as inconsequential and lacking in appeal for the workers, it should be remembered that some fascisms did attempt, and successfully, to base themselves on the workers and peasants rather than the bourgeoisie. This was true in those countries where the working classes or the peasants had not been preempted by Marxist movements. Spain and Argentina provide examples in the West, and it is true of the Iron Guard as well as of the Hungarian fascist movement. To be sure, in those countries the bourgeoisie was not as strong as elsewhere, but another factor is of greater importance in explaining the fascist appeal to the labouring classes. Here, for the first time, was a movement which tried to bring these segments of society into political participation. In under-developed countries, the stress upon the end to alienation, the belief in the organic community, brought dividends—for the exclusion of workers and peasants from society had been so total that purely economic considerations could take second place.

Economics was indeed one of the least important fascist considerations. Jose Primo de Rivera, the founder of the Spanish Falange (which attracted much lower-class support), believed that 'people have never been moved by anyone save the poets', while the Belgian fascist Léon Degrelle called Hitler, Mussolini, and Codreanu 'poets of revolution'. The mystical side of the ideology dominated, the 'magic'; a fascist revolution must recognize the 'primacy of the spiritual'. Not control over the means of production was important, but the 'new man' about whom all fascists talked. He was man made whole once more, aware of his archetype and of those with whom he shared it, an activist in that he was not afraid to join in a revolution which would make society correspond to the longings of his soul. These longings were for unity with the group, for the recapturing of those virtues which were being submerged in the modern world. As Hitler stated clearly throughout his career: a man rooted in the world-view to which he belonged was not afraid to make it come true. Once he had joined he released his creative instincts, his power of will, in the common cause. Triumph meant that the whole nation would now share this creativity and renew itself. Economic well-being was subordinate to the stress upon art, literature, indeed the total cultural endeavour. Fascism was a revolution, but one which thought of itself in cultural, not economic terms.

In spite of the working-class support which it attracted in the more backward countries, in the West this was primarily a bourgeois revolution. The bourgeoisie could have a revolution as an outlet for their frustrations, and at the same time rest assured that order and property would be preserved. But for all that we must sharply distinguish fascism from the reactionary regimes in Europe. To be sure, the Rexists supported the Belgian monarchy and the Flemish fascists did likewise, but the differences are nevertheless far-reaching. Reaction rejected all revolution, opted for the *status quo,* and looked back to the *ancien régime* for its models. It stressed hierarchy, but this was the traditional hierarchy of entrenched privilege. It needs no demonstration that such regimes discouraged activism and mass movements. Moreover, they thought in strictly territorial terms and the 'shared soul' of all nationals or of the *Volk* would have had little meaning for them. For such regimes were not interested in bringing the disfranchised into politics or in ending man's alienation from his society. Their efforts were directed towards keeping men away from politics in order to maintain the monopoly of the traditional ruling class. Culture was not important here, and reactionary regimes gave wide latitude to all sorts of artistic expression so long as it did not encroach upon the monopoly of political power. The description of the Horthy regime by a modern historian is significant in this regard: * Horthy did not intend to allow opposition to challenge his own will, but he did not think it any part of the duty of government to pry into and regiment each detail of his subjects' conduct, much less their thoughts.

Just so the French fascists split from the Action Française because it was not revolutionary enough, as shown by its inaction in February 1934. Francisco Franco destroyed his fascist movement, the Falange, in favour of a Horthy-like dictatorship. Fascism and reaction had different visions, and the two must not be confused.

But what of the differences between the diverse fascisms from nation to nation? These are best exemplified in the problem of racism and anti-semitism. Neither of these was a necessary component of fascism, and certainly not of those sections of the movement which looked to Italy for a model. There, until 1936, racism did not exist. In Belgium and the Netherlands the fascist situation was, in this respect, similar to that of Italy. Léon Degrelle explicitly repudiated racism—hardly surprising in a multi-national nation. What, he asked, is the 'true race' —the Belgian, the Flamand, or the Walloon? From the Flemish side, the newspaper *De Daad* inveighed against race hatred and called on 'upright Jews' to repudiate the Marxists in their midst.

Even Dutch national-socialism under Anton Adrian Mussert at first did not write racism on its banner, and kept silent about the Jews, a silence that the German Nazis were later to find incomprehensible. The French fascist group around the newspaper *Je Suis Partout* did go in for anti-semitism, but even here the Germans were accused of exaggerating the racial issue, for one could have good relations with a foreign people like the Jews. It is not astonishing that the early Falange was free from such ideas, for there were hardly any Jews in Spain. Yet the actual existence of Jewish groups cannot be linked too closely

* Admiral Nicolas Horthy, regent of Hungary, 1920–1944.—Ed.

to fascist anti-semitism—for example both Belgium and the Netherlands had a relatively sizeable Jewish population. To be sure, in those countries a single-minded concentration on Marxism as the enemy tended to exclude all other considerations. But even this does not provide a satisfactory explanation, for the Marxist-Jewish equation could easily have been drawn there as it was in Germany.

This state of affairs did not last. By 1936 Mussolini had turned racist, and not merely because of German influence. Through racism he tried to reinvigorate his ageing fascism, to give a new cause to a youth becoming disillusioned with his revolution. The Italian reversal of attitude on this question seems to have affected the Falange as well, in spite of the absence of a native Jewish population. But here also a need coincided with this change of attitude—namely to make a more powerful appeal to the lower classes. As in Italy, so in Spain, anti-semitism helped to give the movement a greater and renewed dynamic. However, the Falange always rejected secular racism and based itself on the militant Catholic faith of Spain's crusading tradition. Similarly Oswald Mosley's fascists adopted anti-semitism when they found that this could give them a greater dynamic, a true feeling of struggle (and much free publicity) as they paraded through London's predominantly Jewish East End.

It was only in central and eastern Europe that racism was from the beginning an integral part of fascist ideology. Here were to be found the masses of Jewry, and still under quasi-ghetto conditions. They were a wholly distinct part of the population and vulnerable to attack. Moreover, in countries like Rumania or Hungary, the Jews had become *the* middle class, forming a distinct entity within the nation as that class which seemed to exploit the rest of the population through its commercial activities. No wonder the Iron Guard, in appealing to the nationalism of the peasants, became violently anti-semitic and even racist despite their Christian orientation—for they had begun as the legion of the 'Archangel Michael'.

After the First World War, the masses of east European Jewry began to emigrate into the neighboring countries, predominantly Germany and Austria. The account in *Mein Kampf* of how Hitler reacted to the sight of such strangers in Vienna, may well have been typical. However that may be, the facts of the situation in that part of Europe gave fascism an enemy who could be singled out as symbolizing the forces which must be overcome. Moreover, in eastern Europe the struggle for national liberation had become associated with romanticism and racism long before fascism made its appearance on the scene. Hitler captured this tradition, and built upon the 'Jewish question'. This led to a further differentiation of national-socialism from Western fascism. For Hitler the enemy was not a vague Marxism; it was physically embodied by the Jews. Building on the Central-European tradition of a racist-oriented nationalism, he could give to the enemy of his world-view a concrete and human shape. Thus mass terror, and eventually mass extermination, could be built into German fascism as it was not built into other western fascisms. Both in Germany, and during the short-lived dominance of the Iron Guard, mass terror and pogroms became the manifestation of an activism which identified a distinct human group as the enemy.

Mass terror cannot, therefore, be a part of the definition of fascism as a European-wide movement. Hannah Arendt's *Origins of Totalitarianism* is wrong in this regard, and forced to concentrate solely on the German example. There is a difference between fascist violence and street fighting on the one hand, and mass terror on the other, which is explained partly by the predominance of the racial and anti-Jewish direction of the movement in central and eastern Europe.

Mass terror and violence were restrained by another factor within several of the fascist movements. A certain moderation was forced upon the fascisms which identified the nation with the existing state as over against those which sought to liquidate all existing political institutions for the sake of the *Volk*. Thus in Italy Mussolini never attempted to depose the monarchy, and in England, Belgium, and Holland fascism proclaimed its loyalty to the symbol of the state. This was not the case in central and eastern Europe, and as a consequence the activism there could have greater play and a more consistent goal, since *all* existing political institutions were to be abolished and founded anew.

The fascist revolution cannot be understood if we see it merely in negative terms or judge it entirely by the dominance which national-socialism achieved over it by the late 1930s. For millions it did satisfy a deeply-felt need for activism combined with identification; it seemed to embody their vision of a classless society. The acceptance of the irrational seemed to give man roots within his inner self, while at the same time making him a member of a spontaneous not artificial community. Bourgeois youth streamed into its ranks because to them it seemed to offer a positive solution to the problems of industrial and urban society.

The negative side of fascism triumphed in the end. How can the activist dynamic be tamed once the 'eternal verities' have triumphed? Can the emphasis on liturgy overcome the emptiness of a programme fulfilled? The answer was war upon the internal enemy, the adoption of racism; but another general solution lay in the realm of foreign policy. The activism must now be tamed by being directed towards the outside world. Hitler dreamed of his new Europe, Mussolini of the *Mare Nostrum,* Péron of an Argentine-dominated South America, and in Eastern Europe there were enough irridentas to fulfil this function.

The 'new man' of whom fascism had dreamed went down to defeat, the victim of a dynamic which had, after all, not been satisfactorily curbed. The dream turned out to be a nightmare.

2. Fascism as Characteristic of an Era

ERNST NOLTE

The writer who at the end of the nineteenth century had proposed calling his own time the "era of imperialism" would not have found many to agree with him. Yet the term had been in use for centuries and, in spite of many different interpretations, possessed a relatively clearly defined meaning as to content and scope. This does not apply to the term "fascism," with the result that the phrase "era of fascism" does not find ready acceptance even today.

In 1920 the word "fascism" was known to very few people in Europe, and even Mussolini placed it between quotation marks as being a neologism. In 1923, however, the leftist parties throughout Germany staged an "antifascist day," thereby demonstrating as forcefully against the German, Hungarian, and Bulgarian "Fascists" as against Mussolini's victorious Blackshirts. A particular interpretation of the term was an essential before Hitler's seizure of power—that notorious description of the Social Democrats as Social Fascists, with which the Communist party of Germany repeated the fatal mistake of the Italian Communists in extended and crasser form. But at about the same time the leaders of certain groups of the extreme Right proposed

Source: *Three Faces of Fascism* (New York: Holt, Rinehart and Winston, Inc., 1966), pp. 3–21. Translated by Leila Vennewitz. Copyright © 1963 by R. Piper & Co. Verlag, Munich. Translation © 1965 by R. Piper & Co. Verlag, Munich. Reprinted by permission of Holt, Rinehart and Winston, Inc.

to call an "anti-fascist congress." A kind of compromise between the former very wide and the latter very narrow definition was represented, after the great about-face of the Comintern, by the commonly held concept of antifascism which made the policy of the Popular Fronts possible and under whose banners the great world coalition finally fought against Hitler and Mussolini, although this coalition had certainly not been formed under these banners. Today the concept of fascism is still one of direct political significance. The question of whether or not the Franco regime can be called fascist touches upon national interests, and a whole series of new developments has led to a notable revival of the term.

To inquire into the nature of the "era of fascism," then, means to add the specific problem of a still much-disputed term—the scholarly discussion of which has barely begun—to the overall difficulty which every periodization entails. On the other hand, it is obvious that the question of fascism cannot be separated from the question of its era, since no universally acknowledged and meaningful concept of the era between 1919 and 1945 exists. Even if the term "fascism" is taken strictly as a name, that is, to describe an isolated phenomenon, the question remains of the extent to which events in Italy were *not*—in spite of their incalculable world-wide effect—epochal. Whichever way we look at it, the common nature of the inquiry into fascism and the era is inescapable, and it is our task to define the concepts and review the facts.

However, the order in which the thematic material is placed is governed by one helpful limitation. Even though fascism existed after 1945 and has continued to exist since that time, and even though it is still capable of arousing bitter conflicts, it cannot be said to have real significance as far as the image of the era is concerned unless the term be stripped almost entirely of its traditional connotation. Thus the very subject of this study precludes any reference to events of the present day.

Hand in hand with this limitation goes a very tangible advantage; for contemporary history, in so many respects at a disadvantage when compared with its older sisters, has at its disposal a virtually ready-made division of eras, enabling us to trace the course of fascism deductively.

To use the term "era of the world wars" and imply the period from 1914 to 1945 would certainly not be valid for all time; but seen from the present day, the dates of August 1, 1914, and May 8, 1945, represent such profound cleavages in history that their epoch-making character has never been denied. What is disputed (aside from how to divide the subsections) is the context into which the epoch is to be placed and the point in time at which the cataclysmic caesura represented by the outbreak of war caused the new constellations to mature and acquire their first self-awareness. The most important of these concepts imply an answer to the question, whether the chronological and formal criterion might not be augmented by a more meaningful one. It should be enough to enumerate three of the best-known of these concepts:

1. The era of the world wars forms part of an age of revolutions and profound social changes, an age of which the most visible starting point was the French revolution.

2. The immediate roots of this era are to be found in the period of imperialism. It was during this time that all the conflicts developed which merely achieved their climax with the outbreak of war.

3. It was not until 1917 that World War I ceased to be simply a conflict of national states. With the entry of the United States into the war and the Bolshevik revolution, the constellation became a universal one: a general state of civil war and the future splitting of the world into two are already discernible in outline.

From each of these definitions and interpretations it is possible to derive the concept of a new type of political phenomenon.

None of the major political trends in Europe had evolved from a war: liberalism was the expression of the rise of the bourgeoisie; conservatism originally represented the reaction of the threatened aristocratic ruling class; socialism belonged to the proletariat born of the process of industrialization. None of these political doctrines wanted a world war or gave it its unqualified blessing after the outbreak. It was the war that made room for a political phenomenon, which was, so to speak, its very own child, a child which by innate law strove in turn to engender yet another war.

Since 1789, despite all reaction and many political defeats, the social revolution had spread inexorably throughout Europe. It led the bourgeoisie almost everywhere to participate in political power and raised it to a position from which it exerted a determining influence on society; it also provided the bourgeoisie with a new adversary in the shape of the socialistic proletariat. On all sides the newly emancipated class joined forces with the old ruling class against the approaching menace. Although this alliance was only a pragmatic and temporary one, small groups were beginning to transform it into one of principle even before 1914: a historically unique marriage between aristocratic conviction and plebeian reality. At first these groups remained small and unnoticed, but under certain conditions the principle on which they were founded could be of significance for the future since this principle corresponded to a basic characteristic of the social revolution itself: namely, that new auxiliary troops were continually joining the counterrevolution from the ranks of the emancipated, with the result that its face was changing as constantly as that of the revolution.

Before 1914 what was known as imperialism showed itself everywhere to be a compromise between the banal egoism of the national states and the more elusive requirements of the liberal and socialist traditions. Neither Cecil Rhodes nor Theodore Roosevelt nor Friedrich Naumann had any other object in view than to extend their respective "cultural ideas" of their time to the advantage and for the salvation of all peoples within their scope. But was it not implicit in the fundamental nature of this imperialism that it bestow unquestioning approval upon itself?

There is no doubt that the year 1917 represented a cleavage which cut deep into its own time and far into the future. But it is equally certain that the two great powers whose emergence was marked by this cleavage soon withdrew to their own native ground. When the American people opted against Wilson in 1920 it chose two decades of a new isolationism; the skepticism Lenin felt toward the "workers' aristocracy" of the West was soon confirmed. It turned out that the victory of bolshevism in Russia did not prevent its defeat on all the social battlefields of Europe, if it did not in fact actually cause it. Starting not later than 1923, the year of the failure of the last revolts in Germany, the Communist parties were operating everywhere more to the advantage of their enemies' cause than to their own. The Soviet Union became once more an unknown country on the periphery of the world, and Europe was once more the arena of world events. But was it likely that after that fearful interlude the participants should remain quite the same?

The war, the revolution, imperialism, the emergence of the Soviet Union and the United States, were not locally confined phenomena. Neither could a movement which came into being as an outcome of the war, a movement which fought revolution with revolutionary methods, which radicalized imperialism, and which saw in the Soviet Union (and in "Americanism" too, although with less emphasis) the greatest of all threats, be called a locally confined phenomenon, no matter how many differences might be attributable to it due to local conditions. This movement would have found its place in the

Europe of the postwar period even if Mussolini and Hitler had never lived. No term other than "fascism" has ever been seriously proposed for it. This word has the drawback of being simultaneously name and concept; it has the advantage of being without concrete content and of not, like German National Socialism, implying an unjustifiable claim. It is not the business of scholarly investigation to invent a new term just because the one commonly used cannot satisfy all requirements.

If, then, fascism can be defined as a new reality which did not exist before World War I, or only in rudimentary form, the obvious next step is to declare it to be the characteristic political trend of an era in which, owing to the withdrawal of the two recently emerged "flanking powers," Europe can be regarded once more as the focal point of the world. Out of four principal powers in this Europe two, as we know, became fascist within ten years, and after ten more years a continent which had become almost totally fascist (or so, at least, it seemed) had torn the two "flanking powers" from their isolation and challenged them to battle.

When a historian speaks of the "era of the Counter Reformation" he does not imply that the Counter Reformation was the dominant force in all areas of the then known world and that it met with no resistance, nor is he obliged to believe that it contained the seeds of the future. He does not even have to regard it as "necessary." In order to describe a period marked by powerful religious elements he simply uses the religious phenomenon which, being central to this trend, represented its most novel and thus most typical manifestation. In the same way, if we are to name an era marked by political conflicts after the most novel phenomenon in the center of events, we cannot do otherwise than call the era of the world wars an era of fascism.

This definition of the era is not new, and so should not be surprising. At various times it has been used (explicitly or implicitly) by leading representatives of the most disparate parties.

At the peak of his reputation and independence during the years 1930 to 1935, Mussolini often said that fascist ideas were the ideas of the age and that within a few years the whole of Europe would be fascist. On all sides he descried, it seemed to him, "fascist ferments of the political and spiritual renewal of the world"; he defined fascism as "organized, concentrated, authoritarian democracy on a national basis," and did not hesitate to claim for it anything in the world that demanded a strengthening of state power and intervention in the economy.

Mussolini's theory of the imminent fascistization of the world undoubtedly seems prejudiced and vague. Yet Thomas Mann's remarks in his essay *Dieser Friede* ("This Peace"), written at the height of the controversy following Munich from the opposite point of view, are very similar. He speaks of the "complete victory" of the "massive trends of the times which can be summarized in the word fascism" and traces them to "Europe's psychological preparedness for fascist infiltration in a political, moral, and intellectual respect." A little later he calls fascism "a disease of the times which is at home everywhere and from which no country is free." And even after Hitler's defeat he speaks (in his discourse on Nietzsche) of "the fascist era of the Occident in which we live and, despite the military victory over fascism, will long continue to live."

This is somewhat reminiscent of the theory expounded by Georg Lukács in his book, *Die Zerstörung der Vernunft*. Here he attempts to describe philosophical irrationalism as an essential component of and background to National Socialism, as the "reactionary answer to the great problems of the past hundred and fifty years." On Germany's path "from Schelling to Hitler" is to be found practically every name of any stature in German philosophy after Hegel's death: Schopenhauer and Nietzsche, Dilthey and Simmel, Scheler and Heidegger, Jaspers and Max Weber. However, in contrast to many attempts at analysis (particularly in Anglo-Saxon literature), Lukács sees the spiritual foundation of National Socialism as other than exclusively German: he regards the evolution in Germany's intellectual and political life merely as the most prominent manifestation of an international process within the capitalist world.

Of course there are many objections to Lukács' ideas, but this much is undoubtedly true: namely, that, beginning with the close of the nineteenth century, a change took place in the spiritual climate all over Europe, a change which was bound to further—although not create—a new political orientation disaffiliating itself from, and indeed directly opposing, the traditional political environment. With no immediate relevance to the political events of the day, the Nietzschean doctrine, which alone permitted the equation of socialism, liberalism, and traditional conservatism, was adopted and developed by a circle of fascistoid authors: the doctrine of the revolt of the slaves and of the impoverishment of life through Judeo-Christian resentment.

A no less convincing proof of the epochal nature of fascism is the fact that it exerted the strongest possible influence on its opponents. This is true not primarily in the narrow sense that it imposed its own traits directly upon them: in this we are often faced with a matter of parallel development (although they, too, are of great consequence in forming opinion). Fascism forced its adversaries to undertake the most painful self-reappraisal in generations, for it was in their attitude toward fascism that they committed their direst errors and misjudgments.

What was antifascism in its earliest form—the opposition of the Aventine after the murder of Matteotti*—if not the alliance of those who before the March on Rome had been unable to agree and had thereby suffered defeat? What did the slogan "antifascist united front" launched by the Communists after 1935 mean, if not the most revolutionary revision of their own tactics of the previous decade? What, on their highest level, was the content of the discussions and writings of German emigrants, if not the most critical self-examination of the German mentality ever to have taken place? And was not this self-examination at times compelled to admit that the very opposition to fascism often bore fascist traits?

The fascist traits which socialist emigrants from Germany could not help observing in Stalin's Russia were not isolated examples. What was left of the spirit of Lenin and Rosa Luxemburg when "militarism and nationalism, the cult of heroes and Byzantinism" occupied pride of place, and world revolution and the international workers' movement were hardly ever mentioned? How were the enormous differences in piecework wages, the reactionary family legislation, the invoking of the traditions of Peter the Great, to be reconciled with the aims of the October revolution? Did not the trials of Lenin's veteran campaigners mean the start of the worst persecution of Communists the world had ever seen, and was not anti-Semitism secretly fostered by the government? A study of the history of the Soviet Union would, of course, have shown that the beginnings of this trend had their roots deep in Lenin's times. Lenin himself had seen to it that criticism of the party was suppressed; he had replaced local spontaneity with a hierarchical superstructure and had ordered police measures against dissatisfied workers. Was Stalin really a usurper, or was he the executor of Lenin's testament? Was Stalinism only the hard husk pressing on the original kernel to protect it from mortal danger, or was it really the complete

* The withdrawal from the Chamber of Deputies of the opposition to Mussolini after the murder of the Socialist leader Matteotti.—Ed.

antithesis that intended to endure? Today we are not inclined to answer any of these questions with a straight Yes or No and thus concede an essential difference between Stalinism and fascism. Nevertheless, Franz Borkenau's thesis is worthy of consideration: he maintains that since 1929 Russia has taken its place "among the totalitarian, fascist powers." And in any case this much may be said with some degree of certainty: that, since the conflict between Stalin and Bukharin, the question of the attitude toward fascism, has, almost more than any other, determined Soviet policy in all its aspects.

Even Roosevelt's America has not escaped similar reproaches. Dorothy Thompson tried to uncover fascist tendencies in the New Deal: Roosevelt was compared with Mussolini as long ago as 1934; and even in 1940 there were still many Americans who hotly attacked the President for his "Caesarism" and his "Führer principle." Roosevelt himself was so far from regarding the accusation of fascism as negligible that he made a point of explaining his attitude. He did not by any means deny that, in America as well as in Europe, powerful epochal tendencies had brought about the establishment of a "strongly developed leadership." However, it is precisely from this example of Roosevelt that we see how careful we must be not to infer fascism from isolated "fascist" traits. There is no doubt whatever that in his ideas and personality Roosevelt was fundamentally opposed to fascism (and not only to Hitler and the fascism of Germany). Apparently there must be a "fascist minimum" without which the noun would be meaningless and even the adjective "fascist" doubtful. Nevertheless, a careful study of the example of Roosevelt shows that, although fascism was perhaps merely an explosive concentration of principles, most of which were individually necessary, it certainly did not occur as a foreign element in its era, episodic and isolated. Combined with our other considerations and points of evidence, it completes the circle encompassing the thesis that the era of the world wars is identical with the era of fascism.

This only makes the problem of the nature and manifestations of fascism all the more urgent, although it in no way implies a depiction of the era as a whole. Nothing would be more unjustified than to conclude that the other powers of the era, because they cannot be understood apart from their reaction to fascism, constituted no more than this reaction. There is no reason not to suppose that, in the overall relationships of the age, fascism for its part will have to be regarded as being primarily a reaction. Hence the great trends of the age, notably Marxism and liberalism, will always be present in what is to come, and the epochal opponents will keep on appearing, although only in glimpses. Fascistoid thinking, on the other hand, will occupy a good deal of space, if only by one outstanding example, in the form in which it has become a component of fascism. The aim of this study is not to present a picture of the era but a concept of it as far as this can be derived from the nature of fascism. The considerations so far advanced can help to trace the outline of this nature, but they are not sufficient for complete understanding. Detail and clarity are essential to it: without them it is nothing but a soulless diagram.

Up to this point the terrain in which fascism is to be found has been marked out. This terrain now needs to be described in such a way that the multiple nature of the phenomenon clearly emerges. But no phenomenon can be understood if divorced from its surroundings, and the original close affiliation with conservative allies is peculiarly characteristic of fascism. Hence the boundaries that have just been defined must now immediately be recrossed at many points.

Fascist Movements

The year 1919 was a crucial one for fascism, as it was for so many trends of the ensuing decade. Is it a coincidence that the form which was to become the most significant and momentous of all was the first to emerge in embryonic outline from the chaos of the immediate postwar period? For while in the spring of that year Mussolini set up Kurt Eisner as a model for his newly formed Fasci di Combattimento, in Hungary Béla Kun had just taken over the reins of government, and in Germany the combined Reichswehr and peasant-student *Freikorps* overthrew the short-lived Munich Soviet Republic. Of all the revolutionary spasms of that time, this last was the most haphazard, the most doomed, the most idyllic. Triggered by the senseless assassination of the Bavarian prime minister Eisner, who was on the point of resigning, it was the revolt of part of the proletariat under the leadership of a few intellectuals, mostly Jewish and anarchist, in a completely bourgeois city in the heart of a Catholic-agrarian area. By wanton acts of terrorism they managed to injure their own reputation more seriously than their enemies, who for the most part escaped harm. But perhaps it was for this very reason that they aroused so much hatred. And the notion of equating bolshevism with Jewry, and diagnosing both as a deadly disease, took hold more firmly than anywhere else in the mind of the little Reichswehr propagandist Adolf Hitler.

In Hungary the counterrevolution did not bring about the fall of the Béla Kun regime unaided; the advance of the Rumanians sounded the death knell to a revolution which had been just as much a product of national despair and a weapon of national self-assertion as an attack on social traditions. But this was also led mainly by Jews, and the ideas of the young officers who got together first in Szeged differed little from those of their Munich comrades. In 1919 Julius Gömbös was already calling himself a "National Socialist." The numerous patriotic organizations that arose soon afterward can in many aspects be compared to the patriotic groups of Bavaria. Gömbös headed the most important of them as "supreme leader," and in the unfavorable climate of the Bethlen era he wrote pamphlets on international Jewry and founded the new "Party of Racial Defense."

More successful in their external battles, but not really a factor of internal political significance, were the first Austrian *Heimatwehren* of 1919. It was only by degrees that they lost their supraparty position, and not until 1927 did they take the road known as "Heimwehr fascism," which was to become one of the elements of Austro-fascism.

In Poland, too, the threat from outside the country—although it came from Bolshevik Russia and, in contrast with Bavaria and Hungary, actually did represent a deadly threat—did not lead directly to the development of fascist trends. The popular anti-Semitism of the National Democrats and the authoritarianism of the legionaries, who had founded the state, had not yet been joined, so that for some years an extremely liberal parliamentary regime could prevail, until the rebellion of May 1926 brought Pilsudski to the helm.

In Italy the Fiume enterprise of Gabriele D'Annunzio (in September, 1919) marked an important stage on the road of early fascism. The basic traits of its style and symbolism were developed in Fiume, not Milan, and it was here that the poet's socialistic romanticism gave early definition to what was later to become corporatism.

In 1919 in northern Anatolia, Mustafa Kemal Pasha began his struggle for Turkey's heartland in the revolt against his own government and the foreign powers. Although his national defense dictatorship really only belongs on the periphery of this study of fascism, its brilliant success was an encouraging stimulus for all opponents of the Treaty of Versailles.

Also from 1919 stem the rudiments of what was later to become in Rumania the Iron Guard, a student association founded by Codreanu with the object of offering partisan-type resistance to the Red Army invasion he feared was imminent.

In 1919 war and revolution in Europe were more closely contiguous than ever before or since, and that year signaled the starting point of the first fascist parties. Their development progressed at varying speeds, but the years 1922 and 1923 were crucial way stations. During these years the first two fascist parties entered the spotlight of history and world-wide interest; it was chiefly these two which were to keep the world in suspense: one of them achieved a momentous victory, the other suffered a still more momentous defeat. At the end of October, 1922, Mussolini's Blackshirts conquered the capital with their curious "March on Rome," and barely more than a year later Hitler ran impetuously against the reluctantly drawn sword of a government that until then had been consistently friendly and favorably inclined.

A third event from this period is worthy of mention, although it took place in a corner of Europe. On June 9, 1923, the government of the peasant leader Aleksandr Stamboliski—called by his enemies an "agrarian Communist"—was overthrown in Sofia, and the new government of Tsankov steered a bloody course of oppression against the smoldering peasant resistance and in particular against the Communist party. By June 23 the Comintern had issued an appeal to the workers of the world, calling upon them to protest against the crimes of the "victorious Bulgarian fascist clique." Thus in 1922–23 the world saw not only the emergence of the two principal fascist movements under the sign of what was, compared to 1919, a strangely altered battle front, but also the first official appearance of that polemical and universal interpretation which was so vital to the further development of fascism.

From then on fascist movements mushroomed in Europe. In most cases it is hardly possible to say to what extent independent causes or the influence of Mussolini's shining example stood godfather at their birth. It is enough merely to list those groups, parties, and movements which failed to achieve power, or to achieve it unaided. The regimes themselves require a closer scrutiny, as do those countries in which a comparatively uniform trend toward fascism is discernible.

In many cases the splinter groups are the easiest to identify: isolated in their countries, they often looked for a substitute in their boundless admiration for Mussolini and Hitler. Perhaps it is doing an injustice to Léon Degrelle's Belgian Rexists, to the Finnish Lappo Movement, or to the Flemish National Solidarists, to include them here—the Danish National Socialist party of Fritz Clausen, the Francists of Marcel Bucard, the various forms of Swiss fascism, and many similar manifestations in most of the countries of Europe were scarcely more than clumsy imitations.

Possessed of independent roots, and for a short period also of some weight of their own, were the French groups—which, incidentally, greatly enlivened the fascist picture with their diversity and intellectual level (Brasillach, Drieu la Rochelle), and which also, as is generally believed, came closest to seizing power in February, 1934: Georges Valois' *Faisceau*, Pierre Taittinger's *Jeunesses Patriotes*, Colonel de la Rocque's *Croix de Feu*, Jacques Doriot's *Parti Populaire Français*, and finally Marcel Déat's neosocialist splinter group. The British Fascists also had a face of their own. The first of the British groups was constituted as early as 1923, and by 1926 British fascist groups were said to have at least half a million members. The best-known of these was the British Union of Fascists, founded in 1933 by Sir Oswald Mosley, who had been the youngest minister in the Labor party cabinet and in the eyes of many, a future prime minister. The foreign-sounding party label did not prevent it from enjoying a spectacular, albeit short-lived, rise. The Estonian Association of Freedom Fighters must not be overlooked, the only one of all the fascist groups to succeed in legally obtaining the absolute majority vote of the people, but which the government nevertheless brought to its knees by means of a *coup d'état*.

It was not so much their own strength as foreign aid and the chance happenings of war that allowed some of these parties to get into power. Quisling and his *Nasjonal Samling* gave the world a familiar example of this. Their place could have been taken with equal justification by Mussert and the Dutch National Socialist party. German aid also enabled the Iron Guard to come to power (partially and temporarily) in Rumania, and Szálasi's Arrow Cross party in Hungary. Mussolini made the Ustasha leader Pavelić the *Poglavnik* of the Croats. The picture in Tiso's Slovakia is not quite so clear. The Pétain regime was subjected to violent criticism from the Right, and no external influences affected its establishment. Doriot's Sigmaringen power was merely a shadow play and a farce.*

The regimes are another matter; they were typified mainly by the independence of their development, even when they did not remain unsupported. They are outlined here in an order determined by the extent of fascism's disaffiliation from the original alliance with conservative or even liberal forces.

The most striking example was Hungary, where the relationship between the extreme Right and the state, and hence the problem of its form, was revealed in three paradigmatic stages. The policy of fulfillment and renunciation of the Bethlen era may well be compared with

---

* Sigmaringen was the site of a French collaborationist regime established by the Germans after the liberation of France in 1944.—Ed.

the Weimar Republic, the government of Gömbös with the earliest period of Hitler's chancellorship, when the conservatives appeared to have tamed and "contained" their drummers, and the rule of Szálasi with the latter period of National Socialism. Certainly the contrasts were consistently less violent to the extent that, in a country where for eighteen years the flags had flown at half-mast, the general desire for revision of the peace treaty was taken just as much for granted as counterrevolutionary sympathies. The clash of principles, the spark from which fascism first catches fire, was absent. Moreover, Horthy himself was considered to be one of the "men of Szeged." And even Count Bethlen could not seriously be called a (democratic) liberal. Finally, the Hungarians grasped the fact which the National Socialists would never admit: that the fulfillment policy was an inevitable stage on the road to reform. For all practical purposes a Left did not exist, which was why the transition from Bethlen to Gömbös was not in the least comparable to the change-over of January 30, 1933, in Germany. Nevertheless, Gömbös, the man of the people and the supreme commander of MOVE (Hungarian Association of National Defense), was a completely different type from the liberal-authoritative aristocrat Bethlen, and the Jews in particular faced the prospect of his government with some trepidation. But Horthy did not die, like Hindenburg, nor did he let himself be stripped of power, like Victor Emmanuel. Instead he firmly tied the prime minister's hands, and Gömbös was even obliged to renounce his anti-Semitism more or less explicitly. During this period, however, Hungary found its way into the camp of the emerging Axis, and following on his election victory of 1935, Gömbös addressed the assembled crowds in balcony speeches just like his models in Rome and Berlin, with whom he shared a spiritual origin dating from 1919. Horthy's position, true, continued to remain so strong that he was able to consider summarily dismissing Gömbös, and it was only the latter's sudden death that prevented a possible trial of strength. However, if we wished to deny outright the similarity of the Hungarian with the German situation during the first months of 1933, we would have to regard the fascist nature of National Socialism as being rooted in the personal energy of Hitler, the senility of Hindenburg, and the irresponsible actions of von Papen and Hugenberg.*

That Horthy would have voluntarily allowed fascism to assume power in the unmistakable guise represented by Ferenc Szálasi's Arrow

---

* Hindenburg was the President of the Weimar Republic, von Papen was one of his Chancellors, and Hugenberg was leader of the German Nationalist Party.—Ed.

Cross party is quite inconceivable. Although Szálasi was a former officer, Horthy was bound to feel an aversion for everything he stood for: the mysticism with which he steadfastly believed in his mission of saving Hungary, and through Hungary the world; his desire to win the support of the poorer classes and the, at times, emphatically "proletarian" character of his movement; its violence and ruthless propaganda methods; and even the "Hungarianist" program itself, which went beyond the *restitutio in integrum* of old Hungary. Thus it was only under the most dubious circumstances that Szálasi became leader of the government: that is, in the shadow of the violent German reaction to Horthy's armistice offer of October 15, 1944. But he began at a point where Mussolini left off: after the occupation of a country by the enemy and with the unmistakable signs of ultimate defeat. The face of his regime, therefore, took shape solely under the iron necessities of the struggle of despair and did not to any notable extent show spontaneous or typical features of its own.

The "moral dictatorship" set up by Pilsudski in Poland in 1926, with the aim of leading the country to "recovery" (*Sanacja*) by abolishing the "abuses" of the parliamentary system, relied principally on the army. The core of the army consisted of his own legionaries, and even if Pilsudski himself never infringed on the multiplicity of parties and a fairly extensive freedom of expression of opinion, his successors took some forceful steps in the direction of an authoritarian, one-party dictatorship of soldier-statesmen. However, the marshal's regime constantly met with resistance from the Left and with criticism by an organized force on the extreme Right.

If the wholesale suppression of parties and freedom of the press is to be regarded as a sufficient criterion of fascism, it would be necessary to call the "king's dictatorship" of Alexander I in Yugoslavia fascist. But Yugoslavia, even more than Hungary and Poland, lacked the popular movement and the potential single party, a much more distinctive characteristic.

Originally this was also lacking in the Portugal of Salazar, and it has remained to this day an artificial structure. For at bottom the *Estado Novo* is simply a military dictatorship which was lucky enough to find an outstanding civilian who simultaneously strengthened and transformed it. Both the state party of the *União Nacional* and corporatism were and still are merely the means of this strengthening and transformation; they have no independent origin or autonomous will.

In Spain, on the other hand, even before Franco's military revolt there were militant formations of the extreme Right that showed typical rivalry-similarity with the Left. The name of the first of these groups gives us a sufficient clue: *Juntas de Ofensiva Nacional-Sindicalista* (JONS). In February, 1934, it combined with the *Falange Española,* founded by José Antonio Primo de Rivera, and the radical nature of its program (nationalization of banks and the elimination of large landed estates) aroused a great deal of suspicion from the old Right. The outbreak of war, however, cut off its chances of independent development: all the outstanding leaders fell, and in April, 1937, Franco combined the movement—not without some resistance—with the radical-traditionalist units of the Carlist *Requetés* to form the new state party under his leadership: the *Falange Española Tradicionalista y de las JONS.* In its heyday the Falange in Spain played quite a different role from the *Uniao Nacional* in Portugal, yet it is reasonable to suppose that its conservative allies—army, church, and landed gentry—were always stronger than it was, since they were able to maintain a leader from their own ranks at its head.

Austrian "Heimwehr fascism" managed to put the state on a new footing from top to bottom, but Austro-fascism, which finally succeeded the parliamentary system, was not the same thing, and although Starhemberg might be said to have been more of a Fascist than an aristocrat, this would not be true of either Dollfuss or Schuschnigg.*

In fact, of all the fascist movements and trends it was only with Italian fascism and with German National Socialism that a truly popular movement achieved victory, relatively unaided, and swept its leader to the position of supreme head of state. Only here did violent confrontations with the conservative forces continue right up to the final days of the regime and often develop into overt hostility with each side bent on destroying the other. But this view, which considers the relationship of fascism to the traditional system of leadership and code of norms, is not the only one from which a comparison of the different forms of fascism is possible, nor does it permit striking antitheses. For Mussolini had first to turn from a republican into a monarchist before he could embark on the March on Rome, and even during the period of his greatest power he could never contemplate the abolishment of the monarchy. Almost more palpable was the restriction of power which Hitler underwent when he had to allow the major conservative force, the army, a measure of independence of which there continued to be characteristic evidence up until July 20, 1944. Even National Social-

---

* Dollfuss and Schuschnigg were leaders of the corporate state in Austria. Dollfuss was assassinated in 1934 and Schuschnigg was Chancellor at the time of the Anschluss, or union, of Hitler's Germany and Austria in 1938.—Ed.

ism was never the sole determining force except as a trend; and it is this orientation which is the common denominator of all types of fascism, not the particular measure of their success, which continued to depend on a number of chance factors.

It is a peculiarity of the study of history to be concerned with individuality and thus to emphasize the necessity of description. It makes us more keenly aware that such terms as liberalism, parliamentarianism, monarchism, are not fixed quantities but can mean different things in different circumstances. Yet the historian does not for that reason abandon them. That is why he will also insist on the broadest possible empirical basis for the study of fascism. He is in a position to do so since he is familiar with diffuse entities of this kind. For example, nineteenth-century socialism encompasses a vast number of manifestations, and the pupils of Fourier and Saint-Simon were not without reason bitter enemies. Yet there is no question but that a fundamental kinship existed. And just as the historian must protest the exclusion from socialism of all those who do not acknowledge the idea of a phalanstery, so he must object to the narrowing *a limine* of the concept of fascism merely on account of isolated distinguishing marks.

Interpretations of Fascism

One thing, however, the historian cannot do by himself: he cannot evolve a concept on his own authority. He always finds it prefabricated —coined by either supporters or opponents. If he were merely to follow his own bent, he would never exhaust the examination of the smallest of such a term's manifestations, for the associations are endless, and the differences finally lead back to the intangibility of the *individuum ineffabile*. Even the "complexity" (although not the immeasurability) of the phenomenon is only apparent to discerning observation. The original interpretations of political trends, however, are always formed, before objective study forms them, in the confrontations of social existence itself. Applied to a given phenomenon they represent a conception rather than a description. But if the historian has to assume these conceptions rather than initiate them, he will still place them in critical association with each other and with the description, so that in principle it can transcend its premises.

The primary condition for this is the complete and unprejudiced review of conceptions. If the objective study of fascism is made possible by the fact that the phenomenon may be regarded as "dead," this signifies a considerable advance, always assuming that the number of

conceptions is not subject to chance increase but is a matter of con-
clusive necessity.

The oldest of these conceptions is the socialist one. It is, so to speak,
older than fascism itself. When in October, 1914, after a hard struggle
with his conscience, Mussolini went over to interventionism, he definitely wanted this to be understood as socialist interventionism in favor
of attacked nations. His attempt to make the party fall in step with
the new line failed however, and when three weeks after resigning as
editor of *Avanti!* he established his own newspaper, his former colleagues kept on repeating in his former newspaper the inexorable
question: *Chi paga?* (Who is paying?) It is true that this question
could not be unequivocally answered then, nor can it be now, but it
determined the basic outline of the socialist interpretation up until our
own day. Yet it undoubtedly did Mussolini an injustice if it implied
that it was for financial reasons that he carried out the best-substanti-
ated of his political changes of course; it did, however, reveal an
incontestable truth, by associating Mussolini's lack of means with the
high cost of publishing, in the thesis that, at least objectively, he must
be a pawn in someone's game and that this game was primarily an
antisocialist one. This interpretation was painfully confirmed for the
Socialists when their positions of power and their organizations, which
only a few months earlier had spread fear and trembling throughout
the bourgeoisie, were wiped out during 1921 and 1922 by the Fascists
with the open support of agrarians, the big bourgeoisie, and even the
state. The view that fascism is a secondary phenomenon derived from
one of the two fundamental social realities (the bourgeoisie as against
the proletariat), is the basis of all socialist interpretations. Within this
framework they range from a primitive theory of agents to a large
number of diversified theories which attempt to work out the possibilities and limitations of a subjection of the original content by means
of what has been deduced.

However, the attitude of liberalism, even in the case of Italy, does
not absolutely confirm this theory. It is true that, until the March on
Rome, the *Corriere della Sera* under Luigi Albertini supported not so
much fascism as Mussolini, but it then very soon adopted a stance of
sharp opposition. It is also true that the three most respected liberal
politicians—the former prime ministers Giolitti, Orlando, and Salandra
—hesitated, even as late as the crucial date of January 3, 1925. But an
organ of the stature of *La Stampa* had opposed fascism unequivocally
from the very beginning, and its editor, Luigi Salvatorelli, found in the
term *Antirisorgimento* one of the most effective formulas for the battle

with the state party. This term virtually contained the idea of "totalitarianism," and it achieved canonical status when Farinacci and Mussolini deliberately adopted it for the Fascist party in 1925. Leading Italian writers, as distinct from many non-Italian authors, have always strongly emphasized this totalitarian character of Italian fascism; Giuseppe Antonio Borgese followed in the footsteps of the Latin-liberal tradition of regarding Germany as the paragon of modernity and freedom to such an extent that even in 1935 he saw greater chances for freedom and resistance in Germany.

However, the term "totalitarian" was actually evolved by German and American authors as a result of the twin experience of National Socialism and bolshevism. Its interpretation ranges from the political to the metapolitical-metaphysical. The first contrasts the totalitarian state with the liberal-constitutional state and regards it as distinguished by a number of basic features (such as the existence of an ideologically oriented single party) which suspend civil and spiritual liberty. The true nature of the totalitarian state would therefore be a system of uniformity, artificially and compulsorily set up, which presupposes the diversity of the liberal era and hence must oppose it, if necessary by terroristic methods. According to this interpretation, rule by a conservative group must also be totalitarian rule if it forcibly suppresses all other parties and opinions.

A classic formulation of the second interpretation was given by Peter Count Yorck von Wartenburg when addressing the People's Court: "The essential element is . . . the total claim of the state on the citizen involving the elimination of his religious and moral obligations toward God." According to this conception, then, a politically total rule would not actually be totalitarian if it permitted freedom in man's prepolitical and metapolitical relations to other individuals and to God. In its further extension this interpretation is inclined to regard certain features of total claim as denoting totalitarianism's true essence: in terrorism, which proceeds with extreme harshness against the familiar and the traditional; in universalism, which aims at world domination; in perversion, which demands those very things which are contrary to the laws of God and humanity.

How easily this conception allies itself with Christian and conservative beliefs, how greatly it exemplifies the tempering of traditionally antagonistic opinions, is plain to see. However, the specifically Christian-ecclesiastical attitude toward fascism is a separate chapter, and a strange one. For the fact that in most European countries the churches encouraged fascism to a sometimes very considerable degree is something which their adversaries have repeatedly emphasized and which it is hard to deny. Yet it would probably be fairer to speak of an early ambivalence. For even Codreanu, whose allegiance to the church was closer than that of all fascism's founders and whose views had an affinity to those of the Rumanian Orthodox tradition, complained bitterly that, with few exceptions, the clergy did not support the Iron Guard. In Italy and Germany there were also many examples of negative utterances and actions on the part of the clergy even during fascism's preliminary stages. The policy of the Curia, however, remained favorable despite all reservations, the Lateran Pact and the Reich Concordat being well-known instances. Neither pact was able to prevent the early outbreak of violent disputes, primarily concerning the education of the young. In June, 1931, the encyclical *Non abbiamo bisogno* ("We do not need") was directed against Mussolini, as was in 1937 the far better known pronouncement against Hitler, *Mit brennender Sorge* ("With burning anxiety"). Neither achieved the desired goal, but in Italy good relations were nevertheless maintained. Actually a Christian confrontation of uncompromising severity existed only toward National Socialism, and this showed itself less in theoretical works than in testimonies from the death cell and the concentration camp. Moreover, where it found expression in theory, no effort was made specifically to designate National Socialism, which was merely cited as an example of the dangers threatening from secularization and often mentioned in direct association with older antiecclesiastical trends. In any case, the crux lies in the early approval of the churches, even when—and especially when—this approval was attributable to sympathy for a "historic battle of resistance to bolshevism," for, indeed, the inner relationship between National Socialism and bolshevism presents the central thesis.

The inner kinship of what appeared to be antagonistic is also central to the conservative conception, which, of course, took the longest time to evolve. Although it is true that evidence of conservative mistrust is to be found in the preliminary stages, it is equally true that the revolution in Italy and Germany could never even have taken place without conservative collaboration. Perhaps nothing is quite as characteristic as the fact that in England even in the late twenties the number of profascist conservative writings was legion. Long experience, both bitter and profound, was necessary before a change could be wrought. The best example is probably that of Hermann Rauschning, the only high-ranking National Socialist who later became an out-and-out enemy of the regime. His book, *The Revolution of Nihilism,* offers concrete and significant insights into the nature of the new phenomenon which could not easily have been obtained by a socialist or a liberal. It goes far beyond that kind of conservative attitude which finds the plebeian traits of fascism distasteful. But when it comes to tracing ideological backgrounds, both versions unite in making Hitler the final logical conclusion of Rousseau's starting point, and the fascist revolution the continuation of the French revolution.

By this time the essential fact has been clearly brought out that it was precisely this experience of fascism and its hostile proximity to bolshevism that caused the traditional ways of political thought to develop new fronts and new issues. The most significant differences to emerge were, first the political and metapolitical interpretations, and second the opposing views which flowed from them: fascism is either specified, or more or less equated with bolshevism. The socialist and political-liberal conceptions form the first group; the transpolitical-liberal, the Christian, and the principal version of the conservative conception form the second. The democratic-socialist interpretation is the specifying one; the Communist interpretation (in turn identifying fascism with a certain stage of capitalism) is alone in postulating complete antithesis. Even the political-liberal interpretation tends to equate fascism with bolshevism—actually the central thesis of all the other conceptions.

The picture is materially supplemented, however, if we include some more recent interpretations which, although taking a narrower view, still regard the subject as a whole.

First there is the Jewish interpretation, which is based on the most appalling of all human experiences. Nothing is more natural than that this conception should bring the whole weight of this experience to bear in favor of a distinction between National Socialism and fascism. Generally speaking, the anti-Semitic nature of almost all other fascist movements cannot deflect the horrified eyes of the world from National Socialism. Accordingly, the distinction between National Socialism and bolshevism ought to be the next logical step, and very often it is. However, when the nature of Stalinism is seen in its terroristic lust for destruction in contradistinction to the world conspiracy, especially to the Trotskyist one, the equation between fascism and bolshevism can be made here too, and the link with the liberal-conservative conception established.

On the other hand, the psychoanalytical method of observation clearly supports the specifying interpretation. It looks primarily at the style and methods of fascism: the unshackling of primitive instincts, the denial of reason, the spellbinding of the senses by pageantry and parades. It sees all this as the emerging of archaic complexes which are older than nationality. This accounts just as much for the international character of fascism as its antithesis to the much more rational Marxism.

Sociology is, with its basic idea of class structure, a further counterweight to the prevailing equating interpretations. By and large fascism and communism do not recruit their supporters from the same class substratum. This is a point of view, therefore, which, although discredited by the exclusiveness of its claim in the Communist interpretation, cannot be entirely ruled out.

It can hardly be sufficiently emphasized that none of these interpretations has been dreamed up in an ivory tower. Indeed, the chief among them are the fruits of grim ordeals which often brought death to many thousands of human beings. We cannot, then, summarily dismiss one or indiscriminately align ourselves with another. When those of us who come after have access to living experiences from a distance only, we must try to compensate for this deficiency by attempting to co-ordinate the revelatory forces generated by these methods of observation. The demarcation of each will then automatically become apparent.

First Definition

Superficial though it may be, this survey of the phenomenon and its interpretations to date enables us to arrive at a preliminary definition which will serve as a guide and at the same time be subjected to study and demonstration within this analysis.

Neither antiparliamentarianism nor anti-Semitism is a suitable criterion for the concept of fascism. It would be equally imprecise to define fascism as anti-communism, but it would be obviously misleading to use a definition which did not adequately stress, or even entirely omitted, this basic criterion. Nevertheless, the identifying conception must also be taken into account. Hence the following suggests itself:

FASCISM IS ANTI-MARXISM WHICH SEEKS TO DESTROY THE ENEMY BY THE EVOLVEMENT OF A RADICALLY OPPOSED AND YET RELATED IDEOLOGY AND BY THE USE OF ALMOST IDENTICAL AND YET TYPICALLY MODIFIED METHODS, ALWAYS, HOWEVER, WITHIN THE UNYIELDING FRAMEWORK OF NATIONAL SELF-ASSERTION AND AUTONOMY.

This definition implies that without Marxism there is no fascism, that fascism is at the same time closer to and further from communism than is liberal anti-communism, that it necessarily shows at least an inclination toward a radical ideology, that fascism should never be said to exist in the absence of at least the rudiments of an organization and propaganda comparable to those of Marxism. It enables us to understand the extent to which there can be stages of fascism: according to the evolution of the ideology and the predominance of one of its two chief components, the pseudosocialist or the elite—that is, race—element; according to the degree of determination in, and the more or less universal nature of, the will to destruction; and according to the energy of execution. The decisive factors, however, are starting point and direction, for this concept is a "teleological" one, and even the most marked differentiation of stages does not do away with the unity of its essential nature.

II. The Italian Example

The historian A. J. P. Taylor has dismissed Italian fascism as a "fraud," and his professional colleague Denis Mack Smith has described its essence as "rhetoric and blather," although neither would deny the Italian example its sinister qualities. Mussolini and his henchmen, sponsors of a very eclectic ideology fabricated years after their accession to power, may appear a trifle ridiculous, even comical, to later and presumably more sophisticated generations; surely the boasts and actions of the fascist élite appear to have been made with slight esteem for the intelligence of their clientele. Yet it must be remembered that Italy was a country where many citizens nursed a lingering pessimism about the promise of nationhood, where the political class had set itself apart from the mass of the population and had remained indifferent to social and economic problems. Italy was also a third-rate power accustomed to playing the unheroic role of jackal at the side of stronger powers. Indeed, she had been thrown into World War I by callous politicians hungry for territorial reward from the Entente—though her tremendous sacrifice on the battlefields seemingly went unrecognized by the victors at Versailles. And by 1919, Italy was confronted with the possibility of dramatic social upheaval. Against this background, the appearance and appeal of a movement of seeming vigor and purpose, offering a quick exit from a morass of humiliation and frustration, should evoke little surprise. The following readings by Mussolini, by a former socialist comrade who became one of his harshest critics, and by a modern historian should help to define the nature of Italian fascism, explain why it came to power, and why it was to retain power once the postwar crisis had passed.

The Political and Social Doctrine of Fascism appeared in the Enciclopedia Italiana in 1932 under the name of the Duce, although it was most likely formulated by his lieutenants. After several years of proclaiming that fascism was a movement and not a doctrine, Mussolini evidently recognized that perpetuation of his style of authority demanded a definition of what exactly fascism was with only a minimum of doctrinal consistency. Fascism, after all, by then had given its name to similar movements across the continent. This document is instructive not only for Italian fascism but is a splendid commentary on the nature of fascism everywhere. Naturally, it features the customary verbal gymnastics of the Duce, notably as he points with elation to the unoriginal and synthetic character of his creation. Doubtless this doctrinal flabbiness permitted fascism to be defined more in terms of what it was not than in terms of what it was.

For Mussolini, the elemental qualities of fascism were action and faith: "it was born of a need for action," and it "has created a living faith" in its quest for "holiness and heroism." But there is more in these few pages than apocalyptic fervor and a call for collective adventure. Mussolini denies that fascism is the tool of the middle class. Rejecting class warfare, it seeks the amelioration of the living conditions of all, although this vague promise is tempered by the sobering reminder that material well-being must not be equated with happiness! There is repeated deliberate cultivation of the irrational: violence is sanctified; peace is vilified as the shabby refuge of the cowardly and the puny, since great nations must expand as a "manifestation of vitality"; and the liquidation of the allegedly decadent past is demanded along with the elimination of its value system, exemplified in liberalism and socialism. Finally, the state is recognized as the executor of the doctrine. The state instructs, provides order and discipline, and is the guarantor of the vitality of the nation. Who holds state power? The answer, for Mussolini, was too obvious to require lengthy specification.

The second reading is drawn from The Rise of Italian Fascism by A. Rossi, a pseudonym of Angelo Tasca. A prominent socialist intellectual in Italy before World War I, Tasca later gave his allegiance to the Moscow-dominated Third International and figured among the original leadership of the Italian Communist Party. While living in the Soviet Union as a member of the secretariat of the International, he became disturbed by the practices of his soviet comrades, and attacked their régime as "reactionary" for its denial of basic human and spiritual aspirations. Expelled from the U.S.S.R., Tasca took up residence in France where he became foreign editor of the Socialist daily *Le Populaire,* and where he wrote this book, originally published in French in 1938. After World War II, he wrote two highly critical studies of the French Communist Party, which have remained landmarks in the historiography of communism in western Europe.

The Rise of Italian Fascism has been widely recognized as one of the most penetrating analyses of Mussolini's movement and of the factors that accounted for its success. Tasca, perhaps, is too severe with his brother Socialists, especially for their apparent failure to recognize the many-sided impact of the world war. Given to faith in outworn slogans and to timidity in action, he argues, Socialists were so sapped of their vitality that they could offer only anemic resistance to fascism. Tasca makes clear that the "Red Menace" from which Mussolini "saved" Italy was pure fiction, albeit a fiction Mussolini could not have done without. Acknowledging that fascism was the offspring of crisis, Tasca also demonstrates that it received powerful assistance from the established political order. Noting its international character, he considers it to have been not merely a defensive reflex of a threatened middle class, but an offensive drive—a "will to power"—intended to crush every manifestation of the liberating spirit born of the eighteenth-century Enlightenment. Tasca himself was a man of deep humanist commitment, a man whose personal beliefs buttressed his conviction that fascism represented a desperate assault upon the idea of liberation: "An idea is a generation or a succession of generations." "When the fascists kill . . . they know what they are about and do not strike in vain. . . ."

The final selection is reprinted from *Italy, A Modern History*—a generously acclaimed synthesis of Italy's history since her achievement of unification in the nineteenth century—by Denis Mack Smith, a Fellow of the Royal Historical Society and a member of the History Faculty at Cambridge University. These pages are concerned with the theory and practice of Mussolini's fascism, beginning with an analysis of the Fascist Party, the government, and the Duce's techniques of rule over both. The very mediocrity of Mussolini's lieutenants only highlighted the "good show" acted out by the leader, although the contagious intoxication of his performance enveloped those who should have known better, including the Duce himself.

Mack Smith exposes the utter sham of Mussolini's régime: every dictatorship has a vested interest in confusion, so as to prevent the creation of a powerful rival claimant for leadership, but this régime exceeded the limits imposed by prudence in this regard. Mussolini's government had no coherent social or economic policies; its proud corporatism was largely a fraudulent cover for the free play of vested interests. Its cultural policies were lamentable; its educational policies a joke. Like its leader, fascist Italy was arrogant and bombastic, guided by the most appalling banalities. Yet it claimed to have given the world a "new style of living." The trains, of course, did run on time. But Mack Smith's conclusion seems unassailable: "The only truly original contribution of fascism to politics was probably the technique of castor oil" administered to hapless opponents in the most humiliating circumstances.

1. The Political and Social Doctrine of Fascism

BENITO MUSSOLINI

When, in the now distant March of 1919, I summoned a meeting at Milan through the columns of the *Popolo d'Italia* of the surviving members of the Interventionist Party who had themselves been in action, and who had followed me since the creation of the Fascist Revolutionary Party (which took place in the January of 1915), I had no specific doctrinal attitude in my mind. I had a living experience of one

Source: Abridged from *The Political and Social Doctrine of Fascism* by Benito Mussolini, published in *International Conciliation*, January, 1935, No. 306, pp. 5–17, with the permission of the Carnegie Endowment for International Peace.

doctrine only—that of Socialism, from 1903–4 to the winter of 1914 —that is to say, about a decade: and from Socialism itself, even though I had taken part in the movement first as a member of the rank and file and then later as a leader, yet I had no experience of its doctrine in practice. My own doctrine, even in this period, had always been a doctrine of action. A unanimous, universally accepted theory of Socialism did not exist after 1905, when the revisionist movement began in Germany under the leadership of Bernstein, while under pressure of the tendencies of the time, a Left Revolutionary movement also appeared, which though never getting further than talk in Italy, in Russian Socialistic circles laid the foundations of Bolshevism. Reformation, Revolution, Centralization—already the echoes of these terms are spent—while in the great stream of Fascism are to be found ideas which began with Sorel, Péguy, with Lagardelle in the "Mouvement Socialiste," and with the Italian trades-union movement which throughout the period 1904–14 was sounding a new note in Italian Socialist circles (already weakened by the betrayal of Giolitti) through Olivetti's *Pagine Libre,* Orano's *La Lupa,* and Enrico Leone's *Divenire Sociale.*

After the War, in 1919, Socialism was already dead as a doctrine: it existed only as a hatred. There remained to it only one possibility of action, especially in Italy, reprisals against those who had desired the War and who must now be made to "expiate" its results. The *Popolo d'Italia* was then given the sub-title of "The newspaper of ex-service men and producers," and the word producers was already the expression of a mental attitude. Fascism was not the nursling of a doctrine worked out beforehand with detailed elaboration; it was born of the need for action and it was itself from the beginning practical rather than theoretical; it was not merely another political party but, even in the first two years, in opposition to all political parties as such, and itself a living movement. The name which I then gave to the organization fixed its character. And yet, if one were to re-read, in the now dusty columns of that date, the report of the meeting in which the *Fasci Italiana di combattimento* were constituted, one would there find no ordered expression of doctrine, but a series of aphorisms, anticipations, and aspirations which, when refined by time from the original ore, were destined after some years to develop into an ordered series of doctrinal concepts, forming the Fascist political doctrine— different from all others either of the past or the present day.

"If the bourgeoisie," I said then, "think that they will find lightning-conductors in us, they are the more deceived; we must start work at once. . . . We want to accustom the working-class to real and effectual leadership, and also to convince them that it is no easy thing to direct an industry or a commercial enterprise successfully. . . . We shall combat every retrograde idea, technical or spiritual. . . . When the succession to the seat of government is open, we must not be unwilling to fight for it. We must make haste; when the present régime breaks down, we must be ready at once to take its place. It is we who have the right to the succession, because it was we who forced the country into the War, and led her to victory. The present method of political representation cannot suffice, we must have a representation direct from the individuals concerned. It may be objected against this program that it is a return to the conception of the corporation, but that is no matter. . . . Therefore, I desire that this assembly shall accept the revindication of national trades-unionism from the economic point of view. . . ."

And above all, Fascism, the more it considers and observes the future and the development of humanity quite apart from political considerations of the moment, believes neither in the possibility nor the utility of perpetual peace. It thus repudiates the doctrine of Pacifism—born of a renunciation of the struggle and an act of cowardice in the face of sacrifice. War alone brings up to its highest tension all human energy and puts the stamp of nobility upon the peoples who have the courage to meet it. All other trials are substitutes, which never really put men into the position where they have to make the great decision—the alternative of life or death. Thus a doctrine which is founded upon this harmful postulate of peace is hostile to Fascism. And thus hostile to the spirit of Fascism, though accepted for what use they can be in dealing with particular political situations, are all the international leagues and societies which, as history will show, can be scattered to the winds when once strong national feeling is aroused by any motive—sentimental, ideal, or practical.

· · · · ·

Such a conception of life makes Fascism the complete opposite of that doctrine, the base of so-called scientific and Marxian Socialism, the materialist conception of history; according to which the history of human civilization can be explained simply through the conflict of interests among the various social groups and by the change and development in the means and instruments of production. That the changes in the economic field—new discoveries of raw materials, new methods of working them, and the inventions of science—have their importance no one can deny; but that these factors are sufficient to explain the history of humanity excluding all others is an absurd delusion. Fascism, now and always, believes in holiness and in heroism; that is to say, in actions influenced by no economic motive, direct or indirect. And if the economic conception of history be denied, according to which theory men are no more than puppets, carried to and fro by the waves of chance, while the real directing forces are quite out of their control, it follows that the existence of an unchangeable and unchanging class-war is also denied—the natural progeny of the economic conception of history. And above all Fascism denies that class-war can be the preponderant force in the transformation of society. These two fundamental concepts of Socialism being thus refuted, nothing is left of it but the sentimental aspiration—as old as humanity itself—towards a social convention in which the sorrows and sufferings of the humblest shall be alleviated. But here again Fascism repudiates the conception of "economic" happiness, to be realized by Socialism and, as it were, at a given moment in economic evolution to assure to everyone the maximum of well-being. Fascism denies the materialist conception of happiness as a possibility, and abandons it to its inventors, the economists of the first half of the nineteenth century: that is to say, Fascism denies the validity of the equation, well-being-happiness, which would reduce men to the level of animals, caring for one thing only—to be fat and well-fed—and would thus degrade humanity to a purely physical existence.

After Socialism, Fascism combats the whole complex system of democratic ideology, and repudiates it, whether in its theoretical premises or in its practical application. Fascism denies that the majority, by the simple fact that it is a majority, can direct human society; it denies that numbers alone can govern by means of a periodical consultation, and it affirms the immutable, beneficial, and fruitful inequality of mankind, which can never be permanently leveled through the mere operation of a mechanical process such as universal suffrage. The democratic régime may be defined as from time to time giving the people the illusion of sovereignty, while the real effective sovereignty lies in the hands of other concealed and irresponsible forces. Democracy is a régime nominally without a king, but it is ruled by many kings —more absolute, tyrannical, and ruinous than one sole king, even though a tyrant. This explains why Fascism, having first in 1922 (for reasons of expediency) assumed an attitude tending towards republicanism, renounced this point of view before the march to Rome; being convinced that the question of political form is not today of prime importance, and after having studied the examples of monarchies and republics past and present reached the conclusion that monarchy or republicanism are not to be judged, as it were, by an absolute standard; but that they represent forms in which the evolution—political, historical, traditional, or psychological—of a particular country has expressed itself.

·   ·   ·   ·   ·

Fascism has taken up an attitude of complete opposition to the doctrines of Liberalism, both in the political field and the field of economics. There should be no undue exaggeration (simply with the objects of immediate success in controversy) of the importance of Liberalism in the last century, nor should what was but one among many theories which appeared in that period be put forward as a religion for humanity for all time, present and to come. Liberalism only flourished for half a century.

·   ·   ·   ·   ·

Fascism uses in its construction whatever elements in the Liberal, Social, or Democratic doctrines still have a living value; it maintains what may be called the certainties which we owe to history, but it rejects all the rest—that is to say, the conception that there can be any doctrine of unquestioned efficacy for all times and all peoples. Given that the nineteenth century was the century of Socialism, of Liberalism, and of Democracy, it does not necessarily follow that the twentieth century must also be a century of Socialism, Liberalism, and Democracy: political doctrines pass, but humanity remains; and it may rather be expected that this will be a century of authority, a century of the Right, a century of Fascism. For if the nineteenth century was a century of individualism (Liberalism always signifying individualism) it may be expected that this will be the century of collectivism, and hence the century of the State.

·   ·   ·   ·   ·

In 1929, at the first five-yearly assembly of the Fascist régime, I said:

For us Fascists, the State is not merely a guardian, preoccupied solely with the duty of assuring the personal safety of the citizens; nor is it an organization with purely material aims, such as to guarantee a certain level of well-being and peaceful conditions of life; for a mere council of administration would be sufficient to realize such objects. Nor is it a purely political creation, divorced from all contact with the complex material reality which makes up the life of the individual and the life of the people as a whole. The State, as conceived of and as created by Fascism, is a spiritual and moral fact in itself, since its political, juridical, and economic organization of the nation is a concrete thing: and such an organization must be in its origins and development a manifestation of the spirit. The State is the guarantor of security both internal and external, but it is also the custodian and transmitter of the spirit of the people, as it has grown up through the centuries in language, in customs, and in faith. And the State is not only a living reality of the present, it is also linked with the past and above all with the future, and thus transcending the brief limits of individual life, it represents the immanent spirit of the nation. The forms in which States express themselves may change, but the necessity for such forms is eternal. It is the State which educates its citizens in civic virtue, gives them a consciousness of their mission and welds them into unity; harmonizing their various interests through justice, and transmitting to future generations the mental conquests of science, of art, of law and the solidarity of humanity. It leads men from primitive tribal life to that highest expression of human power which is Empire: it links up through the centuries the names of those of its members who have died for its existence and in obedience to its laws, it holds up the memory of the leaders who have increased its territory and the geniuses who have illumined it with glory as an example to be followed by future generations. When the conception of the State declines, and disunifying and centrifugal tendencies prevail, whether of individuals or of particular groups, the nations where such phenomena appear are in their decline.

From 1929 until today, evolution, both political and economic, has everywhere gone to prove the validity of these doctrinal premises.

．　．　．　．　．

For Fascism, the growth of empire, that is to say the expansion of the nation, is an essential manifestation of vitality, and its opposite a sign of decadence. Peoples which are rising, or rising again after a period of decadence, are always imperialist; any renunciation is a sign of decay and of death. Fascism is the doctrine best adapted to represent the tendencies and the aspirations of a people, like the people of Italy, who are rising again after many centuries of abasement and foreign servitude. But empire demands discipline, the coordination of all forces and a deeply felt sense of duty and sacrifice: this fact explains many aspects of the practical working of the régime, the character of many forces in the State, and the necessarily severe measures which must be taken against those who would oppose this spontaneous and inevitable movement of Italy in the twentieth century, and would oppose it by recalling the outworn ideology of the nineteenth century—repudiated wheresoever there has been the courage to undertake great experiments of social and political transformation: for never before has the nation stood more in need of authority, of direction, and of order. If every age has its own characteristic doctrine, there are a thousand signs which point to Fascism as the characteristic doctrine of our time. For if a doctrine must be a living thing, this is proved by the fact that Fascism has created a living faith; and that this faith is very powerful in the minds of men, is demonstrated by those who have suffered and died for it.

Fascism has henceforth in the world the universality of all those doctrines which, in realizing themselves, have represented a stage in the history of the human spirit.

2. The Rise of Italian Fascism

A. ROSSI

I

When the post-war crisis began, Italian national unity had been established for barely fifty years, and the part played by the masses in winning it had been small. After 1870 the old oligarchies had only one aim in view: to suppress the fourth estate and deprive it of every means to direct action and power. On this point the conflicting forces of Vatican and monarchy were agreed. There were no democratic or revolutionary traditions, and the parliamentary system had remained an artificial improvisation grafted on to the life of the nation, whose growth had not been helped by the corrupt methods of Giolitti's reformism.* The only really democratic force was the working-class and socialist movement, but this was handicapped by its narrow outlook and concentration on municipal affairs. Nevertheless the people—workers, artisans and peasants—with the traditions of their own independent institutions, were slowly making their weight felt in the state, when their progress was interrupted by the war. This was begun and

Source: *The Rise of Italian Fascism* (London: Methuen & Co. Ltd., 1938), pp. 323–358. Translated by P. Wait. Reprinted by permission of the Methuen & Co. Ltd., publishers.
* Giolitti was several times Prime Minister of Italy.—Ed.

carried on in Italy as a civil war, and coincided with a grave crisis in the ruling classes. The war was followed by depression and disorder: economic crises in the country, which was exhausted and dislocated by the effort of victory; moral crisis among the people who, 'while being and feeling victorious, were suffering the humiliation and crisis of the vanquished'.

Within these wider causes there were other factors which helped to alter the course and the outcome of Italy's post-war history: the failure of the socialist movement; the reactionaries' and particularly the land-owners' offensive in the form of military action and territorial conquest; the economic crisis of 1921; the help and complicity of the state and its dependent bodies; the discrediting of Parliament; the part played by Mussolini.

•　　•　　•　　•　　•

Most important were the socialist feebleness and mistakes, which were the direct cause, not of fascism itself, which appeared in every country after the war, but of its success in Italy. This becomes evident if one follows from day to day, as we have done, the policy of all the proletarian parties—socialist, maximalist, communist—in the years 1919–1922. It is helpful, though, to look still further into some of their failures and mistakes.

In so doing we may lay ourselves open to a charge of injustice towards the Italian working-class and socialist movement. But this is not the history of that movement, nor the biography of some of its leaders (Matteotti, Turati, Treves, to mention only those who are dead), whose moral greatness was sometimes actually a cause of political inferiority. Nor is this the valley of Jehoshaphat, where faults and merits are meticulously scrutinized. . . . We are combatants who accept, as they come, the tasks imposed on us by the time in which we live. It is our object to record the causes of a catastrophe where results have been grave in the extreme and will take long to repair. But we can only bear the responsibility for the past by a firm determination to avoid, so far as it is within our power, a recurrence of the same mistakes and the same disasters. Only candid and ruthless self-examination can give us the right to draw publicly the conclusions from our experience, and can transform our suffering into a message for others.

The fundamental weakness of Italian socialism in every sphere was due to its lack of true revolutionary spirit. This spirit is drawn by two allegiances: the refusal to accept the injustice, disorder and meanness of existing society, and the will to arrive at a new economic regime, new institutions, arising out of new relationships between men. Condemnation of the present must be enlightened, strengthened and justified by affirmation of the future. Only in this sense is there any truth in Bakunin's saying, 'the passion for destruction is a creative passion'. But it has been truly said of Italy that 'hatred of everything old deadened even the desire for a new order', and that is why this hatred was so impotent.

For a class to be really revolutionary it must, says Marx, 'first be aware that it is not a particular class, but the representative of the general needs of society'. Italian socialism lacked this leaven, which alone could have raised it to victory. With a middle class crippled, clinging to its class point of view in the midst of the great upheaval which had intensified its egoism and its greed, the socialist movement had a great part to play. If it had been strong enough to remain faithful to it, it might have saved the Italian people.

Instead it shirked its task. It lurked in the background all through the post-war crisis. This desertion is the sole explanation of the fascist success. Society, even more than nature, abhors a vacuum, and the forces of barbarism are ever ready to rush in and fill it.

The Italian socialists waited for the middle class to die off naturally, without considering whether its death struggle, as they assumed it to be, if unduly prolonged, might not generate seeds of decay which would infect the whole nation, the socialist movement included. They behaved like the sole heir to an estate who prefers not to turn up till the last minute, just before the will is read. While they waited they confined their activities to 'separating their own responsibilities from those of the ruling classes'. This separation was, up to a point, justified and even necessary. But responsibility for evil committed is always shared by those who have failed to prevent it; and we have no right to connive at others' actions unless we are prepared to step in at the right moment and succeed where they have failed. It is all the easier to separate our own responsibilities from those of the ruling classes if we are able and willing to shoulder our own responsibilities on behalf of an entire nation. If not, it is quite simple to avoid 'legal' responsibilities by pleading a kind of alibi, the last resort of all scoundrels. ('Nothing like a alleybi' was the advice given by Sam Weller's father to Pickwick.) In so doing we incur a much heavier responsibility to history, whose judgments go much deeper than any legal code. Useless, then, to say 'We were not there'. The masses, who have lost all, will want to know why not.

The policy of the Italian communists and maximalists was to let things get as bad as possible. A policy which depends on aggravating a situation the better to control and direct it is justifiable so long as one is ready and willing to intervene at the right moment and restore order in the chaos that follows. Such tactics, which must be employed with the utmost precision, become too easily a game of chance, depending as they do on the blindest and least reversible of forces.

The Italian maximalists and communists had no idea of tactics: theirs was a state of mind that combined demagogy with inactivity and was quite devoid of the prophetic passion which calls down evil in order that virtue may triumph more brilliantly, and of the creative spirit which is capable of bringing about a vigorous transition from lowest to highest.

Such failings always imply a lack of humanity: the syndicate, section, party or class remains hidebound by its own limitations, and instead of regarding them as such, ends by making a fetish of them and loses that power of transcending them, which is the supreme necessity and spirit of socialism. This was the sole cause of the hiatus between the labour organizations, political and syndical, and the mass of the people.

Many of the socialist leaders thought that the vague popular movement which followed the armistice was just a 'war psychosis.' This was doubtless true, but it was not the whole truth. Those who fought in the war came in contact with the 'system' and were swept up and controlled by it for four years. The war had torn them abruptly from their parish pump outlook and given them a stormy introduction to real politics. A whole generation was united in a common experience of an extraordinary nature. Afterwards the mass of ex-servicemen everywhere felt that they were on the threshold of a new life. They revolved vague, half-formulated ideas which led them to seek contact with each other and to feel conscious of the need to fight for their common salvation. As was to be expected after the shock and the bloodshed, their reactions were not always normal. But there was a real feeling that 'we must not be taken in again', a feeling which ought to have been directed towards definite ends. Instead all that was noble and potentially humane in this emotional upheaval remained inarticulate, ignored, until finally it was exploited only to rescue from the past what had better been left there.

The socialist movement failed to realize how the war had thrown the great unorganized masses into the foreground. A movement on such a scale was beyond the old syndicate or party standard. The soldier back from the front found a society at once too unstable and too orderly for his liking. The revolution itself was too orderly—party card, syndicate subscription, membership of the co-operative, difficulties he could not get over, faced as he was by mistrust or tolerance, both equally insufferable. The Italian socialist leaders could no more understand the ex-servicemen of 1919–1920 than the German syndicates understood the unemployed of 1929–1932. Even Turati, so humane and so enlightened, felt that his chicks had turned into birds of prey. His socialism was a matter of conscience and education. In this he was right, but the time had come for the pedagogues, however noble, to give way to the prophets and missionaries. The sheltered flock in the party and the syndicates ought to have been neglected a little in favour of the lost sheep wandering in their thousands over waste land, so that they too could be saved.

Owing to the immense success of their co-operatives, Chambers of Labour, and town councils, the socialists of the Po valley believed they were simply going to absorb the old regime. Every day new institutions were growing up which to some extent foreshowed a society freed from the obsession of profit. But in legitimate pride in the results obtained they lost sight of their limitations, and socialism by remaining local and provincial became the victim of its own success. It went so far as to make a virtue of its faults. It was no longer only the old Italy, but socialism itself, the socialism of Reggio Emilia, which *farà da se*.* There was no point in considering the problem of the state, which supplied credits, grants and public works on demand. 'Here,' explained the socialist chiefs, 'we are already in power. If the whole of Italy becomes a Reggio Emilia the revolution will be made.' This 'socialism in a single province' lost in breadth what it gained in depth; and breadth for socialism is not a matter of mere dimensions, but forms part of its very essence. The rate of its spread decides its nature and its destiny. Through its ignorance or neglect of the peasants of Apulia and the herdsmen of Sardinia it lost contact with the nation and with the reality of socialism. It lost too the sound knowledge that none of its work would last while the 'oases of socialism' were still isolated in a desert whose sands might at any moment submerge them. This kind of socialism not only fails to lead to revolution, but risks losing all its conquests, as it did in Italy. The real essence of local and gradual action is to keep in touch with the state on the one hand and to further the aims of socialism on the other. In the absence of this two-

* 'Will act on its own,' a phrase which appeared during the *Risorgimento*, expressing independence of outside help.

fold outlet the political capacity, to use Proudhon's phrase, that the working class develops in its own institutions is lost to the community. The Italian socialists were utterly incapable of relating their ideals to the tasks imposed on them by circumstances.

Through this lack of perspective a prodigious quantity of devotion and human material, far superior to that behind many other political or religious movements, was wasted, and the chosen people, who had already arrived at the threshold of the new city, were disarmed and vanquished.

The socialists of the extreme left, on the other hand, invoked at every step their final aim of 'proletarian revolution.' On principle everything was sacrificed to this. For them there was no question as to whether their aim was consonant with the general interest; it was an accepted dogma, an historical fact, that it was so. Henceforward human emancipation was the work of the proletariat, and of the industrial proletariat in particular, acting through its leaders and its political party. And in their turn the party leaders became the trustees of the general interest and identified themselves with its progress and its demands. To look back and see if the sanctity of the apostolic succession had survived so many stages was pointless. There resulted a sectarian frame of mind dominated by a theological hatred of all who refused to recognize the divine quality of their mandate. So at the decisive moments in the Italian crisis the communists were fiercely opposed to a 'united front', which they had never seriously or loyally supported.

The ideas and behaviour of the communists over the alliance of the proletariat with other social classes were characterized by the same sort of trickery. These were used as mere pawns in a strategy which was carried on over their heads. The alliance was not conceived of as depending on a common principle to which the proletariat and its allies were bound in equal measure. On the contrary 'partial demands' were discussed, for the sake of an agreement that was only provisional and involved no deep or lasting obligations. While all goes well such differences pass unnoticed, but when the pace slackens the other classes begin to take notice and to claim their independence. This is what happened in Italy.

The alliance was founded on a very impermanent community of interests, and not on a desire for emancipation, which alone could have made it worth while or durable, and it ended not in mere disruption but in actual conflict. For the middle classes fell easy victims to manœuvres aimed at turning them against the proletariat. Fascism gave them an ideology which flattered their worst instincts by allowing them to believe that they were playing an independent and decisive part. The 'arbitration' of the middle class between capitalists and workers was set up against the 'hegemony' of the proletariat. One conception displaced another and the human raw material of the 'revolution' was sacrificed to it.

•   •   •   •   •

The working-class and socialist movement in Italy was therefore defeated largely because, as Filippo Turati said, it was reduced to 'teaching the proletariat to shirk at a time when the country was faced with the most urgent and burning problems'. A graphical representation of the two movements would show them to be in some degree complementary. The socialist curve rises until the spring of 1920, when it fluctuates (defeat of the Turin general strike), hesitates, then rises suddenly with the factory occupations in September. Then there is a continuous fall till the march on Rome. The fascist movement, powerless until the early months of 1920, scarcely revived by the employers' great offensive which led to the occupations, rose steeply during the last three months of 1920 and continued to rise rapidly in 1921. The decline of the working-class and socialist movement was due entirely to internal causes, and preceded and made possible the victorious outbreak of fascism. In an article written at the end of 1920 Mussolini said: 'In the past three months . . . the psychology of the Italian working class has changed profoundly,' and on July 2, 1921, sixteen months before the march on Rome, Mussolini recorded: 'To say that a bolshevist peril still exists in Italy is to accept a few disgraceful fears as the truth. Bolshevism is beaten.' Mr. Bolton King, who has written the best history of the *Risorgimento,* has rightly come to the following conclusion:

> Fascism had no part in the Bolschevist [sic] collapse; it was as yet not strong enough to make itself felt effectively, and Mussolini indeed had smiled approvingly on the occupation of the factories. There is no substance in the myth that it saved Italy from Bolschevism. But the myth is a convenient one and it still lives in dark corners.

In Italy this myth has become the object of an official cult very useful for the purposes of the internal and foreign policy of the fascist regime. It is nevertheless true, however, that it was not fascism which defeated the revolution in Italy, but the defeat of the revolution which determined the rise and victory of fascism.

Why did fascism only begin really to take hold when its historical necessity, or as much as it had claimed for itself, had disappeared? Because the movement was not merely defensive, but a deliberate attempt to wipe out the forces and strongholds of the enemy. In this way alone could the privileged classes and especially the landowners attain their object, which was, not to restore equilibrium, but to profit by its destruction. The retreat of the enemy only whetted their appetite for reaction and revenge. When, for a few weeks towards the middle of 1921, Mussolini toyed with the idea of a general settlement on the basis of a compromise, the fascists in the country districts frustrated his plans and found support for their intransigence in all conservative centres. Aggressive fascism of the *squadrismo* type was born of the union of the capitalist offensive with the ambitions and appetites of various sections of the middle class, left by the ebbing of the tide of war which had carried them along nicely for four years. Thus, to borrow another expression from Turati, 'a revolution in words', which had broken down after October 20, was followed by a 'bloody counter-revolution', a 'posthumous and preventive counter-revolution'. . . .

Just as the capitalist and fascist attack was being launched another factor began to weaken the workers' resistance. The slump became serious after the beginning of 1921, and the industrialists did not hesitate to use it as a weapon, proceeding to make wholesale dismissals of their staffs. The workers' committees and syndicates began by opposing them with their veto, but they could not hope to hold out long with purely passive resistance. The industrialists threatened to close the factories, and the workers no longer had any enthusiasm about occupying them. They tried compromise; with their strong sense of self-preservation and unity, the syndicates and internal factory committees imposed reductions in the hours of work of the whole staff, which they still had power to do, so as to avoid dismissals. This sacrifice by all for all considerably reduced wages all round. Those who were afraid of losing their jobs accepted this as a lesser evil, those who were or who believed themselves safe, eventually began to feel slightly uneasy and incapable of resistance. They became resigned to the elimination of one and then another category of workers: those who had a patch of ground in the sun, those who had no families dependent on them, the latest comers to the factory. This policy of despair gradually impaired the solidarity of the workers' front. Those who were sacrificed, with the tacit or formal consent of those who remained, departed embittered, sometimes desperate. Such a state of affairs could only be tolerated if it led to something better. But the workers, on the contrary, felt that they had reached an impasse, and that their sacrifice was useless, since anyhow the employers managed in the end to reduce their staff as much as they liked. The deadlock might have been ended by a firm policy uniting all the national resources to end the depression and assure at all events a minimum living wage to all workers. But who could have carried out such a policy? Not the socialists, who had been explaining for two years that this was a crisis of the capitalist system, that it was actually the final crisis of this system, and that the *bourgeoisie* must be left to shift for itself. Still less the ruling classes, whose one aim and obsession was the political and industrial enslavement of the workers. Fascism was there to simplify their task.

Consequently the slump, which the socialists had reckoned as an asset, proved their undoing. For every slump starts a process of social disintegration, with results that cannot be foretold dependent as they are upon uncertain human reactions. An exasperated desire to 'put an end to things' somehow may lead to despondency and panic unless it is directed towards some concrete aim, and allowed a glimpse of a new order. The slump crushes those who cannot thus look ahead and are therefore without hope. Its value as a revolutionary factor lies in the forces of order it sets in motion; if these are not the forces of a new order, it only serves to consolidate the old.

· · · · ·

The economic crisis in Italy coincided with a political one. Every branch of the state, police, executive, magistracy and army, gave its support to the fascists, in ways varying from tolerance to direct complicity. The ground was prepared for them, they were supplied with arms and transport, and they were promised immunity from punishment. Government decrees mouldered in files or were used exclusively against socialists. The government itself preferred not to be too deeply involved. For everybody was hoping to make use of fascism: Giolitti, to push the socialists into the government, the conservatives to keep them out, employers and landowners to liquidate working-class syndicalism, the monarchy and the Vatican to buttress the established order. They all relied on fascism as a temporary ally which could easily be disposed of later. As matters stood, the state could only live a hand-to-mouth existence, going from compromise to compromise, from concession to concession. It had no source of strength. The mass of the people was estranged and hostile, and parliamentary crises followed one after the other continuously and without any signs of a solution appearing. Confusion, lassitude, and disgust, skilfully enhanced by controversy, and a kind of 'planned defeatism' prepared public opinion for the justification of dictatorship. Liberty, in whose cause nobody, whether individual or party, was prepared to sacrifice either ambitions or personal wishes, was left defenceless. The threat to the state became a threat to democracy.

· · · · · ·

In addition to the failure of the socialists, capitalist and fascist aggression, the economic crisis, state complicity, and the breakdown of parliamentary institutions, there must be taken into account the personal influence of Mussolini.

During the war he severed all that connected him with his ancient beliefs. At heart, though, he had never been a real socialist. As a young man, consumed by pride and the desire to assert himself, and obsessed by the idea that society was oppressing him, he had broken away and taken refuge in Switzerland. As society would not give him the position he wanted, his will to power took the form of individual revolt. The experiences of his years of exile had a decisive effect on him. Sometimes he had been dependent for his daily bread on the help and goodwill of mere artisans or simple decent socialists, or on petty dishonesty. Sometimes he had had to take the roughest kind of work; he had fallen low, and known extreme poverty. Such a life might have turned him into a saint or a criminal, but he was too ambitious and too unscrupulous to take either way out. He learnt to set his teeth, to calculate, to reject the romantic outlook and to grab his opportunity. Socialism could give him a start and serve for shelter. In a few years he reached the highest position that the party could give him, the editorship of its paper, *Avanti*. By the outbreak of war socialism in its turn had become the obstacle that society had been to him in the years 1900 to 1908. Mussolini did not hesitate to break away a second time. After the armistice he realized that he had to begin all over again and start a third struggle for existence. From that time on his personal fortune is so closely linked with the history of fascism as to be often indistinguishable.

If Mussolini had simply joined forces with the reactionaries in 1919 the flood would have passed over him and he would have been left behind; he would not have found himself in March supported by the ex-members of the 'Fasci of Revolutionary Action' of 1914–1915, nor, a short time later, would he have managed to collect a number of young men and ex-servicemen. Even if he had formed the new *fasci* they would have perished with him. By the end of 1920 the situation had altered: the *squadristi* and the 'slave-drivers', spreading from the valley of the Po, were advancing rapidly and overthrowing the socialist strongholds one after another. Mussolini hastened to make use of this movement, and revised his programme, declaring that 'the reality of to-morrow will be capitalist'. Towards the end of 1921 however, the movement was showing signs of getting out of hand and comprising his political plans. So he tried to frustrate it, denouncing its 'greedy egoism which refuses any national conciliation'; he contrasted the 'urban fascism' of Milan with the 'agrarian fascism' of Bologna, 'fascism of the first hour' with that which stood for the defence of 'private interests and of the darkest, most sordid and most despicable classes now existing in Italy'. Having announced in Florence: 'Our programme is based on facts', he now clamoured for a 'return to principles'. A few months later still, when the situation had developed further, he trampled on the vague tendencies of Grandi * and his friends towards 'democracy' and 'syndicalism', and from their opposition movement he took nothing but the bare principle of armed organization, stripped of any political significance; a simple weapon for the capture of power. Besides, although he disguised his plans in 1921 under a pretended 'return to principles' Mussolini declared one year later that 'to go back to the beginning, as some would have, that is to get back to the 1919 programme, is to give proof of childishness and senility'. His versatility and complete lack of scruple proved an invaluable asset to fascism. It was he who prevented the attack on the Bonomi cabinet in autumn 1921; he who persuaded the group to support the Celli resolution in February 1922 ** and in July succeeded in preventing the formation of an anti-fascist group which might have become a government. If this had taken place fascism would have lost the support, or at least the connivance, of the state, and risked defeat. Finally, if Mussolini had not acted as he did, the march on Rome would have taken place in earnest and fascism would have met its doom.

Mussolini is not a genius; he merely has, as Mr. Bolton King so justly remarks, 'the minor arts of a statesman'. But these he possesses to a very high degree. Much of his strength has come from the weakness of his enemies. In 1919 he was simultaneously outbidding the demagogues and working for the cause of reaction. This could never have happened if socialism had not allowed it. Faced with a construc-

---

* Count Dino Grandi was one of Mussolini's earliest colleagues in the Fascist movement.—Ed.
** The Celli resolution, presented to the Chamber of Deputies, was part of an unsuccessful parliamentary effort to thwart the Fascists.—Ed.

tive, which does not mean a watered-down Socialist Party, based on the traditions, institutions and powerful resources of the Italian working-class movement and free from delusions about soviets, Mussolini's tricks and manœuvres would have fallen flat. From the second half of 1921 up to the march on Rome Mussolini managed to exploit parliamentary action and *squadrismo* at the same time, thus, in Lenin's phrase, combining 'legal with illegal action'. But it was the socialist movement which gave him the necessary freedom of movement, by refraining from all action, legal or illegal, and thus delivering the country into the hands of its enemies. If it had been attacked through these inconsistencies fascism might have been crushed, but because they were neglected and allowed to flourish they became a direct cause of its strength and success.

The Italy of 1919–1922 lacked political leaders. Giolitti's mentality was pre-war, and when he returned to power in 1920 he was in his seventy-eighth year. The others, Nitti, Bonomi, Orlando, Salandra, all suffered from the same handicap: they were good scholars, but too academic to be able to deal properly with the post-war situation. The socialists had a few first-rate men, mostly on the right, but they were hampered by the conflict of doctrines inside the party and the working-class movement. The personal qualities of some of the communist leaders, such as Gramsci and Bordiga, could not outweigh the damage done by hopelessly wrong-headed tactics, and sometimes aggravated it. The maximalist socialists were a body without a head. Lamartine's description of a Girondin chief applied to most of their leaders: 'One of those complaisant idols of which people make anything they wish except a man'.

Italian socialism had need of a man, several men, in order to win, or, which came to the same thing, to avoid being wiped out. This was why Mussolini was able to reduce Italy to his own size and fill the entire horizon. With his advent the rule of 'principle' came to an end, and his own personal adventure became that of Italy itself. For the better understanding of this crisis it is possible and indeed essential to trace back over centuries its remote and fundamental causes: the configuration of the land; the economic and social structure; the long enslavement of the people; the recent liberation, barely tolerated by some, barely assimilated by others. But these causes were not bound, inevitably, to lead to the events of the years 1919–1922 as they actually took place, with all their changes, their possibilities and their final result. New forces were growing up in Italy, alongside the prevalent lethargy, and for a certain space of time these balanced each other. In such cases momentary influences, including luck, may be decisive. The slightest variation may upset the balance and change the whole situation. Then it is that the actions of one man become of first importance, and history becomes a drama in which everything is linked up and nothing pre-determined, in which the epilogue may be changed up to the last minute, so long as the actors—individuals or groups—do not themselves rush towards the catastrophe. Contrary to a common belief, circumstances do not always of themselves create the men who are needed. Past history now provides a proof.

II

Fascism is a dictatorship; such is the starting-point of all definitions that have so far been attempted. Beyond that there is no agreement. Dictatorship of capitalism 'in the period of its decline', dictatorship of large-scale capitalism; dictatorship of finance-capitalism; 'openly terrorist' dictatorship 'of the most reactionary, chauvinist and imperialistic sections of finance-capitalism'; dictatorship of the 'two hundred families'; and so on, until sometimes one meets the definition of fascism narrowed down to the personal dictatorship of Mussolini or Hitler. Someone has said, 'Italian fascism is Mussolini.'

Each of these definitions contains some truth, but none can be accepted as it stands. Further, we shall take care not to produce a new one, which would of course be the right one, a pocket formula, which could be brought out at any moment to clear up our own and everybody else's doubts. Our way of defining fascism is to write its history. We have tried to do this for Italian fascism of the years 1919–1922. A theory of fascism can only be evolved through a study of all its forms, latent or open, modified or unrestrained. For there are many different fascisms, each one made up of numerous, sometimes contradictory tendencies, and capable of developing in such a way that its most characteristic features may be altered. To define fascism is to surprise it during this development, and, in a given country and at a given time, to seize upon its essential differences. It is not a subject with definite attributes which need merely be selected, but the product of a situation from which it cannot be considered separately. The mistakes of the workers' parties, for instance, are as much part of the definition of fascism as the use made of them by the proprietary classes.

The present study of fascism has not been carried beyond the march on Rome, but there is no reason why we should not glance further. Although conditions in Italy ought to be comprehensively reviewed and compared with those in other countries during the years that followed, the present less enterprising method may at least enable us to point out a few common characteristics from which some conclusions can be drawn. For this purpose fascism must be considered in relation to the economic, social, political and psychological conditions from which it sprang; to its own social background and the class struggle; to its tactics, its organization; to its consequences and the regime that it set up; finally to its own programme and ideology.

• • • • •

Fascism is a post-war phenomenon and any attempt to define it by looking for an historical precedent, e.g. in Bonapartism, is fruitless and bound to lead to false conclusions. Foremost among the conditions that made fascism possible was the economic crisis. No crisis, no fascism; and this refers not to any economic crisis, but specifically to the one that settled permanently over the world after the war. The war left the world with industrial capacity beyond its immediate needs and a complete lack of co-ordination between the various branches of production, complicated by a reduced purchasing power in all countries. The result was over-production and famine, inflation and paralysis. We are no longer faced by classical crises, which rise from a terrible slump to a still higher rate of production and consumption. The 'periodic' crises have been succeeded by 'chronic stagnation with slight fluctuations', the 'alternation of relatively short boom and relatively long depression', foretold by Engels more than fifty years ago. Even in the United States, where crises are more oscillatory owing to the possibilities of the home market, the existence of an irreducible mass of several million unemployed points to a new kind of depression. Fascism is bred in these depressions and forms part of the reaction to them. In countries without the large home market of the U.S.A., the British Empire, the U.S.S.R., depressions are more or less incurable. Economic discomfort fuses readily with nationalist aspirations and talk of 'a place in the sun'. This results on the one hand in isolation and the aggravation of the more artificial and parasitical aspects of the economic system, on the other in the illusion that the 'encirclement' can be broken by seeking some violent solution beyond the frontiers. The capitalist system, having to a great extent lost its resiliency, oscillates no longer between depression and boom, but between autarchy and war.

In every country the end of the war and the beginning of the depression saw fairly considerable alterations in social status. The creation of a mass of *nouveaux riches,* and distinct changes in the traditional forms of capitalism resulted in the emergence of a new *bourgeoisie.* Practically all producers had become so used to exceptional war-time profits that they had lost sight of the notion of the rigidity of cost price, while the stimulus of competition had been entirely removed. Such considerations were always resurrected when workers' wages had to be discussed, but they had really ceased to operate, and almost everywhere capitalists were conscious that they could no longer manage without the direct help of the state. Its seizure by any possible means became for them a matter of life-and-death importance.

On the other hand, the war had set the popular masses in movement, and after the war this movement was accelerated. The organization of the workers' parties and the syndicates was breaking down under the pressure of the hundreds of thousands and millions of new members. They had no great stability, and the high tide was quickly followed by a rapid ebb. Moreover, in spite of the growth of the old organizations, there was a large body of waverers who remained outside, ready to rush in any direction. This body has been referred to as the 'middle classes'; but it must be emphasized that they were not the middle classes of the classical period of capitalism, absorbed after each crisis into the machinery of increased production and into a new proletariat. The post-war middle classes no longer had even the chance of joining the proletariat; the depression barred both their rise into the *bourgeoisie* and their descent into the proletariat. This petty and middle *bourgeoisie,* which found itself everywhere excluded, formed the backbone of fascism in Italy and everywhere else. But the expression 'middle class' must be given a wider meaning, to include the son of the family waiting for a job or for his inheritance to *declassés* of all kinds, temporary or permanent, from the half-pay officer to the *lumpenproletarier,* from the strike-breaker to the jobless intellectual. It includes workers who are more conscious of being ex-servicemen or unemployed than of their class, from which they break away in spirit to join the ranks of its enemies.

With the coming of peace the long pent-up demands of the masses were released, at a time when, as a result of the war, there was less than ever to satisfy them. A tendency to hoard available resources rather than find better ways of sharing them brought the problem of power into the foreground. Three factors combined to lead the way to fascism: the intensification of the class struggle, its increasingly political character, and the relative equality of the opposing forces. Given the first two, the third is of crucial importance. Such equality is paralysing to any form of government, whether it be a national coalition, a combination of left-wing parties, or a social democratic majority. So long as it continues and no better form of government is found, the state is at the mercy of blind upheavals caused by some instinct of self-preservation, by the defence of threatened privileges, and by the aspirations of classes that have been upset and thrown out of gear by the depression. By abandoning the attempt to gain a solution by legal methods, the working classes turn to the creation of a 'second power', within the state and opposed to it; the *bourgeoisie* then has recourse either to 'reactionary transformation of the state' or to fascist violence.

Amongst the general conditions of fascism that should be mentioned is the existence of a kind of 'climate', a special atmosphere of excitement and frenzy; this is so indispensable, both before and after victory, that the party leaders have to strain every nerve to keep it up. In this atmosphere all reactions are strained, all sense of proportion is distorted, and ordinary standards vanish. Psychological shock becomes as necessary as drugs to an addict. Delirium is exalted as normality. Fascism cannot be dismissed as mere war psychosis. . . . The history of fascism, however, is one of the most remarkable and disturbing chapters of social pathology.

●   ●   ●   ●   ●

Fascism finds its chief support in the post-war middle class, whose main characteristics we have just described. Must fascism, therefore, be defined as a middle-class movement taken up and exploited by reactionary capitalism? There is much truth in this definition, but it cannot be accepted without reservations. The social significance of a movement is not entirely decided by its social make-up. Although most of the supporters of fascism are recruited from the middle classes, its first historic role is that of the exterminator of working-class parties and syndicates. Afterwards, whatever its pretensions or its supporters, it takes a hand in the capitalist offensive. The suppression of the independent workers' organizations permanently alters the balance of social power. Fascists and capitalists can no longer behave as if these organizations had not been suppressed. Even when fascism pretends to play the part of arbitrator between capital and labour, it puts one of the parties in an inferior position—by destroying its independence—from which it can only free itself by throwing off fascism altogether.

It was chiefly the urban middle classes which were swept into fascism. In July 1919 Mussolini believed, not only that fascism was fated to remain 'a minority movement', but that it could not 'spread outside the towns'. And although Italian fascism was chiefly established, after 1921, through the influx of countryfolk into its ranks, its leaders were largely drawn from the middle classes in the towns, or were the sons of landowners—officers, students—town-dwellers with no desire to play the part of Cincinnatus, once they were back from the front. They were much more anxious to conquer the towns, the first step towards political power, than to be the leaders in their village. Further, fascism was never successful when confined to purely country districts, and the impulse to victory came less from the Po valley campaigns than from Rome and Milan. The big cities always played the leading part.

Fascism finds its chief support in those members of the middle class who either have or think they have no independent economic standing, and are thus easily 'liquidated' or absorbed into the new political framework provided by fascism. It is not pure chance which makes the French peasant oppose fascism so obstinately: he will obviously continue to do so as long as his economic basis—the patch of ground he owns and tills—and his more or less real independence are threatened. In the Balkans all the authoritarian regimes—bred in the great cities—were set up in face of the violent resistance of the peasants, who mostly supported opposition parties (National-Zaranist party in Romania, the Croat peasant party in Jugo-Slavia, the 'Agrarians' in Bulgaria). In all these countries the land reform carried out after the war had created an important class of peasant proprietors, who remained anti-fascist even in subjection; while in contrast the absence of such reforms, or excessive slowness in carrying them out, have made of fascism a danger or a success in Italy, Germany and Spain.

Another theory that will not hold water represents fascism as a revolutionary movement turned reactionary under the influence of the ruling classes. Fascism is reactionary from the start. Its first steps are helped and guided by reactionary influence, and its intervention completely upsets the political and social equilibrium. The coincidence of fascist development and the political and economic offensive of the possessing classes is a common phenomenon. Italian fascism did not begin to be important until 1921, when 'agrarian slavery' appeared in the Po valley, Tuscany and Apulia, at the same time as the industrialists' attack on workmen's wages and collective labour agreements. National Socialism, in embryo in 1923, did not begin to get under way until after 1928–29, when wages were being cut and the policy of deflation had begun. After 1922 Mussolini's policy coincided with that of the 'liberals' of the *Corriere della Sera,* the conservatives of the

Giornale d'Italia, the great landowners and the Vatican, namely, to keep the socialists from any share in power; just as Hitler, in 1930, insisted on the breaking up of the great coalition and the exclusion of the socialists from the Prussian government.

The middle classes had to some extent been caught up by the wave of popular feeling in the years 1919–20, but the inability of the socialist movement to find any solution had cooled them off. Tactless insistence on the 'dictatorship of the proletariat', although this was nothing but a form of words, had helped them to change their minds. Feeling that their pockets and their beliefs were threatened by the socialist movement, they turned towards fascism. All their latent hatred of the man in cap and blouse now came to the surface, finding expression on the one hand in savage attacks on the workers, on the other in a vague desire for independence, and even a kind of idealism. This idealism and the new language it created made its own contribution to the victory of the possessing classes, winning over for them a section of the masses with which they had entirely lost touch.

The relations between middle-class fascism and the capitalist offensive were very close at the start, and have remained so for a long time. Does this mean that they are incapable of development and change? Only a very detailed analysis of these relations in the different countries at different times could lead one to any conclusion on this question; while it must be remembered that, whatever the relations may be, they are always affected and distorted by the absence of a third power, that of a freely organized labour group.

• • • • •

Fascism is not reaction pure and simple, but reaction employing mass effects, which alone are of any use in the post-war world. Hence the use of demagogic slogans and even of socialist terminology: for a long time Mussolini called his paper a 'socialist daily,' and the *Führer's* party still styles itself National-Socialist. As a result the old political parties often find themselves left high and dry.

But the real originality of fascism lies not so much in its mass tactics or its demagogic programme, as in the all-important and independent part played by tactics at the expense of programme. Giolitti used to say, 'Mussolini has taught me that it is not the programme but the tactics of a revolution against which we must defend ourselves.' The fascist method is tactical rather than doctrinal. Its supreme resort is the *fait accompli,* which is of no effect unless it finally leads to the seizure of power. Absolute power alone enables fascism to overcome its inherent inconsistencies and to maintain its advance, for the spoils can be used to satisfy the most varied appetites, the prestige of victory to attract supporters, and the power of the state to crush its enemies into submission for a long while. This is how the fascist writer Curzio Malaparte, in his *Technique of the Coup d'Etat,* describes the political crisis which preceded the march on Rome: 'These same liberals, democrats, conservatives, while they were summoning the fascists to join the National Bloc, were eager to install Mussolini in the Pantheon of the "saviours of the country" . . . but they were not so ready to resign themselves to the fact that Mussolini's aim was not to save Italy in accordance with the official tradition, but to seize the state, a much more sincere programme than the one he had proclaimed in 1919.'

$*$.   .   .   .   .

Hence the importance to fascism of organization, especially armed organization. Every fascist movement has its armed organization, without which it is powerless. This does not mean that every fascist goes about armed, or that the movement has immediate access to arms dumps and arsenals. But its organization is military, with its cadre of officers, discipline, meetings, training, and the firm belief of every member, from top to bottom, that this organization is a necessary and effective instrument for the conquest of power. Fascism always begins by declaring itself 'anti-party' and ends by turning itself into a political party; in all the great countries, however, its military organization remains its chief characteristic. Mussolini was able to enrol the entire party in the squads in December 1921, and in 1936 de la Rocque could convert his squads into a party, with the same aim of saving the military organization by disguising it. This organization lies at the heart of fascism and determines its very nature.

Must fascism be resisted by military means? The question of force is undoubtedly involved. But the force behind a sound policy must come as a natural consequence of that policy. Military organization may be very extensively developed, but if it is out of touch with the country its position becomes desperate; this was the case with the fascist squads in the middle of 1921 and the socialist *Schutzbund* in Austria in February 1934. Both Mussolini and Hitler, on the other hand, won their chief victories on the political field (the Facta crisis in October 1922, and the von Schleicher crisis in January 1933).

It is essential for any anti-fascist movement to be always in close touch with the masses. It must also associate itself with the state. In the event of a complete fusion of the ruling classes and the machinery of state with fascism, there may be no other alternative but direct revolutionary action or fascist dictatorship. Even so the consequence is not inevitably the slippery dilemma of 'bolshevism or fascism', which limits the possible courses of action at a time when they should be as varied as possible. Every example that can be quoted (Italy, Bulgaria, Germany, Austria) proves that a union of the state with fascism is the worst thing that can happen. The policy of the working classes fighting fascism must be to do their utmost to avoid being faced with such a situation.

The working class and the masses should try to cut fascism off from the state, and to neutralise and oppose the influence of those who would subordinate the state to fascism. Fascism can do nothing without the help of the state, and less than nothing as its enemy. But it is difficult for anti-fascism to win if it is simultaneously fighting the state and fascism in their entirety. The Italian communists who declared in 1921 that 'the issue lies between proletarian dictatorship and fascist dictatorship,' and the German communists who in 1932 gave the order for a war on two fronts: 'Against Weimar and against Potsdam', ended by fighting neither fascism nor the state. The struggle against fascism is three-cornered—the anti-fascist front, which must be on as broad a base as possible, the fascist bloc, which has to be broken up, and the state, whose resources must be mobilized for the defence of democracy. Victory is only possible through a political strategy that takes these three elements into account and aligns them in such a way that force is on the side of democracy.

•   •   •   •   •

To complete this analysis of the nature of fascism we must study the fruit it bears: its consequences, not only inside each country, but also on an international scale, which are closely inter-connected.

Wherever fascism is established the most important consequence, on which all the others depend, is the elimination of the people from all share in political activity. 'Constitutional reform', the suppression of parliament, and the totalitarian character of the regime cannot be judged by themselves, but only in relation to their aims and their results. Fascism is not merely the substitution of one political regime for another; it is the disappearance of political life itself, since this becomes a state function and monopoly. Political doctrines circulate, are abandoned or modified, but the people have nothing to do with their adoption or their fluctuations. Even when syndicates, or even a party, continue to exist, they are mere instruments, subordinate branches of the state. By becoming part of the machinery of state their nature does not undergo any change; they merely become instruments in the second degree, the instruments of instruments. With the removal of all freedom and independence from their institutions the people are reduced to a malleable raw material whose properties of resistance and yield can be calculated and controlled. They still take part in parades and demonstrations, and may be kept in a constant state of alertness and tension; but this is simply part of the drill and never approaches the level of political consciousness.

In this system there is no room for the fatal illusion, long held by the communists, that fascism might do some good by destroying 'democratic illusions'. The Italian communists actually announced in May 1921 that: 'It is true that White reaction is celebrating a few ephemeral victories over an enemy which is paying dear for its unpreparedness, but it is destroying the democratic and liberal illusion and breaking down the influence of social democracy among the masses.' And in the resolution of the Presidium of the Communist International, published in January 1934, the following statement concerning Germany may be read: 'The establishment of an undisguised fascist dictatorship, by dispelling the democratic illusions of the masses and liberating them from the influence of social democracy, is accelerating Germany's advance towards the proletarian revolution.' This is not the place for a detailed criticism of this conception, which the Communist International has never abandoned in spite of all its changes of front, and we need only record that fascism suppresses not only 'democratic illusions', but the workers' and socialist movement which is subject to them. Fascism is like a completely successful operation: the patient dies and all his illusions are removed.

By reducing the people to a mere instrument, fascism destroys the nation. This aspect of the system tends to pass unnoticed, disguised by the violent nationalist frenzy that fascism cultivates. National conscience as conceived in the nineteenth century by Mazzini, the prophet of the nation state, is ousted by state expediency. For him nations could not exist without free peoples, any more than humanity could exist without free nations. The winning of political liberty and the winning of national independence spring from the same instinctive urge, and in the best Jacobin and romantic tradition, 'patriot' and 'democrat' are identical. For Mazzini the awakening of national consciousness was no more than an essential step towards the formation of European consciousness: 'Young Italy' could only fulfil itself in 'Young Europe'.

Such conceptions take us far from fascism, while at the same time explaining why the fascists mean to destroy the working-class and socialist movement. Since the end of the nineteenth century socialism has almost everywhere taken the place of democracy in initiating the masses into national life. They have taken their place in the nation and state on social grounds. This has brought difficulties in its train and sometimes confusion and crisis, but it remains a great historical fact that the masses brought the whole weight of their needs and hopes with them into national life, and thenceforward it was impossible for this life to be organized on any but a higher level of conscience, liberty and individual well-being. For the fascists, on the other hand, the people are only the tool of their 'will to power'. This is inspired by a furious nationalism, which takes over the socialists' demands only to adapt them to serve their own purposes. The slogans of the class struggle in its narrowest sense become the passwords of armed strife between nations: 'young' nations versus old, 'poor' nations versus 'satiated', 'proletarian' nations versus 'plutocratic'. Hence in all forms of national socialism the nationalism inevitably absorbs the socialism, and in every fascist 'armed nation' the army swallows up the nation.

This leads equally to autarchy and war. The economic difficulties and contradictions of the fascist regimes speed up the process, but they are not the sole causes. The fascist systems are not only 'driven' into war, all their activities lead up to it, and it provides the opportunities and the atmosphere they need. Though choice there may be, they cannot do otherwise than choose war. Preparation for war at a given moment ceases to be a means, and becomes an end in itself, completely changing the economic, social and political structure of the country. Fascism is committed to this preparation and can only fight its way out. For fascism preparation for war does not mean leaving one of many doors open just in case war should unfortunately break out, but leaving only one open and shutting all the rest. War is not merely a possibility which the state must bear in mind, but a certainty and a necessity to which everything is subordinated. Speaking at the meeting of the Corporations on March 23, 1936, Mussolini explained his policy and his ideas for the future as follows:

Italy can and must attain the maximum of economic independence for peace and war. The whole of the Italian economic system must be directed towards this supreme necessity, on which depends the future of the Italian people. I now come to the crux, to what I might call the plan of control for Italian economic policy in the coming fascist era. This plan is determined by one single consideration: that our nation will be called to war. When? How? Nobody can say, but the wheel of fate is turning fast.

The fascist economy is a closed and planned economy with war as its objective. Cost price, competition and even profit are of no importance in the general scheme. The political aim of preparation for war is more important than any economic consideration, and equally the resulting economic organisation can serve no other aim. In his speech of May 26, 1934 (quoted above), Mussolini said: 'If I wanted to introduce state capitalism or state socialism into Italy, I should now have all the necessary external and objective conditions for doing so.' Can it be said that fascist economy is state capitalism? In spite of several points of resemblance, we believe not. Under fascism the state does not simply take the place of private capitalists as the organizer of the economic system, but forces them to follow its own policy. Fascism is interested in power, not profit. Naturally profit may one day have to be added to power, but between the two there is a wide gulf which the capitalist class, as such, would refuse to cross unless it were forced.

But it is being forced to do so by a new political class, which is a product of the economic evolution of fascism, and which in its turn reacts on this movement by forcing it towards its most extreme consequences. The proletariat, as such, is entirely excluded from this new class. Preparation for war may relatively reduce unemployment and improve the lot of some classes of workers, but under a system of autarchy it is only achieved by sacrificing the standard of living of the working class as a whole. And since it involves a great concentration of industry, trade and credit, and necessitates large-scale agriculture and mass production of cereals a great proportion of the urban and the whole of the rural middle class is more or less ruined. The increasing concentration of industry, the monopoly of foreign trade, the fixing of prices and the many forms of state intervention all tend to the elimination of the lesser industrialists and the small traders and farmers. On the other hand those members of the urban middle class who have no direct share in production benefit considerably from the regime and pocket a nice share of the profits. They are to be found everywhere, occupying numerous places on the executives of the party, militia, syndicates, state institutions new and old. They form part of the immense fascist bureaucracy which is now the country's ruling class. Generally speaking this new class is the result of a compromise between the capitalists and the middle and lower middle class in the towns. It is interspersed with army chiefs, and members of the aristocracy, but the *homines novi* are in a majority, and theirs is the prevailing mentality: a mixture of furious nationalism and state worship, in keeping with both their ideology and their interests. This new ruling class battens on the state, indulging in shameless scrambles for gain, runs through fortunes with ease, exploits and fleeces others, but has no definite place in the economic life of the country. Even when he becomes a landed proprietor or a capitalist this new fascist ruler continues to draw the best part of his resources from the political monopoly of which he is assured, and from the perpetual expansion of the machinery of state, which he encourages with all his might.

Autarchy and preparation for war make this expansion inevitable. The expansion of state machinery in its turn is bound to involve autarchy and war. Nothing inside the country can break this vicious circle. Fascism has successively wiped out the working-class movement, the people, the nation, every restraining influence. Such is the tragic balance sheet of the fascist attack of the years 1921–1922, whose effects stretch far beyond the boundaries of Italy. The flames which destroyed the Peoples' Houses were only the beginning of a greater blaze which threatens to set Europe alight. The blows that shattered the headquarters of workers' syndicates, co-operatives and socialist sections have struck at the foundations of the new Europe: the Europe loathed by fascism, since it means the end of war and fascists alike.

III

For fascism the political programme is a mere makeshift, concocted to meet the immediate needs of political strategy. On the eve of the march on Rome . . . the fascists, like the national socialists, based their candidature to power on the reality of their strength and not on their old or new programme. And it was their strength, directed against the working class and the socialists, which the conservative classes meant to exploit when they helped them to power.

'Our programme is based on facts,' said Mussolini at the fascist congress in October 1919. This remark described not merely the party's intended tactics, but an entire conception of life, which reduces everything to its value in relation to the 'will to power' standard. This is the major difference between fascism and socialism, over which no compromise is possible. The fate of humanity for a long time hangs on the outcome of this conflict, and the issue lies, not, as it may appear, between two rival philosophies, but between philosophy and the negation of all philosophy.

'Action has dug a grave for philosophy,' said Mussolini on his train journey to Rome, where the king was going to charge him with the formation of the new government. This 'realism' that fascism perpetually claims for itself is the high-water mark of its so-called doctrine. Having once arrived in power, fascism, like any other parvenu discovering his noble quarterings, provides itself with antecedents. It goes back to the Guelph tradition, to the Counter-Reformation, to Romanticism: history is ransacked in a feverish search for ancestors. All that survives of these efforts, before as after victory, are the by-products of a crude pragmatism, and the glorification of force, of which a furious nationalism and worship of the state are the outstanding manifestations. Behind it all is the 'pagan' conception of life as struggle and effort which are their own justification. Hence the exaltation of war: 'War alone,' writes Mussolini in the *Italian Encyclopædia,* 'brings all human energies to their highest tension, and sets a stamp of nobility on the peoples who have the courage to face it.'

Certainly fascism always preaches duty, self-denial and discipline, and condemns individual egoisms. But actually fascism is 'anti-individualist' the better to suppress the universal instinct of humanity in the individual conscience, which it frees from its inhibitions so as to avoid the necessity of reckoning with its demands. It sacrifices, not the attributes of individuality, but the conscious being. Apparently everything is saved, since moral life is simply transferred to the state. 'For the fascist everything is in the state, and nothing human or spiritual exists or, *a fortiori,* has any value outside the state.'

'For fascism the state is the absolute, before which individuals and groups are only relative.' And since it is impossible to base a moral imperative on the 'relative', we may well ask the meaning of this 'absolute' which fascism finds in the state. Mussolini himself gives us an answer: 'The fascist state is a "will to power" and to domination.' Having started from the will to power, and subordinated the individuals to it, fascism is bound to find it again in the state. Moral life itself, and all its possible foundations, are locked out. The 'will to power and to domination' has nothing in common with morality, even if, following the Hitlerian formula, this serves the 'vital needs' of a people.

Allowing for its defects, socialism is the greatest attempt to subordinate to the needs of the human conscience everything which, in reality, is hostile and alien to it. Socialism aims at putting human before economic necessities, at 'humanizing' and 'moralizing' nature and preventing its brute forces from spreading unchecked. It studies natural 'laws' in order to make use of them and not to remain bound by them. It fights to save the human soul from outside restraints, and to impose its own internal law on the outside world. Its aim is to control the industrial machine with its huge productive powers as well as the state machine with its great power of coercion, particularly as both the powers and the machines are tending more and more to merge into one. Socialism is a finalist, fascism an instrumental doctrine, a sort of drill, a discipline, a stimulant, and as such it can neither found nor replace a system of ethics either for individuals or for the state.

The negation of philosophy, fascism is thus the negation of politics and religion. 'The democratic conception of life is essentially political, the fascist essentially warlike,' wrote Mussolini in September 1922. Fascism can only tolerate religion if it surrenders what was apparently its own private domain, that of the individual conscience. By helping to break down the resistance of individuals and groups to their absorption by the fascist state, the Church has accepted and smiled on the omnipotence of this state which denies freedom to the independent conscience and to religion itself. Even, or rather particularly, when official honours are being heaped on it, religion only survives under fascism by allowing itself to be used as a tool. Like fascism it becomes merely a discipline, a useful means of consoling and restraining the common people, an indispensable resource that so many atheists, from Voltaire to Mussolini, have invoked. 'Religion for the poor' is thus added to 'imperialism for the proletariat' in the well-filled fascist armoury of *'raison d'ètat.'*

* * * * *

Since fascism exalts action and denies philosophy, must faith in philosophy be signalized by the denial of action? The pundits who take this line betray philosophy twice over by betraying both philosophy and action. No conception of life is true or workable unless it is universally applicable, and in this case 'universally' applies to each individual man, and so to humanity as a whole. Man and humanity are identical terms. It is impossible to affirm what is human in individual man without realizing it in the whole of mankind. Hence the human must be supreme, and impress itself on every branch of life.

There can be no giving way to *faits accomplis,* no surrender to success; the responsibilities that are owed to all men cannot be avoided by an escape into the realm of good intentions. Good intentions by themselves do no good. It is not enough to be in the right; one has got to succeed.

Methods and tactics are necessary therefore; weapons must be chosen, forces combined, the decision made as to where they are to be applied; certain positions must be abandoned in order to win others; progress must be made through advances and retreats and cunning manœuvres whose meaning only becomes apparent with their completion. But tactics, like all the realities of life and history— classes, technique, institutions—have a tendency to develop on their own, forgetful of the end towards which they are directed. Everything tends to grow like a cancer regardless of its surroundings and of the very reasons which brought it into being. This is all the more serious, since a truth derives its value from the importance which is given to it and the position it occupies, for it is one thing if it is kept in the background and quite another if it becomes the centre to which all other factors are subordinated. On the other hand a certain degree of independence in tactics is inevitable and even essential for final success. The tactical 'theme' must be hit upon and renewed in each new situation. The forces available to support it must be summed up and used accordingly, and victory comes only as the resultant of the calculation.

Victory has not only to be won, but won in a given time. Each situation has a 'potential' which is variable but not infinite. Its curve is mobile, but man's action must take place within it, for one day it will fall under the influence of the very forces that have caused it to rise. The point of incidence may be varied a thousand times, but not for ever. Circumstances arise in which a general sense of exhaustion and saturation makes it impossible for action to be postponed any longer, or the opportunity is lost for a long while. Tactics which are inoperable within a given time are valueless; the time factor, itself a variable function, must be taken into account and controlled. In post-war Italy, as elsewhere, there was a great fund of hopes and desires turned towards a new order, but the workers' parties acted as though this capital could be left unproductive or wasted at will. Ten years have been enough to dissipate what seemed inexhaustible, and no one can tell when the impulse and the opportunity will come again.

To win, and to win in time, contact must be made with the great masses, and the help of an organization is indispensable. This does not eliminate the role of individual appeal and protest, the need for both prophets and skirmishers. The chosen few strike the new coinage, but it must be put into circulation, and everything depends on how widely and how quickly this is done. Contact between the idea and the people can be achieved only with an organized system keeping always in close touch with them. This is a liability as well as an advantage, for the go-between, the party, tends to become an independent unit and builds up machinery, which in its turn becomes more or less independent. This hardens into party loyalty, with its defensive and conservative instincts. But it would be a grave error to treat this as a sign of inertia. Some defence mechanism is as necessary to collective bodies as to individuals. The herd instinct is the first victory over chaos; it is a bulwark against the outside world and prevents destruction or dispersal by outside influences before the individuals have found time to get their bearings or realize what is happening. The mass character of post-war social and political action has profoundly altered the conditions for this action. The very fact that action must take place through and on behalf of the masses has made it to some extent inevitable that the struggle should be centralized and more confidence placed in the leaders. A general staff which has to make a public explanation of its tactics every five minutes and justify every step is doomed to defeat. On the other hand, the modern political campaign cannot be carried out without publicity, stage management and much significant symbolism. In it agitation ('the putting of a single idea into many minds') counts for more than propaganda ('the putting of many ideas into each single mind'). Regrettable though this may be, a movement which refuses to adapt itself to these new necessities cuts itself off from the masses and from its goal.

What chiefly stands in the way of this adaptation is an illusion, cherished largely by 'intellectuals', who are inclined to overestimate the value of the tools that they themselves have learnt to handle. For them it is important not only to be right, but to have been right in the past. They are content to prove their enemies' arguments weak or their programme contradictory. The man in the ranks knows that this is only the beginning of a fight which must be constantly renewed. The ideas, plans and promises of the enemy must doubtless be criticised, but it must be remembered that the human mind, as well as the mass mind, is a stream which needs replenishing. If you block the spring, however muddy it may be, another must be provided: one idea can only be replaced by a greater, one passion by a stronger. The masses forget easily; their judgments are based not on the 'contradictions' of the past, but on the consolations of the present and the hopes for the future which are held out to them. But it is the greatest paradox of political life that any war of principles is also, and particularly at critical moments, a war of positions. For no battle is fought without a battle ground, without positions from which to start the attack, put up defences, dig oneself in and hold on in face of the enemy assault. These strategic reasons are obvious, but there are others which go deeper. It is wrong to suppose that an idea goes on living after the men and institutions in which it was embodied have disappeared. In certain conditions it may be resurrected, but there is no certainty that such conditions will return. The fascist experiment proves that an idea is jeopardised when its background is destroyed. 'Ideas cannot be killed' is a sublime and dangerous commonplace, which ignores the fact that an idea needs material support if it is to last. An idea is a generation, or a succession of generations. If the generation disappears and the succession is cut, the idea is submerged and the inheritance lost. When the fascists kill, banish or imprison their enemies, burn their houses and destroy their institutions, they know what they are about and do not strike in vain; especially when they borrow some of the principles of socialism; ideas are menaced as much by falsification as by the destruction of their protagonists. The use of socialist terminology by the fascists is a caricature of socialism, its negation; this ghostly survival is more baneful than death itself.

3. The Theory and Practice of Fascism

DENIS MACK SMITH

The Machinery and Personnel of Fascism

Having overcome the independent organs of public opinion by 1925, Mussolini could spend the next few years a law unto himself, gradually transforming the nature of the state and making it more

Source: *Italy: A Modern History* (Ann Arbor: University of Michigan Press, 1959), pp. 389–427. Reprinted by permission of The University of Michigan Press. Copyright © by The University of Michigan 1959.

authoritarian and personal. All over Italy the nominated *podestà* was to supplant the elected mayor in each town and village. A committee of "eighteen Solons" including Gentile, Volpe, and Angelo Olivetti the ex-syndicalist was appointed in January 1925 to reform the constitution. In December a law gave the prime minister a new legal existence as head of the state, no longer the first among equals but singly responsible to the king. Whereas under the 1848 constitution the king nominated and dismissed ministers, he now could do this only on Mussolini's proposal, and every motion for debate had first to be approved by the Duce. Mosca was a lone voice in opposition to this. A law of January 1926 then gave Mussolini power to issue decrees having the full force of law—there were to be more than one hundred thousand decree laws issued under fascism, making administration and justice impossibly complicated. Mussolini's person was declared inviolable, and after the attempts on his life by Colonel Zaniboni in 1925 and the Irish Miss Gibson in 1926, capital punishment was prescribed for those who so much as contemplated his death.

By a law of December 1928 Mussolini was to enter the plentitude of power, for the king then lost his right even to select the prime minister. The Grand Council of fascism was empowered to list the names from among whom Mussolini's successor should be chosen, and the king not only agreed to this but apparently he was once given such a list. This promotion of the *Gran Consiglio* of the fascist party into an organ of state was a constitutional innovation of which Mussolini was particularly proud. Its secretary continued to be secretary of the fascist party. Mussolini alone could convene it and determine who should attend; he was its president by right, could decide its agenda, and use it as a check on the cabinet. He even gave it a right to intervene in the succession to the throne itself, since the heir Umberto was reputedly lukewarm in supporting the regime. Behind all these theoretical attributes, however, there is no evidence that the Grand Council had any importance in practice until in July 1943 it turned on its creator and toppled him.

A new electoral law of May 1928 also changed the representative system once again, receiving only fifteen hostile votes in the Chamber. Parliamentary candidates in future were to be selected from a list drawn up by unions of workers and employers, and from the names on this list the *Grand Consiglio* would chose the candidates who were then put to the electorate for approval or rejection en bloc. Only in the impossible event of their rejection were second elections to be held between competing parties.

Mussolini told the Senate when presenting this bill that universal suffrage was merely a conventional fiction and that the constitution was dead and buried, not because it had been abolished, but simply because Italy was now profoundly different from what it had been in 1848. The senators who sat quietly though this kind of talk were still very largely the liberals appointed by Giolitti and Orlando, and a counterresolution presented by Ruffini on this occasion received forty-six signatures. Albertini made the point that the victors in World War I had been the free peoples, "while those ruled by more or less despotic forms of government were either defeated or else fell out of the struggle before its end. . . . I am a survivor of a liberalism that even though defeated cannot accept dishonor, and mindful of the oath taken in this very hall of the Senate, I feel it my duty in this hour to reaffirm my unshakable faith in those principles which the bill before us denies." Hundreds of new senators soon swamped these antediluvian survivors, and because it became *de rigueur* for the whole body sometimes to wear black shirts and shout ritual slogans, the liberals preferred to stay away.

In 1929 when elections were held, 136,000 votes were officially declared to have been cast against the national list of candidates, but this number may have been pure guesswork. The next elections in March 1934 showed only fifteen thousand votes for the opposition, though 95 per cent of the electorate was said to have voted. These were absurd figures in view of the number of policemen and political prisoners who testified to the strength of popular resistance. Plebiscites of this sort were a bogus test of public opinion and merely indicate how easily such elections can be manipulated to give a required result.

But this is not to say that Mussolini was unrepresentative of his country. Opposition there may have been, but it could not be very vocal, and where most people wanted security and prosperity above everything, Mussolini could easily persuade them that he had these gifts at his disposal. The plebiscitary dictatorship was in its own way a manifestation of democracy. Other politicians in history had already discovered that liberty and equality could be exclusive as well as complementary, and that by careful handling the mob could be used to make a dictator more autocratic. The argument for Leviathan grew ever more attractive to the generality of people as international relations became more perilous and as the problems of government escaped further from their knowledge and experience. Internal liberties might seem to be too expensive when they meant delay, division, and inefficiency. And so Mussolini was able to establish what he called an "authoritarian, centralized democracy," in which he could talk contemptuously of the "putrefying corpse of liberty" to the applause of a uniform nation.

The central organ of the revolution was the fascist party itself, and parallel with each existing institution of state there grew up a new one which was dependent on the party: the fascist militia alongside the army, the Roman salute with the military salute, the special tribunals cutting across the ordinary law courts, and the federal secretary at the side of each provincial prefect. There was also the Palazzo Venezia which after 1929, when Mussolini made it his private office, overtook the Quirinal palace as a fount of patronage and power, and there was the party song *"Giovinezza"* which, to the king's disgust, began to oust the *"Marcia Reale."* At the apex, the Duce of fascism was simultaneously the Head of the Government, and these two offices were soon considered identical. Gradually, the party was thus absorbing the state. Fascist law became the only effective law, and the nationalization of the fascist militia transferred an onerous burden from the shoulders of the rich party backers onto the taxpayer. Emblazoned on the state coat of arms was the party emblem of the lictor's fasces. The party secretary in the end assumed ministerial rank and attended cabinet meetings; he came to be a *de jure* member of the defense council and the board of education and was given precedence in ceremonial processions and court functions.

Another tendency was for the party itself to become increasingly centralized, and throughout 1923 there was a purge of its provincial directorates, as local fascist units were subordinated to the center at Rome. Several times before 1922 the local ras had rebelled and overruled the leader, but never again for the next twenty-one years. After 1926, instead of the *Gran Consiglio* being elected at the annual party congress, nomination was introduced from the top—"supermen elect themselves," declared Mussolini. The *Gran Consiglio* then chose the party secretary, and the latter appointed the provincial secretaries who together made up the national council. These provincial secretaries then appointed the lesser officials of the local *fasci*.

Membership of the party fluctuated considerably in number, for there was a ridiculous oscillation between considering the party as a mass and as an elite. At one moment the *tessera fascista* was a document requisite for many types of employment. At another, large expulsions were decreed when the party was suddenly thought to be unwieldy or ridden with factions. Its hard core was the "fascists of the first hour," the *sansepolcristi* who had inaugurated the movement in 1919 and who continued to set the tone. These obtained special privileges, as did all real or self-styled "pre-march" fascists, and for this reason the hooligan element remained on top.

Few of the party leaders were more than mediocre men, and few were even efficient. Most of them were unintelligent, grasping, jealous, and incompetent, and jockeyed for place by telling tales against their rivals, or else boosted each other's morale by organizing "spontaneous" crowd demonstrations for one another. With the possible exception of D'Annunzio, there seems to have been no living Italian for whom Mussolini felt any admiration. When he later claimed that the party leaders had let him down, the answer must be that he had the subordinates which he deserved and whom he had himself advanced. No doubt he deliberately promoted their rivalries and conflicting policies. Frequently, he replaced nearly all the ministers and party leaders in a sweeping "change of the guard," and he publicly boasted in 1929 that he used to announce these wholesale changes without even consulting first with the people he intended to appoint or dismiss. This was a revealing manifestation of *ducismo*.

Each party secretary was quickly superseded by another, so as to prevent anyone like Goering from winning too much influence or building up a private empire within the state. In 1923 Michele Bianchi was displaced as general secretary by Giunta. In 1925–26 the post was held by Farinacci, one of the more illiterate and brutish of the hierarchy, anticlerical and anti-Semitic. The term of his successor, Augusto Turati, ended when he was charged with immorality, suspected of lunacy, and confined at Rhodes. He was succeeded in turn by Giurati, Starace, Muti, and Serena; of these only Serena reigned long enough to have much influence, his consulship extending from 1931 to 1939. Then, with Vidussoni in 1941 was appointed a party secretary still in his early twenties, of whom no one knew anything at all except that he had failed his examinations and had a medal for valor. After him came Scorza.

Mussolini's sons were but shadows of their father. Bruno was involved in running an airline to South America, and Vittorio tried to assume direction of the film industry. Edda, their sister, had a more forceful character. Mussolini's elder brother Arnaldo was the most worthy of the family, a man of some conscience and religion, and one of the few men to keep Mussolini's affection and confidence. His job was the running of *Il Popolo d'Italia*.

Of the other leaders the Duce was always a little suspicious, sometimes with reason. Emilio de Bono was fifty-six years old in 1922, a white-bearded, somewhat puny army general who helped organize the militia and whom Mussolini was to execute in 1944. Italo Balbo in 1922 was only twenty-six, thirteen years younger than Mussolini. The most genuine and gallant of the fascists, he was always a *frondeur,* with his own private aims and ambitions which often differed from Mussolini's, and he was suspected of courting Prince Umberto in the hope of some time succeeding to supreme power. Mussolini was a little afraid of Balbo it seems, as well as envious of his youth. Eventually, this potential rival was to be shot down by Italian antiaircraft guns in 1940, probably by accident. A more senior and more absurd figure was Cesare de Vecchi, created count of Val Cismon, poetaster and pseudo academic, who was the general butt of his colleagues and eventually helped to remove Mussolini in 1943. Dino Grandi was another young "first hour" fascist, and a callous squad leader in his youth. He also had some ambition to succeed or replace Mussolini. His chief official task was to fill up the ministry of foreign affairs with party hacks; later he took over the London embassy during the thirties. Grandi was a competent diplomat, but fawning and obsequious toward Mussolini until he too deserted the sinking ship in July 1943.

The younger generation was represented by Galeazzo Ciano, whose father, Costanzo, was an admiral who had done very well financially out of running the ministry of transport. The younger Ciano rose rapidly to become foreign minister in 1936 at the age of thirty-four. He compared moderately well with his associates, being generally good-natured, and having something of wit and even intelligence to make up for lack of education, but he was corrupt and self-indulgent, superficial to a degree, idle, frivolous, and quite without weight of character. Ciano was an exhibitionist who lived for the camera, and sometimes used to play irresponsibly with the destiny of nations just out of vanity or pique. He is said to have been liberal in giving away vital public secrets to friends in high Roman society, who found in him almost alone of the fascist leaders a man of conversation and polish, and he defended their interests against the quasi-socialist elements which occasionally threatened to dominate the party. The old-guard fascists of the first hour resented him as an upstart and were more than enraged when in 1930 he was chosen by the Duce as a son-in-law. For years Ciano remained the dictator's favorite, until in

1944 his father-in-law had him shot in the back for treason in order to placate the Germans.

On the left of the party was Rossoni, leader of the fascist labor unions and an erstwhile revolutionary agitator in the United States. Bianchi and Professor Bottai also inclined toward this left wing, together with other ex-socialists like Farinacci and Bombacci on the extreme fringe. The relative importance of this group is hard to gauge, but union leaders in general gained in power and prestige from the new centralized organization of trades and professions. More and more individuals in search of a job after 1922 had to adanbon the socialist and Catholic unions and join the fascist syndicates. Under government pressure, in October 1925 the Confederation of Industry and the Confederation of Fascist Trade Unions singed the Vidoni pact, when their spokesmen, Gino Olivetti and Rossoni, each recognized the other as representative of his whole class. Olivetti, however, was far more genuinely representative than Rossoni, and Mussolini thus obtained industrial peace at his own price, although workers were placed in a clearly inferior position by the abolition of strikes and penalizing labor unrest. Clearly, the left wing of the fascist party was not very strong in itself until Mussolini reverted to his earlier socialism toward the end of his life.

It will not be very helpful to list many of the numerous laws decreed by fascism, because in any case they rarely corresponded with achieved results. But one reform obtained particularly wide publicity, and it must therefore be noted how the socialistic and bureaucratic tendencies in fascism together resulted in creating the so-called Corporative System. Mussolini was eager to demonstrate that his movement, despite appearances, was not simply conservative, but was simultaneously full of new and seminal ideas. The party intellectuals were therefore enlisted to expound and apply his oracular assertion that "the Corporative System is destined to become the civilization of the twentieth century."

This was one of a number of concepts which he borrowed from the nationalists. Its author, the nationalist Rocco, became minister of justice in January 1925; a new ministry of corporations was created in 1926, and in 1930 a National Council of Corporations was called into theoretical existence as a deliberative assembly. To it were attached all the workers in the state through their respective trade organizations. When at last the system took more positive shape in 1936, there were said to be twenty-two separate categories for various trades and industries—for instance, the fifth for the sugar and beet industries, the ninth for metallurgy, the twenty-second for the professional classes and artists. All workers were fitted into an appropriate category, and each category was given political as well as economic functions. The union officials were of course appointed from above, because this was good fascist theory and because jobs had to be found for party members. The workers themselves had but to pay their subscriptions and do what they were told, for instead of being citizens with rights and independence, they were now cogs with a function. Having abolished political liberalism by 1925, Mussolini thus buried economic liberalism soon afterward.

The idea of corporativism seemed so attractive and typically fascist that Mussolini's claims for it far outdistanced actuality. In November 1933 he promised the National Council of Corporations that they might one day replace the Chamber of Deputies: "The Chamber has never been to my taste; it has now become anachronistic even in name; as an institution it is foreign to our fascist cast of thought, and presupposes a plurality of parties which no longer exists." Two years later he shamelessly assured them that they were "perhaps the most imposing assembly in the whole history of Italy." Finally, in 1939 the Chamber of Fasces and Corporations was created, and the old parliamentary system disappeared in name as well as in fact.

Imposing though the name of this new body may have sounded, the corporations were more an aspiration than an actuality, and Salvemini* rightly called them an elaborate piece of imposing humbug. In practice the new system was simply an attempt to keep a tight hold on the workers in straitly centralized unions. The machinery of corporativism was tremendously expensive, and this invited much jobbery and corruption, while a vast organization had to be built up to do things which voluntary unions did more willingly and more efficiently elsewhere. Whether they performed any genuine function which had not been done before is still a mystery.

Mussolini in March 1936 told the Council of Corporations that he "did not wish to bureaucratize the entire economy of the nation," but in practice the extension of governmental activities everywhere brought with it a top-heavy organization, slow and unresponsive, and quite out of close touch with ordinary people. Party members and officials constituted a huge new vested interest, since the party, the militia, and the corporations provided what was admitted to be as

* Gaetano Salvemini, historian and critic of Mussolini's regime.—Ed.

many as a hundred thousand jobs for secretaries and organizers. Fascism in this way helped to satisfy that deep-rooted desire among Italians to find a respectable post in government service, poorly paid but easy work and a sure pension. The census returns of 1931 and 1936 reveal strikingly how the greatest increase in occupation statistics was made by administrative and professional categories. The bureaucratic capital, Rome, now regained the lead in size (lost about 1875) over the industrial capital, Milan. A writer in the London *Economist* thus described the position in 1935: "The new corporative state only amounts to the establishment of a new and costly bureaucracy, from which those industrialists who can spend the necessary amount can obtain almost anything they want, and put into practice the worst kind of monopolistic practices at the expense of the little fellow who is squeezed out in the process."

With all this increase in government expenditure and patronage, corruption became the besetting sin of the regime, even though the Duce personally did not seem to profit from the graft which riddled every department of state. While he was in prison on the island of Ponza in 1943, the local policeman explained to him why the tap in his room did not run: although money had been lavished on an aqueduct, most of it had been channeled into the pockets of good party men and their friends. In every locality the party hierarchs or *gerarchi* were petty tyrants with an unlimited call on public money and the assurance of being acquitted of any crime. As they were almost invariably bad men to begin with, this conscious immunity often had shocking results.

Authenticated and unauthenticated stories of malversation were legion. Mussolini's friends, unfortunately, included people interested in the marble trade from Carrara, and the monstrous public buildings erected in the best *stile fascista* all over Italy and its colonies are probably not unconnected with this fact. Fictitious "industrial zones" were declared to exist so that state subsidies would be forthcoming, and mock factories were built for this same purpose, though they were never apparently intended to produce anything. There was a lively trade in titles. In another field, Farinacci the railroad clerk easily picked up an honorary doctorate of law, and the incontrovertible nature of his forensic arguments secured him the rewards of a good legal practice. Ciano was also said to have used his inside knowledge to buy up ships prior to the Ethiopian war. And thus the ungodly flourished.

In most cases this corruption was no doubt petty and unimportant.

For example, even an unfriendly American press agency could usually buy up a monopoly of pictures from a party official on any newsworthy event, and a reporter with ready cash could jump an important story even when a simultaneous release had been promised. But sometimes matters were not so trivial. High civilian and military officials are known to have diverted funds away from aircraft development, and as there were always enough people who would keep silent for a consideration, Italy lost World War II before hostilities had begun. Salvatorelli, who is the safest historian of this period, concludes that this corruption became really scandalous only from the moment when Mussolini began his liaison with Clara Petacci in the middle thirties; thenceforward, it was not only something normal and unconcealed, but even regulated and taxed.

That this rickety machine kept running so long was due largely to the personality of its leader. Mussolini lacked all nobility of character, but he knew the Italians and knew how to make them serve him. He was always able to inspire confidence and make people think him sincere, whatever his beliefs or lack of them. Skill consciously employed was here allied with a fascination he exerted almost unconsciously.

In 1932 Mussolini dropped some revealing remarks to Emil Ludwig: "Today people have not so much time to think as they used to have. The capacity of the modern man for faith is illimitable. When the masses are like wax in my hands, when I stir their faith, or when I mingle with them and am almost crushed by them, I feel myself to be a part of them. All the same there persists in me a certain feeling of aversion, like that which the modeller feels for the clay he is moulding. Does not the sculptor sometimes smash his block of marble into fragments because he cannot shape it to represent the vision he has conceived? Now and then this crude matter rebels against the creator." His interlocutor asked whether a dictator could be loved. "Yes," answered Mussolini with renewed decisiveness, "Provided that the masses fear him at the same time. The crowd loves strong men. The crowd is like a woman."

Mussolini was a play actor who knew how to produce himself in public. With his bulbous and unsmiling face he created a legend of the strong man who was victorious and always right, the wise man who knew the inmost thoughts of people, the industrious servant of the public frequently photographed when toiling in the harvest field stripped to the waist. Foreign diplomats were impressed and frightened when they had to move past a double column of his unpaid corps of pugnacious-looking black-uniformed musketeers with daggers held out at arm's length, and any reception in Mussolini's gigantic marble study was always carefully staged to humble the visitor. His most important quality was thus that of being a stupendous poseur. His mixture of showmanship and vulgarity appealed to the common people, who liked to hear of his adulterous relationships and illegitimate children because he then became more human and virile. They were not allowed to know about his ill-health or his use of eyeglasses, and foreign journalists would be expelled if they mentioned his ulcer, let alone if they hinted at syphilis.

Only in retrospect do we notice Mussolini's deep inferiority complex and his extraordinary timidity and reluctance to decide between alternative lines of conduct. What was stressed at the time was the carefully contrived swagger and braggadocio of a Benvenuto Cellini. On top of this was superimposed the quite different legend of a temperate man who did not smoke, who seldom drank wine, and ate little but fruit, milk, and vegetables. A light would burn in his study far into the night to persuade people that he was at work, when in reality he was asleep, or dallying in the dark with Signora Petacci. Stories circulated of his skill on the violin, and his abiding affection for Dante, without which no Italian politician can pass muster for long—it was even claimed that he knew whole cantos of the *Divine Comedy* by heart. His fencing and horsemanship were legendary, for he had to excel in everything, and a public fall from his horse would be stringently concealed from the newspapers. Since there was no possibility of contradiction, he even convinced himself of his ability as a brave soldier, a daring aircraft pilot, and (most dangerous of all) a great strategist and war leader. In his "autobiography" he was childishly vain about driving cars so fast that experienced drivers were astonished.

Some of this deceived nobody except himself, and even the witless party leaders had their private laugh when requested to record some flatulent mot for posterity. But propaganda makes people gullible and uncritical, and fascism bred an astoundingly low average of sense and discrimination. After one visit Mussolini paid to Genoa, a journalist was not ashamed to write: "To die without lament, and with a vision of light in one's eyes, and an infinite sweetness in the heart, that is what we should be glad to do after the experience of today, while our hands still keep some of the warmth of his masculine hand which we kissed, our hearts in tumult and full of a sense of liberation." When people began to turn against fascism, it was not so much for its tyranny and bellicosity as for this sort of contemptible bad taste which permeated the whole of public life.

There was perhaps some slight excuse for foreigners to approve of Mussolini from a distance when Italians found so much to idolize on the spot—and in this connection one may note that Italians living abroad were wheedled at great cost to the exchequer into becoming his most blatantly enthusiastic fans and propagandists. Croce* later tried to exculpate himself for supporting Mussolini in 1922–24 by describing fascism as a disease which came to Italy from abroad and largely because of foreign help (as also he insisted that it was brought to the South from northern Italy and by northern Italians). Croce even took this piece of patriotic consolation to the point of asserting that fascism was wholly alien to Italian traditions and temperament. The evident sophistry of this thesis must not make us ignore its tiny germ of truth. Among the British, Bernard Shaw whimsically defended the Ethiopian invasion. Winston Churchill in 1927, after an hour with Mussolini, spoke of his charm and gentleness and praised those Italians who backed fascism against the Reds. Churchill and Lloyd George both referred to the Corporative System in Italy as a highly promising development. One British foreign minister was accused of giving the fascist salute at a press conference in Rome, and the wife of another on a celebrated occasion was seen to be wearing the party badge. From the United States many useful loans were advanced to fascist Italy until the Debt Default Act was passed, and one version of Mussolini's "autobiography" was apparently written for him by an ex-ambassador of the United States at whose house he used to stay.

There was a fair amount of uninformed foreign approval for fascism, though no one has been able to prove that this had much effect in practice. Those Italians who say that Britain and America ought to have condemned Mussolini should pause to think whether foreign interference in domestic affairs does not usually have the reverse effect of strengthening a regime, as indeed happened later over sanctions. All that foreigners could see was the applause which the Italian press and parliament (and the electorate) gave to fascism in 1922–24, and by 1925 the damage was done irretrievably, short of war. One may add that the shopwindow aspect of fascism was deliberately dressed with an eye to foreign inspection. When Axel Munthe asked him to make Capri into a bird sanctuary, Mussolini saw the advertisement value of the idea to impress sentimental foreigners—though his forgetfulness or his discourtesy was such that he is said to have given Munthe

* Benedetto Croce, philosopher and historian.—Ed.

skylark pie for lunch when the latter arrived to thank him for his benevolence.

Mussolini's flair for publicity is undoubted, but it masked a profound lack of skill in policy and administration, and so in one sense was to prove his undoing. His journalistic bent is revealed in the periodic anonymous articles he continued to write for the press, and it was on the profits of journalism, authorship, and newspaper ownership that he lived, for it was claimed somewhat dubiously that he never took his ministerial salary. Press clippings from abroad were diligently studied and became lamentably influential on policy, while Mussolini's own mental processes never ceased to be governed by slogans and cight-column headlines. This was to prove disastrous. Mussolini was a facile assimilator of superficialities and possessed an ephemeral but sometimes surprising secondhand culture—"forgive my learned references" was a phrase which used to amuse his entourage. He preferred to argue and speechify rather than to penetrate behind words to reality, and so never properly dissected a problem, but thought he could solve anything after a cursory survey. Fascism, which affected to despise speeches and talk, was itself essentially rhetoric and blather. Mussolini was a moderately good talker, and some good listeners said they found his conversation delightful, but he was a terribly bad administrator, and his policy was too often empty, contradictory, and misapplied.

The motto "Mussolini is always right" was nevertheless stenciled on waysides houses all over Italy, winning credence by repetition—it was even embossed by *devots* on their notepaper. And yet his opinions were inconsistent as well as shallow. On and off he preached and then abandoned socialism, anticlericalism, republicanism, anti-imperialism, and pacifism, and one should remember his campaign in April 1919 against dictatorships of every kind. At one moment he claimed to be the categoric antithesis of democracy, at another its most perfect manifestation. His one constant belief was that action was for the sake of action and consistency mattered not a whit, so that ideas and opinions were of minor importance, simply tactical means to win the alliance of the Church or the conservatives or the trade unionists. Patriotism meant little to him, and, to judge from his abuse of them, he despised Italians even more than he did humanity in general. He glorified Italy only in so far as this redounded to his own glory, and he as readily handed her over to German occupation and civil war when she threatened to fall short of that purpose.

Mussolini was easily influenced, and his lieutenants quickly discovered his vexatious habit of always agreeing with the last person he had spoken to. But perhaps no one held any continuous influence over him until the Petacci family cornered him in his premature dotage. He was no respector of persons and had little sense of loyalty to former friends and collaborators. Indeed he despised friendship. He boasted to Senise that he had never possessed a friend in his life, and very few people were ever asked home to the Villa Torlonia. The truth was that, apart from an impressive interview technique, he never shone when dealing with individuals, whereas he loved crowds and felt enlarged when addressing them. He was as self-consciously unsure of himself in private as he was self-consciously aggressive in public.

Mussolini was careful to take upon himself all the credit for any success, because this not only fed his vanity, but it also prevented his lieutenants from gathering any popular support and becoming anything but abjectly subservient to his person. For the same reason he discouraged them from taking any bold political initiative. In return they were allowed to strut in fine uniforms and amass private fortunes, the chief losers being the Italian people who consequently were exploited and misgoverned by the dregs of the nation. Yet though Mussolini tried to monopolize the credit for success, he always found someone else to blame for failure, and perhaps he reached that last fatal pitch of delusion where he genuinely thought that he could do no wrong. This divorce of power from responsibility was ruinous, and it was, for example, to allow Mussolini to declare war without full appreciation of Italy's inordinate unpreparedness. Such was the deliberate concentration of power in himself that there was only himself to blame for the result. In 1926 Mussolini personally held the offices of prime minister, president of the council, foreign minister, minister of the interior, minister for the Corporations, minister for all three of the service departments, and commander in chief of the militia. At other times he was also minister for colonies and for public works. Mindful of the Code Napoléon, he also had to put his own amateurish stamp on the new codes of law which were introduced in 1930–31.

This was quite absurd, for no one could attend to so many jobs, and power thus became confusedly dispersed through a jungle of undersecretaries, *gerarchi,* and ras, who were frequently changed, and who were seldom given either the time to carry out any reform or the authority to consider policy over a broad enough field. The dictator's personal permission was needed before the police could change into their summer uniforms, but high policy went disregarded, and as minister of war he confessed to Bottai in 1939 that he had had no idea that the artillery then in use dated from World War I. Again and again he buried his head in the sand, either from ignorance and carelessness, or from a genuine fear of having to take the responsibility for policy decisions, and unfortunately he could never abide the existence of a vice-Duce to supply his deficiencies.

Economic and Social Policy

Fascism began with no particular economic policy; its doctrines of planned economy were one day to be called typically fascist, but in fact they were developed late and as an afterthought. The first minister of finance, De Stefani, started the regime off on a completely different tack by reducing government expenditure and giving freer rein to private capitalism. He also partly rationalized the tax system, and in the years 1924–26 the budget once again was balanced. Italy was meanwhile sharing in the general prosperity of contemporary Europe, and liberal economists could approve of government policy.

In July 1925 the economist De Stefani was succeeded for three years by the financier and industrialist Count Volpi, and the situation at once began to change in the direction of protection and central planning. First, import duties were heavily increased on grain, sugar, silk, and other commodities. Then the currency was revalued, mainly for reasons of prestige and in order to put the lira on a par with the franc. Note circulation was heavily reduced, and credit was so restricted by the banks that the value of the dollar fell from 32 to 18 lire in the single year 1926–27. This raised export prices and severely damaged trade, though it benefited the bureaucrats and those of the middle classes whose salaries had depreciated during the postwar inflation. Meanwhile, the trade unions were emasculated by the Vidoni pact in 1925, and thirty rather vapid aphorisms were officially coined in 1927 and issued with the grandiose title of a Charter of Labor. Mussolini in 1926 then opened up his national "battle for grain," followed by a "battle for population." The new trend of the times can be seen in decrees issued for reducing the size of newspapers to save wood pulp, for diluting gasoline with alcohol made from wine or grain, and for allowing a nine-hour working day again. Gradually, a planned economy was introduced, at least on paper. Self-sufficiency had become the principal aim by the early 1930's, and the Leader had declared that "laissez faire is out of date." No one could obtain employment without a special worker's pass, and on this pass were included details of a man's political as well as his industrial experience.

The immediate postwar economic recovery began before fascism came into power, and so reflected no very positive credit on the government. But the slump in Italy started earlier than the collapse of the bull market on Wall Street and must be ascribed in great part to Mussolini's policy of revaluation and autarky. Tourism and the trade in luxury commodities fell off. The rich began to complain that the lira was valued too highly and that the multiplying bureaucracy ate up too much of the community's taxable wealth. Accordingly, the salaries of government employees were cut by 12 per cent. Those affected by this cut and by parallel wage reductions found it cold comfort when Mussolini told the Senate in December 1930 that "fortunately the Italian people were not accustomed to eat much and therefore feel the privation less acutely than others." When recovery commenced after 1933, he contrived to attribute it to fascism, but he then started preparing for war and this began the progressive ruin of the whole economy.

Fascism found it hard to alter Italy's dependence on foreign imports —in 1925 this dependence included 99 per cent of her cotton and mineral oil, 95 per cent of her coal, and over half of her metals. Industry did make considerable progress, but mainly in the field of military supply. Production of electricity was subsidized and increased about fivefold between 1917 and 1942. The automobile industry was said to be producing some 34,000 cars a year by 1941. In an attempt to modernize shipping, bounties were given for the scrapping of old vessels, though unsound investments were made in big prestige liners such as the "Rex" and the "Conte di Savoia" which might win the "blue ribbon" for a brief year but could not compete economically in transatlantic traffic. Moreover, shipping construction seems to have declined in the 1930's, owing to the high cost of steel plate which resulted from exorbitant protection and the system of trusts. Schemes were devised to build oil refining installations at Bari and Leghorn, and perhaps Mussolini believed his own statement that he would make Italy self-sufficient in oil and gasoline by 1938. But achievements fell ludicrously short of this aim, and had he taken the trouble to discover the real precariousness of Italian industry, he might have been less bellicose in foreign politics.

Mussolini was no mere instrument of business and agrarian interests, yet his ignorance about economics and human nature left him an easy target for sharks who wanted protective duties or who extracted money from the state for quite impossible schemes of industrialization. Fascism seems to have had a close reciprocal understanding with the big trusts from which both sides gained, and several presidents of the *Confindustria* became ministers. When Count Volpi of the Banca Commerciale Italiana took over the ministry of finance, this began another involvement of banking with politics which aroused as much talk of scandals as the Tanlongo affair in the 1890's, only this time the talk was suppressed. In 1928 the heavy taxes on company amalgamation deeds were reduced. The industries of the Ansaldo group, which had collapsed in 1921, clearly banked heavily on a government which would stimulate armament production and "nationalize" their losses. A new steel cartel arose in the early thirties which helped to keep inefficient firms alive, its express intention being to maintain high prices and restrict production, and consumers thus compulsorily subsidized inefficiency in order to prevent a large uneconomic investment from losing its value. With such help, the Edison electricity company, Montecatini chemicals, Snia Viscosa artificial silk, and Pirelli rubber lost none of their dominant position. The Agnelli family, which controlled Fiat, became responsible for four-fifths of Italian automobile manufacture, as well as for numerous other operations which ranged from mining and smelting to making vermouth, cement, and newspapers. These were private concerns. Italian economy under fascism was not typified by direct state ownership, but in 1933 the *Instituto per la Ricostruzione Industriale* was founded by the government to subsidize industry and to save those banks which had been too liberal in giving long-term credit. By the time the war came, the I.R.I. controlled many of Italy's leading firms in the heavy and mechanical industries and had interests stretching over a wide field of banking and manufacture.

Nevertheless, as employers found it increasingly necessary to go to Rome for credit, permits, and protection, they were bound to be irked by the delays and restrictions involved in this growing dependence upon the government. Milanese businessmen had welcomed fascism's nationalization of labor unions, but in the thirties they felt the brunt of capital levies, compulsory loans, and the high taxes which imperialism demanded. The war industries doubtless continued to thrive, but even here it is evident from Italy's weakness in 1940 that billions of lire must have been misappropriated. By a paradox, the obverse of dictatorship was inefficiency, and such a fact cannot have helped to ingratiate this type of government with the generality of businessmen.

Wages and conditions of labor did not improve under fascism, and as early as 1926 the hard-earned eight-hour day was surrendered. The official index of wages told such a tale that its publication was suspended in 1927, the year in which a general wage reduction was decreed. Figures given by the International Labor Office in 1930 suggested that real wages in Italy were lower than anywhere in western Europe, including Spain. Even the *Corriere della Sera* admitted that they had been reduced by almost half in the four years before 1932, and Professor Chabod, after trying to reconcile many conflicting statistics from various ministries, now concludes that between 1926 and 1934 farm laborers lost 50 to 70 per cent of their wages. Unemployment figures still showed a million out of work in 1935.

By a typical *volte-face* Mussolini abandoned his boast about increasing prosperity, and in May 1936 bragged instead that he was enforcing a more vigorous way of life: "We must rid our minds of the idea that what we have called the days of prosperity may return. We are probably moving toward a period when humanity will exist on a lower standard of living." Mussolini had by this time engaged on a policy of war and was taking money away from welfare in order to invest it in imperialism. People have estimated on official figures that three or four hundred thousand Italians at this time were still living in hovels made of earth and sticks, and many others in caves or crowded ten to a room. To these classes of the abjectly poor a showy apparatus of social services was offered, which was much more than the liberals had ever considered, but in great part this was just another piece of window dressing, and expenditure on social services probably absorbed less of the national income than in nearly all other European countries. Foreign visitors would not notice the increase in child labor, but punctual mainline trains and strict police action against beggars would impress them, and depreciation in other far more important regards might thus pass unobserved.

These twenty years witnessed a big exodus from the land. The census of 1921 gave three-fifths of the working population as still employed in agriculture, but that of 1931 gave less than half. Mussolini strongly disliked this drift to the cities, in particular because industrial labor was factious and socialistic, and a law was therefore passed in 1930 to stop workers moving except by permission of the prefects. The landowners were grateful for this, because it kept their peasants tied to the soil and wages low. But rural overpopulation thereby became worse, so much so that proprietors were sometimes obliged to employ a fixed proportion of workers per unit area of land. Nobody liked this increasing degree of coercion all around, and one is not surprised to find it only in part effective.

Mussolini maintained that Italy was the classic land of the small-holder, but on the one hand some seven thousand small properties a year continued to lapse to the exchequer for failure to pay land tax, and on the other hand nothing was done to divide up the large estates. A bill had already passed through the Lower House in 1922 by which part of these large estates should be given out to the peasants, and indeed this was a policy which *Il Popolo d'Italia* had itself specifically proclaimed in January 1921, but after 1922 Mussolini was too much in thrall to the agrarians, and the bill was quietly dropped. Some fifteen noble families such as the Borghese, Caracciolo, Chigi, Colonna, and Torlonia continued to hold between them well over a million acres of land, which in a small and crowded country was a sizable proportion of the total agricultural area. It was estimated that in 1930 there were some 3,500 *latifondi* each over 1,200 acres in size, together comprising a fifth of the land under cultivation, while 15,000 people held other estates of 250 acres or more; all these together covered half the cultivable area of Italy. No doubt many of these large farms could not be split into small holdings without loss in productivity. Nevertheless, satisfaction of land hunger was probably the only way to reconcile the peasantry and prevent that flight from the countryside which Mussolini so deplored.

Some idea of the principal imports and exports of Italy at this time may be gained from the following tables for 1933:

IMPORTS (*in million lire*)

Raw cotton	737
Coal and coke	685
Wheat	504
Machinery	365
Wool	361

EXPORTS (*in million lire*)

Fruit and garden produce	1,091
Raw and artificial silk	820
Cotton fabrics and yarn	676
Cheese	241

It will be noted how much Italy was still an agricultural nation and yet how dependent she was upon imports of grain.

Perhaps the most striking alteration in her economy under fascism was in domestic production of wheat. Ever since 1870 the annual production had been little more than forty million quintals, but by 1930 Mussolini had raised this to sixty million, and by 1939 to eighty million quintals. This *battaglia del grano* was highly successful. Medals for the most successful farmers were distributed each April 21—this date being now set up to rival the socialist May Day—and progress was such that wheat imports were cut by 75 per cent in the ten years after 1925. The price paid was, however, dangerously high. Cereals were a type of agricultural product which long experience had shown to be the least economical for Italy, and the result was to lower the total output of agriculture and with it the national income. Mussolini's obsession about self-sufficiency drove him to produce the maximum quantity of wheat at any price, instead of as much as could be produced economically. Marginal land was therefore changed over from cattle pasture, fruit, and olives, thus quite upsetting the economy, and the cost of Italian wheat was 50 per cent higher than of American.

While the large-scale cereal growers grew fat on government subsidies, consumers were not in the best position to make their voices heard. As wheat cost more, some Italians simply had to eat less of it, and the switch in land usage also meant that there was less livestock and olive oil. Political motives thus played havoc with Italian agriculture, and autarky added to Italian economic problems instead of solving them as Mussolini had assumed. The relative index of variations in consumption per head given in the *Enciclopedia italiana* shows the effect of a rising cost of living:

	1922–29	*1930–38*
Wine	123	101
Wheat	100	91
Tobacco	99	81

With this decline in consumption of basic foodstuffs, it is small wonder that the infant mortality figures remained twice or thrice those in Scandinavia.

Another fascist "battle" was that for land reclamation, under the generalship of undersecretary Serpieri. Mussolini soon discovered the advantages of *bonifiche* as an ostentatious testament to his own skill and enterprise, and in 1928 large government funds were appropriated to schemes of water regulation and mountain conservation which were beyond the scope of individual proprietors. Positive achievements were the Emilia canal, and the partial colonization of the Volturno Valley and the Pontine marshes. The Agro Pontino was near Rome, and hence its reclamation was a particularly useful advertisement with foreign visitors. Several hundred thousand acres were reclaimed, and hundreds of peasant families were settled in a more ambitious and successful scheme than any previous ruler of Italy had attempted. Here again, however, the work was marred by its primarily political motivation, and it was said that proprietors who had the ear of some *gerarca* diverted the money to land of their own which was in good shape already. When Mussolini turned away to pursue his grandiose schemes of imperialism after 1934, payments on land reclamation dried up. Many of his improvements were then lost in World War II, for as soon as dikes were left unrepaired, water crept back over the old marshland. Farm buildings scattered irrationally over the Sicilian *latifondi* also had to be abandoned when insufficient investment was forthcoming to change the prevailing type of extensive agriculture.

Progress was maintained in the development of communications. The mainline tourist trains did run punctually, and by 1939 some five thousand kilometers of track had been electrified. Fast traffic roads called *autostrade* were built to connect the principal towns and tourist centers in northern Italy, Turin to Milan, Milan to the Lakes, Florence and Rome to the sea. The aircraft industry never developed quite as successfully as Italian skill in automobile manufacture might have predicted, but Italian planes won the Schneider trophy in 1920, 1921, and 1926, and Major de Bernardi set new world speed records in 1927 and 1928 with a Macchi seaplane powered by a Fiat motor. It is interesting to note these dates, for the gradual encroachment of fascism over the whole of Italian life was reflected in a diminution and not an increase in this kind of success, and only 11,000 planes seem to have been produced in World War II. Prizes and subsidies were liberally offered, and by 1939 Italy's civil airlines covered a considerable mileage, but the war found her deficient in types of warplane and industrial capacity. Mussolini boasted that he could blot out the sunlight with his air force, but he had no idea of the inefficiency and corruption attending his sort of totalitarianism.

The eighth national census in 1936 showed that Italian cities had absorbed two million more people during the previous fifteen years as the industrial fever took hold. Between 1871 and 1943 Rome grew to seven times its former size, and Milan to six. In the period 1921 to 1931, Rome increased its population from 690,000 to over a million. The coastal towns, Taranto, Bari, Genoa, and Spezia also expanded considerably. The drying-up of overseas emigration contributed powerfully to this movement, and after 1922 urbanization continued despite attempts by the government to stop it.

The damming of the stream of emigration was one of the biggest changes of all in postwar Italy. In 1920 the current still ran strongly, and about 350,000 Italians entered the United States alone. Then came the American immigration law of 1921 which laid down an annual quota for every nation, namely 3 per cent of its share in the U.S. foreign-born population as of 1910. The Italian quota was thus reduced to about forty thousand, and the Johnson Act of 1924 cut this figure to under four thousand. After other countries had followed suit, there were often more old emigrants returning to Italy each year than new ones leaving, especially as Mussolini was shortsighted enough to encourage this trend. This lowered the standard of living in emigration areas, and reduced the remittances sent home by emigrants. By 1939, as links with the homeland became severed, the sum of these remittances had dropped from about five billion lire to about five hundred million a year, a not inconsiderable loss in the balance of payments.

This drastic fall in emigration might have been compensated in part by a fall in the birth rate. But Mussolini for some reason thought that national honor demanded a high rate of fertility, and so launched a "battle for births" with the fantastic target of increasing the population by one-third to sixty million before 1960. When the incredulous asked how such a number could live in Italy, the reply came in typical fascist language that they would live because they could not die, adding that such questions were pernicious and insidious and revealed a weary or anemic mentality. A large population meant more cannon fodder, and would perhaps impress foreigners with Italy's need for colonies; it would also keep wages conveniently low. Faced with Italy's most chronic and intractable problem, it is interesting to see that Mussolini aimed to make it worse and not better, for he harked back to a pre-Malthusian age when the birth rate might have been considered an index of a nation's virility.

Mussolini therefore subsidized matrimony. Fathers with conspicuously large families received higher wages, and the most prolific mother in each region was made an honorary member of the fascist party and might even be ceremonially received by the Duce. Loans were advanced to newlyweds, to be repaid only if there were children or not enough, and specially favorable insurance poli were distributed by the officiating priest along with a copy of Pius XI's encyclical *Casti connubi*. Being unmarried was a serious impediment in most careers, and in February 1939 it was declared an absolute bar to promotion in government service. A progressive bachelors tax was introduced in 1926, and exemption allowed only to clergy and disabled veterans. This interference in family life was taken to the point where parents were forbidden to give their children names which might sound like an offence to fascism. Women were also encouraged to stay at home so as to have more time for children and to reduce unemployment. There was the feeling that women as schoolteachers might be too religious and too pacific for the planned indoctrination of Italian youth, and in the end they were dismissed altogether from jobs in government service. The potential labor force of the country had thus been heavily reduced just at the moment when war preparations were beginning, and there was no corresponding gain elsewhere to make up for it.

Results were once again incommensurate with intentions. Excluding the war period, 1932 was the first year since 1876 in which there had been fewer than one million live births—a fact which perplexed and infuriated the Duce.

Fascist Doctrine

Fascism at first boasted of being a movement and not a doctrine. Action, said Mussolini, was of primary importance, even when it was a blunder, and the theory or purpose behind action was largely irrelevant. The battle was what mattered, no matter for what cause. "Believe, obey, and fight" was his motto for Italians, inscribed in Article 4 of the fascist party constitution, yet the belief to which he was referring was not in a creed but in a person.

The success of fascism in 1919-22 was due less to any interior logic or merit of its own than to the vacuum left by the failure of other parties. Hence no doctrine was required, and indeed victory was even helped by this negative philosophy, for fewer people were antagonized. Mussolini's life had been a succession of negations, against the state, the socialists, and the Libyan war; against law and order, and then against disorder; against parliament and liberalism, Versailles and the League, bolshevism and democracy. When asked to replace these negations with something positive, he became evasive and contradictory, for he had no serious beliefs of his own, and any positive statement was likely to offend some possible ally. In this way, astoundingly enough, Mussolini came into power before people had more than a vague idea of what he stood for, and the fact that such a person as Croce could think fascism empty of doctrine and therefore innocuous was a powerful motive in neutralizing potential opposition.

The only truly original contribution of fascism to politics was probably the technique of castor oil. Nevertheless, from this unpromising start, Mussolini skillfully maneuvered after a few years into a position where he was actually claiming that for the first time in modern history the Italians had given the world a doctrine, a philosophy, a new style of living. This he did by making a patchwork of bits and pieces collected from friend and foe. He had learned the theory and practice of revolution from the socialists; his foreign policy, after a few false starts, was taken bodily from the nationalists; the liberals around Gentile contributed a pseudophilosophical terminology; and from certain authoritarian parties abroad he discovered how Catholicism could be used to underpin a strong state built on order and obedience.

This strange amalgam was never given quite enough time to set, and Mussolini went on mouthing negative or meaningless slogans of doubletalk long after he had decided that fascism was after all a doctrine as well as a movement. Indeed, this doubletalk was thoroughly typical of him. Sometimes he instructed fascists to live with a high seriousness and passionate conviction; sometimes they were prescribed the "could not care less" attitude summed up in their uncivilized motto *me ne frego*. Relying on people's forgetfulness, he said that he was a friend of England and yet her irreconcilable enemy. He was the only disinterested champion of the League, and yet also its destroyer—both these incompatible facts being treated as matter for boasting. He meant to bring both peace and a sword:

> We represent a new principle in the world, the clear, final and categoric antithesis of democracy, plutocracy, Freemasonry, and the immortal principles of 1789.

> The ideals of democracy are exploded, beginning with that of "progress." Ours is an aristocratic century; the state of all will end by becoming the state of a few.

> Fascism is the purest kind of democracy, so long as people are counted qualitatively and not quantitatively.

This last remark is taken from the famous article on fascism in the

Enciclopedia italiana, an article which was written about 1931, signed by Mussolini but obviously composed by a number of hands including that of Gentile. Here at last it was boldly asserted that fascism had a doctrine, that of the Ethical State which manufactured its own system of morality and owed no allegiance to anything outside itself, that of the Nation in Arms which had to fight in order to justify its own existence:

The fascist conception of the state is all-embracing, and outside of the state no human or spiritual values can exist, let alone be desirable.

Perpetual peace would be impossible and useless. War alone brings all human energies to their highest state of tension, and stamps with the seal of nobility the nations which dare to face it.

Mussolini's article became the last word in philosophic speculation, just as his speeches had already become a bible for the faithful from which texts could be dug out to suit all occasions. Every few hundred yards along the roadside the traveler would see emblazoned in large letters on the whitewashed walls of a house the terse and pregnant quotations which every schoolboy had to know by heart: "He who has steel has bread"; "Better to live one day as a lion than a hundred years as a sheep"; "Nothing against the state, nothing outside the state"; "Nothing is ever won in history without bloodshed." In order to immortalize these great principles of 1922 a fascist faculty of political science was established at Perugia in 1927, followed by the creation of a "School of Fascist Mysticism" at Milan to debate what these principles meant. The true fascist, said a decree on the militia, must have his mind "pervaded by a profound mysticism." Groups of professors were given lectures by visiting party bureaucrats on not trying to put their own reasoning capacity on a level with the Duce's for between them and the leader was "a simply astronomical gap."

One of Mussolini's chief mentors in establishing the intellectual content of fascism was the Sicilian philosopher, Giovanni Gentile, who had split away from Croce and his fellow liberals in 1921-22. Early in 1925 Gentile drew up a fascist manifesto to send to important foreign intellectuals, signed by Pirandello, Ungaretti, Soffici, Pizzetti, and Panzini among others; to which Croce drew up a counter-manifesto signed by Einaudi, Ferrero, Fortunato, Mosca, Salvemini, Salvatorelli, and others who formed a far more distinguished list. Gentile became minister of education, member of the *Gran Consiglio*, president of the *Istituto Fascista di Cultura,* and general editor of the

Enciclopedia. He was a person of intelligence and it seemed also of integrity, but his vanity was tickled when fascism adopted the philosophical jargon of Actual Idealism. Croce, who had formerly been his friend, had also once preached the necessity of a strong state, yet drew back as soon as he realized what was happening. Gentile on the contrary turned somersaults to prove that all true liberals must be fascists, and he had insufficient self-respect to rebel when Mussolini contemptuously declared that "one *squadrista* was worth two philosophers."

Gentile's official task was to justify fascism theoretically, to rationalize its boasted anti-intellectual bias, to demonstrate how its proclaimed lack of a philosophy might be itself a philosophy, and how its frequent changes of policy could be theorized and comprehended into a program of higher opportunism:

> Often the Duce, with his profound intuition of fascist psychology, has told us the truth, that we all participate in a sort of mystic sentiment. In such a mystic state of mind we do not form clear and distinct ideas, nor can we put into precise words the things we believe in, but it is in those mystic moments when our soul is enveloped in the penumbra of a new world being born that creative faith germinates in our hearts. . . . The fascist spirit is will, not intellect. . . . Intellectual fascists must not be *intellectuals.*

Again, with another paradox, he adapted Croce's Hegelianism to attract right-wing Italian liberals into the fascist party:

> The *Duce* once discussed whether action should be by force or consent, and concluded that the authority of the state and the liberty of the subject are counterparts and inseparable. . . . Fascism does not oppose authority to liberty, but sets a system of real and concrete freedom against an abstract and false parody. . . . Even in the nineteenth century people were beginning to think that a strong state was necessary in the interests of liberty itself. . . . One can even say that the new Corporative State, by stressing the identification of liberty with authority, and through a system of representation which corresponds better with reality, is actually more liberal than the old.

There was apparently sufficient speciousness in all this to appeal to many of those steeped in the fashionable idealist philosophy. It was easy to make fun of the skeptical prewar liberalism

> . . . which dared do nothing because it believed in nothing and saw no point in sacrifice; which used to measure the national fortunes by the standard of individual well-being, but never liked to compromise itself or

to get heated about anything, preferring to put on one side any question that might imperil *quieto vivere;* which threw the cold water of prose upon the enthusiasm of poetry, and recommended moderation at all costs.

Nevertheless, Gentile leaned over backward to the other extreme, justifying the cruelties of *squadrismo* and writing pages of nonsense about the economy and austerity of the *stile fascista.* He was bold enough to say that in the corporative system the Italian genius was once again leading the world, for the first time since the age of the Renaissance.

Many of Gentile's ideas were later repudiated to his great chagrin, for Mussolini never liked people who were clever, and his use of an umbrella indicated that the professor was out of touch with the true fascist style. One of his *gaffes* was the attempt to set up a special fascist university at Bologna, as if any other sort of university might still be extant. He also made an unguarded remark about fascism being a minority movement and had to be publicly disavowed. Then after 1929 came Mussolini's reconciliation with the Church, which was most upsetting to those who had first been attracted to fascism by its anticlerical leanings. Gentile's own educational reform of 1923 had been inspired by the belief that the dogmas of the Church were no more than a useful halfway house to the truth, and suitable for primary schools alone. When fascism sensed the need of full alliance with the Church, Gentile fell from grace. He remained on and off an officeholder, and was eventually assassinated by the antifascists in 1944.

Mussolini's inspirational method of extempore speechmaking sometimes led him to pose as a philistine and say that he cared not the least bit for the past, but in his contrary pose as an intellectual he set great store by rooting his movement in Italian historical traditions. Research was vigorously organized for this purpose under De Vecchi, who set up a control of historical publications, and under whose aegis facts and documents were sometimes treated with scant regard for the truth. One deliberate intention was that fascism should be differentiated from everything in Italian history that was unwarlike, parliamentary, or bourgeois, and in this sense, said De Vecchi, history knew no more profound revolution than that of fascism. On the other hand the regime had to be linked with Mazzini, Foscolo, Dante, and the great names of the past. Both in history and politics it had to be simultaneously ultraconservative and ultrarevolutionary.

Imperial Rome was a favorite hunting ground for moral lessons and heroic exemplars. Mussolini thus announced that Caesar was the greatest man who had ever lived, and he innocently and comically called Shakespeare's *Julius Caesar* the finest school for statesmen. The fascist symbol had itself been derived from the lictors of ancient Rome, and such words as consul, cohort, and centurion were now halfheartedly and self-consciously resuscitated. Archaeology therefore came into its own. "Fascism," said the egregious De Vecchi, "has solved the most formidable problems of archaeology and of art through the mind and will power of the *Duce*." An ambitious excavation of the Forums at Rome was started in 1924, and in ten years had completely altered this region of the city, bringing to light what was Roman at the expense of what was Christian and medieval. A monumental Via dell'Impero was built as an ugly scar through the city, and there was even vandalistic talk of opening up another imperial route between the Pantheon and the monument to Marcus Aurelius in Piazza Colonna. Meanwhile, large outdoor maps in marble relief showed the extent of the Roman Empire, with the implication that what Rome had done once she could do again. In the new penumbral jargon, life had to be lived *romanamente*. Mussolini set the example in his revival of pagan rites, and in October 1928 instituted a ceremony in which patriotic citizens presented their national savings certificates as a burnt offering on an ancient altar of Minerva specially brought out of its museum for the purpose.

The great names of other periods were likewise taken as forerunners and examples. The Middle Ages were deliberately played down as a period of weakness, though Dante was transmuted into a premature nationalist. The Duce used to recall listening to his father read Machiavelli's *Prince* aloud by the family fireside, and he himself frequently quoted it and chose the theme of this book when he wrote a slight disquisition for his honorary doctoral degree at Bologna. The Renaissance itself was not, however, uncritically accepted in the new canon, as it was said to have diverted Italians into a ruinous individualism, and works of art were generally anathema to Mussolini. Renaissance rulers had spent money on beauty instead of on making a strong and victorious state.

The nineteenth-century *risorgimento* showed more of the authentic fascist ebullience and gave Mussolini the comfortable feeling that he was the fulfillment of a logical process of history. Garibaldi had been a Duce with a colored shirt and was marked as a precursor by his acts of piracy, his balcony speeches, and his militarized youth corps. Newspaper correspondents with Garibaldi had commented on the electrifying communion of mind between him and the masses, and on the religion of Garibaldianism for which people were ready to die. Benevolent and liberal-minded though he was, Garibaldi had chosen the title of dictator when he ruled over half the peninsula, for in his own words, "I had become more and more convinced that the only way to get Italians to see eye to eye and agree with each other is by using armed force, nothing less."

The official professors similarly had an easy time with Mazzini, who had spent much of his life crusading against parliament and socialism, and against what he called the excessive individualism of the Americans. Mazzini, as a collectivist, had come near to suggesting that the individual had only duties, while the state alone as a moral entity had rights. His ideal state looked like a totalitarian theocracy, in which there was no distinction between Church and state and no conflict between classes. Mazzini and Garibaldi would certainly have opposed much of fascism, but with much of it they might also have sympathized, and together they represent an authoritarian tradition on the radical Left to which some of the fascist leaders belonged.

On the Right, a parallel tradition could be traced back to the time of Cavour, and especially to those of Cavour's colleagues like Spaventa who followed Hegel in theorizing about the state. Some of these right-wing liberals had from the start advocated an extension of governmental controls, and it was the Right not the Left which had first advocated nationalization of the railroads. Bonghi, although a good liberal, had concluded that Italian parliamentary government worked well only when a man of genius like Cavour had coerced it into operation. The young Orlando, likewise disillusioned with parliament, had written in 1884: "Our only hope is in the appearance of a *deus ex machina*, that is to say a man of such demonstrably superior qualities, and such determined intention, that he would seize the rudder of the state and pervade every aspect of peoples' lives with a sense of positive government action." The arrogant Crispi had been vain enough to imagine himself just such a superman, and had had good reason to think that Italians would welcome a disciplined authoritarian state. The pessimists pointed out that, except for a brief and imperfect interval since 1860, absolutism had been the sole political experience of most Italians. Furthermore, while other countries had inherited a disbelief and an individualism from the Reformation, Italians had nearly all been brought up in a church which demanded perfect obedience.

These historical facts no doubt help in part to explain why parliamentary government had broken down in 1922. Fascist historians were able to find precursors everywhere and to suggest that arbitrary rule came naturally to the national temperament. From Rienzi to Masaniello and D'Annunzio there had been many notable demagogues before Mussolini, and Gregorovius in the nineteenth century said that he found three types constantly recurring in Italian history—Machiavelli, Cesare Borgia, and the *condottieri*. Enlightened despots, Jacobins, Bonapartism, national unification by conquest and plebiscite, irredentism and imperialism, all of these were wrought into an arid and melancholy pattern by obedient official historians. The intent was to confer an aspect of inevitability on the events of 1922 and to make Italians feel that by nature and history they were destined for this high fate. All roads led to Rome, to the Third Rome in which Mussolini aimed to outdo all the Caesars and Popes.

The Standardization of Culture

Artists and intellectuals can be as unreliable as anyone when dealing with politics. Pirandello signed the manifesto of fascist intellectuals and put on the gaudy fascist uniform of Mussolini's new academy. Shortly before his death, Puccini gave his blessing to fascism and was made a senator for his trouble. The *doyen* of Italian economists, Pantaleoni, was also made a senator and so was the sociologist Pareto. Marconi, too, had his pride caressed when he was created a marquis and his advice was asked on politics. Mussolini later wrote of this period as "the time of the carrot and the stick," and his own experience taught that these two weapons were effective with most people in attaching them to the regime. A decree of 1933 prescribed, on paper at least, that party membership was necessary for any administrative post, and Croce and the Church both agreed that this was a formality which could be accepted even by nonfascists if it were needed for office or promotion. Few people in fact could afford to hold out.

Croce himself, though his writings might be removed from schools and libraries, possessed an integrity and an economic independence which allowed him to remain adamantly distinct from fascism after 1925. D'Annunzio, on the other hand, easily capitulated to the grant of a pension, and a palatial villa was bestowed on him as a national monument in which he could indulge his unamiable eccentricities. Since he was never able to throw off the memory of the absolute power he had enjoyed as Regent of Fiume, he was also presented with the forecastle of a naval ironclad which he erected in his garden by

Lake Garda; sentries stood on duty there, and the poet used to welcome visitors by a salute of guns corresponding to their merit or title, just as though he were still a sovereign power. D'Annunzio was also created Prince of Monte Nevoso, one of the few examples of princely rank conferred in modern Italian history. The old aristocracy resented the way in which fascism cheapened titles and granted them in batches. Mussolini invented several completely new titles for himself, and he made De Pinedo a marquis for flying around the world in 120 days.

The intellectuals were drilled into corporations like everyone else, because fascism liked to have everyone and everything organized and wanted to prevent any untidy leftovers or people who claimed some vestigial independence of thought. After 1933 compulsory uniforms were introduced even for teachers and civil servants as a symbol of their new uniformity of mind, and medals were distributed annually for fascist achievements in art, culture, and sport. A National Council of Research was created, over which Marconi and Marshal Badoglio were to preside, which had considerable patronage. There was also a Fascist Institute of National Culture under the presidency of Gentile, which published periodicals and set up libraries for the study of fascism.

Between 1926 and 1929 the Fascist Academy was conceived to coordinate all work in the arts and sciences, to "preserve for our intellectual life its national character according to the genius and the tradition of our race, and also to favor its expansion abroad." There were to be sixty academicians, all chosen by Mussolini, paid a salary, addressed as "Your Excellency," receiving free first-class travel, and given a mock-antique uniform complete with plumed hat and gilt sword. Pirandello, Marinetti, and Panzini were obvious choices as inaugural members, and its secretary was Volpe, the best of the fascist historians. Tittoni, Marconi, D'Annunzio, and Ferderzoni, successively its presidents, wore ostrich feathers and had perquisites on an even more luxurious scale.

In return, the duties of academicians were negligible. They awarded titles and decorations, banned words of foreign derivation, and decided that every good fascist ought to address his neighbor only in the stilted language of the second person plural. Inevitably, they were a dull body, chosen generally for their artistic and political orthodoxy and suffocated by worldly success. Most of them became as much at home in fascist parades as in the arts and sciences, and the photographs of them goose-stepping at the Roman salute have a macabre fascination. Papini and the composer Mascagni look oddly placed in this *galère*. But the honor and perquisites did without doubt cause many a crisis of conscience among an important class of people. Some of the signatories of Croce's antifascist manifesto in 1925 had become apologists and even propagandists for the regime ten years later, because Mussolini used the carrot to good effect.

A mild rap with the stick was also used to conscript the intelligentsia when professors in 1931 were required to swear an oath of loyalty not only to the king but to fascism. This oath, too, was generally considered a mere formality, and the Church again held that it was a legitimate claim by the government for obedience. The world-famous mathematician Levi-Civita added a private reservation, and the government showed that it was quite ready to accept the substance without the form. About twelve hundred professors did as they were bid. Orlando and De Viti de Marco preferred to resign before the oath was put to them. Eleven others made their names celebrated by refusing to swear, and so forfeited their posts. They included De Sanctis the ancient historian, Lionello Venturi the art historian, Ruffini the canon lawyer, and Buonaiuti the modernist theologian who had come under ecclesiastical ban. The students were incited to mob those teachers who refused to burn their pinch of incense, but sometimes had the sense to respect such signal courage and integrity. Nevertheless, the oath was a big success for the regime, and if only there had been several hundred refusals instead of eleven it would have been a sharp challenge which would have carried weight with public opinion and abroad.

When the racial laws were introduced in 1938, ninety or more scholars were dismissed, the two leading Italian mathematicians, Volterra and Levi-Civita, among them. Others who had Jewish friends and relatives followed these into voluntary or involuntary retirement and exile. The physicist Fermi had already refused to return home after receiving his Nobel prize in Oslo, and as two of his leading followers in Rome also left, the loss to Italy in the field of nuclear physics was incalculable. Together with the bureaucratization of universities and the selection of professors for political reasons, this persecution helps to explain the backwardness of Italian science in assisting the war effort after 1939.

In literature and history some of the party bosses put their names to —and perhaps even wrote—articles and books purporting to be serious contributions to scholarship. In Croce's magazine, *La Critica,* a true scholar like Omodeo was able to expose some extraordinary examples of plagiarism in their work, but he had to pay for his courage and irony, and not many people were thus ready to risk their careers. The vagaries of the censorship were notorious. Fisher's *History of Europe* was confiscated from bookstores in 1939 by order of a new dignitary called the Minister of Popular Culture. An index of prohibited books was also drawn up for libraries, in which, along with Robert Graves and Axel Munthe, Machiavelli and Boccaccio were in 1939 declared "unsuitable to the fascist spirit." By this time the lunatic elements of fascism were clearly in full control. It may seem surprising that good work could ever be done in such an atmosphere, and yet the pervasive inefficiency, plus a certain amount of good-natured tolerance, allowed much more freedom of expression than was ever possible in contemporary Germany.

It is too early to estimate what posterity will find durable in the artistic and cultural achievements of the last thirty-five years. The arrival of fascism seemed to coincide roughly with the end of a period. Pascoli and Fogazzaro had disappeared before the war; Modigliani the painter died in 1920, Pareto in 1923, Puccini and the Duse in 1924. The leaders of the next generation were of smaller stature, and the central controls of fascism were inevitably a brake and a hindrance upon them. Political motives also helped to weaken the literary and aesthetic links with France and so to cut off Italy from the most vital source of challenge and renewal. German influence was more encouraged, especially as Mussolini himself had acquired a fair superficial acquaintanceship with German culture and went on taking German lessons to the end of his life. Beethoven and Wagner he much preferred to Puccini, or so he said, but Vittorio Mussolini often saw his father asleep during Wagner's operas.

Mussolini intended fascism to be strikingly creative and sought hard to discover for it a cultural identity. Successive experts thus restlessly pursued one novelty after another, though there was an absence of strong traditions to build on, and the results usually lacked individuality and character. The ubiquitous but hazy "fascist style" was eventually dragged into art as well as into manners and even religion. Dragged is the only word, for Mussolini himself in his poverty of spirit had no love of art, and he had welcomed Marinetti's fantastic suggestion to dispose of the national galleries in exchange for good foreign currency. What he would have liked, he told Ciano, was fewer pictures and statues and more enemy flags captured in battle. He boasted that he had never set foot in a museum or art gallery until

Hitler took him on a minute examination of the Pitti and Uffizi, and the boredom and physical exhaustion of this occasion was to remain a painful memory.

Marinetti the futurist had been the earliest literary influence in fascism, but futurism had been more talk than achievement, and in any case was passé long before the fascists had caught on to its usefulness. The religious conversion of Papini about 1918 was symptomatic of an already existing return from these futuristic excesses back to order, discipline, and traditional language, and Papini too became a keen fascist. Bacchelli, Baldini, and Ungaretti were turning to more classical models of prose and poetry after the crude paroxysms of yesterday's *avant garde*, but these people were too intellectual for Mussolini. In an attempt to show what the fascist style meant in literature, the Duce himself set up as a playwright, and so did the barely literate Farinacci, with unimpressive results.

Pirandello's best work was already written by the end of 1921, in which year he had composed *Enrico IV* and *Six Characters in Search of an Author*. In 1934 he won a Nobel prize for literature. But he was never outstandingly popular in Italy, and after the first performance of *Sei personaggi* he had been hissed into the street. In his lugubrious characters it is possible to glimpse something of the spiritual emptiness of postwar Italy; they believed that life was a bad joke, vain and useless, and that private illusions alone afforded any protection—an apt enough commentary on fascism, even though not Mussolini's idea of the *stile fascista*. Among the younger generation, Moravia's brilliant novel of 1928, *Gli indifferenti*, held another mirror up to fascist Italy, and described a cynical, existentialist world, peopled with sensual, repugnant characters and devoid of belief and purpose.

In sculpture and painting, fascism lacked both attractiveness and character, an understandable state of affairs in an organized and artificial culture where the prizes went to those who depicted fascist successes and martyrology. Since the death of Canova a hundred years before, the academic school of sculpture had been coasting on its past momentum, and the *risorgimento* had brought only a horrid outcrop of heroic groups and rhetorical statues in most *piazze* up and down the kingdom. Then at the turn of the century, the embellishments on the Vittorio Emanuele monument in Rome demonstrated official art at its biggest and unhappiest. Fascism inherited no ready-made school or tradition except this, together with an indigestible ferment of fashionable novelties, and not much success was registered in creating a new style which reflected the inner nature of Mussolini's revolution. Advanced artists such as Carrà and Chirico, metaphysical painters and surrealists, neocubists, neorealists, tonalists, hermetic poets, and all the rest, managed to exist alongside the safe academic art which flourished on official patronage.

In architecture the fascist period showed more character. It has been said that architects flourish under a dictatorship as much as lawyers in a democracy. Buildings can become good publicity, and countless post offices and town halls proved to be effective vehicles for the grandiose and magniloquent impressions which fascism hoped to convey. A veritable building fever overtook the regime. Compared with the baroque Rome of Bernini, the much larger "Humbertine" Rome palpably lacked a consistent style and is remembered mostly for its gigantic official follies. The new fascist style was unashamedly modernist. It transplanted, or rather translated and traduced, Gropius and Le Corbusier, using harsh geometrical lines and large white plain surfaces to replace the pilasters, loggias, and elaborate façades which had for so long been used to soften the glaring sunlight of Italy. At its most successful there was Michelucci's railroad station at Florence, and a younger school of engineers led by Nervi and Ponti was to show an artistry in reinforced-concrete hangars and office buildings which won world-wide admiration after 1945. At its worst, Mussolini's taste showed a reversion to the classical and "Roman," almost always spectacular and violent, and usually vulgar. At international exhibitions, the Italian pavilion had if possible to be higher and showier than others, and the unfinished tower of Babel outside Rome is today a melancholy reminder of shoddiness and vainglory.

The history of these twenty years was not, of course, synonymous with that of fascism. There were Toscanini and the other exiles abroad, and even in Italy there was always some nonconformity to interrupt the monologue which issued from Palazzo Venezia. It is tempting to say that the only interesting creative work came from the nonco-operators. There were fine works of historical scholarship by Omodeo, De Sanctis, De Ruggiero, Chabod, Salvatorelli, Spellanzon, and many more. The better novelists of Bacchelli's generation showed no purely official qualities in their novels, and much of Treccani's huge and impressive *Enciclopedia italiana* is naturally quite free of political slant. Above all loomed the majestic figure of Croce, who as a writer, thinker, and critic of art and literature had an immeasurable influence on all intelligent people. In a hundred ways Croce exposed the bad taste and shoddy thinking which were in danger of typifying a whole generation of Italians, and luckily he was himself too big a figure with too great a world reputation to be suppressed.

Fascism was too casual, and perhaps too self-consciously on the defensive, to be as insidious and deep-rooted an evil as nazism. Nevertheless, despite the few creative artists who had the courage, integrity, and means of livelihood to hold aloof from official direction, the damage done was incalculable. Many writers, artists, and thinkers had to depend on official money, and this made it the more disastrous that a policy of artistic autarky ran parallel with that of political and economic autarky. The music and drama of "sanctionist" states was thus forbidden during the Abyssinian war, and jazz was always deprecated as something alien to the race. Such a doctrine of cultural self-sufficiency betrayed a lack of confidence and an unwillingness to compete which was both a symptom and a cause of artistic decay.

The education of the young was vitally important for a government which boasted of upsetting all the conventional standards of morality, justice, and civilization. Official policy laid down that Italians must be brought up to be more warlike and tough, less artistic and less "nice," and to be always "desperately serious." Above all they had to become less individualistic and more amenable to discipline.

The education act of 1923 sponsored by Gentile was passed before Mussolini knew what he wanted. It had allowed considerable freedom to private schools and greater autonomy to universities. It stressed the value of humanist education and promoted the teaching of philosophy at every level. It also laid down the sensible doctrine that examinations were to test not facts learned by rote, but understanding and expression. Gentile's philosophical method became vacuous and rhetorical in the hands of lesser men, and it could be argued that Italy's chief need was not for more philosophy but for that very scientific and technological education which Croce and Gentile thought to be of minor importance. Nevertheless, Gentile's reform contained few of the usual fascist banalities, and it helped to preserve some independence of mind in education during the dark days to come.

It was again typical of fascism that one reform should cancel out another. Instead of the stability which Mussolini had promised to bring, he soon had to invert his thesis and proclaim that fascism was not a revolution once and for all but a perpetual revolution. His own ministers changed almost as rapidly as their predecessors. Eight ministers of education, eight ministers of public works, and nine ministers for the colonies followed each other in the fourteen years after 1922; the syllabus and curriculum for schools were repeatedly changed; textbooks were rewritten when Fedele wanted more religion, or when Ercole wanted more economics, and yet more radically when De Vecchi ordained that every detail of education must be infused with the highest fascist principles. Bottai then put an end to mixed schools, since male supremacy was a fascist principle. But the basic problems of education remained unsolved, and the seventh national census in 1931 still gave 20 per cent of illiterates (48 per cent in Calabria), while the eighth in 1936 pointedly omitted to give any figures at all.

"Fascist culture" and "corporative law" were introduced even into the schools, although the teachers must have been puzzled as to what these topics really meant. The subject of history was said to have been hitherto too disorganized and piecemeal, and henceforth was going to be disciplined in order to illustrate the primacy of Italians. Out of 317 history textbooks, 101 were forbidden by a special commission in 1926, and ten years later a single standardized text was in compulsory use. The polarization of history around the year 1922—*anno primo*—was indicated by a new calendar superseding the outmoded reckoning of dates from the birth of our Lord, and no one was allowed to point out that this was just aping the French Revolution. Balbo's description of his flight across the Atlantic in 1933 became Italian literature and a set text for secondary schools. Foreign literature was represented among other books by translations of Benjamin Franklin and Samuel Smiles. The Italian language was enriched with new words coined by Mussolini which Panzini had to include in his dictionary, and books were written to analyze the subtlety and vigor of the leader's literary style—though his more scatological expressions were if possible concealed from the public eye. The words chosen for spelling lessons were connected with fighting, and children were taught how Italy had saved Britain and America in World War I and how Mussolini had now made Italy again "the first nation in the world."

Selected phrases from the compulsory reader issued for eight-year-olds in 1936 give some indication of the kind of education which fascism now intended to impart.

The eyes of the Duce are on every one of you. No one can say what is the meaning of that look on his face. It is an eagle opening its wings and rising into space. It is a flame that searches out your heart to light there a vermilion fire. Who can resist that burning eye, darting out its arrows? But do not be afraid; for you those arrows will change into rays of joy.

A child, who, even while not refusing to obey, asks "Why?," is like a bayonet made of milk. . . . "You must obey because you must," said Mussolini, when explaining the reasons for obedience.

How can we ever forget that fascist boy who, when near to death, asked that he might put on his uniform and that his savings should go to the party?

To the victor who has conquered the Abyssinians we owe eternal gratitude and obedience for winning the greatest colonial war that history has recorded. . . . The Empire has been created by the rooted conviction in us that "Mussolini is always right."

An essential part of fascist education was the conscription of youth into quasi-military units. At the age of four a child became a "son of the she-wolf" and put on his first black shirt; at the age of eight he joined the *Balilla,* at fourteen the *Avanguardisti*—Balilla was the nickname of an unknown Genoese boy who was said to have thrown the first stone against the Austrians in a civic rebellion of 1746. These children were trained to military discipline, and special toy machine guns were made for their entertainment. They were also instructed in *cultura fascista*, which they were then expected to retail among their families. Official chaplains were attached to the *Balilla*, and this partially appeased the Church for the fact that a monopoly on youth clubs had been obtained by organizations which were pagan in fact and militaristic in both fact and theory. Millions of Italian boys and girls passed through this poisonous process of indoctrination, though no doubt it was often applied or absorbed in a casual and slipshod manner.

Other methods of propaganda were limited, since most Italians had not yet acquired the habit of radio or even of newspapers. Even the provincial Catholic press had to fill three of its four pages with fascist nonsense in order to purchase the use of one page for the bishop's letter and events of the ecclesiastical calendar. Mussolini made his first broadcast speech over Marconi's new system in 1924, but a technical hitch made his words unintelligible and for fear of ridicule he was cut off. Radio was of course monopolized by the government, and a law of 1927 set up a special organization which later became *Radio Italiana*. A policy was eventually laid down for radio programs to be governed by "a rigorously autarkic cultural spirit," and when the minister of culture announced this to the fascist Chamber he was greeted with loud applause. Mussolini himself only two or three times in his life gave talks specially for the radio, because he quickly discovered that impersonal fireside chats were not much in his line.

The Italian film industry was not organized until relatively late. Historical films were always a favorite in Italy, as they could give full scope to the feeling for pageantry and national greatness. Lucrezia Borgia, the battle of Lepanto, the last days of Pompeii, Nero, Julius Caesar, even Dante, all were filmed at least once. On the introduction of talkies about 1926, another speciality was opera and dramatizations of the lives of composers such as Verdi and Bellini. After 1929, films with a fascist bent became more common, but people found them dull, and American importations were more diverting as well as technically superior. Mussolini had films specially shown for him most evenings. He himself preferred comedies to tragedies. He tried at first to forbid films with foreign dialogue, and then allowed foreign products a quota of only one to ten instead of ten to one. This caused American companies in 1939 to withdraw from Italy, and the consequent decline in foreign competition gave Italian producers a guaranteed market however poor their efforts. For this reason, and because of the demands of propaganda, good films such as the *Siege of Alcazar* were exceptional. Yet subsequent development of the new realist school with De Sica and Visconti revealed a fund of latent talent, and with the removal of central direction and ideological prejudice, Italy was ready to take a front place in the world of cinema.

A totalitarian regime had of necessity to stake out moral dominion over every sphere of individual life, and this included recreation and sport. Here national prestige could be asserted ostentatiously, and the nation's physique could be improved against a day of bloodier battle. The vogue of sport, like the word itself, had been introduced from Great Britain late in the nineteenth century. About 1858, Englishmen were forming the first Alpine societies, and the first ascent of Mont Blanc was in 1865. In 1870 the first cycling club was founded in Milan, and after 1909 the *giro d'Italia* became one of the big events of the year. The second favorite sport was football, for which a club was started as early as 1890 in Genoa. From 1908 when the first Italian championship was held, football spread rapidly, until there were ten thousand recognized clubs. Fox-hunting also was brought in from England, and there was a golf society in Rome by 1903.

Mussolini did his best to organize these miscellaneous importations, and one party secretary even tried to instill the fascist style into sport through a new and short-lived game called *volata*. The organization of leisure was a paramount aim of the new ideology, so *"il weekend"* was abolished and in 1935 became by law *"il sabato fascista."* Sport eventually became a fascist monopoly: for example, the Olympic Games committee had to be affiliated with the party, and the party appointed the president of the Italian chess association. The physical education of the young benefited incidentally from this official encouragement, and the *Dopolavoro* institution provided excellent cheap vacations and recreation for workers. Many international victories were also won in bicycle and motor racing, and in 1933 the carpenter Primo Carnera beat Sharkey at New York to become world heavyweight boxing champion, the newspapers being carefully instructed never to show pictures of him knocked down in the ring. Boxing, said Mussolini, "was an essentially fascist method of self-expression." In February 1939 the Italian lawn tennis association decreed that all players in international matches should wear fascist uniform and should respond with the fascist salute when their opponents offered to shake hands. Once again, thinking to aim at the sublime, the movement had fallen by an internal and inevitable logic into the ridiculous.

The football industry was purged as early as 1926, and reorganized on lines "more consonant with the new life of the nation." The game was said to be not a foreign importation, but a development of the old Tuscan *calcio*, which had long ago been forbidden because of the casualties it caused and then had been taken to England. Its control now passed from local clubs to a central body with a honeycomb of divisional, zonal, and federal directions. By 1937 there were 52,000 players licensed by their membership cards to play, and 2,700 authorized referees under the chief referee at Rome with his gold whistle. As a "typically Italian creation," there was a new official, the *commissario di campo*, who was sent by the federal director to "invigilate" both the behavior of the public and any fouling on the field which might escape the referee. No one knew who he was, but he drew up a private report on the game and sent it to the zonal Directorate of Football, where it was then compared with that of the referee. Sport, as in other countries, was thus encouraged to pass from dilettanti to professionals, and also from the countryside to the large metropolitan towns, for only big stadiums could pay for the grand spectacles which were part of the choreography of fascism.

III. Hitler and National Socialism

Germany is the great modern tragedy. How and why she slipped into catastrophe are questions demanding more than satisfaction of historical curiosity. Apparently destined for greatness, Germany's moment of ascendancy was brief: forged by Prussian power in the wake of military triumph in 1870, German hegemony in Europe was smashed by military defeat in 1945, and the prospect of its early renewal appears dim. The roots of disaster may be traced in German history since 1870, and indeed before. Nazism was the inheritor as well as the manipulator of several strands of the German past, and was hardly the original creation of a single man or movement. Few would deny the legacy of history in the origins of Hitler's Germany, whether it be the political legacy of Bismark's Empire, which accustomed Germans to firm rule by the man at the top; or the legacy left in many minds by the persistence in German thought of anti-democratic and racial doctrines. But, as the authors of these readings would hasten to add, although National Socialism was cast in a recognizably German mold, it was also part of a European inheritance.

The Weimar Republic, born in 1919 in the aftermath of defeat, toppled by Hitler less than fourteen years later because too few Germans were willing or able to defend it, was compelled to live with an inheritance of adversity, including the lie that its creators had stabbed the army in the back in 1918 as well as the simple fact that many Germans were ill-prepared for an experiment in liberal democracy. The story of Weimar's abbreviated life is too dismal and too familiar to warrant extensive analysis in these readings. The "objective" criteria in the Republic's failure are easily catalogued: an infirm political system, characterized by a multiplicity of parties; the existence of sworn enemies of the régime on its left and right; constitutional weaknesses, the most critical being the ability of the President to act arbitrarily; the political unreliability of the army; the stigma of the Versailles Treaty and the reparations; economic crises; social unrest; and the treachery or stupidity of key political, business, and military figures in assisting Hitler's rise to power. What is less comprehensible is why so many Germans were willing to accept the Hitlerian solution, an avowedly extremist one, at a moment when the twin crests of economic and political crisis seemed to have passed. Why was it that Hitler, now considered a monstrous if not mad criminal, should have been able to draw upon strains of fervent idealism and have appeared as a hero to millions of his countrymen? Why did Germans give their allegiance to the Nazi leaders, who seem striking only for their very ordinary appearance, the crudeness of their utterances, in a word, for their banality, and who are remembered for the hideous deeds which they perpetrated? The purpose of these readings is to offer at least partial answers to these questions. Rather than an intensive exploration of German history and a specific analysis of the failures of the Weimar Republic and its citizens, attention has been given to the nature of Hitler's revolution, the Nazi ideology, the techniques of Nazi rule and structure of the Party, and to a portrait of the Führer.

The opening selection is a vital chapter entitled "The Nazi Revolution" from *The Rise and Fall of Nazi Germany* by T. L. Jarman, Reader in Education at the University of Bristol and well-known author of several books in modern European history. Jarman demonstrates that Hitler's revolution did not precede, but was the consequence of, his accession to power in January 1933. He further states that Hitler was installed as Chancellor of Germany not because of revolutionary upheaval but because of political jobbery and his ability to cast the Nazi movement as a viable alternative to the alleged weaknesses and decadence of democracy. Specifically concerned with the years 1933 and 1934, this excerpt describes how Hitler was able to attain dictatorial power by sweeping aside his enemies and some of his friends, many of whom were solid Nazis, by employing the coercive apparatus of the state, and even by resorting to murder. Noting the ease with which the Führer carried out his task, Jarman believes that Hitler "had little to fear from the German people," and concludes that by mid-1934 the Nazi revolution was complete, since it had achieved its only real goal—power.

Power and the Nazis' fateful fascination with its workings are the theme of the second reading, drawn from a book published in 1939 by the only high-ranking National Socialist to leave the Party and become its declared enemy. Dr. Hermann Rauschning was a Nazi leader in the Free City of Danzig, but withdrew from the Nazi fold because he could not disobey his "duty and conscience" when he was instructed to persecute Catholics and Jews. *The Revolution of Nihilism* is perhaps the best known of Rauschning's writings, although his accounts of Hitler's conversations have been invaluable to historians.

A personal testament to the steady erosion of the author's confidence in the Führer and to his disgust with the broken promise of the Nazi ideology, *The Revolution of Nihilism* also provides, as Ernst Nolte put it, "concrete and significant insights" into the fascist phenomenon. Rauschning detected the mainsprings of National Socialism—violence, the cultivation of destructive revolutionary dynamism, the deliberate choice of immoral methods, and outright destruction—mainsprings which served no higher aspiration, no goal other than the consolidation of power in the hands of the ruling élite. Nazism's sole objective, argues Rauschning, was to secure the victory of the Party, to cement the triumph by a continuous "intensification of the process of revolutionary disintegration."

Rauschning's keen appraisal of the techniques of his ex-colleagues unmasked the nature of German totalitarianism long before the defeat of Hitler's régime permitted more sophisticated scholarly inquiry. Demonstrating the potent appeal of the irrational in Nazi policy, Rauschning shows how the masses were persuaded to become voluntary partners in their own repression. In an extensive commentary upon Nazi rule, the author emphasizes its machinery—especially the use of overlapping authorities and a sense of omnipresent power—and its trappings—notably the incessant marching, systematic lying, and "permanent pugnacity" vital to its perpetuation. Rauschning's is perhaps a unique contribution to our understanding of fascism. Attracted to National Socialism by its promise of renaissance, appalled by its immorality and worship of power, he perceived that its very existence depended upon the maintenance, even the acceleration, of the use of violence. Unlike Jarman, who considered the revolution complete with Hitler's acquisition of dictatorial power, Rauschning demonstrates that, by its own inner logic, the Nazi Revolution had to be unfinished.

In the third selection, a chapter taken in its entirety from *Three Faces of Fascism,* Ernst Nolte is also concerned with power and destruction, arguing that they were inextricably intertwined in Nazi doctrine. Tracing National Socialism from its shabby origins as a message of hope and hatred to its fulfillment in destruction, Nolte claims that it sought from the outset to "preach a doctrine" and that doctrine demanded the liquidation of its enemies. Like Rauschning, Nolte emphasizes the sheer violence of the Nazi movement; even its meetings were vicarious battlefields where marching columns symbolized the alleged beauty of struggle, and, like Italian fascism, these columns were meant to convey the image of an irresistible tide. The annual Party gathering at Nuremberg is fully described and analyzed in this reading. Featuring martial music, drills, ceremonies, stirring speeches about the soil, the dead, and German greatness, and climaxed by the Führer's harangue, it was less an exercise in self-congratulation than a celebration of the ideology itself. Conquest and annihilation, according to Nolte, were the permanent, unremitting aspirations of National Socialism. Thus, a "will to destruction," actualized during World War II, was at the heart of Nazism.

Undoubtedly the most celebrated work on Nazism is Alan Bullock's *Hitler: A Study in Tyranny,* first published in 1952 and reissued in a completely revised edition in 1962. The concluding reading in this section is composed of a chapter entitled "The Dictator" and the "Epilogue" from this biography. Although scholars have begun recently to apply the tools of psychology to studies of Adolf Hitler, it may be several years before Bullock's portrait of the dictator is superseded. Bullock's Hitler is complex, even contradictory: impervious to criticism and famous for his rages, the Führer was a master politician, patient, sometimes kindly, and not without genius. A "consummate actor," he mesmerized the crowd, yet he gradually became the victim of his own acting and of his unlimited capacity for hatred. Like

Rauschning and Nolte, Bullock considers power and force to have
been Hitler's chemistry; his striking originality lay in the ruthless pursuit of his fantastic ambitions.

The final pages serve well as a conclusion to this entire section.
Bullock reviews the several explanations of Hitler and National Socialism; and, while he admits the German character of the master and
his creation, he confirms that both must be seen as manifestations of a
European malaise. Finally, Bullock concurs with Rauschning and
Nolte: Nazism, whose only goal was domination, was a "revolution
of nihilism," since it produced nothing.

1. The Nazi Revolution

T. L. JARMAN

The Nazi Revolution did not precede, but followed Hitler's becoming Chancellor of the German Reich. Hitler was called upon in legal
fashion by the President to assume the Chancellorship; he did so as
the result of bargaining with Papen, and political bargainings in one
form or another had been going on for a long time. Papen thought
that, as a result of his bargain, he would be able to control and
moderate Hitler. The Nazi leader came to power as the result of the
failure of the other parties in Germany to combine against him—that
is, of their failure to realize in time how small were their own dis-
agreements when compared with the magnitude of the menace which
threatened them. The Nazis, before Hitler came to power, never won
more than slightly over 37 per cent of the votes cast in an election.
But the other parties were hopelessly divided in their opposition: the
Social Democrats were not strong enough alone, the Communists
hated the Social Democrats almost more than the Nazis, the Nationalist Party in its nationalistic outlook sympathized with the Nazis. Thus
Hitler was able to strike his bargain with the influential Papen and
Hugenberg, the leader of the Nationalist Party; Hitler became head
of a coalition government. At first, therefore, he had to go carefully;

Source: T. L. Jarman, *The Rise and Fall of Nazi Germany* (New York: New
York University Press, 1956), pp. 147–166. Reprinted with permission of the
New York University Press.

it took him just five months to consolidate his position and make himself dictator.

In Hitler's coalition Government Papen was Vice-Chancellor; he was also Reich Commissioner for Prussia, and these two offices appeared to give him sufficient power to hold Hitler in check. Of the remaining posts only two were held by Nazis: Frick was Minister of the Interior, and Göring Minister without Portfolio (and also Minister of the Interior for Prussia). Two posts were given to men of Hindenburg's choice: the diplomat von Neurath became Foreign Minister, and General von Blomberg Minister of Defence. The other posts went to the Nationalists, Hugenberg, Seldte (leader of the Nationalist private army, the *Stahlhelm*, comparable to the S.A.), and others of their party. It certainly looked promising enough for Papen; he had persuaded Hindenburg to overcome his fears of making Hitler Chancellor, and now with the new coalition Government it seemed evident that the wild man was under firm control. But Papen had a lot to learn.

The Nazi-Nationalist coalition held 247 seats in a Reichstag of 583. Hitler's first task was to find a secure parliamentary majority. Hitler might have gained the support of the Catholic Centre; negotiations were opened, but Hitler saw to it that they broke down. It was his aim to fight an election with the State machinery on his side; it had long been his aim not to revolt against the State, but to take over all the machinery of state, and use it to make the Nazi revolution. Papen was beguiled into the trap and persuaded Hindenburg to dissolve the Reichstag: Germany was to go to the polls once more. 'The struggle is a light one now', wrote Goebbels, 'since we are able to employ all the means of the State. Radio and Press are at our disposal. We shall achieve a masterpiece of propaganda. Even money is not lacking this time.'

Hitler presented the Nazi Party as an alternative to the weakness and futility of the old regime, of the democratic system which had rested chiefly on the Social Democrat and Catholic Centre parties. 'In fourteen years the system which has now been overthrown has piled mistake upon mistake, illusion upon illusion.' The other parties, he argued, had failed in foreign policy, and had brought economic ruin at home. He even avowed that his Government was more Christian than the Centre, whose members had sat with Socialist atheists. How different, he argued, the Nazis would be! 'I ask of you, German people, that after you have given to the others fourteen years you should give to us a period of four years.'

Neither funds nor force were lacking in the Nazi campaign. Göring played a prominent part in raising funds; he called a meeting of the great industrial leaders, including Krupp and Dr. Schacht, and a sub-scription list from the leading Germans firms was drawn up. To ensure that the force of the State also was on the Nazi side, Göring used all his ruthless energy. As Minister of the Interior for Prussia, he was in charge of the Prussian police and Prussian state administration; since Prussia was by far the largest state, Göring in fact was in charge of nearly two-thirds of Germany, and was of greater importance than the Reich Minister of the Interior (who, in any case, was the Nazi, Frick). Göring proceeded to purge the Prussian civil service and police; he dismissed those officials whose loyalty to the new Government was doubtful and replaced them by Nazis. He formed an auxiliary police into which he drafted large bodies of men from the S.A. and S.S., and supplied them with arms. He warned the regular police that they must co-operate with S.A., S.S., and the *Stahlhelm*. And, above all, he told the police to use their firearms 'without regard for the effect of their shots'. With Göring in charge of the coercive machinery of the Prussian state, German citizens were helpless; the law afforded no redress to Nazi violence.

The main Nazi attack was directed against the Communists, which was good propaganda and sound tactics. It was announced that, in a raid on the Communist headquarters, the police had found the plans for a Communist revolution. But these were never published, in spite of promises by Hitler and Göring to do so. Then on the night of 27 February the Reichstag building caught fire and was burnt out. This was but part, so went the official explanation, of a campaign of Communist terrorism. A young Dutch Communist, van der Lubbe, was caught in the act of starting fires. Actually, it appears certain, the Nazis themselves had used an underground passage leading from the palace of the President of the Reichstag (Göring) to the Reichstag building to fire it, and used the Dutchman as a cover-up. The subsequent trial at Leipzig was embarrassing to Göring: the judges acquitted the accused Communist leaders (the German, Torgler, and the Bulgarian, Dimitroff, who with great audacity scored well off Göring during the trial.) Van der Lubbe only was executed. Hitler had wanted the immediate hanging of the Dutchman outside the Reichstag—and is said to have wanted a St. Bartholomew's Night of vengeance throughout Germany. The coalition Government, however, demurred; Hugenberg and Papen wished the army to intervene, but Blomberg opposed its intervention in politics.

The Nazis were restricted, but not stopped. The burning of the Reichstag served its purpose. Hitler issued a presidential decree 'for the protection of People and State': to protect the people, it suspended the clauses of the Weimar Constitution guaranteeing personal liberty. Göring arrested the Communist Deputies of the Reichstag and a number of Social Democrats as well. Nazi violence against the Communists increased—meetings were broken up, newspapers suppressed, leaders and speakers beaten up. The Communist Party was not banned, however; it was wiser to leave it to split the working-class vote at the election, and so avoid any accession of strength to the Social Democrats. Hundreds of people were injured and fifty-one officially admitted killed during the election campaign. Moderate people everywhere were intimidated, either by reports of the intended Communist revolution or by the Nazis' terrorism itself. Hitler was able to dramatize his election campaign as a struggle to save Europe from Bolshevism. In an interview with the *Daily Express* correspondent, he denied charges that the Reichstag fire was a put-up job. 'But I will tell you another thing', Hitler said. 'Europe, instead of suspecting me of false play, should be grateful to me for my drastic action against the Bolshevists. If Germany went Communist, as there was every danger of her doing until I became Chancellor, it would not have been long before the rest of civilized Europe fell a prey to this Asiatic pest.' Hitler concluded the interview by saying: 'We must crush Communism out of existence.' But he said that normal freedom would then be restored—an empty promise. Göring epitomized the ferocity behind the campaign when he declared at one of his meetings: 'Fellow Germans, my measures will not be crippled by any judicial thinking. . . . I don't have to worry about justice. . . . This struggle will be a struggle against chaos, and such a struggle I shall not conduct with the power of the police. A bourgeois State might have done that. Certainly, I shall use the power of the State and the police to the utmost, my dear Communists, so don't draw any false conclusions; but the struggle to the death, in which my fist will grasp your necks, I shall lead with those down there—the Brown Shirts.'

The German nation polled on Sunday, 5 March, after weeks of oratory, threats, street violence, vast meetings, demonstrations, and torchlight parades, which all helped to create the impression of an invincible mass movement advancing to victory. Nearly 90 per cent of the electors voted. The Nazis polled 17,277,200 (increasing their vote by 5½ millions) out of a total of 39,343,300, which gave them 288 seats in a Reichstag of 647 members. With their allies, the Na-

tional Party of fifty-three members (with a poll of 3,136,800), the
Nazis thus had a bare majority. The remarkable thing about the election results, however, was how steady had been the reaction of the
great opposition parties to the Nazi campaign: the Social Democrats
lost one seat only, polling over 7 millions; the Catholic Centre increased their votes, and polled nearly 4½ millions; and even the
Communist Party, though it lost 1 million votes, polled nearly 5 millions. As far as the figures went, the Nazi victory was by no means
overwhelming. But it was sufficient. If the Communists were absent—
and most of them were under arrest—the Nazis would have a majority
in the Reichstag without the support of the National Party. And that
would make Hitler independent of Papen and Hugenberg.

Hitler's task was to make himself supreme by destroying, or reducing to a subordinate position, those other institutions or organizations
which could in any way challenge, check, or hamper his power as head
of the Reich government. This process was one of *Gleichschaltung,* or
co-ordination: the whole life of Germany was to be brought under the
control of the Nazi Party. Hitler had to deal with the Reichstag and
the political parties, with the trade unions, and with the federal states,
or *Länder.*

At first Hitler showed himself conciliatory, for he wanted the Reichstag to pass an Enabling Bill to give the Government special powers. To
do this, which meant an alteration of the Constitution, would require a
majority of two-thirds. To win the support of all the conservative
forces, he staged a splendid ceremony at Potsdam, just as he had said
privately he would, to mark the reconciliation of old and new in Germany. The ceremony on 21 March was to mark the opening of the
new Reichstag, but the Garrison Church at Potsdam evoked memories,
not of Weimar and a democratic Germany, but of the military spirit of
the Kaisers. The Army and the S.A. formed guards of honour as President and Chancellor arrived. Inside the church were the surviving
high officers of the old imperial Germany, headed by Field-Marshal
von Mackensen, and all in uniform. The Nazi Deputies in their brown
shirts, the Nationalist members, and the Catholic Centre were drawn
up in rows. The Kaiser's chair was empty, but behind it sat the former
Crown Prince, representative of the Hohenzollerns. Hindenburg, bow-
ing low to the ex-Crown Prince, spoke briefly of the mandate given
by the people to the new Government, of its heavy tasks, and of his
hope for a united, free, and proud Germany. Hitler, in civilian morning
dress, followed. He spoke of 1918 and the collapse of the nation, and
said: 'In a unique revival, in the last few weeks our national honour

has been restored and, thanks to your understanding'—addressing Hindenburg—'the union between the symbols of the old greatness and the new strength has been completed. . . . We pay you homage, *Herr Generalfeldmarschall.* . . . Providence places you over this revival of our nation.' Hitler shook Hindenburg by the hand; and the old warrior stepped down alone into the crypt to lay a wreath upon the tomb of Frederick the Great. Then the roar of guns in salute broke the silence and, a little later, in the clear spring sunshine outside, the troops and detachments of the S.A. and the Stahlhelm marched past in review.

Two days later, on 23 March, the Reichstag met in its temporary accommodation at the Kroll Opera House. The building was surrounded by S.S., and inside were men of the S.A. But Hitler, in proposing the Enabling Bill, spoke in a conciliatory tone; he had, indeed, already made certain worthless promises to the leaders of the Catholic Centre, and he now made more to the members of the Reichstag as a whole. 'The Government', he said, 'offers to the parties of the Reichstag the opportunity for friendly co-operation.' Only the Social Democrats dared to oppose—their leader, Otto Wels, having the great courage to stand up in the hostile throng and say that his party would vote against the Bill. The Communists were in gaol; the Catholic Centre voted for the Bill. The result was announced by Göring: for the Bill, 441; against, 94. When Hitler, with the Cabinet, appeared on the balcony, the crowd went wild with delight. Again and again it shouted, *'Heil Hitler!'* By the new law, the Government was given the power for the next four years to make laws without the Reichstag; such laws were to be drafted by the chancellor, and they might modify the constitution. Hitler was independent of the Reichstag—he was a dictator.

The policy of *Gleichschaltung* was soon applied to the political parties and the trade unions. Many of the local trade union offices had, indeed, already been pillaged by the Nazis, but on 2 May, after the people of Berlin had been dazzled on May Day by a gigantic Nazi demonstration and spectacle on the Tempelhof field, the trade union offices all over the country were occupied by men of the S.A. or S.S. The union officials were often beaten up and thrown into prison or concentration camp. The union organizations were then taken over by the Nazis, and re-formed into the new German Labour Front. The Nazis followed up their blow to the trade unions by one against the Social Democratic Party itself. On 10 May its property—buildings, offices, newspapers, and funds—was seized. In June this Party was formally banned. The Communists had not been allowed to take their seats; their Party property was also confiscated. The other parties, though less roughly handled, saw the danger of a similar fate. At the end of June and the beginning of July the small Democrat Party, the People's Party, and the once-important Catholic Centre Party all liquidated themselves. Hugenberg, in spite of his protests, could not save his own Nationalist Party; it also liquidated itself at the end of June, and Hugenberg was forced to resign his ministerial post. Seldte, the leader of the Stahlhelm, joined the Nazi Party, and his organization was eventually merged in the S.A. On 14 July the Government issued an official order declaring that 'The National Socialist German Workers' Party constitutes the only political party in Germany.

Meanwhile—indeed, ever since the election victory of 5 March— the process of *Gleichschaltung* had been applied to the federal states. Prussia was already under Göring's control. On March 5, on the initiative of Göring, the Government of Hamburg was seized by a coup. On 9 March General von Epp acted for Hitler in Bavaria, where there had been since Hitler's becoming Chancellor of the Reich some talk of secession and restoring the Wittelsbach monarchy; Epp turned out the Bavarian Government and filled up the posts with Nazis. Between 5 and 16 March the other federal states passed under Nazi control, Frick, as Minister of the Interior, sending in *Reichskomissars* to replace the state governments by Nazi ministers. Early in April Hitler appointed for each state a *Reichstatthalter,* or governor, with powers to appoint and remove the state government and dissolve the state parliament. At the same time Papen was pushed aside altogether in Prussia (where he had been nominally superior to Göring), Hitler making himself *Reichstatthalter,* with Göring as Minister-President. On 30 January 1934 a new law abolished the elective state parliaments altogether, and transferred their once sovereign powers to the Reich; the *Reichstatthalters* and state governments were made subordinate to the Minister of the Interior of the Reich. Thus, under Hitler, German administration reached a degree of centralization previously unknown. As Frick explained the new law: 'The historical task of our times is the creation of a strong, national, unitary state to replace the former federal state. . . . The state governments from today on are merely administrative bodies of the Reich.'

Hitler was now dictator, with the machinery and powers of a great state in his hands. But as a former Nazi revolutionary he was still surrounded by revolutionaries—men who were violent and fanatical, good fighters in a revolutionary movement, but inconvenient and embarrassing when once the revolution had succeeded. One makes a revolution with one set of men; one governs with another—as Mussolini was reported to have said later on to Hitler. Then there were many in the Nazi Party, and many who had joined it later in its time of success, who had hoped to get something out of it. Some of them were disappointed, and some did not do as well as they had hoped. At first there were excitement and expectancy, then anti-climax. Disappointment and discontent were rife and had to be reckoned with, and there were also the old rivalries and jealousies among the Party leaders which had shown themselves as early as Hitler's imprisonment in 1924. There were, too, the very natural fears of the established civil servants in their ministries, of the Foreign Service, and of the higher officers of the Army for the new men who were being placed in positions of authority. The capitalist elements of Germany, the great industrialists and also the small traders and shopkeepers, feared the radical, socialist demands of the Left wing of the National Socialist Party. Outside of Germany there was the reaction of foreign states to be watched—for example, the nervous reaction of France, Poland, and Russia. There were protests from abroad about the atrocities inside Germany, for it was soon reported that terrible things were happening—secret arrests, beatings and torture, imprisonment without trial. Göring's secret police were gaining notoriety. Prisons and concentration camps began to fill up, and against the Party the ordinary person had no redress. Ordinary Germans, who had not suffered, were apt to excuse themselves with a shrug of the shoulders. 'You know the times we live in', they said.

Nevertheless, the Nazi movement had behind it a powerful revolutionary force, which had gathered to itself a large mass support in the country. It was wrong to suppose, as Socialist and Communist elements in foreign countries tended to do, that the Nazi régime was a dictatorship imposed by force on an unwilling people. It was even more wrong to imagine that the German people were awaiting an opportunity for revolt. The extraordinary thing is that Hitler had been able to carry through his policy of *Gleichschaltung* without serious opposition. Reichstag, parties, trade unions, the federal states had all given way without a struggle. Hitler himself was surprised by the collapse of the opposition. The Nazis had shown great energy, determination, and will power; unfortunately, the moderate, reasonable, liberal elements had shown nothing comparable, and even the Communists and the Social Democrats, with their theoretical attachment to the idea of social revolution, had not dared to make a stand. Indeed, the violent elements in the Communist Party were attracted by the Nazis. And Röhm, it seems, welcomed them into the S.A. 'It's easier to control

Communist elements inside the S.A. than by closing the ranks against them', he said. 'They can't undermine the S.A.—some of my best men are former Communists. Let them call them "Beefsteaks" [i.e. red inside, brown outside, as Berlin put it]. I like them radical.' Hitler's success was a measure of what could be achieved by an unscrupulous and determined leader, and how easily the masses could be cajoled, seduced, and led away. Hitler had nothing to fear from the German people. But he had to fear a crisis in his own Party.

Hitler was faced with three problems: the problem of the second revolution, as it was called; the old problem, which had given trouble before, of the relation between the S.A. and the Army; and the new problem raised by the declining health of Hindenburg. And these problems were not distinct and separate; they were interconnected.

Hitler himself was not interested in the details of government and administration; nor was he an economist or socialist. Promises of social and economic reform were useful to beguile the masses, but the work of managing the economic system he was prepared to leave to industrialists and economic experts so long as they provided employment and produced the goods. Hitler wanted time: time to consolidate his régime and to prepare for the great tasks of foreign policy which were his main interest. But he was being pushed by the forces in his party pressing for a second revolution, and he was aware of a divergence in the Party between the conservative, national and capitalist element and the socialist element. Hitler himself sounded a note of warning. In a speech on 1 July 1933 to S.A. and S.S. leaders, he explained that the first three stages of the revolution—preparation, the seizure of power, and the achievement of totalitarianism—were over. The chief requisite now was order. The idea of a second revolution or 'revolution in permanence' could not be tolerated. 'I will suppress every attempt to disturb the existing order as ruthlessly as I will deal with the so-called second revolution, which would lead only to chaotic conditions.' And a few days later he addressed the Reichstatthälter, assembled in Berlin. Once again Hitler said. 'The revolution is not a permanent state of affairs, and it must not be allowed to develop into such a state. The stream of revolution released must be guided into the safe channel of evolution. . . . We must therefore not dismiss a business-man if he is a good business-man, even if he is not yet a National Socialist; and especially not if the National Socialist who is to take his place knows nothing about business. In business, ability must be the only authoritative standard. . . .' And again, a week later, in speaking to the Nazi *Gauleiters,* he said that there must be no 'radical breaking up of existing conditions which would endanger the foundations of their own life'.

Others in the Party, and especially in the S.A., thought otherwise. Goebbels had often attacked the reactionary forces of the right; Gregor Strasser, though he was now living privately since throwing up his job in the Party, looked on Hitler's advent as the first stage in a revolutionary process; his brother, Otto Strasser, stood for simultaneous attack on bourgeois capitalism and international Marxism, and had broken with Hitler because he regarded him as a reactionary. Most important of all, however, was Röhm, because he was Hitler's friend and comrade since the early days and was now chief-of-staff of the S.A. with between 2 and 3 million men under his command. But revolutionary Nazis did not agree among themselves, and were kept apart by personal jealousies and fear. Ludecke, according to his own account, had tried several times, and especially in 1932, to bring Röhm and Strasser together, but without success. Ludecke's personal story in 1933–4—an old Party member imprisoned first on Göring's orders and then put away in a concentration camp on Hitler's orders, finally being forced to escape over the frontier—is some indication of the intrigues going on in the Party. In June 1933 (shortly before the Gestapo arrested him on Hitler's directions) Ludecke had a long talk with Röhm, and the two men discussed the prospects of 'a house-cleaning of the Party' and an extension of the revolution. One difficulty was that Röhm could always be attacked by his enemies in the Party on the ground of his private vices. 'Those hypocrites!' Röhm exclaimed. 'I've suffered enough from that. . . . Homosexuality isn't a reason for removing an able and honest leader from any position, so long as he is discreet. Such a more or less natural abnormality is nobody's business. . . . Haven't I worked all my life for this land and given Hitler all I had? Where would he be without me? Hitler had better look out—the German revolution is only beginning!' Then Röhm tossed over to Ludecke a copy of a Nazi monthly, in which a bold message from Röhm himself headed, 'S.A. und deutsche Revolution', was published: 'One victory on the road of German revolution has been won. . . . The S.A. and S.S., who bear the great responsibility of having set the German revolution rolling, will not allow it to fall asleep or to be betrayed at the halfway mark. . . . If the Philistines believe that the national revolution has lasted too long . . . it is indeed high time that the national revolution should end and become a National-Socialist one. . . . We shall continue our fight—with them or without them. And, if necessary, against them. . . . We shall watch relentlessly to keep the half-hearted and the opportunists from hanging themselves like so much lead on the Führer's sacred, socialistic will. . . . We are the incorruptible guarantors of the fulfilment of the German revolution.'

Bold words! Rash words! And Hitler had read the article, so Röhm avowed, and Röhm had said more to Hitler than he had thought proper to put in print. Röhm had a clear, if rather naïve, view of things. 'The cowardly surrender of the opposition surprised Hitler', he said, 'more than it surprised me. He can't get over it. Why doesn't he put the money-bags where they belong! If he didn't know it before, he knows now that I'll never allow our revolution to fizzle out. Of course, he's in a quandary and, as usual, shuns a clear-cut decision. . . . But if he thinks he can squeeze me for his own ends for ever, and some fine day throw me on the ash-heap, he's wrong. The S.A. can also be an instrument for checking Hitler himself.' Röhm, too, had a view of the wider, world situation: he saw the possibilities—the German Army High Command hand in hand with big business and looking for a military alliance with Russia; or Hitler as dictator with the Army under his thumb marching eastwards against Russia. For his own part, Röhm (and Ludecke) thought to work with Russia and against capitalism in Germany and the West. Again, in a speech in April 1934, Röhm expressed his view that the German revolution was 'not a nationalist, but a National Socialist revolution, with special stress on the word "Socialist". . . . There are still men in official positions today who have not the least idea of the spirit of the revolution. We shall ruthlessly get rid of them if they dare to put their reactionary ideas into practice.'

It was, indeed, a clear picture Röhm had given. Röhm and his S.A. were after the fruits of Socialism, the spoils and pickings of revolution —though this was not altogether unnatural when one recalls the long years of depression and unemployment, and how the S.A. had offered hope to unemployed workers and professional men and ruined members of the middle classes. Hitler was interested in power, and to secure the power he had achieved he must retain the support of the Army and ensure his succession to the Presidency. The Army was now bitterly jealous of the S.A., and feared it, for the S.A. was many times larger than the Army, and Röhm wished to use it as the basis for a new people's army. And the Right-wing conservative forces behind the President hated and feared the radical, socialist element in the Party headed by Röhm. Hitler was indeed in a quandary. For the S.A. could still be useful to him; he could use it to bring pressure, blackmail, if necessary, on the Army and the Right-wing forces of industry and finance; he could use it as a bargaining counter in foreign policy—for example, by offering to reduce its strength when Mr. Eden visited Berlin in February. And perhaps, too, Hitler suffered genuine qualms in turning on his old friends; he certainly had a strong sentimental feeling for the early days of struggle, the *Kampfzeit*. But Hitler was a realist: at all events he must retain on his side the real forces of the country, the Army and large-scale industry.

Hitler tried conciliation, as he had done before with Röhm and with the Strassers. He made Röhm a minister in the Reich Government in December, and wrote him a most friendly, personal letter at New Year, 1934. Hitler thanked him and his leadership of the S.A. for 'making it possible for me to win decisively in the struggle for power'; he thanked him for his 'imperishable services' and declared: 'How grateful I am to destiny for being allowed to number such men as yourself among my friends and comrades-in-arms.' But Röhm was not satisfied. Göring had been made a general and Hitler had promised Blomberg a field-marshal's baton. 'And I!' said Röhm to Ludecke. 'I am still minister without portfolio.' Then, referring to the New Year letter from Hitler: 'He can't fool me. . . . Yes, we still need him. Unfortunately, half the nation already sees a demi-god in him. But we must push him soon, lest the others push him first. . . . If Hitler is reasonable, I shall settle the matter quietly; if he isn't, I must be prepared to use force—not for my sake, but for the sake of our revolution.' On 4 June Hitler spent five hours with Röhm. 'I implored him for the last time', Hitler reported later, 'to oppose this madness of his own accord', and to 'use his authority so as to stop a development which in any event could only end in a catastrophe'. But apparently Röhm was neither won over nor intimidated. For the immediate future, Hitler ordered the S.A. on leave for July, and Röhm himself went on sick leave on 7 June—but not without a message to his men which contained a challenge to the enemies of the S.A.: 'At the hour and in the form which appears to be necessary they will receive the fitting answer.' To Röhm there seemed no immediate danger. Like so many others, he, too, underestimated Hitler.

But the intrigues went on in Germany, and tension grew. Schleicher had appeared again in the background.* The full story of what went on is not known, and probably never will be. However, it seems certain that Hitler managed to reach an understanding with the generals:

---

* General Kurt von Schleicher, ex-Chancellor, had been involved in the tangled politics that helped bring Hitler to power.—Ed.

the Army should remain the national source of power and the S.A. be kept in a subordinate place; Hitler, in spite of conservative hopes of a restoration of the Hohenzollern monarchy when Hindenburg died, should succeed to the presidential power.

Then, on 17 June at the University of Marburg, Papen made a bold speech. It was a warning to Hitler of the anxieties of the Right, of the conservative and respectable forces in Germany, and indeed voiced the doubts and fears of decent elements throughout the nation. He dealt severely with the idea of the second revolution:

Whoever toys irresponsibly with such ideas should not forget that a second wave might be followed by a third, and that he who threatens to employ a guillotine may be its first victim.

Nor is it clear where such a second wave is to lead. There is much talk of the coming socialization. Have we gone through the anti-Marxist revolution in order to carry out a Marxist programme? . . . Would the German people be better for it, except perhaps those who scent booty in such a pillaging raid? . . . At some time the movement must come to a stop and a solid social structure will arise. . . . There is no upbuilding amid everlasting eruptions.

He went on to ask for confidence and understanding rather than propaganda. 'It is time', he said, 'to join together in fraternal friendship and respect for all our fellow countrymen, to avoid disturbing the labours of serious men and to silence fanatics.' Papen's speech was something of a sensation. Goebbels, as Minister of Propaganda, took steps to ban its publication. Papen saw Hitler and threatened resignation. Hitler also received a warning from the President and a threat to declare martial law. A few days later, appearing publicly in Hamburg, Papen received an ovation. In the last week of June tension reached breaking-point.

On 30 June Hitler struck. Behind him he had the S.S., and the Army. It was in the Hotel Dreesen at Godesberg on the Rhine, on the afternoon of the 29th, that Hitler made up his mind. That very night he flew from Bonn to Munich to confront Röhm in person. Early on Saturday morning, the 30th, with Goebbels, who had rapidly put his radical views aside, and other Nazi leaders, and well guarded by the S.S., in armoured cars, Hitler drove out to the hotel where Röhm was staying at Wiessee. The S.A. leaders on whom they could lay hands were dragged out of bed, accused of plotting a *coup d'état,* carried back to Munich, where Hess was waiting for them, and shot by S.S. guards in the old Stadelheim Prison. The notorious Heines, found sleeping with a youth, was shot there and then, according to one account. Röhm, shut in a cell with a loaded revolver, refused to commit suicide, and was shot by one of the S.S. In Berlin Göring and Himmler directed operations. Executions of S.A. leaders went on during the Saturday and Sunday. Karl Ernst, seized when setting out on a voyage with his wife, is said to have died shouting, *'Heil Hitler!'* He thought that Hitler had been betrayed. At the same time, a number of others, some of them supposedly dangerous, were disposed of individually in their homes, offices, or elsewhere—the ex-chancellor General von Schleicher and his wife, his friend, General von Bredow, Gregor Strasser, and two of Papen's staff, von Bose and Edgar Jung. Papen himself narrowly escaped, though placed under house arrest for several days. Prominent Catholics were shot, including Dr. Klausener, leader of Catholic Action. There were many executions in other parts of Germany. Hitler's old opponent, von Kahr, former premier of Bavaria and now a man of seventy-three, was dragged from bed in the night; his body was later found hacked to pieces. Willi Schmidt, the Munich music critic, was done to death by reason of his name; the S.S. were looking for a different Schmidt. How many died altogether is not known: estimates varied from the official figure of seventy-seven to a figure of over 400. There may have been many more. 'Like a black panther on a dark night', Hitler was reported as saying, 'so I spring on my enemy by surprise and destroy him.'

Whether there was any real or definite plot against Hitler cannot be decided for certain. No valid evidence was produced, it is unlikely that all these very different people could have been involved in the same plot, and the fact that Röhm was on holiday and caught completely unawares does not indicate that he was on the point of making an immediate coup. But by his action, Hitler relieved the pressure on him from Left and Right, and disposed of men who might have been dangerous. Hitler defended his action in a speech on 13 July to the Reichstag—to a Reichstag which since the *Gleichschaltung* of the political parties consisted of Nazi members only. He made the most of the known vices of the S.A. leaders, Röhm and Heines, of their homosexual practices, and also accused them of drunkenness, extravagance, and luxurious living on Party funds. But these things had for a long time been no secret. Hitler did not, however, hide what was their real crime—the threat of a second revolution. He spoke of them as 'uprooted', and said that they had become 'revolutionaries who favoured revolution for its own sake and desired to see revolution established as a permanent condition'. They had found 'in Nihilism their final confession of faith'. Hitler made a grandiloquent plea in his own defence: 'Mutinies are repressed in accordance with laws of iron which are eternally the same. If anyone reproaches me and asks why I did not resort to the regular courts of justice, then all I can say to him is this: in this hour I was responsible for the fate of the German people, and thereby I became the supreme justiciar of the German people. . . . And everyone must know for all future time that if he raises his hand to strike the State, then certain death is his lot.' In other words, stripped of its grandiloquence, what Hitler was saying meant that, like a Chicago gangster, he had succeeded, and, having succeeded, he now disposed of his fellow-gangsters lest they might prove dangerous.

Some people hoped that Hitler's action would at last open German eyes. This, however, was a complete error. People said instead: 'Leave me in peace with your terror stories. I don't want to know of them. . . . Hitler saved us from a far worse civil war.' Hitler, too, doubtless wanted to forget. Months later there was still on the walls in the Dreesen Hotel a photograph of Hitler and a group of Nazis, which had originally included Röhm. But now Röhm was covered by a figure cut from another photograph and pasted skilfully over the dead S.A. leader. Röhm was hidden lest Hitler on subsequent visits should remember.

It remained for Hitler to put the final touches to his position of absolute power. On 2 August President von Hindenburg died—at a lucky moment for Hitler. At once a law, dated 1 August, was issued, uniting in the person of Hitler the offices of President and Chancellor. Hitler was thus in theory as well as fact head of the State. The title 'President' was, perhaps, too republican in flavour for Hitler. He did not use it, but was known as *Führer und Reichskanzler.* But he wanted its powers; with the presidential function he became commander-in-chief of the German armed forces. Officers and men now took the oath of allegiance to Hitler, mentioned by name in the form of words: 'I swear by God this holy oath that I will give unlimited obedience to the Führer of the German Reich, Adolf Hitler.' On 19 August by plebiscite the German people were asked to approve. Out of 45 million voters, over 38 millions voted 'Yes'. The Nazi revolution, Hitler's revolution, was complete. Hitler's sense of personal power grew. For him there was neither law nor morality—for him all that was old-fashioned sentiment.

2. *The Revolution of Nihilism*

HERMANN RAUSCHNING

The Aims of National Socialism

"Our aims are perfectly clear. The world is only surprised at our attitude because it does not know us." The German propaganda leader wrote this, with his characteristic pregnancy, on the occasion of Lord Halifax's visit to Germany in 1937. "The aims of National Socialism are being achieved, one after another. . . . It will come. It is coming, bit by bit. We have time!" he continued. It is true enough that the world still does not know National Socialism, but it is not correct to say that the aims of the party were clear. We have to combat two views, one that the course followed in the Reich was carefully planned and thought out and directed toward definite objectives fixed once and for all, and the other that National Socialism is guided on the whole by doctrinaire program points. There are many who will contend that National Socialism reveals a broadly conceived, dogmatically defined philosophy, possessing absolutely definite doctrines in regard to all human relations which must be unreservedly accepted by every loyal citizen. Nevertheless, we must ask: is National Socialism doctrinaire? It is, of course, beyond question that it is the product of doctrinaire ideas and that doctrinaire personages play a part in it to this day. Of much greater importance is the question of the connection of what was regarded as National Socialist doctrine with the two elements that characterize the movement, the irrational passions that undoubtedly play an important part, and its leading personalities. A sharp distinction must be drawn in National Socialism between this genuinely irrational revolutionary passion, affecting not only the mass of followers but the leaders themselves, and the very deliberate, utterly cold and calculating pursuit of power and dominance by the controlling group. We may generalize: The doctrine is meant for the masses. It is *not* a part of the real motive forces of the revolution. It is an instrument for the control of the masses. The élite, the leaders, stand above the doctrine. They make use of it in furtherance of their purposes.

Source: *The Revolution of Nihilism* (New York: Alliance Book Corporation, 1939). Translated by E. W. Dickes.

What, then, are the aims of National Socialism which are being achieved one after another? Certainly not the various point: ` its program; even if some of these are carried out, this is not th .ning that matters. The aim of National Socialism is the complete revolutionizing of the technique of government, and complete dominance over the country by the leaders of the movement. The two things are inseparably connected: the revolution cannot be carried out without an élite ruling with absolute power, and this élite can maintain itself in power only through a process of continual intensification of the process of revolutionary disintegration. National Socialism is an unquestionably genuine revolutionary movement in the sense of a final achievement on a vaster scale of the "mass rising" dreamed of by Anarchists and Communists. But modern revolutions do not take place through fighting across improvised barricades, but in disciplined acts of destruction. They follow irrational impulses, but they remain under rational guidance and command. Their perilousness lies in their ordered destructiveness—it is a misuse on a vast scale of the human desire for order—and in the irrationality and incalculability of their pressure for the "victory of the revolutionary new order." This pressure is completely uncalculated, unconsidered, the pressure of men with no program but action, instinctive in the case of the best troops of the movement; but the part played in it by its controlling élite is most carefully and coolly considered down to the smallest detail. There was and is no aim that National Socialism has not been ready for the sake of the movement to abandon or to proclaim at any time.

The National Socialist revolution, at the outset a nationalist seizure of power, is viewed much too much in the light of historic precedents. There are no criteria and no precedents for the new revolutions of the twentieth century. The revolutionary dictatorship is a new type, in its cynical, unprincipled policy of violence. The outsider overlooks above all the essential distinction between the mass and the élite in the new revolutions. This distinction is vital in every field. That which is intended for the mass is not applicable to the élite. Program and official philosophy, allegiance and faith, are for the mass. Nothing commits the élite—no philosophy, no ethical standard. It has but one obligation, that of absolute loyalty to comrades, to fellow-members of the initiated élite. This fundamental distinction between élite and mass does not seem to have been sufficiently clearly realized, but it is just this that explains many inconsistencies, many things done, that leave the outsider dumbfounded.

There has scarcely been a single old National Socialist who attached

any importance to the program and program-literature of the party.
If any section of the party was in it for action and nothing else, and
completely uninterested in programs and ideologies, and strong for
that very reason as the real backbone of a brotherhood, it was the
section of the party that was its vital element, the Storm Troops. Their
repugnance to programs was well known, there was no success in
training them in "theories." And the National Socialist "Bible," that
remarkable book which is now accorded the sanctity of verbal inspiration, was far from playing its present part among old "Pg's" (*Partei-
genossen*), old members of the party; they paid no particular attention to it. Nobody took it seriously; nobody could, for nobody could
make head or tail of it. The mass understood and understands nothing
and does not want to understand. Each individual holds to whatever
he can comprehend in it, to any particular bit that concerns him
personally. The things that stir most men and fire their enthusiasm
are the rhythm, the new tempo, the activity, that take them out of
the humdrum daily life: with these things much can be done, the
masses can be inflamed. They are matters of emotion, with much the
same appeal as the call of the first *Wandervogel* * movement, which
brought men away from the security of their homes and sent them on
a roving life: an emotion compounded of romance and boredom. The
initiated member, the old Pg, knew that the whole tableau of philosophical outlook and party doctrine was only of symbolic value,
something to stir men's imagination, to divert their thoughts from
other things, to discipline them. It was a cover for realities which
must not be "given away" to the masses. He himself, the old Pg, was
a Catilinarian, a mere *condottiere*; or, if he was an idealist, in his
progressive liberation from the crude ikon-worship of the National
Socialist masses he felt a pride of partnership in the reality behind it,
the heroic nihilism of the party, inculcated in the young men as soon
as they were old enough for the senior groups of the Hitler Youth. If
we try to understand what it is that tempts Hitler again and again
to dwell on Freemasonry, on the Jesuits, or on the Teutonic Order,
we come close to the essential secret of the National Socialist élite,
the "mystery," as the Teutonic Order called it, the esoteric doctrine
confined to the brethren who were called to initiation. It was the piecemeal character of their initiation into secret aims, the aims and
methods of a ruling class, by stages of discipline, enlightenment,

* The "Roamers," a youth movement, were inspired by the *volkish* message.
—Ed.

liberation, that set the eyes of National Socialism in envious rivalry on such organizations as Freemasonry.

The movement has no fixed aims, either economic or political, either in home or foreign affairs. Hitler was out even in 1932 to liberate himself from all party doctrines in economic policy, and he did the same in all other fields; and this "realist" attitude was adopted, and still is, not only by the leader but by every member holding any official position in the party, or admitted at all into its confidence. The only objective was the victory of the party, and even favorite doctrines were abandoned for the sake of this. The rise of National Socialism compelled the élite of the movement to become realists, and when they came into power they made this acquired pragmatism the foundation of the fanatical activity of the movement in the new, national field. It is no doctrinaire commitment of the movement that drives National Socialism into lines of action which from a realist and rationalist standpoint are incomprehensible, but its revolutionary, irrational character, which continually prompts it to any possible revolutionary destruction of existing institutions.

The fight against Christianity is not a matter of doctrine or program; this is clear to any reader of *Mein Kampf* or of the party program; yet it has come, simply because it lies more than anything else precisely in that direction of the destruction of existing institutions. For all practical purposes it should suffice for the racial State and for independence from all alien, supernational, superstate powers, if a German National Church were started. But the revolutionary destruction of the Christian basis goes much farther than this. A schismatic separation of German Catholicism from Rome, inevitable as it seems to-day, has already been put out of date by the developments in Germany. It will be a brief episode on the way to the comprehensive aim of destroying the Christian faith as the most deep-seated root of Western civilization and of the social order. It will be a stage that will assist the revolutionizing of the soul of the masses, not the actual final aim. Similarly the fight against Judaism, while it is beyond question a central element not only in material considerations but in those of cultural policy, is part of the party doctrine; but, for all that, it is now an element in the revolutionary unsettling of the nation, a means of destruction of past categories of thinking and valuation, of destroying the liberalist economic system based on private initiative and enterprise; it is also a sop to the destructive revolutionism of the masses, a first lesson in cynicism.

This irrational element in National Socialism is the actual source of its strength. It is the reliance on it that accounts for its "sleep-walker's immunity" in face of one practical problem after another. It explains why it was possible for National Socialism to attain power almost without the slightest tangible ideas of what it was going to do. The movement was without even vague general ideas on the subject; all it had was boundless confidence: things would smooth themselves out one way or another. Give rein to the revolutionary impulse, and the problems would find their own solution. An open mind and no program at all—that is what enabled National Socialism to win through in its own way with its practical problems. Its strength lay in incessant activity and in embarking on anything so long as it kept things moving. Conversely, it abandoned anything that could hinder it, such as the construction of the Corporative State and the reform of the Reich. What it needed and intuitively took up were the opportunities of revolutionary dislocation.

Nothing is more idle than to engage in heated discussions of the capitalistic and monopolistic character of National Socialist economic policy, or of the question whether Socialism or Reaction has been the driving force in its schemes of social reconstruction. National Socialist "anti-capitalism" is similarly just a bargain-counter, like almost everything else. If there is one thing that does not and cannot exist among the National Socialist élite, it is a genuine sense of social solidarity with the propertyless classes of the nation. One may count on finding just the opposite, and it is easily discernible in Hitler himself—an unconcealed contempt of the crowd, the common people, the mob: they are there not to be served but to be used.

National Socialism is action pure and simple, dynamics *in vacuo*, revolution at a variable tempo, ready to be changed at any moment. One thing it is not—doctrine or philosophy. Yet it has a philosophy. It does not base its policy on a doctrine, but pursues it with the aid of a philosophy. It makes use of its philosophy as it makes use of all things men have, and all they want, as fuel for its energy. Its policy is exactly what a critic of the era of William II said of the policy of that time: it is "opportunist policy," though in quite a different, a much more "realist", sense. It is opportunist policy in the sense of making use of every opportunity of doing anything to increase the movement's own power, and to add to the elements under its domination.

National Socialist policy is in the highest degree subtle and sly, aimed at keeping to the front a system of "inflammatory ideas," in order the more effectively and the more startlingly to seize each opportunity. People used to say that any policy of important scope always needs justification by a great idea. But that was intellectual, ideological generalizing. It assumed that there are still ideas in which men believe. To the conscious nihilist there are no ideas. But there are substitutes for ideas which can be foisted on the masses by suggestion, and he has little hesitation in imposing on them whatever they can swallow.

The National Socialist "philosophy" is not the outcome of any lofty intuition; it is deliberately and carefully manufactured. Originally it developed out of much the same doctrines as those which Sorel formulated in his gospel of violence: a myth must be created to give the masses the energy for action. Thus the ruling consideration in the production of the National Socialist philosophy is its power of influencing the masses by suggestion, of instilling into them the sense of the duty of obedience. The great paradox of this revolution is that its lack of principle is one of the main secrets of its effectiveness. It is its strength; it is precisely in this characteristic that the actual revolutionary power of the movement lies, and its character of a "permanent revolution," impossible to bring to a close. The naïve element among its mercenaries has largely been removed by the decimation of the Storm Troops, but the subtler and far more effectual element, the élite under the leader's protection, has remained. This élite keeps alive the revolutionary spirit, in spite of all announcements of the ending of the revolution. National Socialism cannot abandon this dynamic element; in doing so it would be abandoning itself. And the question becomes more and more insistent, how long can a State, a nation, a society, endure a governing élite devoid of all principle, without disintegrating?

Error and Deception

Error or deliberate deception? Which was it? Was the National Socialist party in doubt as to its own real character; did it genuinely regard itself as a movement of national rebirth, or did it cleverly and deliberately adopt that disguise in order to attain power? Undoubtedly both the one and the other. There was an honest belief among a great number of the members of the party, and among its followers, that they were laboring in the service of national recovery. Even among the élite the consciousness of the actual part they were to play came only with the first great successes. But there were some among them who knew how matters stood, probably long before the arrival in power. Hitler himself pursued carefully calculated tactics: he damped down the Socialist tendencies in the movement and brought the Nationalist ones into the foreground. He was out to gain powerful patrons and friends who could help the movement into power. The temporary veto on the anti-capitalist propaganda desired by Gregor Strasser was due to his insistence. And this was not because Hitler was himself a reactionary, but because at that moment the Socialist note would have interfered with the political developments envisaged. It was precisely at this point that Hitler showed his real superiority over his élite: at the right moment he took a course which was extremely awkward for him and an extremely unpopular one, but which alone led along the road to power—the camouflage of the "dynamic" revolution as a movement of national renewal. He put up with the dissatisfaction and disgust of his élite, and allowed them to abuse him for his "inadequacy" as an "advocate," and for his supposed idea that he could attain power by means of speeches and parades, threats and extortion, and secret deals with bankers and soldiers, industrialists and agrarians. Yet from the point of view of the movement and of its aims his course was the only possible one. He was justified in the outcome, and encouraged to continue in that course. He brazenly joined forces with the monarchists; brazenly denied his own views and affected to be a reactionary. With a technique of camouflage unprecedented in Germany, he arranged the deal that associated his party with the national rising which ended in the National Socialist revolution. He succeeded in a concealment of the true facts on a scale never before known. The deception continues to this day—a presentation of the revolution as an innocent affair, middle class and moderate. Deliberately concealing the true nature of the National Socialist revolution, the new élite successfully occupied Germany. Under its disguise it succeeded in foisting on the country, in place of an authoritarian State, an instrument of dominance that serves simply and purely for the maintenance of its own absolute power. Under the mask of a movement of national liberation, it achieved the despotic repression of the nation, with the voluntary assistance of the middle classes and large sections of the working class.

Only these facts provide the standpoint for a judgment of what National Socialism regards as its creative achievements, its work in the field of constitutional, social, and economic affairs. The outstanding feature to-day in these fields is beyond question their universal subjection to despotic control. A machinery of absolute and universal dominion is being erected in an entirely disorganized State. Nothing is more mistaken than to talk of a "totalitarian State" or a "classless society" within the realm of a nihilist revolution. In the place of these there is the machinery of absolute dominion, recognizing independence in no sphere at all, not even in the private life of the individual; and the totalitarian collectivity of the *Volksgemeinschaft*, the "national community," a euphemism for an atomized, structureless nation.

The retrogression from the conception of the State to that of the party in what a German sociologist has defined as its primitive sense, that of an organization for rule by violent means, is paralleled by the retrogression from the sphere of legality and constitutionalism to the primeval conception of Leader and Followers and the principle of absolute power and blind obedience. Within this organization of dominance which has replaced the State, there has developed as the indispensable means of rule the segregation of a privileged élite from the totally unprotected and disfranchised mass. The control of the remnants of the State by a party ("the Party commands the State") may be regarded as a phase in the process of the dissolution of the old forces of order by the revolution. This process ends with the absorption of the State and its functions by the "organization for rule by violent means." To-day the State is nothing but an administrative machine. There is no true sphere of the State in the Third Reich.

The Doctrine of Violence

National Socialism does not mean the crushing of the "mass revolt" but the carrying of it to completion. The astonishing thing is not that this could have happened, but that it could be done under the mask of a movement in the opposite direction, without those affected realizing the reversal of the course. To-day, after six years, there are, to say the least, still many respectable people associated with German "dynamism" who have not yet realized that their imagined national and racial rebirth amounts to nothing more than the adoption of the revolutionary system of "direct action" as the fundamental principle of the carrying of the "mass revolt" to completion.

Direct action is defined as "direct integration by means of corporativism, militarism, and myth"; this is to replace democracy and parliamentarism. But the true significance of direct action lies in its assignment of the central place in its policy to violence, which it then surrounds with a special philosophical interpretation of reality. Briefly this philosophical system amounts to the belief that the use of violence in a supreme effort liberates creative moral forces in human society which lead to social and national renewal. "Civilization is the endeavor to reduce violence to the *ultima ratio*," writes Ortega y Gasset. "This is now becoming all too clear to us, for direct action reverses the order and proclaims violence as the *prima ratio*, or rather the *unica ratio*. It is the standard that dispenses with all others." Violence, says Sorel, is the basic force in life. When all other standards have been unmasked by scepticism of all doctrines, reason itself is robbed of all force. The anti-intellectual attitude of "dynamism" is not mere chance but the necessary outcome of an entire absence of standards. Man, it holds, is not a logical being, not a creature guided by reason or intelligence, but a creature following his instincts and impulses, like any other animal. Consequently reason cannot provide a basis for a social order or a political system. The barbaric element of violence, which reformist Socialism and moderate Marxism would place in safe custody under lock and key, is the one element that can change a social order. That is why revolutionary direct action has won the day against the responsible, non-revolutionary Socialism of the working class, just as it has violently eliminated the middle class itself as the ruling class. Hostility to the things of the spirit, indifference to truth, indifference to the ethical conceptions of morality, honor, and equity—all the things that arouse the indignation of the ordinary citizen in Germany and abroad against certain National Socialist measures—are not excrescences but the logical and inevitable outcome of the National Socialist philosophy, of the doctrine of violence. This hostility to the intellect, to individualism and personality, to pure science and art, is not the arbitrary invention of a particularly vicious system of racial philosophy, but the logical outcome of the political system of revolutionary direct action with violence as its one and only historic motor.

The New Elite

The Leader-and-Followers principle simply destroys the possibility of building up a State. When this principle is dominant, the State can no longer exist. Nor can a social order endure. While still permeated with the idea of the "idyllic state of the rule of responsible middle class people," the nationalists confused their desire for the restoration of a regime of this type with the essence of the doctrine of violence, the principle of personal conspiratorial pledges of élite to Leader, which could produce a dictatorship ruling by violence, but never a monarchical restoration. In bringing the National Socialist Party into the "combination" they imagined that they had placed the reins of government in the hands of the aged President Hindenburg, assigning to the party leader the function of whipping up the enthusiasm of the country by his oratory. But the outcome was not as innocent as these self-styled realists expected. The special feature of the German development is the segregation out of the masses of a special élite which shares the privileges of power, and the atomization of the organized nation, which is reduced to an amorphous mass held together in new official mass groupings. It is the élite that actually organizes the revolutionary process; at the same time it controls the machinery of government. It represents the actual "Following" of the "Leader." Only in that capacity is it privileged. This National Socialist élite is nothing but the class that, in Pareto's phrase, is "arriving," forming, independently of any doctrine, the real kernel of a revolution. Pareto holds that a revolution is possible only when a ruling class that has lost its strength of will and is physically decadent, and no longer able to defend its hold of power by forcible means, is faced by a new class that has set out to take its place. In any case, the National Socialist revolution resembles the process described by Pareto, the rise of a new class and the abdication of an old one.

On the problem of the political élite, of the "ruling element with a historic mission," the monarchists, proceeding from a different starting-point, had developed much the same ideas as those underlying the National Socialist enterprise of creating a new upper class as an instrument of dominance. Some of the monarchist groups expected themselves to become the new upper class of the National Socialist mass movement, and their anticipation helped in no small degree to bring into existence the "combination" of 1933.

National Socialism, with its sharp elbows, pushed all these lofty aspirations rudely aside. It had no need either of an intellectual or of a social élite. *L'élite, c'est moi*, was its attitude. The ponderous and self-conscious discussions among the nationalists of the problem of the élite and the political leadership were in strong contrast with the unscrupulousness of the National Socialists in the practical task of selecting their élite. To them the formation of an élite was not a problem in political theory but a practical process connected with their struggle for power. They did not dream of introducing fresh blood into their élite from outside their own ranks. They were not interested in the slightest in the qualities of outside candidates, their intelligence, their capacity, or their social standing. These outsiders were just "pigmies," in the Propaganda Minister's phrase. What the National Socialists did take over was the language of those rivals. By appropriating for lip-service the ideas and standards of genuine political and social élites, they have succeeded to this day in deceiving a naïve nation, and masking the true fact that National Socialism brought to the top a primitive, vulgar élite under the cover of national and social aims. The fiction that every element associated with National Socialism in the struggle for power proved itself by that fact to be by nature and character a part of the élite exposes the mechanism of this primitive but effective method of selection. But the secret of the union of the élite is their lack of doctrine. No allegiance to any sort of philosophy merited membership in the actual élite, but the simple fact of having fought for its power. The actual selection, said the National Socialists, is our affair. Neither by intelligence nor capacity nor noble birth nor special standing were men qualified for entry into the élite, but simply by denial of the traditional decent citizen's outlook. Ordinary life gives the true leader's nature no opportunity for success, only temptations, which end his respectability. To have come to grief in ordinary life is no disqualification for revolutionary leadership—on the contrary. With the full momentum of their demagogic resources, and with the readiness to gamble of the true desperado, who has nothing to lose and everything to gain, this gutter élite were able to carry the day with ease against the rather too cautious and anemic members of the aristocratic clubs.

Their success was facilitated by their adoption of their rivals' political language. The National Socialist leaders concealed their true objectives so well that many members of the élite only realized after a considerable time that they had been drawn into a double existence, with fictitious spiritual, national aims, and one very real one, the pursuit of power. The actual participants in power within the National Socialist Party are a ruling minority of super-careerists. This cream of the élite use the power they have seized to feather their nests. The most outstanding quality of the élite is "the accurately chosen and ruthless application of all the physical and material power at its disposal." Here again the National Socialist leaders carried into practice the new doctrine of violence, the doctrine that spiritual assets are of value for the legitimation of political power and for nothing else; such things have no intrinsic authority, no value in themselves: there is nothing that counts, except force; it is by force alone that an élite comes to the top. Force is applied at all times, for the one purpose of maintaining the élite in power—and applied ruthlessly, brutally, instantaneously. But it is discreet to provide a reasoned justification for this application of force, through a suitable ideology. The true élite is entirely without scruples and without humanitarian weaknesses. Where these appear, where the use of force is hampered by scruples, the élite becomes decadent and opens the way for the rise of a new élite. Thus it is virtually a duty for every member of the élite to undergo training in brutality. It prefers at all times the most violent means, the most violent solution. Only in this way does it retain its position. In this way, as Pareto points out, the simple biological struggle for existence is transferred, in the struggle between the élites, into the sphere of human society.

Such are the views of the National Socialists, not systematically taught in public, not collected into a system at all, but conveyed from member to member in the actual cadres of the élite, and made the basis of all action. This is the attitude which is plainly adopted by the élite in actual practice. This attitude gives them their ruthlessness in the use of their power and resources, their rapidity of action, their readiness to take risks, and through all this their notorious superiority to all earlier ruling classes, all political groups, capitalist or Socialist. There are those who praise the rapid and ruthless action of the National Socialist leaders in home and foreign politics; all this implies is that the new élite make use of their power and resources mainly in order to maintain themselves in power and to extend their power.

But these practical rules and maxims of political leadership, adopted consciously or unconsciously by National Socialism, are applicable only in the course of a revolution permanently in progress. The revolutionary élite can maintain itself in power in its permanently critical situation only by continually pushing on with the revolutionary process. In its effort to hold on to power it is compelled to destroy the old social and political institutions, since it is in these that the strength of the old ruling class lies. When the political structure of the country has been razed to the ground, the élite will march over the frontier, to upset the existing international order.

The right men in the right place—that is a typical rule in civil life in peaceful times. In revolutionary times, and then only, there is no need for the "right" man. Any man will do who will exercise power with ruthless brutality. Only in a revolutionary period can the difficult problem of selection of personnel be treated with the negligence, indeed the criminal negligence, shown by National Socialism. But this can continue only so long as there is little or no effort at genuinely constructive work, little being done beyond the using up of accumulated reserves, and revolutionary destruction. For such work, the less education the leaders have the better.

The new élite of National Socialism is an affront to all historic and traditional standards. It is a deliberate breach with the past and the seal of a new order. The "ruling element with a historic mission" is formed by the National Socialist élite, and by them alone. This is due to their determined struggle for power after the coup-by-arrangement of January 30th,* while the élite of the capitalist parties rested content with the externals of leadership, with posts from which they were driven out one by one as opportunity offered.

After all this it will surprise nobody that the National Socialist revolutionary élite are entirely without moral inhibitions, and that individually they reveal so strange a mixture of extreme nihilism with an unashamed adoption of the ways of the half-educated lower middle class. The cool and calculating resolution that marks the political dealings of this élite has hitherto been associated in people's minds with outstanding intelligence or at least versatility—at all events, when not dealing simply with criminals. In these people we find, however, a mixture of qualities, a naïve mixture of qualities always regarded up to now as irreconcilable with one another. But the unusualness of the mixture must not blind us to the fact that the operative part in the duality of these natures is a hard, resolute, ruthless will, even if their German is ungrammatical and their intellectual equipment manifestly of the lowest. It is characteristic, too, of National Socialism that it is only in exceptional cases that its leaders are removed on account of incorrect dealings—to put it euphemistically—under the civil code. Lack of morals in civil life is not frowned on: it is no ground for suspicion of a member's National Socialist orthodoxy. National Socialism demands, indeed, of its sworn élite that all personal moral scruples shall be overridden by the needs of the party. Anyone who reveals that he is allowing himself the luxury of guidance by his own conscience has no place in the élite and will be expelled. It is not surprising to find that absence of moral scruples in the private life of a member of the élite is dealt with very gently by the party authorities. It is impossible to demand scrupulous correctness in a member's private life when any crime may be required of him in the interest of the party. Demands have actually been made of individuals in order to have a future hold over them, or to test their readiness to obey. In Danzig the Senator for Public Health was required, against the clear medical evidence, to declare in the case of the death of a National Socialist "militant" that the man had been killed by a blow struck by a political opponent. The Senator refused

* January 30, 1933, the date of Hitler's accession to power.—Ed.

to make an official declaration in conflict with the truth; he was deprived of his office and his senatorship. This is one instance of a method pursued deliberately in order to make the élite a following sworn to blind obedience, a company from which every member's escape is cut off, because he has been incriminated.

The Divine Inspiration of the Leader

In the center of the movement stands the figure of the Führer, the Leader. This central figure cannot be replaced by anything else, a group or committee or board. Any such suggestions overlook the essential "charismatic" element of the leader, the element of his "divine inspiration." This element in the mass leader, the great demagogue and revolutionary is a reality that cannot be dismissed even by those who personally are not under its influence. A great deal of the nimbus of the revolutionary leader seems manufactured and is in fact manufactured; but the root of his mesmeric influence lies, like that of the revolutionary "dynamic" urge in the movement itself, in an irrational element, in the medium-like gift of the revolutionary. Hitler is a revolutionary and mass leader with the medium's gift of thrall, a thrall in which he is himself caught. "Then came the great thrill of happiness," wrote the *Arbeitsmann* (organ of the National Socialist Labor Front) of the effect of the personality of the leader on the masses. Another impression: "I looked into his eyes and he into mine, and at that I had only one desire, to be at home and alone with that great, overwhelming experience." This extravagant outburst came not from an "intense" woman supporter but from a judge in a high position, talking to his colleagues. I can vouch for this case from my personal knowledge. "For I am among you, and ye are with me"— the leader must speak in a religious mood, in lapidary phrases that can be used with suggestive force. "Our divine service," wrote the newspapers of a party congress, "was a turning of the thoughts of each one of us to the root of all things, to the Great Mother. That was in truth divine service." In the eternal battle between light and darkness, acceptance and rejection of life (to quote Ley, the leader of the Labour Front), the German, with his new faith in the leader, is faced with the great decision. He is also faced with the lighting effects and the orders for applause, the special platform and all the other gadgets of a glamour-machine.

Hitler is deliberately and unceasingly held up to the masses as a deity. One of the principal devices for securing National Socialist dominance is this deification of the man, his raising to the altitude of the sole savior of the nation. "We all believe on this earth in Adolf Hitler, our leader"; "we acknowledge that National Socialism is the faith that alone can bring blessedness to our people." These are official pronouncements by the party élite. The Messiah-figure of the leader is the indispensable center of their propaganda, as carefully devised as the whole of the apparatus of power. Some time before the seizure of power a prominent National Socialist expressed to me his opinion that the figure of the leader must be withdrawn more and more into seclusion and surrounded with mystery. He must only come visibly into the presence of the nation by means of startling actions and rare speeches at critical moments in the national destiny. Except for that he must withdraw from view—just like the Creator behind creation—in order to heighten his effectiveness by his mysteriousness. The very rarity of his appearances would make them events. No great leader should wear out his greatness in the daily drudgery of administration. And, declared this old "Pg," he could conceive that at a critical turning-point in the national history the leader might be more deliriously effective if he were dead. He might even have to be sacrificed in order to complete his work. Sacrificed by his own Pg's, his own party comrades, and his faithful followers. Only when Hitler had really become a mythical figure would the whole depth of his magical influence reveal itself. All this I was told in perfect sincerity and conviction. It was spoken out of a genuine faith, which at that time still existed, in a spiritual mission entrusted to National Socialism.

Our age, said Burckhardt, readily indulges from time to time in the awe of adventurers and visionaries. We may add that it permits itself to be carried away by brutality in the guise of religious ecstasy, and by any storm over national and social affairs if it involves hatred of some third party. The effective principle in this is the "magic of extremism." In its presence, Burckhardt found, argument becomes completely impossible. Once more we may observe the degeneration that struck observers in the age of the decay of Hellenism—faces and figures grown ugly; nowhere any nobility, either of physical heritage or of intellect or of soul; no sign left of any inner struggle or any genuine repose; only eyes that flash for a moment and then are blind again; brutal expressions, sinister gestures, puffy or distorted features, the grimaces of the inane. The magic of leadership is magic primarily for such types as these. They reveal not only the "fury of partisanship" but the enviousness and the lust for domination of the lower middle class.

But this process of the mesmerizing of the masses is only made possible by the general revolutionary disintegration of all the genuine elements of national welfare and public order. Thus neither the devotion to the leader nor the faith in him is of purely artificial production. Their appearance is due less to the foisting of a "Messiah" on the masses than to the loss of validity of the old and genuine standards and allegiances. The question still remains how such immense dynamic power could proceed from petty and contemptible sources. It is characteristic of the present time that an appearance of gigantic achievements can be created with no basis in fact. The technical and organizing resources available enable any sort of phantasmagoria to be given for a time the semblance of reality. Politics are bound up today with the existence of a specialized "machinery."

The Machinery

Darré, who stands out among the national leaders of National Socialism on account of his organizing ability, is head of the Reichsnährstand or National Food Estate. This agricultural organization was created relatively late by the party; Darré himself calls it the *"agrarpolitischer Apparat"* (political machinery for agricultural issues), or "aA" for short. In so doing he reveals the nature of all National Socialist organization. He had not the slightest intention in organizing the National Food Estate of creating anything resembling a true guild corporation, a real administrative body for the agricultural occupations. The Reichsnährstand is nothing but a machine for the complete control and direction of agricultural production and of the farming population itself by the party. Here, in the sector of agricultural policy, there was revealed at the outset the system which, thanks to Schacht,* was extended much later, by means of currency control and the Four Year Plan, to the whole economic system of the country —the control and supervision of the whole field of trade and industry, as a means to the control of the population engaged in trade and industry. All the gigantic organizations created by the National Socialists, some during the "period of struggle," some after the revolution, are machines for the control of the whole life of the nation. These are not new self-governing bodies, not organs and links in the State or the social order: they are political machines, machines for control, for propaganda, for supervision, for terrorist dominance. They are machinery for the influencing of opinion, never organs of independent

* Reich Minister of the Economy, 1933–1937.—Ed.

formation of opinion. They are machinery that conveys a drive always in one direction, from above downwards, from the central political control right down to the private household, right into the most intimate elements of family life.

In this respect the National Socialist organizations differ from all other associations. They are mainly concerned with nothing else than the safeguarding of the resources of power with which the dominant élite exercises its dominion. They include also a number of checking systems which appear to the careless observer as a senseless duplication of the organization; in reality these are based on the principle of reciprocal supervision by rival parallel organizations. The "struggle for power" became a training of the harshest sort for the leaders of the party; not so much through the conflict between Socialist and anti-Socialist as through rivalry between groups in the élite. It has, perhaps, been the greatest feat of the National Socialist Party that it has preserved its organization intact and endured the load test of eight years of ostensible legality, while in its own ranks the rebellious revolutionists by temperament, the desperadoes and gangsters, the despairing patriots, the ambitious, and the ideologues carried on their personal intrigues and separate moves. In the competition for power within the party, for places and allies, in an absolutely nerve-wracking and soul-destroying struggle behind the scenes, the great tactical experience of the party has developed and the ideas for the building up of its organization have been clarified, becoming then, after the arrival in power, the principles of domination in public life.

It is unnecessary to give an elaborate description of the organization of the National Socialist Party, which to this day baffles even the German party member. A better idea of the nature of this truly gigantic effort may be obtained by a few reflections on the tasks the organizations have to fulfil as the machinery of domination, and on the way the ruling élite protects itself from the tendencies towards sectional independence within the party. Such tendencies are implicit in every organization, and might lead to dangerous splits, rivalries, cliques, and, in short, to a new party structure and so to the crippling of the whole machinery and the ending of unified control. I give here the essence of the instructions which are "hammered" again and again into the National Socialist officials of all grades all over the country. The need for them is frequently enough exemplified in the shortcomings of various prominent leaders, their weaknesses and kinks, which simply have to be put up with, and provided against by closer collaboration between all the organizations. The personal shortcomings of certain of the eminent members of the élite are discussed quite openly among the higher officials. They cynically admit the rivalries and mortal enmities between leaders; and they mention the tendency of leaders to form their own private armies as an entirely natural result of the existing system. But this admission of personal weaknesses is certainly itself no sign of weakness. What is of prime importance is the determination, in spite of these admitted weaknesses, under no circumstances to allow the unity of the party to be broken and the instrument of dominion to be thus destroyed.

Is National Socialism the "Salvation Army of German patriotism," as a cynical critic maintained? There is something in the idea. The movement has made the small traders and lower middle class its backbone, instead of the Storm Troopers. And the whole machinery of the party is built up out of lower middle class elements. But it would be a great mistake to overlook the essential feature of the organizations, their very practical and extremely effective character as instruments of dominion, as the machinery of continuous terrorism and repression. The tasks the machinery of domination has to fulfil are: the permanent revolutionizing of the mass of party followers, the keeping alive of their will to fight, and the maintenance of the dynamic character of the movement. The rank and file have to be kept continually on the move and continually under tension. They have to be controlled down to the smallest detail in their whole lives. They have to be kept entirely dependent and under supervision, and prevented from giving way to any undisciplined impulse of their own. Each member of the rank and file of the party must be made to associate his whole existence with the party, and to identify himself entirely with the party, by the continued fear that if he does not do so he will be robbed of his livelihood. The rank and file must be made to feel that they are continually under observation, and must be kept in continual restlessness and insecurity, in a permanent state of uneasy conscience and fear. These tasks yield certain principles of organization, which amount in the end to this: the machinery must be absolutely watertight, and it must embrace every side of life. There must be no zones of immunity.

A further principle, that of finding as far as possible some official duty for everybody, in order to keep everybody actively associated with the movement, and to create a universal sense of participation in direct action, is regarded as an "important link in the national community." Every part of men's lives is drawn into the field of party responsibilities, and in this way everyone's private existence is rooted in the party, his vital interests are bound up with the party for good or evil, and no one can do anything in independence of the party. It is the principle of the ubiquitousness of the party and the ending of individual private existence. In this way the instrument of power becomes also an eternally vigilant machinery of espionage.

A very important principle is that of twofold organization. For every group of duties parallel bodies are trained, to cover the same field of work from different sides, with the principal object of watching one another and holding one another in check by their rivalry. This principle is regarded as so important that it is carried through right up to the top. A further principle of organization is the delimitation and grading of the fields of work of all party officials by the two regulative disciplines of leadership and blind obedience. The fact that every person in an official position in the party is harnessed to the disciplinary mechanism in several directions, participating both in the responsibility of leadership and in the duty of absolute obedience, has developed a very practical and tightly drawn system of supervision and counter-supervision, from which no official can possibly escape. Finally, this whole system is kept under observation by a secret party tribunal and jurisdiction, completely independent of the State, whose activities are supervised in turn by special inspectors. The whole gigantic apparatus is centered on the single supreme individual; his final decision is only needed in exceptional cases, the self-acting mechanism disposing of most matters in lower stages of the hierarchy. Thus the whole machinery remains free for all practical purposes for the transmission of orders from above, and in critical matters from the supreme leader, down to the extreme limits of the organized party. A grandiose and certainly a unique instrument of the leader's will.

Its gigantic scale and its absolute comprehensiveness are not the products merely of an idle interest in organization, but of a measure of necessity. Nothing in the whole machinery is there for its own sake. With all its stages and ramifications, in appearance a product of the German mania for organizing, the system is really the result of no comprehensive scheme or idea; it is simply the product of the needs of the years of struggle, aimed at securing the personal power of the élite over their own forces. It had the further aim of forming an all-comprehending instrument of dominion, of the maintenance of the power of the dominant élite over the country, after the arrival in power. These aims account also for the complete "co-ordination" with the movement of all existing organizations, down to those of the canary breeders and the stamp collectors. It would be an altogether superficial view to regard all this as the mere outcome of personal ambition. In order to assure its power, National Socialism could not afford to leave in freedom even the most insignificant zone, even an entirely unpolitical one. It was compelled for its own security to subject every sort of activity to its machinery of control, not because there was any need, for instance, for canaries to be trained on National Socialist lines, but because it was necessary that each individual should come up against the all-embracing party at every step, so as to be under direction and supervision and influence even in his hobbies.

This *Gleichschaltung* of old organs of a rich social and cultural life inevitably robbed them of all initiative and creative energy, and sooner or later they were bound to wilt in their captivity; but this did not disturb the new élite. Commercial and industrial associations may retain their usefulness even if they are organized less for the representation of the interests of their members than for the domination of those interests by a jealous party authority. Their practical tasks will still have to be determined on definite lines. But associations that owe their existence not to any necessity but to free choice, all the cultural, social, humanitarian associations which placed their wealth of creative effort in the service of the advance of civilization, can have no function as instruments of domination and are doomed from the moment when they are *gleichgeschaltet*.*

This leads us at once to the question how any machinery of domination of this sort can continue indefinitely to function. A nation and society thus brought into bondage is bound with mathematical certainty to lose its creative capacity. It is bound to do so quite apart from the unendurability of the intense and continuous effort demanded of every person by the party organization. Even the élite will not keep it up, and most certainly not the mass of the population. Sooner or later after any revolution the time is bound to come when the newly arrived upper class it has created must modify and relax the totalitarian apparatus of power. The question will then arise whether it has so accustomed the country to its rule that it no longer needs the complete machinery. But the "dynamic" or continuing revolution seems in this respect again to have its own peculiar character. It is a permanent movement for the sake of continuing change, and it cannot abandon its revolutionary character. So long as the movement remains, it cannot dispense with its apparatus of power, cannot rely on

---

* Co-ordinated, or, to abandon euphemisms, made to "toe the line."—Translator.

reconciling the country to its dominion. All hopes of any gradual abandonment in the Third Reich of the system of compulsion, of any scrapping of the machinery of domination, are thus illusory.

The confidence of the National Socialists in their hierarchy is not justified. A critical situation will inevitably develop, with a further degeneration of the dictatorship. We may at once point to a weakness which will not be removed either by the National Socialist groups in the factories or by the counter-revolutionary cadres of the S.S. (the "Black Guards"), or even by the subtle safety device of the party judicature. The greatest weakness in this instrument of power lies exactly where the party sees strength—in its totalitarianism and centralization. The system might lose and replace subordinate elements, but it certainly cannot afford to lose its head. It is thus conceivable that the whole gigantic apparatus of power might collapse in a night in complete impotence through a single mishap, might fall into an amorphous heap of debris without a trace of life left in any of its sections. The federative principle and the delegation of power to free and independent bodies in genuine self-government do not mean decadence; they are the indispensable condition of any high standard of state and social life. They are also the first condition of the permanence of any system of public order. Such domination as that of the parvenu groups of National Socialist leaders may be able to last for a few years with the aid of their apparatus of violence. But the day will come when National Socialism will reach its end, and then it will give place to a true system of public order; or else the nation will itself come to ruin under National Socialism. There is yet another circumstance that must not be overlooked. Sooner or later a rule of this sort must come to grief owing to the character of its officials.

The Tactics of Domination

Next after the hierarchy in the means of dominion come the methods of forcible disciplining and of destruction of the earlier elements of orderly government. In this connection it would be natural to consider all the methods of violence, old or newly elaborated, which are used by modern revolutions—concentration camps, political terrorism, the secret police system, the employment of special cadres of the party for purposes of intimidation; and also the more subtle methods of spreading fear and of breaking men's character and independence. I must refrain, however, from pursuing this subject in detail, since the modern methods reveal such subtlety and such inventiveness that it would be necessary to quote concrete cases in order to bring conviction to readers in general. The time will not fail to come when this part of the story becomes generally known. After the events of June 30th, 1934, a high official of the Gestapo (the secret police) horrified at what had happened, said to me in Berlin that he wished a happy fate might preserve the German people from ever learning the truth. Perhaps it is not right to wish this. In any case, merely to mention these things is to bring oneself under the suspicion of carrying on atrocity propaganda and consequently to destroy the value of what one has to say. I must leave it to some experienced police official to write the necessary specialist work on modern methods of violence, on the comprehensive system of public cruelty which has been elaborated. I will devote only a few words to the National Socialist tactics of domination.

National Socialism pursues in general a fairly uniform plan in this field, but varies it in detail in relation to particular groups of persons. The art of carrying on an interrogation, the technique of tiring out an intellectual and upsetting his nervous balance, the adjustment to idealists or to the characteristics of persons of lower middle class extraction, are already a regular tactical system. There is no softness or urbanity or cautious leading up to the point; the method is always to pounce on the victim, to corner him, startle him, browbeat him, and in general to rely on roughness.

At the back of all National Socialist activities is a thoroughly marked preference for immoral methods. The immoral course is always more effective, because it is more violent. The immoral course also gives the illusion of strength and daring in persons who are merely underhand by choice. It is a fundamental principle of National Socialist tactics to strike fear by deliberate and pronounced incivility and violence, and by making a show of readiness to go to any length, where the same purpose could be achieved without difficulty by milder means. But National Socialism is never single-mindedly in pursuit of anything; it always has the additional aim of further shaking the existing order with every success it gains. Its robust methods are deliberately calculated. And most of the roughness of manners and habits and of the barbaric style of government aims at producing the illusion of an elemental strength which the system does not in reality possess, an illusion for which there is no need where a certain reserve of strength is always in hand.

This preference for violence as the typical revolutionary method is not inconsistent with the crafty and very successful appeal of National

Socialism to the lower middle class self-righteousness. Its violent character is only superficially inconsistent with its practice of posing always as the champion of justice, denouncing wrongs that cry aloud to heaven. Everything it does is represented as done simply in the defence of a sacred right and a moral mission. It could beat its breast, for instance, over the detention camp in which National Socialists were placed in Austria, as though there were no atrocities in the German concentration camps, and could denounce the intention it alleged of falsifying the Austrian plebiscite with an assumption of supreme unconsciousness of its own terrorist methods. Every lie is adorned with a show of virtue. Always National Socialism is defending a right, always pursuing honor and faith. Moral indignation comes next after brutality in the National Socialist armory of effective propaganda. It takes the place of reasoned argument. The revolution is true to type in its eternal moralizing, in its defence of "virtue" like the great French Revolution, in its sentimentality and emotionality. Its "Leader" always has sobs and tears at his command, exciting wrathful derision in the old militants of the party. This assumption of virtue and morality falls short, it is true, of the primitive naïveté of a genuine revolution. In its insincerity it is entirely in character with the brutality and the cynical amorality revealed in the everyday activities of the National Socialists.

Should terrorism produce discontent, there is always a public enemy to be discovered. Public indignation is poured over him from time to time, so that collective outbursts of rage may provide a diversion for accumulating private resentment. To provide continual diversions, and never to leave the citizen to himself with nothing to do, is another tactical rule of general application. It is an effectual method of treatment not only for the masses but for all opponents, including opponents abroad of German foreign policy. Keep people busy, give them something to think about, startle them, never allow them time for reflection; always lie in wait, ready to pounce; always take the initiative and so maintain the lead.

Hitler's very realistic estimation of the masses was revealed in *Mein Kampf*. It may be said in general that at the back of the whole tactics and method of propaganda of National Socialism there is a complete contempt of humanity: the whole system is based on taking men as they are and pandering to their weakness and their bestiality. Such is its universal recipe. National Socialism banks on human sloth and timidity—just as much in the case of the intellectuals, the middle classes, and the old ruling classes, as with the masses. It does so especially with foreign countries. In Germany it yields a much more effective means of domination than would the exclusive dependence on terrorism. The exploitation of envy and ill-will, of the lowest human instincts, the sowing of dissension between opponents, and the appeal to their ignoble qualities and notorious weaknesses have thus far unfailingly helped National Socialism to success, incidentally destroying the basis of a general sense of morality which was weak enough to begin with.

The system owes its internal strength to the general voluntary co-operation in the work of the secret police, the general acceptance of denunciation as a patriotic duty. But the completely amoral regime of National Socialism steadily ignores the fact that this resort to the worst of human motives, and to the extreme of brutality and violence, to hatred, vengeance, envy, ill-will, to licentiousness, to robbery, to lying on principle, its resort to all these motives and methods has set in motion a ruin of the national character on a scale hitherto unimaginable, which must inevitably recoil in the end on the ruling élite themselves. The élite are clearly untroubled by the dangers of this whole course, because in spite of their bombastic declamations about the thousand years of their "Third Reich" they have a very strong subconscious sense that their furious, hysterical onward drive has not a very long course ahead of it. In any case, the greatest statesmanship could not set up a "revolutionary new order of this world" on a nihilistic moral foundation of this sort.

The Reichstag fire, organised for political purposes by party members on the instructions of German Ministers, is a thoroughly illuminating example of the method universally adopted by the party. It is the party's special device, applicable universally. Crimes are arranged and attributed to opponents. The people are kept in a state of fear, utterly intimidated. At the same time they are stirred up into a blaze of indignation, given the sense that they have been saved from destruction, and made to feel thankful to a strong regime that gives them security. Hundreds of times this plan is carried out on varying scales. National Socialism is always ready to make play with its Bolshevist propaganda-bogey on a vast scale. The nation is kept in a state of alarm, and meanwhile, in the same breath, the regime takes credit for the maintenance of peace and order. Few things are more characteristic of the regime than its unscrupulous, lying glorification of an existing law and order which it destroys or publicly insults by whatever it does.

One word, finally, on the simplest and most elementary, but perhaps most effective and most characteristic method of domination employed by National Socialism—the marching. At first this marching seemed to be a curious whim of the National Socialists. These eternal night marches, this keeping of the whole population on the march, seemed to be a senseless waste of time and energy. Only much later was there revealed in it a subtle intention based on a well-judged adjustment of ends and means. Marching diverts men's thoughts. Marching kills thought. Marching makes an end of individuality. Marching is the indispensable magic stroke performed in order to accustom the people to a mechanical, quasi-ritualistic activity until it becomes second nature. No less an authority than the pseudo-German Rosenberg, in his *Gestaltung der Idee,* has given the classic explanation of this occupation with marching: "The German nation is simply out to discover at last its own style of living, a style of living that is fundamentally distinguished from what is called British Liberalism. . . . It is the style of a marching column, no matter where or to what end this marching column may be directed." At the back of all these night marches, marches out, marches back, these mass demonstrations and parades, was the consideration that the sense of primitive community through functional integration is created and fostered by marching in columns, military drill, military evolutions, the rhythm of a host in step. Nothing could show more shockingly, more grimly and indeed spectrally, the utter emptiness of a political movement and its concentration on mere externals than this elevation of marching to be its motto and essential principle. We have it here admitted that the nation is marching aimlessly, just for the sake of marching. It is a confession of the lack of any sort of doctrine in this revolution for revolution's sake, this hustling activity just to distract men's minds.

A Philosophy for Show

It is perhaps not generally known, at all events I do not remember any public mention of the feature, that Hitler has a deep respect for the Catholic church and the Jesuit order; not because of their Christian doctrine, but because of the "machinery" they have elaborated and controlled, their hierarchical system, their extremely clever tactics, their knowledge of human nature, and their wise use of human weaknesses in ruling over believers. Hitler wants to see the points of the National Socialist program regarded as analogous to the Church's venerable *Credo,* the confession of faith. He is aware that for fifteen hundred years the Church has withstood all assaults from logical criticism on its ancient creed. He sees that anything can be done with a creed of that sort, no matter how irrational or inconsistent. The flock of believers will accept anything, and will listen to no reasoned opposition. But there is one thing that, he knows, must never be done: no change must ever be made in a creed, even if the creed no longer has any practical significance in men's lives, if it is no more than an ancient monument. Any change would only perplex and unsettle the faithful.

These considerations must be borne in mind in examining the National Socialist philosophy. What the National Socialist leaders require is just the opposite of what a non-revolutionary leader needs: the more inconsistent and irrational is their doctrine, the better; the more sharply defined are its outlines. Only the inconsistent has vitality. The National Socialist leaders know that their followers can only take in details, that the masses can never see the wood for the trees. Anyone capable of appreciating generalizations must either be brought into the élite or fought as an intellectual, a Liberal. Thus, in the elaboration of the National Socialist philosophy everything that might have gone to the making up of a systematic, logically conceived doctrine is dismissed as a trifle, with sovereign contempt. And anything that seemed useful has been incorporated, whether or not it was logically consistent with what was already in the program.

But the much-discussed "philosophy" of National Socialism needs also to be considered in relation to historic tendencies in men's ideas if its actual revolutionary bases and its practical aim are to be understood. One effective element was considered to be a real belief in a new myth that can take the place of Christianity, to serve the needed rejuvenation of the nation. But it was considered no less important to bear in mind the practical indispensability of a philosophy for show. The present-day "philosophy" is certainly a very diluted substitute— the dilution was very necessary—for Hitler's first vague and tentative ideas for one of stupendous grandeur. Here again Hitler felt himself called upon to proclaim the true doctrine to the German nation of the future. But the essential element in the philosophy of today is that it is a very effective and an indispensable means of revolutionary destruction of the old order. Consequently it has long been no more than an instrument in the hands of the élite of the party. This élite has passed beyond all belief even in its own substitute for a logical system, and has fallen into complete nihilism. It has accordingly, in the main, turned away from its leader in his capacity of prophet. It may be that the leader is already no more than an isolated, antiquated requisite of the earlier period of the growth of the revolution, destined ultimately to be of no further use except as a stage property.

In any case, all these things are merely things for show, means of propaganda, doctrines foisted cynically on the nation by an élite who are themselves completely indifferent to them. The brilliant achievement which National Socialism managed to palm off as its philosophy developed was the grafting of all sorts of different fruits on the stem of the common crab-apple planted at the time of its first meetings in the vaults of a suburban beer-house in Munich. There were all the elements of the patriotic summons to the defence of the country, taken over from the last years of the world war. Clearly associated with these were the ideas of the pan-German, "racial" policy. These two conglomerates of ideas were among the earliest stock of the original nucleus of the party. Two further ideas had to be brought in with some difficulty, for they were diametrically opposed to one another. One was the Socialist re-ordering of society, and the other the return to monarchy and to the dominance of the old ruling classes. Traditionalist and nationalist ideas had to be brought in, such as the Prussian spirit, with which great play was made later on, at the Potsdam congress of the party. Middle class nationalism, with its keen interest in the traditions of the State, had to be worked in, and attention paid to the hereditary standards of the army officers. Finally, account had to be taken of the outlook of the Christian churches; room had to be found for the ideas and aspirations of the farmers, the artisans, and the small employers; and above all, attention had to be paid to the youth of the country.

All these considerations formed the framework of the National Socialist philosophy, which next had to be set out, as a matter of the first importance, in fiery phrases that would work on the masses and serve as the starting points for continual appeals to the emotions, in order to produce intoxication and ecstatic response. Everything had to be brought in that appealed to the indignation or aroused the enthusiasm of each person present at the meetings, each member or follower of the party, producing a fluid, anonymous crowd, open at all times to the force of suggestion. "Talk in generalities," was the continually repeated instruction from the National Socialist leaders in the "period of struggle," in every field of propaganda, big and little. Talk in generalities above all at times of threatening crisis, with signs of unrest. And never enter into discussions, never attempt to be informative, never appeal to good will or to sober reflection. Speak in terms of innuendo, of menace, whip up enthusiasm by showing it, storm, appeal, promise, talk of the great supermundane mission of National Socialism. No details, no concrete promises. Such were the instructions. And they were justified by results; they showed the National Socialist "philosophy" working successfully. Concrete promises divide, generalities unite. So effectively, so undiscriminatingly, in such elementary terms, intelligible to the most simple-minded of propaganda corporals, was the philosophical training imparted. Its supreme purpose was the collecting of the crowd, the emptying of its mind, the rousing of its feelings, the summons to a pretended higher existence, on a heroic scale; or to a happiness as one of a herd—Strength through Joy, Beauty of Labor, Enjoy Life. Simple but effective, for it is not meant for the despised intellectual, who is no more than an odd individual here and there, but for the masses, to place them under a spell and lead them by the nose.

There can be no denying the evidence of all these necessary ingredients in the so-called philosophy of National Socialism. It bears the scars of its past history in the totally contradictory ideas of its spiritual forefathers. In the words of Mephisto, it collects anything and everything for stuffing into the respectable citizen's cranium, and succeeds in "uniting great-heartedness with guile." It is not a whole, and it is absurd to treat it as a whole. It is of functional importance only, a means and nothing more. It is the main element in propaganda. The question to be asked of it is not its meaning but its purpose. It serves mainly for the propagation, in a form assimilable by the masses, of revolutionary aims which can be harbored at first hand only by a small élite. The function of the philosophy is to keep alive the fighting character of the movement. "Train them in the philosophy," "constantly impress on the men the fighting character of our movement," "when we have won, our real fight will be only beginning"—these were the instructions given over and over again to the National Socialist propagandists during the so-called *Kampfzeit,* the "period of struggle" (for power). "Dynamism" is kept alive in the masses only in the form of permanent pugnacity. The masses tend all the time to grow slack, and need constant stimulating. Nothing is of more importance to National Socialism than the possession of "enemies," objects on which this pugnacity can sharpen its claws. This is the root explanation of such senseless and horrible myths as that of the totally evil character of the Jews. If there is no other enemy available there is always the Jew, whose despised figure can always be made to serve as fuel for the fighting spirit, and at the same time to keep alive the happy feeling of belonging to the company of the elect. Whenever during the "period of struggle" the attention of the masses had to be turned away from existing problems, or simply when it was desirable to rouse the fighting spirit of the followers of the movement, the Jew-Freemason record was regularly set going.

All these elements, so primitive and threadbare in their psychology, are nevertheless thoroughly effective in practice. It would be a great mistake to suppose that so cunning an individual as the German Minister of Propaganda is not perfectly well aware that the atrocity propaganda against the Jews, including the "Protocols of the Elders of Zion," is preposterous nonsense, that he does not see through the racial swindle just as clearly as those compatriots of his whom it has driven out of their country. It would be simply foolish to imagine that any member of the élite truly and sincerely believes in the bases of the "philosophy." They have been deliberately concocted for their demagogic effectiveness and for the furtherance of the party's political aims. They have also been chosen with a cunning realization of the needs of the masses and particularly of the German masses. Other representations of good and evil, of hero and weakling, may "work" in other countries; the selection for Germany was already indicated by the experience of the pan-Germans and the anti-Semitic "racial" parties. They had proved already the effectiveness of anti-Semitism and of racial mystification with the masses. The popular attractiveness of nationalist ideas of expansion by conquest had also been revealed even before the War. All that National Socialism did was to work up these ideas, already propagated among the middle classes under the past regime, into yet more demagogically effective shape.

In recent years there have been important and growing changes. Not only the leaders, but the masses, and the army of minor officials, have been brought face to face with realities. The elemental force of a revolution transforming the whole life and outlook of the country is breaking through the papier mâché world of make-believe and semi-romanticism, and revealing to every man, no matter how eager his desire for a secure existence, the impossibility of reversing the engine or even of stopping it. No one to-day can resist the impression—sincere supporters of the regime regretfully admit it in confidence—that this platform philosophy is betraying a staleness that prevents it from stirring up revolutionary enthusiasm any longer even in the best-drilled mass demonstration. The philosophy is beginning to reveal its insincerity. It is losing its propaganda value as a means of suggestion. It is becoming an actual stumbling block for the followers. It is revealing, in such persons as the Jew-baiter Julius Streicher, the lower middle class character of its origin. The question for the future will be whether the party can survive a gradual modification of its philosophy, whether, while retaining essential parts of the old philosophy, it can introduce harder, more masculine elements, closer to the kernel of the actual doctrine of dynamism, of direct action, of violence, and develop a new myth, perhaps of Social Revolutionary type. Beyond question, for the new recruits, the youthful elements, the old tune has lost its catchiness. Party members are beginning to laugh at the Leader's spiritual outpourings, his sermons on art, his mediocre German, his crude economics. Party leaders are getting apprehensive about his speeches: they are "dreadful." Only among the faithful laity are they still taken seriously as revelations of supreme wisdom.

The Revolution Without a Doctrine

It is paradoxical, and must seem illogical, to describe a movement which comes before the world in the heavy armor of a comprehensive and absolutely binding philosophy as a revolution without a doctrine. Yet the recognition of this fact is the first and most fundamental condition for the ending of the present situation in Germany.

It is certainly difficult to liberate oneself from the popular conception and to realize that the philosophy of National Socialism has not the quality of doctrine, of a rational body of principles for the German revolution. But there will be still more objection to the view that not even the nationalist pan-German tendencies of the movement have any longer a foremost place in present-day German aims. It is, of course, possible to bring forward overwhelming evidence that nationalist objectives influence the internal politics of the existing regime, as well as its foreign policy. But the National Socialist revolution is not confined to these nationalist tendencies; they represent only the first, preparatory phase in the struggle for power. National Socialism has reaped the benefit of the justified national agitation for liberation from the Treaty of Versailles and its dictated provisions. It has also reaped the benefit of the militarist and pan-German ideas and aspirations in leading circles of the army and of the civil population. But these are not the whole of its aims. It makes use of them for their effect as elements in the spreading of revolutionary feeling, but its aims stretch far beyond them, and to-day it regards them as elements of minor importance. National Socialism is not a nationalist movement but a revolution, a process of destruction, making an end even of nationalist conceptions and achievements. The revolution owes its nationalist appearance to the facts that it began as a nationalist movement and that it achieved the first great steps in home and foreign policy under the banner of nationalism.

It is necessary to realize the completely new character of the modern doctrineless revolution. It is necessary to get away from the idea that what still attracts the principal attention both of opponents and of adherents of National Socialism represents the essential element in what is happening in Germany. It will have to be realized that what is more likely is that we are at the outset of a movement with incalculable possibilities of development. At present it is nothing but destruction, the dissolution and annihilation of the old elements of public order. It is destroying everything it lays its hands on. What positive qualities it has, what sort of a function it might have in the building up of a new order, nobody can yet say. What it calls its new order is nothing but a vast misuse of the human aspiration for ordered conditions. Those who still rest their hopes on the reactionary character of National Socialist dynamism will be just as deluded as the genuine Socialists who fail to realize its nihilistic and revolutionary character, and consequently are at cross-purposes in their fight against it.

National Socialism has not only destroyed the achievements and the past power of the working class, a fact that might justify its description as a counter-revolutionary movement; it has also destroyed the political and social power of the capitalist class and of the former ruling classes of society. It is also proceeding to the total and irrevocable destruction of the economic position of those classes. The National Socialist revolution is thus at least two things at once—social revolution and counter-revolution. This implies, however, that in the strict sense of the words it is neither.

In our day there are no longer any revolutions in the sense of liberation through a doctrine. In the realm of nihilism there can be none. Nihilism, as the total rejection of any sort of doctrine, must develop of necessity by its own logic into an absolute despotism. The development from Leninism, the backbone of which was, after all, an unshaken belief in human reason, to Stalinism, the expression of total nihilism, has been logically and historically inevitable. In the last two decades the destruction of the last of human political valuations has been complete. By many of the older generation, with their firm faith in rationalism, the process has not been realized. But in this period the tendency to complete moral scepticism has not only destroyed the last vestiges of human valuations in the element of theory, but has produced a complete rejection of every sort of doctrine in practical affairs. This fact is masked, it is true, by the fact that political nihilism has dressed itself up in the paradox of an absolutely binding, more or less rationally argued, "philosophy" or doctrine, which it has raised virtually to a religion. But the variety of the doctrines and philosophies of the revolutions that have broken out in various countries cannot conceal their essentially uniform character of totally despotic and totally destructive systems.

It might be tempting to demonstrate a close relationship between Fascism, Bolshevism, and National Socialism, to describe each of them as a special type of the dynamic movement, the doctrineless revolution, and to find distinctions between them only in the degrees and shades of their revolutionary impulse, or in the historical occasion of their initial phase. It is not long since the leader of Fascism himself arrived at the conclusion that Stalinism represents the development of Bolshevism into a sort of Fascism, the Fascism, it is true, of a Genghiz Khan. This assessment is justified in so far as Stalinism is nothing more than the jettisoning of the Communist doctrine of the Russian revolution and its development into something else. One thing is certain: the German movement is only at the outset of its revolutionary career, while Stalinism seems already to have come to the end of a career. There are, at all events, essential features common to all three of the European anti-democratic movements. But their anti-democratic political and social order does not necessarily imply a common revolutionary attitude.

There is, however, another bond of union between the three anti-democratic dictatorships, the constantly growing belief that a complete overthrow of all existing institutions is the indispensable prelude to a national renaissance. It is especially among the younger generation that the new ideas are widespread and vitally operative, the idea that all doctrines, nationalist and socialist alike, have become out-of-date and meaningless, and the idea that all that is necessary is devotion to the revolutionary movement for its own sake, a movement that is its own meaning and purpose, as the outlet to a new, unknown and dangerous life, but at all costs a life of strength and energy. These young people already see the one essential common element in the great revolutionary processes in their destructive character, and they no longer attach any importance to the doctrines that divide them. They have already got beyond the narrow limits of nationalism and imperialism, but they have also dismissed the dogmatic theories of a "just" social order as the source of earthly happiness. They see life's meaning in its perils, life's purpose as domination, the means as violence, and the goal as the worldwide totalitarian empire.

3. Practice as Fulfillment

ERNST NOLTE

1919–1923

In calling the National Socialist practice "fulfillment," what is meant, of course, is the fulfillment of Hitler's "doctrine," for without this practice the doctrine would indeed never have been anything but the distortion of a diagram which had long since been implemented by superior thinkers and not least by Maurras.* At the same time it is not advisable, any more than it was with the Action Française, to describe the practice *after* analyzing the doctrine, for here too it is intimately linked with its history. And again, this history could not be told without outlining the doctrine. At this point, therefore, the meaning of "fulfillment" has been established in a preliminary sense, yet sufficiently.

Unlike Italian fascism but like the Action Française, National Socialism seeks from the very beginning to preach a doctrine. But its practice, as against that of the Action Française, is not a mode or action proceeding logically from a carefully developed conviction. In its specific nature it is rather an integral part of the proclamation of the *Weltanschauung,* of ideology, itself, and it is the practice which gives this ideology its real effectiveness. In *Mein Kampf* Hitler with good reason placed the power of the spoken word far above that of the written word. It is unlikely that his book won him many supporters for National Socialism, whereas his speeches fascinated the masses over and over again. But on every occasion a Hitler speech was staged and protected. The staging and protecting of these speeches was the very heart of early National Socialist practice; that is why Hitler could say of propaganda that it attempted to *force* a doctrine on the entire population. Since indoctrination is achieved by force, it is permissible to call the practice fulfillment even in the early days; after the seizure of

---

* Charles Maurras was one leading personality of the Action Française, a movement devoted to "integral nationalism". See the article below by Robert J. Soucy.—Ed.

Source: *Three Faces of Fascism* (New York: Holt, Rinehart and Winston, Inc., 1966), pp. 365–401. Translated by Leila Vennewitz. Copyright © 1963 by R. Piper & Co. Verlag, Munich. Translation © 1965 by R. Piper & Co. Verlag, Munich. Reprinted by permission of Holt, Rinehart and Winston, Inc.

power it amounted primarily to implementation, without ever quite losing the first meaning.

But this definition requires the study of two essential conditions without which National Socialism could never have been born and which distinguish it considerably from Italian fascism.

Anyone trying in the Red Bologna of 1920 to preach the National Socialist ideology, or force it onto his audience, would hardly have escaped from the city alive. National Socialism and fascism developed on two totally different types of soil. Even when Mussolini was already the most powerful party leader in Italy, in the summer of 1922, the city administration of Milan was still in socialist hands. In Ferrara, in Bologna, in Mantua—everywhere the Fascists had risen up in bitter fighting in the midst of revolutionary-minded masses. In Munich, on the other hand, the Reichswehr and the Home Guard were in control after the downfall of the Soviet Republic; the other voices in the political concert were provided by the Bavarian People's party and the German National People's party. After the terrible bloodletting and vengeance of May, 1919, there were virtually no more Communists, and the Social Democrats of the majority were more bourgeois than anywhere else in Germany. In this city Röhm and his friends "nationalized" the masses by having the café orchestras play patriotic songs and beating up anyone who did not immediately rise to his feet. Here many organizations of the radical Right had continued to operate even under the Soviet Republic. And the popular mood was just as much against the Jews in Bavaria as against the "Bolsheviks" in Berlin— even if not always from the same motives. In other words, in the Munich of 1919 onward, there could be absolutely no question of that threat of "bolshevism" which in Italy was a reality. And it was this that enabled the proponents of a most intense anti-Marxist *Weltanschauung* to set about forcing their outlook on the predisposed masses.

However, young National Socialism would presumably never have emerged from the many other similar groups had it not—unlike fascism—been motived by a *Führungsimpuls,* a leadership urge, which nothing could withstand. It is true that for nearly two years Hitler was only the director of propaganda for the party and took orders from the party executive, of which Anton Drexler was chairman. But there is no reason to doubt his assertion that he never brooked interference in his own field, and what was the youthful NSDAP without its propaganda? In July, 1921, Hitler managed to terminate the first party crisis by becoming first chairman with dictatorial powers and being only *pro forma* responsible to a remains of democratic control by members and leading executive bodies. Mussolini could not possibly have served as a model here, for it was just at this time that he was entering upon his bitterest conflicts with the new Fascists outside Milan, and not even before the March on Rome could he be called the "dictator" of his party. In terms of both relative and absolute time, the leadership principle became paramount earlier in National Socialism than in Italian fascism.

At first Hitler's leadership urge was directed solely toward increasing the size and frequency of rallies and the care with which he organized them. In the very earliest days, his restless drive for publicity and proselytizing constituted a real revolution for Drexler's and Harrer's publicity-shy group. It began with a few dozen listeners in smoke-filled back rooms in obscure taverns; the program rally already took place in the Hofbräuhaus, and in February, 1921, Hitler could risk hiring the huge hall of the Krone Circus. Yet although he managed to attract bigger and bigger crowds and to bring them under his spell, it was hardly the novelty or perceptiveness of his *Weltanschauung* which were responsible for these triumphs. More than any of the other similar personalities of his kind in Munich, he had the gift of *communicating an emotion*.

But this communication had to be protected from disruptive influences. Hence the important thing was, from the very beginning, to turn his listeners from an audience into a community. The system of guarding the hall and maintaining an *Ordnertruppe* is attributable to this basic requirement no less than to the alleged terrorist fighting methods of the Marxist foes. For the ordinary citizen was at that time still accustomed to heckle and argue during political meetings. And the "Marxists" were only more brutal inasmuch as they had developed habit into a method and sometimes tried to "blow up" hostile meetings by noise and catcalls. But hecklers were thrown out of Hitler rallies long before the "Gymnastic and Athletic Division of the NSDAP" was officially founded in August, 1921. A paragraph from one of those naïve reports the Reichswehr group command had drawn up illustrates this; it was dated August 14, 1920: "Then Herr Hitler spoke about this subject, but he became enraged and shouted so loud that at the back it was impossible to understand much. When Herr Hitler spoke, a fellow always shouted 'Pfui,' while the others always backed him up with 'quite right.' But this fellow was soon taken care of. He was thrown right across the hall, on the steps he was immediately protected by a policeman, otherwise perhaps he would not have got home in one piece. In *Hitler's Table Talk* Hitler himself described the remarkably rough methods he used to silence women who attempted to embark on arguments and whom he could not very well have thrown out by the hall guards. There is little reason to take for granted those sections of his report on the early days which were anxious to give the impression that Munich was a city ruled by the Red mob. A more likely reason for the loving care Hitler expended on the organization of the *Ordnertruppe* was his endeavor to safeguard the communicating of emotion from *any* kind of interference.

This is not to imply that organized attempts at interference did not take place. It was here that the typical difference in fighting methods became apparent. Wilhelm Hoegner reported that Social Democratic workers tried to disrupt the meeting of February 24, 1920, but that armed National Socialists made mincemeat of them with life preservers, rubber truncheons, and riding whips. If even in Italy the difference between red and white terror could hardly be ignored, in the Munich of the years following the Soviet *Putsch* this difference reached proportions of complete incommensurability.

It was also present in the famous brawl in the Hofbräuhaus of November, 1921, which Hitler described in such glowing terms and which was the immediate cause of the *Ordnertruppe* being given the honorable title of *Sturmabteilung* (SA). For it is clear from his description that the Marxist majority which had infiltrated into the hall intended to break up the meeting merely by making a lot of noise or at most hurling beer mugs around, according to local custom. Even superhuman bravery would not have enabled the weak *Ordnertruppe* to stand up to a crowd twenty times as strong if only some of the other side had had real weapons and the intention to attack. However, that was so patently not the case that the speaker was able to remain calmly in his place. From then on, according to Hitler, there were no more organized attempts at disturbance—although even before that they were few and far between—and so the unrestricted monopoly which the National Socialists had always claimed for their assemblies was maintained, and the dissemination of the new ideology never failed to find an audience in the proper frame of mind.

Thus Hitler had learned from his enemies and to a certain extent outdone them by creating a qualitatively new style of assembly. This also applied to the propagandist preparation of the rallies. Who had ever heard of a "bourgeois" party having its posters printed in bright red, of having a red flag carried at the head of its parades? Who else but the proletariat had till then (although no longer precisely in Munich) ridden on red-draped trucks through the streets? But these posters were covered with short, inflammatory words which were much more intelligible to the man in the street than Marxist expressions; the men who waved from these trucks were no longer the shabby proletarian figures of past days, but young soldiers whose shouts met with a warm response on the part of the people in the streets. Although the flag was blood-red, that alarming expanse of a single color was now embellished by a symbol (albeit strange) of salvation and hope in the middle. Moreover, this group worked harder than any other party. Armies of men pasting up posters were at work at all hours, either armed themselves or guarded by escorts with rubber truncheons, steel rods, and pistols. Great swastikas appeared on house walls and bridges everywhere. It was not long before as many as six or even twelve assemblies were arranged for one evening, and at each one of them *der Führer* held forth. This growth in the direction of the gigantic was bound to alter the functions of the SA. The propaganda troops were no longer limited to staging and protecting speeches: they acquired an importance of their own as a demonstration of will and energy. The protection of the Führer became the special duty of the *Stosstruppe Hitler,* from which later grew the SS; the SA as a whole soon split up into units of a hundred men and assumed more and more the character of a private army. But Hitler wanted it to remain a party army and a body of propaganda troops whose job it was to rule the streets and with giant parades wage the "war of annihilation against Marxism." "What we needed and still need," he said in *Mein Kampf,* "was not and is not a hundred or two hundred bold conspirators, but hundreds and hundreds of thousands of fanatical fighters for our ideology."

The concealed polemic of these words was aimed at a third characteristic that the SA was increasingly assuming under Röhm's influence and which could not fail to remove it from the area of the ideological battlefield: the character of a volunteer unit (*Wehrverband*). Although as a volunteer unit it received arms and support from the Reichswehr, it was also removed from the absolute control of the party leader; it became absorbed by secret military training and took its place among other volunteer units. In this matter, however, Hitler had to yield in 1922–23, and thus his own most personal creation, the SA, acquired for him something of the aspect of the moon, which always only turns one side toward the earth. There are many instances in *Mein Kampf* of this first serious intraparty bone of contention.

At the heart of its practice, therefore, early National Socialism was quite distinct from early Italian fascism. Fascism at first had nothing to do with the preaching of an ideology, it did not fight its battles in meetings, its fighting troops were not a body *beside* the party, and no one tried to detach them from it. Common to both were basic intention and basic character, both fought a war of annihilation against Marxism by adopting and typically transforming Marxist methods. The "fascist minimum" certainly did not exclude deeply rooted differences.

In those points where the organization was determined directly by the stronger leadership urge and the requirements of ideological propagation, the differences are obvious. They unfold in two main directions. From the leadership principle proceeds the postulate that the entire effort first be concentrated in one single place and that *Ortsgruppen* be formed only when the authority of the headquarters in Munich could be considered unquestioningly acknowledged. Hence National Socialism never had anything like fascism's *Ras*; on the other hand, until the November *Putsch* it remained a local phenomenon limited to Bavaria and in fact to Munich. Its revelatory character gave rise to an extremely sharp distinction between "members" and "followers," between activist nucleus and merely listening, sympathizing crowds. The extent to which Hitler regarded his people as an object, while the masters and potential occupants of the "nerve centers of the state" were to remain a small number of members, is to be seen with matchless clarity from some pages of his book printed in bold type. If the SA was separated more strictly from the NSDAP than the militia from the Fascist party, this applied even more to the associated organizations of which some—communications corps, youth league, motorized detachment, for instance—had been founded in the early days.

The most obvious points in which the two parties agree were probably those of *style*. It is easy to see why: both parties could be regarded as the expression of those military divisions which had never been spiritually demobilized. Hence their appearance in public was always determined by a paramilitary style—parades, bands, flags, escorts—although this style, taken by itself, was not enough to typify fascism as such, since it is also common to nonpartisan veterans' associations and other volunteer groups. Fascism was distinguished by the ability to transform this style typically and to make it the hallmark of the whole party and, ultimately, of the population. At first both these elements were present in both parties in rudimentary form only. Gabriele D'Annunzio's theatrical genius set an example which for the time being both Italian fascism and National Socialism could only approach. The National Socialist storm troops of 1923 were essentially mere groups of civilians shouldering rifles, with only a hint of uniform in their armbands and windbreakers. In the great parades of patriotic associations they were hardly distinguishable from the other formations. However, at the mammoth demonstration in August, 1922, against the "Law for the Defense of the Republic" the SA was the only group to carry banners and for this reason was applauded at the Königsplatz with special warmth. But Hitler spoke as one among many, and at no time during this period did the NSDAP control a joint rally with the monopoly and pre-eminence of the Fascist party at the rallies of Trieste and Bologna. At German Day in Nuremberg Hitler, wearing a raincoat, stood among a fairly large group and took the salute at ground level. Whenever the SA adopted a decidedly military note and drove up on motorcycles with the "swastika on their steel helmets," it did so in its capacity of volunteer unit. Nowhere was the "fascist salute" yet in evidence, nor was the brown shirt.

What was genuinely new and typically transformed was the party flag. The swastika did not, like the lictor's bundle, recall a remote but nevertheless still tangible historical era: as an ancient and prehistoric symbol of salvation it was supposed to proclaim the future victory of "Aryan man." Just as Mussolini's oratorical style, even in its worst outbursts, seemed controlled and moderate when compared to Hitler's, so the recalling by the Fascists of the Roman imperial tradition seemed, despite its dubious aspect from a national standpoint, concrete and historically valid when compared with this appeal to the prehistoric and the archaic. Not only in ideas: in sight and sound, too, the extreme nature of the young movement, although its fighting methods were much less bloody, is easily recognizable in comparison with fascism.

1925–1932

After Hitler's return from Landsberg* there was a far-reaching change in certain elements of National Socialist practice, particularly in their mutual relationship. For a considerable time Hitler was banned from public speaking, and this affected the very heart of past practice. Dissemination of the ideology was transferred to the newspaper and, more specifically, to the propaganda activities of the principal men under Hitler. His book did not attract much attention to begin with. The successes in North Germany of Strasser and later Goebbels made it clear that Hitler and National Socialism were by no means identical, and that a pan-nationalist movement had a considerable future quite apart from his personality. Although the question of whether a non-

* Prison.—Ed.

fascist National Socialism could have developed under Strasser's leadership is not an idle one, it cannot be discussed in this context. Similarly, what went on during the political struggle between the Strasser and Hitler wings is of no interest here. The only fact to be emphasized at this point is that Hitler succeeded in establishing his position of power in the newly founded party on a statutory basis and in further developing the organization to a highly remarkable degree. While all the other elements in the practice evolved normally—although quantitatively rather than qualitatively—Hitler (with the considerable assistance of Strasser) gave the party an organization which was no longer even remotely comparable to the rudimentary beginnings of the early Munich days.

The refounding of the party in February, 1925, was sufficient testimony to Hitler's unbroken authority, and after the satisfactory termination of the leaders' conference in Bamberg new statutes were laid down at a general assembly on May 22, 1926. They declared the cornerstone of the party to be the National Socialist German Workers' Union in Munich, the leaders of which were *eo ipso* identical with the leaders of the party as a whole. This body consisted of a collective organ—made up of the executive, the chairmen of the committees, and the chief administrator—but the first chairman was not subject to majority decisions, and this gave him dictatorial powers, especially as it was he who appointed the chairmen of the subcommittees—that is, for propaganda, organization, athletics and gymnastics (SA), and investigation and arbitration (*Uschla*)—and the two other members of the executive (secretary and treasurer) were in any case appointments of no political influence. The sole safeguard against arbitrary action was the provision of a right of control on the part of the members of the general assembly over the first chairman; since, however, these consisted by statute entirely of members of the Munich *Ortsgruppe,* the whole of the rest of the Reich party found itself in the position of a completely dependent province. Thus it was quite consistent with the spirit of these statutes that the *Gauleiter* were also to be appointed by Munich.

It is here that the difference is to be found as against the comparable Fascist party statute. There the regional deputies, who were not appointed from above, corresponded to the Munich committee chairmen. In Germany there had never been room for more than a minute degree of local spontaneity: the election of the *Ortsgruppen* leaders by the members. But by 1929 even this had been abolished.

From the committees there very soon developed the central offices of the Reich administration, and by 1928 their most remarkable characteristic was already established, for in fact there were two organizational divisions, the "attack department" under Gregor Strasser, and the "development department" under Konstantin Hierl. The first had subsections for foreign countries, press, and organization; the second for agriculture, race and culture, internal affairs, and so forth. The first took care of the day-to-day tasks of the organization and hence wielded more practical influence, while the second—in the midst of the Weimar period—planned the National Socialist state and for this reason was by far the more interesting. It had no counterpart in the Fascist party before the March on Rome, whereas Strasser's department can very well be compared with the fascist general secretariat, and the SA under Pfeffer von Salomon with the militia under Balbo. The men of the "development departments," like Hitler himself, were already living in the Third Reich. It was here, for instance, after his appointment in 1930, that Walter Darré, who was in charge of agrarian-political affairs, planned those laws which were to give a large section of the German farmers the unique position which could be described as "serf-aristocracy."

These offices were continually being augmented by new bureaus and sub-departments, so that by 1932 a bureaucracy of considerable dimensions had been created which stood ready to occupy the nerve centers of the state—to use Hitler's expression in *Mein Kampf*. It will be enough to name some of the bureaus of the five chief sections: internal affairs, juridical affairs, national health and race, national education, military and foreign affairs, civil servants, NSBO (trade-unions organization), press, federations of doctors, lawyers, teachers and students, areas of currency, finance, and production, horticulture, stock market, the Eastern territories, settlement, poultry-farming. Even if in 1933 the immediate occupation of all the corresponding government offices by this parastate party administration was not feasible, the NSDAP had nevertheless prepared itself for its seizure of power much more thoroughly than was within the power or intention of any other totalitarian party.

Moreover, it was essential that it should do so, seeing that the terms and conditions for its struggle had radically altered. After 1925 it was no longer the sheltered, cherished ally of the governments. What else could Hitler do but adopt a tactic of legality—in other words, avoid getting into an altogether hostile relationship with the state? Yet had he really ever pursued a tactic of illegality and revolt? In 1923 the whole of Bavaria had wanted to march on Berlin, and all Hitler had wanted was to take the lead. In the early Munich days he had had to fight more against his anonymity first, and later his own partisans, than against actual political adversaries. It is significant that before November 9, 1923, the movement did not have a single death to its name.

After 1925 all this changed. The attitude of the ruling party in Bavaria toward the traitor released from prison was surprisingly generous, although by no means cordial. Throughout Prussia and in Berlin a hard fight had to be fought. The Reichswehr had dissociated itself from the National Socialists. Until the plebiscite against the Young Plan, the party received almost no support. It managed to keep going essentially on the strength of its own efforts, thereby refuting the argument that a fascist party can *only* thrive on the support of powerful financial and political circles. The fact that after 1930 it could become the largest mass party in German history was something it had chiefly itself to thank for—that is, Hitler's power as an orator and his will to leadership, an organization already geared to an assault, the untiring energies of some tens of thousands of activist supporters, the susceptibility of the German people to its style, and not least the absence of a program in the social field which allowed it to be all things to all people. The world economic crisis was merely the wave which lifted up the superbly prepared swimmer. Nevertheless, it was important to meet with plenty of sympathy from leading social circles without encountering any determined antagonism on the part of the state. The connection between these two phenomena is revealed in a number of utterances made by the Reichswehr command, which was not nearly as favorably inclined as the Italian army in 1921–22 or the Bavarian Reichswehr of 1921–23. The manifest result was that Goebbels, for example, could afford to behave in his speeches with an insolence toward the Weimar "system" in "Red" Berlin which today seems incredible and yet which became one of the hallmarks of reconstituted National Socialism.

On the whole the style developed consistently and with continuity, enriched by the essential element of honoring the dead and the "blood banner." At the Weimar party conference in the summer of 1926, the SA columns marching past Hitler already wore their brown shirts and held their right arms outstretched, while Hitler took the salute standing in a large open car, his arm extended unwearyingly in salute. During the years that followed, the marching brown detachments became an ever more familiar picture in Germany, with new additions to their uniforms and insignia showing elaborate gradations of rank, occasionally involved in street-fighting, but usually parading in a peacefully threatening manner, never resorting to open battle, like the Italian Fascists, against the institutions of the enemy. Even in 1931–32 there was certainly no civil war in Germany, and yet under altered circumstances and on a larger scale there was a repetition of the picture of 1918 and 1919: the columns of Communists, in which thousands of ill-dressed civilians, shouting "Hunger" and raising their fists, marched behind a vanguard in shabby uniforms and at most a primitive brass band, were matched by the parades of the National Socialists, and here behind banners and flags, to the accompaniment of shouted commands and military music, company after company of jack-booted men marched in strict discipline and perfect step. Fifteen years earlier, the crowds of poorly armed Spartacists had likewise faced the detachments of the uniformed *Freikorps* as deadly enemies. The configuration was now radically altered: the state had long ceased to fear the Communists in their isolation, but the victors of those days had multiplied their ranks much more swiftly and showed a more determined face.

Hitler evidently judged the German people of his era more correctly than Rosa Luxemburg had done when he said in 1927: "We have a third value: the sense of battle. It is there, merely buried under a jumble of foreign theories and doctrines. A powerful great party tries to prove the opposite, until suddenly a quite ordinary military band comes along and plays, then sometimes the hanger-on wakes up from his dreamlike state, all of a sudden he begins to feel himself one with the marching people, and he falls in step. That is how it is today. Our people have only to be shown this better thing—and you see, we are already on the march." It seemed as if the people of Mars had merely rediscovered and renewed their old style when, under Brüning's government, the SA military columns, stretching away as far as the eye could see, marched past the party leader Hitler in front of the Brunswick Palace just as the guards and fusiliers had once marched past their Kaiser.

But how great the difference actually was could be seen from every rally at which this Führer spoke. As early as 1927, when the speaking ban was lifted even in Prussia, this was where the heart of National Socialist practice lay. By 1932 the dimensions had expanded enormously: Hitler spoke to tens and hundreds of thousands, he was the first German politician to make frequent use of the airplane, he knew how to maintain tactical silence on many subjects, and he had long since cast off his previous awkward manner with people. But the essential element remained quite unchanged. He still, to use the words of the reporter of those early days, "flew into a rage," he still communicated an unbridled emotionalism to the expectant crowds and received in return wave upon wave of delirious rapture. Indeed, if the appeal to soldierly traditions and the magic of the military style decided this political battle, they were implemented by a man who could not have been further removed from the traditional nature and ethos of the soldier. This paradoxical synthesis, however, was vital to victory.

1933–1939

It must not be imagined that with the seizure of power the practice of National Socialism immediately and uniformly became the practice of state and society but in every direction the process of integration or totalization began without delay. In the field of propaganda, a new National Socialist creation replaced the institutions of the old state which had been but barely developed—whereas the Catholic Church could maintain and even legally reinforce its independent position, although at the cost of severe sacrifices and considerable loss of prestige. The party's agricultural section provided the existing ministry with its head and principal functionaries, while the foreign affairs bureau did not manage to make the leap into the foreign office, and it remained comparatively without influence. The SA tried in vain to obtain control over the Wehrmacht; the SS, on the other hand, after a few attempts took over the police. According to their differing personalities, the *Gauleiter* gained varying degrees of influence over the administration of their regions, while a number of National Socialist ministers were captured, as it were, by the large established apparatuses of the central sections with the aid of some concessions. In some spheres of life, the introduction of the leadership principle met with what was often a felt need, in others it led to absurd results. Some measures, the book-burning, for example, produced cries of horror all over the world; others, such as the vigorous steps taken against the Communists, met with considerable approval—overt or tacit—in many foreign circles.

The task of presenting the whole process in its stratified unity and its *specific* efforts toward totality is one which, despite some significant initial attempts, cannot be considered complete. In this context it cannot even be a matter of outlining certain points of view or observation methods. The first limitation derives from the comparison with fascist Italy. A second consists in the fact that events which in a narrower sense may be called political must be excluded here. But even then the task would be much too extensive. For instance, it would be highly interesting to examine the relationship between the "corporative state structure" in Italy and the "regulation of national labor" laid down in Germany by the law of January 20, 1934, and especially how the institution of the German Labor Front which, of course, comprised employees *and* employers, is to be evaluated when compared with Italy. But a precise answer requires a relatively too extensive examination, while no research is necessary to grasp that it was a system of party-state definition of the relationship between capital and labor which in the practical field greatly favored the employers but which was not without danger to them. Of no less interest would be a comparison of the educational system of both parties, in which the German system with its Adolf Hitler schools and *Ordensburgen* (training institutes) was undeniably ahead. It would also be valuable to examine the various degrees of undermining and impoverishment in the various sciences and their institutions.

The only possible method is by selection. It may seem arbitrary because in each case one must neglect or overlook some essential item. In making this selection it would not be right to try and counterbalance the twelve years of extravagantly staged lighting effects by illuminating only the cellar regions of the building where the spotlights never fell, or by letting so-called justice attempt to balance the "positive" and the "negative" fairly and symmetrically. It is much more important to realize that, in the specific practice of National Socialism as well as in its history and ideology, the so-called positive and the so-called negative constitute a closely knit whole deriving from uniform roots.

Since historical description must to a large extent depend on documents which did not come to light until later, the only examples selected will be those manifestations which were generally known during their own time. In each of these the elements of National Socialist practice must be so recognizably combined that a detailed analysis is superfluous; each must be comparable, although to a varying degree, with an Italian counterpart. The following will therefore be briefly discussed: (1) A Reich party conference; (2) Legislation on race and hereditary health; and (3) Evolution and self-evaluation of the SS. As the 1937 party congress, occurring as it does immediately before the start of the big changes in foreign policy, seems to be the most suitable for this study, points 1 and 2 will be reversed.

The National Socialist race policy was developed during the peace years in three principal legislative thrusts, with considerable intervals between them, in order evidently to stabilize what had been achieved and accustom the population to the new laws. The turbulent beginnings in 1933 were followed by a year and a half of comparative quiet, until the Nuremberg laws pitched developments another substantial step forward. Then for two and a half years nothing much happened, but early in 1938 one new measure followed rapidly on the heels of another, and only for their climax in November, 1938, was the crime of Herschel Grynszpan taken as a pretext.* At the same time the geographical expansion of the race legislation began. This expansion had always been aimed at Jewish property and even before the outbreak of war it constituted a wartime measure.

The beginnings of the anti-Semitic policy were disguised as a reaction to the "atrocity stories" of the Jewish emigrants. A committee headed by Julius Streicher appealed to the public for a boycott of Jewish shops and businesses, and on April 1, 1933, members of the SA spent the day on sentry duty in every town and village in Germany, holding placards and challenging the citizens, with more or less threatening looks, not to patronize the businesses of this particular group of their fellow citizens. It was a pseudorevolutionary action—a feast for the cameras of all the foreign journalists and offensive also to the order-loving German people who, with all their enthusiasm for the national revolution, must at that moment have experienced their first inkling of things to come. The action was hurriedly called off, and Julius Streicher never again took the spotlight in such a significant and obvious capacity. But the thinking of the new men was disclosed by the most recently appointed Reich minister, Dr. Goebbels, more effectively than whole weeks of boycott could ever have done, for in his broadcast speech of April 1 he had the following to say about the German Jews: "If they maintain today that they cannot help it if their racial brothers in England and America drag Germany's national regime down into the mire, then we cannot help it if the German people take it out on them." And he threatened that the boycott would be resumed in such a way "that German Jewry will be annihilated."

This was the kind of sophistry that till then the Germans had delighted in dubbing "Jewish," and anyone who, on the strength of the reports of some emigrants (or, worse still, of the universal reaction

* Grynszpan was the assassin of the German legation secretary vom Rath in Paris.—Ed.

of world opinion), used this argument to declare as hostages hundreds of thousands of human beings because of their "blood," could not be surprised if he was held capable of the most dire deeds and intentions.

From now on the "elimination of Jews from the body of the German nation" was undertaken not by way of mass demonstrations and revelatory speeches, but by legal measures. The *Gesetz zur Wiederherstellung des Berufsbeamtentums* (law for the restoration of the civil service) of April 7, 1933, laid the foundation; this was the first law to contain the "Aryan paragraph" and thus to pension off all civil servants of non-Aryan descent, with the exception of veterans and their dependents. This paragraph was very soon extended to include first lawyers and doctors under the municipal health schemes, and soon afterward writers and artists, university and high-school students; it was not long before "proof of Aryan descent" became a matter of vital concern for most Germans.

On June 28, 1933, Reich Minister for the Interior Frick made a speech before the newly appointed "Advisory Council of Experts for Population and Race Policy." In it the concepts of the National Socialist policy of racial health for the nation were officially presented, and distributed in pamphlet form. The minister began by pointing out the impending racial death of the nation as a result of the decline in the birth figure, and calculated that the "reproductive output" of German women was some thirty per cent below what was required merely to ensure maintenance of the population figure. But increase must be the objective. To achieve this, particularly strenuous efforts were needed since by no means *every* German child was welcome. In cautious and yet scarcely mistakable phraseology, the minister mentioned that, according to some authors, twenty per cent of the German population must be considered biologically impaired from a hereditary standpoint, and that propagation on the part of these people was therefore not desirable. Liberalism and industrialization had, he said, brought about a sharp deterioration of the family, and that was all the more dangerous since the neighbors to the East and the inferior layers among Germany's own population showed a very high birth rate. Miscegenation was contributing toward further debasement of the race. Above all it was necessary, apart from the elimination of the Jews, drastically to reduce expenditure on asocial and mentally unfit members of the community; the state must use its resources for the healthy and valuable members, the continuance and racial improvement of the people were its objectives. Tax adjustments would favor large families, economic measures would return working wives to their families, instruction in race hygiene must be assured of a place in schools. One must once again have the courage to classify the body of the nation according to its hereditary values.

The first legal measure to be forecast by the speech was implemented on July 14, 1933: the *Gesetz zur Verhütung erbkranken Nachwuchses* (law for the prevention of progeny suffering from hereditary disease). The hereditary diseases named varied greatly in character and diagnostability (that is, schizophrenia and manic-depressive madness appeared side by side with hereditary blindness and deafness), but its crucial and novel feature was that, instead of the wishes of the patient or his legal representative being the yardstick, the official doctor or director of the institution could apply for sterilization of the patient, and such applications were decided on by a "tribunal for hereditary health."

The same day saw the announcement of the *Gesetz über den Widerruf von Einbürgerungen und die Aberkennung der deutschen Staatsangehörigkeit* (law concerning the revocation of naturalization and the annulment of German nationality). This made it possible for "undesirable" naturalizations between 1918 and 1933 to be revoked, thus fulfilling an old postulate of the party, but in principle it also abolished the continuity of the state. A state which deprives a section of its citizens of citizenship, through no fault of their own, in fact abrogates all other contracts and commitments from the past. Practically speaking, the depriving of emigrants of their citizenship identified state and regime, yet it is much less novel than the first part of the law. It punished the deed, and that links it to the ancient traditions of European justice.

Here was where the Nuremberg laws differed. They punished "a state of existence," thereby constituting a fundamental break in the course of German justice. From the narrow juristical standpoint, they could, it is true, be regarded as a codification and hence improvement of an arbitrary practice, and it can be taken for fact that the experts involved saw to it that the draft most favorable to the Jews was adopted. But as long as principles differ qualitatively from mere customs and circumstances, September 15, 1935, will remain a date of cardinal importance. It can be objected, of course, that it was after all only a discrimination, not a punishment, and that many analogies can be cited: the United States "race legislation" has been repeatedly put forward as an example. In actual fact, however, this argument merely proves a lack of understanding of historical fact and the distinction between "implementation" and "cancellation." It might also be said that the Soviet Union deprived whole strata of the population of their political rights and, as a logical conclusion of certain measures, condemned them to death. But there is a great difference between social and biological existence, between a "law" and a "wholesale procedure." It is impossible to avoid the conclusion that the Nuremberg laws represented an entirely new departure in history.

The *Reichsbürgergesetz* (Reich citizenship law) distinguished between the ordinary citizen and the Reich citizen, the sole beneficiary of full political rights, and thus implemented the fourth point of the party program.

The *Gesetz zum Schutze des deutschen Blutes und der deutschen Ehre* (law for the protection of German blood and German honor) rendered sexual intercourse between adults of mixed "blood" a criminal offense—it even prohibited a mere presumed *proxima occasio*. Incidentally, the restriction of the threat of punishment to the man alone was an indication of the new-old evaluation of the sexes.

Of the utmost practical importance were the regulations governing the execution of these laws. These regulations facilitated the tightening of laws in some cases and the removal of certain restrictions in others. The tendency to equate Jewish veterans with the rest of the Jews followed logically from the intention of these laws. On the whole, however, this thrust forward was followed by a long period of quiet; and it was a proof, not, indeed, of a humane attitude, but of the shrewdness of National Socialist policy, that Jews could participate in the economy, although impeded in many ways, for another two years or more.

However, even during 1936 and 1937 these matters were not lost sight of, as events in Upper Silesia showed. There the Jews had invoked the regulations for the protection of minorities contained in the agreement on Upper Silesia inaugurated by the League of Nations, and the Reich government had been forced to recognize this interpretation. But when the regulations expired in 1937 the race laws were immediately introduced.

1938 saw the vigorous resumption of the policy of "the recovery of racial health." New regulations governing the implementation of the *Reichsbürgergesetz* revoked the licenses of Jewish doctors and removed the exceptions still existing for lawyers and patent attorneys. This was followed by a "purging" of the country's entire medical system. In 1938 even the laws governing taxes underwent a "racial" extension: for instance, tax exemptions for the children of Jews were discontinued. A decree of Göring's concerning the reporting of Jewish property gave a hint of the future course of events. In July the practice of certain trades was prohibited. In October the passports of all Jews were ordered to be stamped with a "J". The law of January 5, 1938, dealing with the changing of family and first names had already had the same end in view. Like naturalization, the assimilation of names was now also revoked. In August a regulation made the addition of one Jewish first name (Sara or Israel) mandatory.

Following the assassination of the German legation secretary vom Rath in Paris, the line of "direct action" which had been so hurriedly abandoned in 1933 was resumed. Organized giant pogroms and special taxes amounting to a billion marks can only be comprehended if they are regarded as the acts of primitive tribal warfare; likewise all the legal measures which, instead of being merely the revocation of political emancipation, now forced the Jews back into the pariah existence they had led during the Middle Ages—the only difference, and a far from negligible one, being that now even their financial resources had been taken from them. The Jews' affection for Germany must have been immense if *such* measures were necessary to compel them to emigrate. In actual fact the explanation was much more commonplace. It is impossible to exert strenuous efforts to rearm and at the same time finance an extensive emigration with foreign currency. With idle talk about emigrating to Madagascar (which was French, after all), people tried to hide the fundamental fact that through its own policy Germany had been turned into a prison for the larger, less prosperous section of the German Jews and those among them with few connections abroad. It is fair to ask, however, whether the intelligence of the leaders must not be assessed somewhat higher. Rosenberg, at least, stated on February 7, 1939, that Jewish emigration was an *international* problem of the most far-reaching significance, thus complicating still further what was already an extremely difficult situation. And *could* Hitler in his notorious threat to the Jewish warmongers really not fail to see that *his* war had begun long ago and had dispossessed the enemy to an extent far beyond anything that any war in the history of Europe had ever so much as contemplated? In the summer of 1939 Jews were no longer permitted to take part in German cultural events, or to show themselves at certain hours and in certain places, or to drive any motorized vehicle. With the swiftly mounting danger of war, virtually only two possibilities remained open. The first was for Germany to acquire living space for them by force of arms. The second was death. Even before the war broke out, only a thin wall stood between them and death. A system such as National Socialism made the most extraordinary things possible; but it was incapable of what appeared to be the simplest of all: to come to a halt and go no further.

Once again, it is very helpful to look at Mussolini's Italy to discover the particular features of the National Socialist population and race policy. Frick's speech offers a good starting point. There is no doubt that it cited a number of measures which were acknowledged in every country as more or less correct and desirable. What gave the speech its fascist flavor was that he overemphasized the intentions in question, made them the elements of a secular process of salvation, and linked them undeniably and pre-eminently with the military potential. All this comes through just as clearly in Mussolini's speeches and decrees on the population policy; indeed, some of his ordinances are even sharper than their German counterparts. For example, in Italy in 1938 marriage was made compulsory for the obtaining of high administrative posts. What was entirely absent in Mussolini, however, was the tendency to classify the body of the nation according to its hereditary biological values, and to declare the progeny of considerable sections of the population to be undesirable. Actually this tendency never materialized to any great extent in Germany, but its potential existence is in itself sufficient to warrant its being regarded as the radical-fascist element in the German population policy.

In regard to the race laws, as has been shown, a comparison is also not entirely out of the question. But on the whole it is not particularly helpful, the National Socialist race policy being too much *sui generis* for it not to be subjected to an isolated scrutiny.

The insights which it forces on the observer are bitter in either direction: bitter for the Jews, more bitter still for the Germans—even if, and especially if, moral judgments on individuals are avoided and its further expansion during the war is not considered.

For to suppose that Hitler could have provided the Germans with victims in the form of Jehovah's Witnesses or alcoholics instead of Jews as a substitute for the forbidden class warfare is incorrect. It is true that Germany with its Jewish population of one per cent knew no such sociological Jewish problem as Rumania or Poland, but the fact remained that in some professions and occupations a proportion of Jews had been reached which could not be maintained indefinitely. Anti-Semitism is by no means a relic of the Middle Ages or the expression of petit-bourgeois social envy; in an age of the growing awareness of national and social differences it is under certain conditions an element of national consciousness itself. Even liberals, far from being philo-Semitic, were hostile to the idea of "Jewish national self-segregation," although, of course, they were also against segregation counter to the will of those concerned as carried out by the proponents of racial anti-Semitism. However, the consciousness that the Jews were not merely a religious community but a people had been roused just as much by Zionism as by anti-Semitism. It may sound hard, but it remains a fact that German Jewry, as a group which, though not without its own differentiations, was on the whole readily distinguishable, faced an inexorable decline after the deceptive upsurge of the first years of its complete emancipation; it could not escape being crushed between the two extremes which it had itself generated—complete assimilation and Zionism. Even with the most terrible of his deeds Hitler did not simply fly in the face of history: here, too, he rode its trends which he then manipulated so that they could operate in reverse. In this way he transformed the inevitable restoration of Germany into a war of aggression, the expansion of German influence in the world into the conquest of living space, the spiritual self-dissolution of German Jewry into physical annihilation.

However, this last transformation, even in its early phase before the war, was no less fatal to Germany than to the Jews, however little public evidence of this catastrophe there was.

In its most universal sense, the legislation dealing with the Jews meant the revoking of emancipation. It follows that Germany thereby denied the advantages which it had itself derived from emancipation. When in the name of Germany, Hitler even excluded Jewish veterans from the German "national body," he clearly denied nationhood itself which above all else means "common destiny," and in this way rendered Germany's legal claim to nationality problematical.

Because Hitler did not even grant the Jews the rights of a national minority (as was demonstrated by the affair in Upper Silesia), he virtually rendered the German minorities in Eastern Europe defenseless also, and threw away one of the trump cards which Germany had obtained from the Versailles Treaty.

By making hundreds of thousands of Jews answerable for the deed of one man, the leaders of the state were preparing the soil for the day when millions of Germans were to be made responsible for the deeds of one man.

There was nothing clandestine about any of the laws, measures, and speeches which have been cited; that they grew out of one central impulse toward leadership was explicitly announced by Hitler in his proclamation at the Reich party congress of 1937: "Germany has experienced the greatest revolution, however, in the national and racial hygiene which was undertaken for the first time on an organized basis in this country. The consequences of this German race policy will be more decisive for the future of our people than the effects of any other law. For they are creating the new man."

Nevertheless, they did not appear in the full illumination of open publicity. Inasmuch as this is part of the National Socialist style, it would seem appropriate to give a brief description of this Reich party congress in 1937. In doing so, we shall try not to minimize the spell which, according to many witnesses, was cast by these events, and the description will therefore closely follow official reports.

The ninth party congress of the NSDAP, designated the Reich Party Congress of Labor, lasted from Monday, September 6, to Monday, September 13, and took place in Nuremberg as it had done ever since 1927.

Adolf Hitler arrived in Nuremberg late on the Monday afternoon and began by inspecting his personal bodyguard, which received him in perfect formation, with fixed bayonets and wearing full-dress uniforms. To the ringing of church bells he drove through the sea of flags in the gaily decorated city to the town hall; there, standing in the enormous open car, his arm raised constantly in salute, he greeted the cheering populace which lined the streets and waved from every window. With a fanfare of trumpets he entered the great hall, on the façade of which the swastika banners framed the shrine of the Reich insignia, and there, ready to receive him, stood the entire leadership corps of party, state, and Wehrmacht, all in uniform. He was welcomed by the mayor, who praised the great progress made in laying out the Reich party congress grounds. In his reply Hitler also spoke of the realization of his gigantic plans for the grounds. On his way back he was again greeted by the cheers of the multitude. The official report states: "like a storm it breaks over everyone. The Führer is here, now the city is truly alive."

On Tuesday morning the Reich party congress was ceremonially opened in the Congress Hall. Wave upon wave of marching columns and hurrying people filled the city from early morning. The vast hall was crowded with delegates from every party organization and many guests of honor, among them a delegation from the Fascist party of Italy. Once again to a fanfare of trumpets Hitler entered the hall with the opening notes of the "Badenweiler March." The "blood banner" (the swastika flag that had been carried in the Munich *Putsch*) was borne into the hall, reverently saluted by all present, and placed immediately behind the speaker's rostrum. Behind it, the standards of every corner of Germany formed serried ranks. The overture to *Tannhäuser* began, followed by the old Netherlands hymn of thanksgiving.

Rudolf Hess proceeded to pay homage to the dead, and in his speech he sounded the keynote of the congress—the contrast between National Socialism and its will to rebuild and its joy in work, and communism with its decay, forced labor, and hopelessness. The Führer's proclamation, read by a *Gauleiter*, dealt with the same theme; it contrasted Bolshevik chaos and will to destroy with National Socialism's staggering archievements in reconstruction, as a result of which unemployment had been completely eliminated. Under the impact of this message the tens of thousands of listeners broke into prolonged and rapturous cheering.

That evening the cultural session took place at the opera house, where for the first time the newly created "national prize for art and science" was awarded. The session signified "the proclamation of German sovereignty in cultural achievements and art," and in a highly meaningful sense, for Hitler had banned the acceptance of the Nobel Prize by Germans for all time. The first prize winner was Alfred Rosenberg. The Führer himself gave a long address attacking modern art as well as the literary clique which had resulted from this disgraceful "retrogressive trend." By contrast, National Socialism made the cultural achievements of the past accessible to the broad masses and was itself creating buildings which were among the greatest and noblest architectural achievements in German history.

Wednesday morning saw the parade of the Reich Labor Force on the Zeppelin Field, and its morning service at which the massed voices of tens of thousands uttered songs, speeches, and vows: "A service in the cathedral of the German countryside."

In the evening the congress was continued; the most outstanding speaker was Alfred Rosenberg, who gave an interpretation of the times and history from the standpoint of the eternal struggle between creation and destruction, a struggle which aligned National Socialism against bolshevism in the same way that Rome had once confronted the Syrian plague spot of Carthage. Reports on the achievements of the *Winterhilfe* program and health policy brought the evening to a close.

On Thursday, "in a solemn act of thrilling beauty," the Führer laid the cornerstone of the giant German Stadium, at the same time opening the National Socialist Athletic Contest, at which the main emphasis was on team and military sports. In the evening Goebbels violently attacked Spanish bolshevism; it was destroying the churches, he said, and yet being defended by Western intellectuals and churchmen, who were devoid of sound instincts. Hans Frank gave a report on "Law and Justice in the National Socialist Reich." He stressed the fact that during the previous year the last stipulations of the Versailles Treaty to restrict the sovereignty of the Reich had been removed, so that the "restoration of Reich sovereignty" was now a *fait accompli*. Otto Dietrich, head of the Reich press, unmasked the innate falsity of the liberal "freedom of the press."

Friday morning was given over to the police and the demonstration of its unity with the SS. The Führer dedicated its new flags by touching them with the "blood banner," and interpreted this act as the integration of the police "with that great unified marching column of the German *Volksgemeinschaft*."

Impressive figures were contributed to the congress in the reports of Darré, Amann, and Todt. No one could accuse Dr. Todt of lying when he said that a few years previously the progress made in building the *Autobahnen* would have been beyond the dreams of the boldest civil engineer, and that these achievements had only been possible as a whole through the impulse of a powerful will unhampered by parliamentary institutions.

In the afternoon "the women [marched into the hall] in long columns." They listened to a report given by the Reich Leader of Women on the many ways of safeguarding the German family. The Führer himself explained to them the ultimate goal of all National Socialist efforts: the German child. Brought up as a hardy race, in future the men would provide the women with a "true and genuine protection and shield." "Seemingly endless applause" followed his address.

Perhaps the most impressive event of the congress was the roll call of the one hundred and ten thousand political leaders Friday evening on the Zeppelin Field. With military precision the thirty-two *Gau* (district) columns marched toward the field from all sides and met exactly on time for their entry. Shortly before ten o'clock the Führer arrived. Standing stiffly at attention Dr. Ley reported all present. "At that moment the surrounding darkness is suddenly flooded with white light. The beams of the hundred and fifty giant searchlights shoot up like meteors into the obscurity of the black night sky. High up the columns of light join on the cloud ceiling to form a flaming square wreath. It is an overpowering sight: moved by the gentle breeze, the flags on the stands all around the field wave slowly back and forth in the shining light. . . . The northern side is closed off by the main reviewing stand. The huge structure is bathed in brilliance, crowned by the golden rays of the swastika in the wreath of oak leaves. On the end pillars to the left and right, flames leap up from great bowls. . . . The crowd stands waiting in awestruck silence." With a fanfare of trumpets the Führer strode to the main rostrum.

Then came the banners: thirty-two thousand of them. The banner song of the men of the Vogelsang *Ordensburg* rang out through the air: "What took a thousand years to come, the Führer forced into existence. With flags and banners flying, it rolls on roaring to eternity." Then the Führer spoke of the sufferings of the time of struggle and of the happiness of the present, now that a people imbued with faith had found its place in the "united battle front of the nation," which would never let go of and never abandon its people from the *Jungvolk* via the *Hitlerjugend*, *Arbeitsdienst*, and Wehrmacht through to the party and its organizations. The old guard of the National Socialist revolution had brought this miracle to pass, and to the accompaniment of protracted demonstrations of enthusiasm and emotion he formulated the innermost secret of this miracle as follows: "That you have found *me* and that you have believed in me, this is what has given your life a new meaning, a new task. That I have found *you*, this is what has made my life and my struggle possible." He closed with a *Heil!* for Germany, and from a hundred thousand throats the "Song of the Germans" surged forth "like organ music." Then the Führer left the rostrum, passing through the lane formed by his bodyguard, accompanied by shouts of *Heil!* But for a long time the shining searchlight wreath remained in the night sky "like a cathedral."

On Saturday morning there was the solemn ceremony of one hundred and fifteen thousand eighteen-year-olds swearing their oath of allegiance to the Führer. Confronted by his young people the prophetic spirit came over Adolf Hitler once more: "Just as you stand before me today, so year after year for centuries the young generation will stand before future Führers and will continue to bear witness to their devotion to the Germany that we have fought for and won today."

This was followed shortly afterward by the annual conference of the German Labor Front. Robert Ley deployed his principles for the solution of the social problem: "Same step, same pack, same march: then there is nothing to tell me outwardly whether the man is an employer or a worker." The concept of "soldier of labor," he went on, will finally overcome class distinction. In the evening a long report stressed the achievements of the *Deutsche Arbeitsfront*, with special reference to the social services of the National Socialist community "Strength through Joy" and the organizations "Leisure Time" and "Beauty of Work."

Sunday morning was devoted to the parade of the political fighting units of the party for the great roll call in the presence of the Führer. To the more than one hundred thousand men in their brown and black uniforms, Adolf Hitler spoke of the discords of the past and the people's new sense of ethnic unity (*Volksgemeinschaft*)— achieved by such fanatical struggles—which now followed one command, one order, as a single bloc. Massed around their symbol of triumph, the symbol of their blood, he said, the people, certain of victory, turned their eyes toward the banner of the old foe, who "confounds the nations." After the dedication of the new flags and banners, Dietrich Eckart's song, "Germany Awake," brought the parade to an end, and shortly afterward "the army of one hundred and twenty thousand" marched for five hours past their Führer. A particularly powerful impression was left by the parade of the black cadres of the "*Schutzkorps* of the Movement," among whom the units of the special duty detachment and the bodyguard were the most striking.

Monday was Wehrmacht day. There were military maneuvers of extreme precision on the field, while many hundreds of planes of the fighting squadrons roared across the sky. The "unique method" of presentation was so perfect that the onlookers obtained "a co-ordinated and thrilling picture of the course of a modern infantry battle." The "unity and power" of the parade which followed whipped the audience to one storm of applause after another.

In the evening the great final address of the Führer brought the ninth Reich party congress to a close, after the standards of the movement, to the strains of Wagner's "March of the Nibelungs," had been carried into the hall. Adolf Hitler spoke of the ineradicable impression made by "a new generation's confession of faith founded on a national ideology," he explained his historical philosophy from the creative race nuclei to his description of the dictatorship of the proletariat as a "dictatorship of Jewish intellectualism," and he declared in impassioned language that the National Socialist state would tolerate no shift in the balance of power in favor of bolshevism in Europe, beginning with Spain, and that, in the case of a threat, it "would stand up and fight for its existence with a fanaticism different from that of the bourgeois Reich of old." Many hundreds of thousands, he said, had marched in Nuremberg, "in uniform ranks like the grenadiers of the best regiments," borne up by an inward harmony of soul and yet still merely the vanguard of the great people's army of Germany, just as the soldiers, whose maneuvers had been admired, were after all only "the point of a sword" which protected their native land. He closed with the words: "The German nation has indeed obtained its Germanic Reich." Thunderous applause surged toward the creator of this Reich, and the songs of the nation, accompanied on the organ, mounted solemnly to the sky. At midnight the congress came to its traditional close with the tattoo and taps of the Wehrmacht.

Indeed, after all this what could strike one more forcibly than the thought that no boyhood dream ever attained a more complete, more brilliant fulfillment? Had it not become a reality, "the Reich" of which Hitler had so often spoken to Kubizek? Had it not been created, this united body of the nation of which he used to preach: impervious to Jewish intellectualism, fixed in its own purposes, proceeding along the paths of nature? Had not the abyss of the past actually swallowed up all that had once posed as political reality—conservatism, liberalism, and socialism, Center and Social Democrats alike? A dispassionate opponent would presumably have answered by saying that all Hitler had done was transform the old Prussian-German barracks state into one single state barracks, and that this was the basis of all his successes. But it was precisely in this transformation that the problem lay. For it was not a matter of "backward" but of "forward," of modernization. Hitler had succeeded in imparting mass-effectiveness and mass-accessibility to those things which had formerly been the preserve of small sections of the population. To this end he had made use of the most modern means offered by technology. And his actions were based on certain premises the truth of which was not acceptable to many of his opponents. Even if a hundred thousand people in Nuremberg stayed home or clenched their fists in their pockets: a rejoicing of this kind is quite impossible among a people which was and is really imbued with an irreducible class enmity. National Socialism was as good a proof as Social Democratic revisionism of Lenin's thesis concerning the workers' aristocracy. All the elements of this style were already present in the style of fascist Italy; however, the difference in quantity and relative timing is of qualitative significance here.

Nevertheless, the objection has an obvious merit, although perhaps it should be formulated less tritely and less polemically: the old god had blessed his people again when, after straying briefly from the path, it found its way back to him. But was everyone aware of the sacrifice necessary to make this blessing a lasting one? Hitler knew it: two months after his Reich party congress he summoned the chiefs of staff to the Hossbach conference.*

For today's observer, the picture of all that rejoicing and marching, all those uniforms, raises one paramount question: How could it happen that such an overwhelming display of total mobilization inside and outside Germany—a display that could have only one implication— was not universally taken for what it plainly was, a declaration of war? And if this picture of a people which in peacetime had turned itself into a single shining well-equipped army was not enough: How could the meaning of "Germanic Reich" and "safeguarding existence" as interpreted by *Mein Kampf* have been overlooked? How could the people themselves—once known as the nation of thinkers—seriously suppose that their Führer was a wizard who, alone among all earth-dwellers, knew how to create employment and economic recovery out of nothing while producing quantities of unproductive weapons? There are probably three main factors capable of offering some explanation of the inexplicable:

1. Paralysis in the face of the unheard-of and the unprecedented. When the German imperial army slightly increased its peacetime strength, France introduced three-year conscription. When Hitler increased Germany's military potential tenfold, a hundredfold, France was as petrified as the proverbial rabbit confronted by a snake.

2. The hope of a lightning conductor, that is, the expectation that, in view of the anti-Bolshevik attitude of the regime, the Soviet Union would have to foot the bill.

3. The unique position of the German people in process of "secularization." This people had never become reconciled on its intellectual levels with the process underlying its rise to the position of foremost economic power in continental Europe. It still hankered after metaphysics, unity, and profundity, and National Socialism meant the translation of these things into politics, however much—and with good reason—it would sooner or later repel the best representatives of this nostalgia. Under the dome of light on the Zeppelin Field, in the

* The conference of November 5, 1937, where Hitler allegedly revealed his plans for European war.—Ed.

thunder of mass cheering, a German was justified in believing that this unity was for its own sake alone.

However, the study of this party congress or of any other similar rally can also convey valuable insights into the nature of totalitarianism.

Under the immediate impact of war there has been an excessive tendency to identify totalitarianism with "terror" and "horror." But "totality" is in the nature of all great achievements which challenge and embrace individuals and groups. In them enthusiasm precedes terror—which is merely the obverse of enthusiasm, directed at hostility and resistance. The question is, what generates such enthusiasm and when; what are its characteristics and those of the terror that may result from it? Experience and reflection seem to show equally well that keeping up with industrial developments under unfavorable conditions is the only great social task which must today be tackled with enthusiasm and hence in a totalitarian manner. In other words: under certain circumstances that often concealed and yet all-dominating technological and economic revolution (which until 1918 was a seemingly isolated phenomenon and took place everywhere in more or less liberal guise) must assume political shape and force everything into total subjection. It was the Bolshevik revolution of 1917 which marked this crucial point in world history. It founded a system which carries out that development in a completely different, that is, totalitarian, form, and which has proved itself equal to the task with terrible concomitant manifestations and in the face of enormous resistance. Those who regarded a lead in development as an eternal birthright were bound to feel threatened. What complicated matters still further was that the revolutionary power rested on a theory of revolution based on entirely different premises, namely a nontotalitarian revolution to emancipate the individual in the most advanced countries. The disparity between ideology and reality could not but enhance the sense of being threatened, especially in the neighboring countries. Yet, it was anti-Bolshevik propaganda, with its polemic against the starvation and misery in the Soviet Union, the "Bolshevik chaos," that proved how it could not possibly be a manifestation of military aggressiveness. The Soviet Union was not imperialistic before the Hitler-Stalin pact, and, even after it, only in the sense of desiring a glacis fortification in the face of threatened attack—not for reasons of virtue, but because it had to catch up, laboriously and under the most adverse conditions, with a development of several decades. It *had* to be totalitarian, and thus did not need to look to war as its final stage. An industrial power, on the other hand, which had its place in the front ranks of development, could not in Hitler's era want anything but war if it embarked on a totalitarian effort.

Seen thus, fascism appears to lack inherent necessity: a totalitarianism with no *raison d'être*. But that does not mean there was no motive for it. According to motive and character, it shows various levels. Italian fascism, born of bourgeois resistance to the attempted Communist revolution, did not deny the Soviet Union its right to exist and its own kind of historical necessity; with this as an example, it would be possible to discuss the important question of whether a fascism can, legitimately and permanently, be a "development dictatorship." German National Socialism, the offspring of defeat in war and a temporary economic depression, saw itself as the implacable enemy of a "world danger." However, for National Socialism the Soviet Union represented a "world danger" not merely in its capacity of imaginary "plague spot" and center of the Jewish conspiracy, but also in a more real sense, because an industrialized Eastern Europe meant *eo ipso* the negation of total, that is, primarily military and geographical, German sovereignty. Hence the specific totalitarian nature of the German form of fascism *had* to be military, with the whole colossal striking power aimed principally at its great neighbor to the East and its "necessary" totalitarianism.

The similarity between certain manifestations ought not to allow one to forget the fundamental differences. It would, of course, have been possible—for theoretical hindsight, at least—to combat bolshevism solely on account of its bloody excesses and world-revolutionary ideology, in order then to provide the peoples of Eastern Europe with another and no less effective form of confrontation with their basic problem. In this way it might have been possible to demonstrate that bolshevism was *not* a necessary totalitarianism but that, even without it, Russia could have kept up with the headlong development in Europe and the U.S.A. But in that case would totalitarianism—with the premises of the race doctrine—have been worth the effort? That would have meant an affirmation in principle of this course, the acknowledgment of it as a universal necessity, whereas it was not even possible to affirm it with a clear conscience as a racial privilege! Hitler was always fully aware of these relationships, and Rosenberg wanted to ensure that the peoples of Eastern Europe were as agrarian peoples protected from the assault of centralizing bolshevism. A fascist Germany was incapable of doing otherwise than carrying on its war in Eastern

Europe in order to achieve unqualified sovereignty; and it could only hope to safeguard itself finally against what it felt was the threatened development of the peoples of Eastern Europe if it could discover and eliminate the agent of these processes.

This law of existence for National Socialism can be deduced from a study of the Reich party congress no less clearly than from an analysis of Hitler's ideas. But for the totality of his political intentions, all the cheering and enthusiasm, all the military precision and discipline of the Reich party congress, are not enough. The Wehrmacht stood ready to ward off the assault of an enemy; there was no problem in winning over the masses who were members of the National Socialist armed units for an attack on bolshevism; but for the true ends of the totalitarian war of National Socialist Germany, neither of these two factors sufficed. Hitler needed a body of men who stood unconditionally at his disposal for all his political intentions, because they knew what was at stake and because they desired it. All the signposts of the 1937 demonstration of power pointed toward the SS.

The place occupied by the SS in the system can therefore be deduced. At this point it is enough to trace the historical development in outline and then (without for the time being resorting to documents which remained secret for many years) to allow the group to present its own image of itself, as formulated with the greatest authority by Heinrich Himmler.

Hitler had always striven for a politically oriented body of men which would be at his exclusive disposal. When in 1923 Röhm and Kriebel turned the SA more and more into a military unit, the *Stosstrupp Hitler* (Hitler shock troop) was organized, the principal function of which was the personal protection of the Führer. The setting up of a personal *Stabswache* (staff guard) under Julius Schreck in March, 1925, had a similar objective; it was a countermove to Röhm's *Frontbann* plans. During the late summer of 1925, the *Stabswache* became the *Schutzstaffel* (guard detachment), which was extended beyond Munich and at the party congress in Weimar was accorded a significant privilege: Hitler handed over the "blood banner" to it for safekeeping. With the reorganization of the SA it lost in importance; yet in its small number (as compared to the mass movement of the SA) was contained the potential of its elite character and, in its specific bodyguard function, the direct link with the Führer.

The man who perceived its innate possibilities and vigorously followed them up was Heinrich Himmler, son of a Bavarian schoolteacher; he had gone through the period of the Bavarian Soviet Republic as a very young officer's candidate and had later been Gregor Strasser's secretary for many years. When he took over the SS in January, 1929, it had less than three hundred members. He insisted on having photographs of new recruits submitted to him and inspecting them for racial traits, and he only accepted men over five feet seven inches in height. The reasons for this were at first as pragmatic as they were typical. He indicated them in a later speech as follows: the "Soldiers' Soviets types" of 1918 and 1919 had all had "something funny" about their appearance, and that must be attributable to an admixture of foreign blood. "To have good blood" meant for Himmler: to be soldierly and unconditionally counterrevolutionary. Before long he was bound to hit on the idea that a body of men of good blood contained that "racial nucleus" of which Hitler had so often spoken. However, this racial nucleus could only be permanently dominant if it had a clear awareness of race and the determination to preserve it. Himmler therefore singled out the SS from all other formations by the "Betrothal and Marriage Order of the Reich SS-Führer" of December 31, 1931. This made marriage for SS men dependent on the Reich SS-Führer's consent—that is, stipulated a racial inspection of the fiancée and her genealogy by a race department established expressly for this purpose. The SS was to be more than a mere association of men: it was to be a community of genealogically high-grade families. Since Himmler was an *Artamane* and an agriculturist by profession, it is not surprising that the office of inspection soon turned into a department for race and settlement under the direction of the Minister of Agriculture and Chief of the Reich Peasants, SS-*Obergruppenführer* R. Walter Darré. The SS distinguished itself in 1931 by helping to suppress the SA uprising of Captain Stennes; on that occasion Hitler gave it the motto: "SS man, your honor is called loyalty." And finally, also in 1931, there began the organization of its own intelligence service under the onetime naval lieutenant Reinhard Heydrich. When Hitler seized power, the SS was still, with its fifty thousand members, a small organization and under the authority of the chief of staff of the SA, but the seeds of its future significance were already present.

In March, 1933, Hitler created from its ranks a new *Stabswache* under Joseph Dietrich; this later became the *Leibstandarte Adolf Hitler* (Adolf Hitler's personal bodyguard), while armed special units of the SS in other cities became the matrix of the subsequent special duty SS. This secured for Hitler an armed force of his own stamp permanently at his disposal: it was "part of neither the Wehrmacht nor the police," and bound to him by a more personal and less specific oath than that which attached the soldiers to the Wehrmacht. The full implication of the SS oath became apparent for the first time on June 30, 1934. No firing squad of the Wehrmacht would have been permitted to kill the SA leaders without process of law: for the SS there already existed only the will of the Führer as sole law above and beyond all regulations and principles. There was little reason to believe that this formation would ever refuse to carry out *any* order of their Führer.

In March, 1933, with the appointment of Himmler as provisional chief of police in Munich, the SS began its penetration of the police. Within a year Himmler was given control of every regional police force in Germany, and in June, 1936, he was appointed chief of the German police. Since the Röhm crisis he had been head of an independent branch of the party: now both offices were combined in a single institution, the "Reich Führer of the SS and Chief of the German Police" was accorded a position unique in the constitution, one which a formal subordination to the Reich minister for the interior did not weaken but reinforced. For through this steady coalescing of SS and police, a sphere was created which, while protected by the state, was at the same time removed from the control of the state, a field which was becoming less and less subject to the control of regular state administration, and this was what made it so useful for the carrying out of the Führer's own revolutionary decisions. The unity of state and nonstate elements was henceforward to be the, at times, opaque characteristic of the principal institutions of the SS. Special obligations entail special rights: thus every member of the SS was given a privilege which singled him out from his fellow citizens—the right to defend his honor with arms.

In his speech of January, 1937, on "The Nature and Functions of the SS and the Police," Himmler named five "pillars" of the SS. The *Allgemeine SS* (general SS) consisted, apart from its top leaders, of men earning their living in civilian life. Its regional organization corresponded to that of the Wehrmacht; it passed on its young candidates to the army and received them back again, to maintain their health and hardihood through sports and athletic contests, in the process of which it also formed a counterbalance to the dangers of urban living and misuse of alcohol.

The *Verfügungstruppe* (special duty unit) was to fight in the field but was also, by way of constant exchange, involved in the activities of the police; for in the coming war the police was by hook or by crook to keep the home front (the "fourth war theater, inside Germany") "healthy," since bolshevism as a subhuman organization would try to stir up the dregs of this home front and incite it to a new stab in the back.

The third pillar was the *Totenkopfverbände* (death's head units), formed from the guards of the concentration camps. Their function was also the immediate safeguarding of the internal security of the Reich. They had custody of the "dregs of the criminal world, a mass of racially inferior trash," including many professional criminals kept in preventive and usually permanent confinement.

In fourth place Himmler named the *Sicherheitsdienst* (security service), "the great ideological intelligence service of the party and ultimately of the state." The fifth pillar was the *Rasse- und Siedlungshauptamt* (department of race and settlement), whose functions were of a positive nature: processing of marriage applications and genealogical histories submitted (as far back as 1750), problems of settlement and ideological instruction, as well as the furthering of science insofar as it was of political value.

Thus each of the five pillars in its own way served a single objective: the *Gesundung* (restoring to health) and safeguarding of "blood," threatened as it was in such multifarious ways. The SS was therefore simply the most complete organizational concretization of Hitler's doctrine. The concluding words of Himmler's address show that an analogy to Hitler's fear was not unknown to the SS leader: coming decades would represent "the war of destruction of all the subhuman enemies in the world against Germany" as the leading nation of white humanity, a war which, so Himmler apparently believed, could only be survived because a fortunate circumstance had allowed it to occur in a time "in which once in two thousand years an Adolf Hitler is born."

Himmler gave this address to officers of the Wehrmacht, and it was printed "for official purposes only." But two years earlier, in 1935, the Reich SS-Führer had already conveyed his ideas about the SS to the public at large on the occasion of the *Reichsbauerntag* (Reich Peasants Congress) in Goslar, and under the title of "The SS as an Anti-Bolshevik Combat Organization" these ideas had been widely disseminated.

The most typical feature of this speech is that it starts off by depicting the eternal and universal nature of the Jewish-Bolshevik mortal enemy with a forcefulness and naïveté that remind one instantly of Dietrich Eckart's *Zwiegespräch*: the Bolshevik spirit had at one time led the Jews to exterminate the best Aryans from among the Persian people, in Verdun the eternal enemy had brandished the executioner's sword of Charles the Frank over thousands of Saxon chieftains, by means of the Inquisition(!) it had dealt Spain a mortal blow, in the French revolution it had slaughtered the fair-haired and the blue-eyed, and finally in Russia, with the aid of the Jew Kerenski, it had opened up the way for the Jewish GPU to its work of destruction. For centuries the Jew had been hurling poison and murderous weapons at the Aryan peoples, he had allowed whole tribes which were not desirable to the Jews to starve to death, in this secular strife there were only victors or vanquished, and in this case to be vanquished meant the death of a people.

It is in this perspective that Himmler deliberately placed the character of the SS. Through a process of constant selection it filtered a stream of the best German blood. The positive side of its will permitted the SS to understand the value and sacredness of the soil, to perceive its goal in settlement, and to stand beside the German farmer as his most faithful friend: it was no mere accident, Himmler pointed out, that as the Reich SS-Führer he himself was a farmer. But the negative side of its will enabled the SS to be "a ruthless executioner's sword" toward all forces of the Jewish-Bolshevik subhuman revolution at the slightest attempt at revolt. The concluding sentences of the speech were frequently quoted in National Socialist literature: "So we have assembled, and according to immutable laws we march as a National Socialist, soldierly order of Nordic men and as a sworn community of their clans on the road to a distant future, and we desire and believe that we may be not only the grandsons, who fought it out better, but beyond that the ancestors of later generations necessary for the eternal life of the German Germanic people."

If one bears in mind *what,* according to Hitler and Himmler, was to be "fought out," what an "eternal life" of the German people presupposed in the eyes of these men, one sees that it was possible even in 1935 to describe the SS with accuracy: an unconditionally obedient *tool* in the hands of the Führer for the implementation of the true aims of his policy—the safeguarding of an eternal sovereign life of the Germanic-German Reich by settlement-conquest on the one hand, by annihilation of the mortal enemy on the other; but at the same time also the highest *goal* of this policy, as that racial nucleus of the best— that is, soldier-peasant—blood destined to be the ruling class of the Reich.

One might say that in Italy the development of the party army followed a more fortunate course. The *Moschettieri di Mussolini* never amounted to anything more than an insignificant prestige unit, because they were not required to shoot the commanders of the militia. Moreover, before the war this militia had been a larger and more renowned army than the *Waffen-SS,* having victoriously fought a full-scale war in Spain. There had, of course, been problems with the national army, but these had been overcome. Could not the SA with a little more luck have evolved in this direction? Yet this comparison shows how vitally necessary the SS was to the National Socialist regime. For, in keeping with its origin and structure, the SA was primarily the mass auxiliary formation of the Wehrmacht for purposes of national restitution. The doctrine which had now become the state itself—that of the creative race nucleus, its laws of existence and the deadly threats to it—needed just such an incomparable elite formation for the attainment of its real objectives. In spite of the many random happenings and incongruities in the historical development (for example, even up to the end of the war there was never complete identity between police and SS), there is no doubt either of the indispensability of the SS to the regime or of its inner solidarity.

1939–1945

National Socialist practice, as distinct from fascist practice, underwent considerable changes during the war. When, for instance, the wavering German front was stabilized during the winter of 1941–42, Hitler displayed a hitherto unsuspected leadership drive. It was undoubtedly an innovation in style when, after the victory over France, field-marshal generals were appointed en masse at the Reichstag session of July 19, 1940. The war organization as such, in its penetration of the spheres of state, party, Wehrmacht, and SS, is a subject meriting thorough exploration. But even in such a remarkable phenomenon as the *Einsatzstab Rosenberg* (Rosenberg operational staff), typical traits came to light which had to remain hidden in peacetime.

However, among all the institutions of the National Socialist state, the SS was the most powerful in its evolution and its consequences. It is true that there was nothing exactly new in this evolution, but its extraordinary logicality makes it a fascinating object of study. Here, too, however, it is not really possible to obtain a detailed view of the whole. For example, the increase of the *Waffen-SS* from barely thirty thousand men to a gigantic army of nearly one million did not begin until after the outbreak of war; only then were the legal foundations actually laid and the authoritative statements made. It was at this juncture that the elite corps saw itself exposed to all manner of influences, and it became a heavily stratified and not readily definable structure.

Once again the selection of three manifestations, taken this time from a single area, will serve to throw light on some of the most typical aspects of National Socialist practice. This area is the activity of the SS in three fields of primary importance. These fields cannot be completely separated, although essentially they can be allocated to certain subdivisions of the organization: the consolidation of the German people, the ferreting out and disarming of all adversaries, and the destruction of the chief enemy.

The first task was allotted to the Reich SS-Führer as the Reich Commissar for the Consolidating of the German People (RKF), by a secret decree of Hitler dated October 7, 1939. It was broken down into three separate measures: return of Reich ethnic Germans (*Volksdeutsche*) from foreign countries; elimination of the harmful influence of foreign elements among the population; and establishment of new settlement areas by resettlement. This was a program made to order for the SS; here negative and positive measures were to balance each other with pristine clarity. But in addition an energy and loyalty to principles were demanded which could not be expected of ministerial departments and which could only be displayed by a "political" organization, that is to say, one which was not bound by traditional standards. Hence Himmler as RKF "made use of" these government authorities but demoted them to the position of mere tools, without right of veto or control. After certain initial difficulties, especially with its own Department for Race and Settlement, the bureau of the RKF achieved considerable power and was given a place in the circle of twelve chief SS departments.

The legal basis for the negative aspect of Himmler's activity as RKF was the decree concerning Polish property of September 17, 1940, which in the incorporated Eastern European territories—the vast area of West Poland with over eight million Poles—officially abolished Polish private property, although in practice its existence had already been completely ignored. Himmler defined the implementation of this decree as follows: "The prerequisite for potential confiscation according to Section 2, Paragraph 2a, is present objectively when, for example, it is a case of land belonging to a Pole. For all Polish landed property is required without exception for the consolidation of the German people."

Thus by very simple means the department in charge of land distribution created the *Lebensraum* for those German groups brought back from all over Eastern Europe which had played such an invaluable role in German *ethnic* influence but which were now being taken back by the RKF's resettlement commission to reinforce German *state* power. But in July, 1942, Himmler as RKF was also responsible within the *Generalgouvernement* for a brutal action of expulsion and resettlement designed to make the city of Lublin and its surrounding territory the first German settlement bulwark in the Polish heartland. Yet all this was a mere trifle compared to what was planned for the postwar period. At the conference of group leaders in Poznań, Himmler disclosed some of these measures: "If the SS together with the farmers, and we together with our friend Backe, then pursue the settlement in the East, without restraint, without ever concerning ourselves with what is traditional, with *élan* and revolutionary zeal, then in twenty years we shall have thrust back the ethnic boundaries five hundred kilometers further to the East."

The identity of the "negative" and "positive" intentions is obvious here. In 1939 and 1940 a number of portentous measures were already aimed at serving this identity. A valuable insight into Himmler's positive ideas is provided by the instructions for the agricultural development of the new Eastern European territories which he promulgated in his capacity of RKF on November 26, 1940. It is particularly revealing that, although the creation of medium-sized hereditary farms was regarded as the basis of German ethnic (*Volkstum*) policy, social gradations were carefully specified; the lowest level of the hierarchy was to be occupied by German farm laborers, but on the higher levels the farms were to encourage the "stabilization and creation of a new class of indigenous leaders." Layout and architectural style of the villages and farmhouses were prescribed in detail. Dwellings of Polish farm laborers had to be located at a distance from the German settlement. Special attention was to be given the planting of trees and shrubs, since this would set the stamp on the German settlement of Eastern Europe. The inherited love of Germans for trees, shrubs, and flowers had to be preserved: hence the village oak and the village linden tree were to be present everywhere. Each village had to contain a party building, each town a hall for functions. The individual farmhouses were "to be the visible expression of a new German peasant culture." Old architectural styles and harmonious integration with the landscape were to be combined with the demands of modern hygiene and technology.

A third function of the RKF was likewise positive, but here he had to watch his step. It concerned the retrieving of dispersed Germanic blood. A regulation dating from 1940 reveals the principles by which Himmler was guided and the objectives he pursued: "Necessary though it is for a lasting purification of the German Eastern territories that the foreign elements living there should not be permanent or allowed to become permanent, it is equally essential that the German blood present in those areas be retrieved for the German nation in cases where the person of this blood has become Polish in his religion and language. It was these very people of German blood who provided the former Polish state with those leaders who—whether from blindness or in conscious or unconscious failure to recognize their blood relationship—adopted the most intensely hostile attitude toward their own German ethnic origin." Soon the "prevention of any further increase in the Polish intellectual class" and the "increase of the racially desirable population growth for the German people" were announced as immediate objectives. Accordingly many Poles were scrutinized by experts as to their "Germanness" and where necessary transferred to a German environment for "renationalization," in the process of which there was in principle nothing to prevent children being taken from their homes and being taught, against the will of their parents, to hearken to the true "voice of blood." So the old theoretical destruction of the concept of nation by the nonhistorical race doctrine was implemented a thousandfold in practice. But one can hardly fail to recognize the underlying fear in Himmler's words with their false ring of truculence: "Either we obtain the good blood which we can make use of, and integrate it with our nation, or, gentlemen—you may call it cruel, but nature is cruel—we destroy that blood." Never again, he said, was the enemy to obtain capable leaders and commanders; any false pity at the present time would imperil the existence of the German people in the future.

For the German people was surrounded by enemies, indeed they were to be found everywhere in its very midst. Himmler cited as enemies: all Communists, all Freemasons, all democrats, all convinced Christians, all nationalists even. If one adds Himmler's not entirely unfounded doubts as to the political reliability of the Wehrmacht officers' corps, it could be supposed that the SS alone was the true German people and that its enemies were as legion as the sands on the seashore. How was it to defend itself against these enemies now, as well as to safeguard its pre-eminence for all time?

The institution established by the SS specifically for investigating and combating all enemies was the *Reichssicherheitshauptamt* (Reich Security Department), a veritable model of the blending of "state" and "party" authorities and interests. It came into being in September,

1939, by combining various police and SS bureaus and was placed under the command of Reinhard Heydrich as Chief of Security Police and the SD (Security Department). A glance at the organization chart (of October 1, 1943) shows its functions.

Of the seven bureaus, the most interesting in this context is Bureau IV, the office for the "Investigating and Combating of Enemies." It was identical with the former Gestapo and was headed by the Gestapo chief, SS-Group Leader Müller. In common with all the other bureaus, it was divided into groups and subsections. Group IV-A concerned itself with "enemies, sabotage, and security"; the various subsections dealt among other things with Communists, Marxists, and affiliated organizations, reactionaries, the opposition, legitimists, liberals, also with the products of ideological opposition such as sabotage, illegal propaganda, or political counterfeiting.

Group IV-B dealt with political Catholicism, political Protestantism, sects, other churches, and Freemasons. In charge of Jewish affairs, among other things, was Subsection IV-B4, "Political Church, Sects, and Jews," headed by SS-*Obersturmbannführer* Eichmann.

The chief function of Group IV-C concerned protective custody; Group IV-D dealt with foreign workers, enemy aliens, and emigrants. The remaining groups were concerned with the regular duties of the political police such as security and passports.

Bureau VII, "Ideological Investigation and Evaluation," was directly concerned with the specific enemies of National Socialism. This was the scientific counterpart to Bureau IV, with its own subsections for Freemasons, Jews, political churches, Marxists, liberals, political emigration, separatists, pacifists, and reactionaries.

Other bureaus too, in particular the Foreign Intelligence Service (VI) under SS-*Oberführer* Schellenberg, were concerned in many different ways with the enemies not only of the German state but also of the National Socialist ideology. "Positive" work was also undertaken in the Reich Security Department, especially in Bureau III, "Spheres of German Life" under SS-*Brigadeführer* Ohlendorff, which included groups for ethnic affairs and culture with subsections for (among other things) "Racial and National Health," "Science," and "Education and Religious Life."

Thus Hitler's doctrine of the enemies had grown into a gigantic organization whose significance increased from year to year. It is noteworthy that the concentration camps—to the outside world the best-known consequence of National Socialism's systematic combating of enemies—developed from relatively small beginnings. In 1937, after the initial phase of uncontrolled terror, conducted mainly by the SA in improvised camps against its enemies, there were only three camps left, under the "Leader of the Death's Head Units and Concentration Camps." These camps contained a few thousand inmates, not all of whom were political prisoners. It was no mere chance that National Socialism had achieved victory by riding the wave of its alliance with the nationalist revolution, and if it did not immediately deal severely with all its enemies, this was partly because it had not yet revealed to all the scope and intrinsic nature of its opposition. But 1938 already saw a marked increase in the number of inmates, especially in the wake of the pogrom of November, 1938. From then on, "protective custody," which the Gestapo was empowered to decree, took the place, both in extent and severity, more and more of the regular punishments of the law, and during the war the German concentration camps soon became in size and importance the institutions the world later came to know. Nevertheless, this was not due *solely* to a striving for power on the part of the Reich Security Department, any more than was the increasing take-over of the functions of the courts, which found notorious expression, for example, in the agreement between Himmler and Thierack.* Rather, one must take into consideration the fact that as the years went by, the enormous and implacable opposition which National Socialism had created for itself emerged with growing clarity and self-confidence, and that the center of the attack on this opposition, the SS and the Reich Security Department, had to increase the severity of its measures to match the increasing resistance which this severity called forth.

And so the transition is made to the final and most terrible chapter of all. This is not to imply that the *will to destruction* emerged only during one stage of the ever-intensifying battle. On the contrary, it is highly typical that this will was palpable in the very first days of the war, that it exerted its influence in many areas, that it pursued its course with the participation of the most varied departments: in other words, it formed part of the original severity. However, this does not preclude the fact that it became more intense as time went on till it finally could give the impression of being impelled.

September 1, 1939, is the date of a decree of Hitler's which became the basis for the Third Reich's program of euthanasia. Soon after the defeat of Poland, Hitler ordered Frank to eliminate the Polish intelli-

* Thierack, Reich Minister of Justice, agreed with Himmler in 1942 that prisoners in certain categories could be "worked to death."—Ed.

gentsia. The decree relating to the commissars ordered the wholesale elimination of the political commissars of the Red Army.

Nevertheless, for Hitler and Himmler as well as for posterity, the emphasis was entirely on the annihilation of the Jews. This process differed essentially from all other extermination actions, both as to scope and to intention. It is impossible here to go deeply into its organization, just as its history could not be depicted earlier in this study. A few indications should be enough to show what these events meant in the light of practice.

A secret decree of Hitler's in the summer of 1941 apparently gave the signal to begin this gigantic task. It was directed by a small subsection of the Reich Security Department headed by a man with the rank of *Oberregierungsrat* (chief privy councilor). There is reason to believe the statement of one of the participants that scarcely more than a hundred persons were directly involved in this undertaking.

The extermination camps themselves were planned and administered by a section of the Economic and Administration Department of the SS, the existence of which was probably hardly known to most of the members of this enormous apparatus (who were chiefly concerned with the arming of the *Waffen-SS*). The selections and the extermination process itself were handled by only an infinitesimal number of SS men, since the actual burden was shifted onto Jewish prisoners.

Even those men who were principally concerned with the execution of the plan were not criminals by nature and had no criminal tendencies in the legal sense. The commandant of Auschwitz, Rudolf Höss, had had a strict Catholic upbringing and had volunteered during World War I as an enthusiastic sixteen-year-old. Admittedly he had been found guilty of political assassination and sent to the penitentiary (Martin Bormann had also been involved in the same incident), but while there his aversion to common criminals increased, and as an *Artamane* he dreamed of sunlight and new settlements until he finally ended up in the "death's head unit" and under the strict discipline of Theodor Eicke, who taught him that an SS man must be able to destroy even the members of his immediate family circle if they transgressed against the state or Adolf Hitler's ideas. On the whole he was probably less of a criminal in the conventional sense than a sentimentalist.

Himmler's ideas are well illustrated by a letter he wrote to the commandant of a concentration camp he visited. He was indignant that a young girl of racially good appearance should be employed in the camp bordello. Only old, completely degenerate prostitutes were to be used for such purposes; he never wanted to have to reproach himself for forsaking a young member of the *Volksgemeinschaft* without cause, and abandoning her once and for all to crime; the SS must not place itself on a level with the law, in whose prisons young people were corrupted for the rest of their lives.

There is a third noteworthy aspect. The transportation of Jews robbed the Wehrmacht of precious freight space, the number of armament workers was reduced in defiance of all economic reason; the closer the Russian armies approached, the more fanatically did Eichmann endeavor to see that the Hungarian Jews were also carried off to their fate.

All this leads to the following conclusions:

This procedure, kept secret though it was, nevertheless corresponded to the central intention of National Socialism. In his Poznan speech Himmler said: "We had the moral right, we had the obligation toward our people, to kill this people which wanted to kill us." A bacillus had been exterminated; now the important thing was to survive the operation without suffering injury to the soul, to the character. National Socialism had been talking for twenty-five years about this bacillus and the world sickness it caused. Alfred Rosenberg may have all his life considered the talk of "extermination" and "elimination" to be metaphorical, but Hitler and Himmler at any rate were more logically consistent.

Not only were they more consistent: in terms of their own thinking they were also right. One cannot make implacable enemies of Communists and democrats, reactionaries and Christians, Russians and Anglo-Saxons, and still believe in a lasting victory without assuming that all this opposition aroused by one's own demands is attributable to an identifiable "instigator."

In Hitler's extermination of the Jews it was not a case of criminals committing criminal deeds, but of a uniquely monstrous action in which principles ran riot in a frenzy of self-destruction.

The fact that National Socialism had to execute the very essence of its doctrine as a clandestine process, but that it also was unable and unwilling to keep it sufficiently secret for it not to be suspected gradually by the uninitiated, had a curious and very characteristic result. When Hitler's retinue of leaders were on trial at Nuremberg, there was not one who had not been inspired by moderate and sensible views. Sabotage of Hitler's extreme commands had—it now became apparent —begun with the next man in line in the government and was effectively carried out down to the lowest levels in the chain of command. Even the chief of the Security Police and the Security Service, SS-

Obergruppenführer Kaltenbrunner had, according to his testimony, endeavored to apply the brakes and improve the situation wherever he could, and in the end whatever he did was done out of regard for the future of his native land Austria. After the Führer's death the core of leadership of the National Socialist state snapped back, like a steel spring wound up too long, to its original position and became a body of well-meaning and cultured Central Europeans.

The astonishment of many prosecutors, who had naïvely imagined a fascist dictatorship to be a conspiracy of bandits, was no doubt considerable. Not a single one of the accused made any attempt whatever to justify the extermination measures. Not one testified defiantly to the necessity of the war for the conquest of living space and its unprecedented methods. These men had been better people than most of the world had assumed. But they had been weaker in spirit than one might have supposed. They wanted German sovereignty, but they did not, like Hitler, take into account what sovereignty means today. They wanted a war-efficient state, but they did not, like Hitler, consider what a modern and autonomously waged war implies; they vigorously defended the social order in the traditional German sense, but they did not realize the sole means by which it could be finally secured. They combated the Jews, but they failed to recognize that even a complete emigration, according to the intrinsic meaning of the National Socialist doctrine, could not accomplish any genuinely essential changes. No wonder they became the prey of the more logically consistent mind.

But what is the meaning of a consistency which no one is prepared to profess any more? Even after a total defeat of the Western democracies, countless people would have clung to the conviction which is the very cornerstone of liberal and democratic belief—that personal inviolability and dignity must be the boundary and objective of all politics. Even after a destruction of the Soviet Union, countless people the world over would have defended the doctrine which is the heart of communism—that only socialization of the means of production can open up the path to a better world. The core of National Socialism, the doctrine of world salvation through the elimination of the disease-spreading Jews, was forsaken after the defeat even by the innermost circles among the leaders. All that remained was a few trivialities and shallow claims. It was not the documents of the prosecution but the documents of the defense that set the final seal on Adolf Hitler's death. And this death meant, if not the end of fascism, certainly the end of its era.

4. The Dictator

ALAN BULLOCK

I

In the spring of 1938, on the eve of his greatest triumphs, Adolf Hitler entered his fiftieth year. His physical appearance was unimpressive, his bearing still awkward. The falling lock of hair and the smudge of his moustache added nothing to a coarse and curiously undistinguished face, in which the eyes alone attracted attention. In appearance at least Hitler could claim to be a man of the people, a plebeian through and through, with none of the physical characteristics of the racial superiority he was always invoking. The quality which his face possessed was that of mobility, an ability to express the most rapidly changing moods, at one moment smiling and charming, at another cold and imperious, cynical and sarcastic, or swollen and livid with rage.

Speech was the essential medium of his power, not only over his audiences but over his own temperament. Hitler talked incessantly, often using words less to communicate his thoughts than to release the hidden spring of his own and others' emotions, whipping himself and his audience into anger or exaltation by the sound of his voice. Talk had another function, too. 'Words,' he once said, 'build bridges into unexplored regions.' As he talked, conviction would grow until certainty came and the problem was solved.

Hitler always showed a distrust of argument and criticism. Unable to argue coolly himself, since his early days in Vienna his one resort had been to shout his opponent down. The questioning of his assumptions or of his facts rattled him and threw him out of his stride, less because of any intellectual inferiority than because words, and even facts, were to him not a means of rational communication and logical analysis, but devices for manipulating emotion. The introduction of intellectual processes of criticism and analysis marked the intrusion of hostile elements which disturbed the exercise of this power. Hence

Source: "The Dictator" and "Epilogue" from *Hitler: A Study in Tyranny*. Completely Revised Edition, by Alan Bullock. Copyright © 1962 by Alan Bullock. Reprinted by permission of Harper and Row, Publishers, and British publishers Odhams Books Limited.

Hitler's hatred of the intellectual: in the masses 'instinct is supreme and from instinct comes faith. . . . While the healthy common folk instinctively close their ranks to form a community of the people, the intellectuals run this way and that, like hens in a poultry-yard. With them it is impossible to make history; they cannot be used as elements supporting a community.'

For the same reason Hitler rated the spoken above the written word: 'False ideas and ignorance may be set aside by means of instruction, but emotional resistance never can. Nothing but an appeal to hidden forces will be effective here. And that appeal can scarcely be made by any writer. Only the orator can hope to make it.'

As an orator Hitler had obvious faults. The timbre of his voice was harsh, very different from the beautiful quality of Goebbels's. He spoke at too great length; was often repetitive and verbose; lacked lucidity and frequently lost himself in cloudy phrases. These short-comings, however, mattered little beside the extraordinary impression of force, the immediacy of passion, the intensity of hatred, fury, and menace conveyed by the sound of the voice alone without regard to what he said.

One of the secrets of his mastery over a great audience was his instinctive sensitivity to the mood of a crowd, a flair for divining the hidden passions, resentments and longings in their minds. In *Mein Kampf* he says of the orator: 'He will always follow the lead of the great mass in such a way that from the living emotion of his hearers the apt word which he needs will be suggested to him and in its turn this will go straight to the hearts of his hearers.'

One of his most bitter critics, Otto Strasser, wrote:

Hitler responds to the vibration of the human heart with the delicacy of a seismograph, or perhaps of a wireless receiving set, enabling him, with a certainty with which no conscious gift could endow him, to act as a loudspeaker proclaiming the most secret desires, the least admissible instincts, the sufferings, and personal revolts of a whole nation. . . . I have been asked many times what is the secret of Hitler's extraordinary power as a speaker. I can only attribute it to his uncanny intuition, which infallibly diagnoses the ills from which his audience is suffering. If he tries to bolster up his argument with theories or quotations from books he has only imperfectly understood, he scarcely rises above a very poor mediocrity. But let him throw away his crutches and step out boldly, speaking as the spirit moves him, and he is promptly transformed into one of the greatest speakers of the century. . . . Adolf Hitler enters a hall. He sniffs the air. For a minute he gropes, feels his way, senses the atmosphere. Suddenly he bursts forth. His words go like an arrow to their target, he touches each private wound on the raw, liberating the mass unconscious, expressing its innermost aspirations, telling it what it most wants to hear.

Hitler's power to bewitch an audience has been likened to the occult arts of the African medicine-man or the Asiatic Shaman; others have compared it to the sensitivity of a medium, and the magnetism of a hypnotist.

The conversations recorded by Hermann Rauschning for the period 1932–4, and by the table talk at the Führer's H.Q. for the period 1941–2, reveal Hitler in another favourite role, that of visionary and prophet. This was the mood in which Hitler indulged, talking far into the night, in his house on the Obersalzberg, surrounded by the remote peaks and silent forests of the Bavarian Alps; or in the Eyrie he had built six thousand feet up on the Kehlstein, above the Berghof, approached only by a mountain road blasted through the rock and a lift guarded by doors of bronze. There he would elaborate his fabulous schemes for a vast empire embracing the Eurasian Heartland of the geopoliticians; his plans for breeding a new élite biologically pre-selected; his design for reducing whole nations to slavery in the foundation of his new empire. Such dreams had fascinated Hitler since he wrote *Mein Kampf*. It was easy in the late 1920s and early 1930s to dismiss them as the product of a disordered and overheated imagination soaked in the political romanticism of Wagner and Houston Stewart Chamberlain. But these were still the themes of Hitler's table talk in 1941–2 and by then, master of the greater part of Europe and on the eve (as he believed) of conquering Russia and the Ukraine, Hitler had shown that he was capable of translating his fantasies into a terrible reality. The invasion of Russia, the S.S. extermination squads, the planned elimination of the Jewish race; the treatment of the Poles and Russians, the Slav *Untermenschen*—these, too, were the fruits of Hitler's imagination.

All this combines to create a picture of which the best description is Hitler's own famous sentence: 'I go the way that Providence dictates with the assurance of a sleepwalker.' The former French Ambassador speaks of him as 'a man possessed'; Hermann Rauschning writes: 'Dostoevsky might well have invented him, with the morbid derangement and the pseudo-creativeness of his hysteria'; one of the Defence Counsel at the Nuremberg Trials, Dr Dix, quoted a passage from Goethe's *Dichtung und Wahrheit* describing the Demoniac and applied this very aptly to Hitler. With Hitler, indeed, one is uncomfortably aware of never being far from the realm of the irrational.

But this is only half the truth about Hitler, for the baffling problem about this strange figure is to determine the degree to which he was swept along by a genuine belief in his own inspiration and the degree to which he deliberately exploited the irrational side of human nature, both in himself and others, with a shrewd calculation. For it is salutary to recall, before accepting the Hitler Myth at anything like its face value, that it was Hitler who invented the myth, assiduously cultivating and manipulating it for his own ends. So long as he did this he was brilliantly successful; it was when he began to believe in his own magic, and accept the myth of himself as true, that his flair faltered.

So much has been made of the charismatic nature of Hitler's leadership that it is easy to forget the astute and cynical politician in him. It is this mixture of calculation and fanaticism, with the difficulty of telling where one ends and the other begins, which is the peculiar charatceristic of Hitler's personality: to ignore or underestimate either element is to present a distorted picture.

II

The link between the different sides of Hitler's character was his extraordinary capacity for self-dramatization. 'This so-called *Wahnsystem,* or capacity for self-delusion,' Sir Nevile Henderson, the British Ambassador, wrote, 'was a regular part of his technique. It helped him both to work up his own passions and to make his people believe anything that he might think good for them.' Again and again one is struck by the way in which, having once decided rationally on a course of action, Hitler would whip himself into a passion which enabled him to bear down all opposition, and provided him with the motive power to enforce his will on others. An obvious instance of this is the synthetic fury, which he could assume or discard at will, over the treatment of German minorities abroad. When it was a question of refusing to listen to the bitter complaints of the Germans in the South Tyrol, or of uprooting the German inhabitants of the Baltic States, he sacrificed them to the needs of his Italian and Russian alliances with indifference. So long as good relations with Poland were necessary to his foreign policy he showed little interest in Poland's German minority. But when it suited his purpose to make the 'intolerable wrongs' of the Austrian Nazis, or the Germans in Czechoslovakia and Poland, a ground for action against these states, he worked himself into a frenzy of indignation, with the immediate—and calculated—result that London and Paris, in their anxiety for peace, exerted increased pressure on Prague or Warsaw to show restraint and make further concessions to the German demands.

One of Hitler's most habitual devices was to place himself on the defensive, to accuse those who opposed or obstructed him of aggression and malice, and to pass rapidly from a tone of outraged innocence to the full thunders of moral indignation. It was always the other side who were to blame, and in turn he denounced the Communists, the Jews, the Republican Government, or the Czechs, the Poles, and the Bolsheviks for their 'intolerable' behaviour which forced him to take drastic action in self-defence.

Hitler in a rage appeared to lose all control of himself. His face became mottled and swollen with fury, he screamed at the top of his voice, spitting out a stream of abuse, waving his arms wildly and drumming on the table or the wall with his fists. As suddenly as he had begun he would stop, smooth down his hair, straighten his collar and resume a more normal voice.

This skilful and deliberate exploitation of his own temperament extended to other moods than anger. When he wanted to persuade or win someone over he could display great charm. Until the last days of his life he retained an uncanny gift of personal magnetism which defies analysis, but which many who met him have described. This was connected with the curious power of his eyes, which are persistently said to have had some sort of hypnotic quality. Similarly, when he wanted to frighten or shock, he showed himself a master of brutal and threatening language, as in the celebrated interviews with Schuschnigg and President Hacha.*

Yet another variation in his roles was the impression of concentrated will-power and intelligence, the leader in complete command of the situation and with a knowledge of the facts which dazzled the generals or ministers summoned to receive his orders. To sustain this part he drew on his remarkable memory, which enabled him to reel off complicated orders of battle, technical specifications and long lists of names and dates without a moment's hesitation. Hitler cultivated this gift of memory assiduously. The fact that subsequently the details and figures which he cited were often found to contain inaccuracies did not matter: it was the immediate effect at which he aimed. The swiftness of the transition from one mood to another was startling: one moment his eyes would be filled with tears and pleading, the next blazing with fury, or glazed with the faraway look of the visionary.

* President Hacha of Czechoslovakia yielded to Hitler's demand for the dismemberment of his country in 1939.—Ed.

Hitler, in fact, was a consummate actor, with the actor's and orator's facility for absorbing himself in a role and convincing himself of the truth of what he was saying at the time he said it. In his early years he was often awkward and unconvincing, but with practice the part became second nature to him, and with the immense prestige of success behind him, and the resources of a powerful state at his command, there were few who could resist the impression of the piercing eyes, the Napoleonic pose, and the 'historic' personality.

Hitler had the gift of all great politicians for grasping the possibilities of a situation more swiftly than his opponents. He saw, as no other politician did, how to play on the grievances and resentments of the German people, as later he was to play on French and British fear of war and fear of Communism. His insistence upon preserving the forms of legality in the struggle for power showed a brilliant understanding of the way to disarm opposition, just as the way in which he undermined the independence of the German Army showed his grasp of the weaknesses of the German Officer Corps.

A German word, *Fingerspitzengefühl*—'finger-tip feeling'—which was often applied to Hitler, well describes his sense of opportunity and timing.

No matter what you attempt [Hitler told Rauschning on one occasion], if an idea is not yet mature you will not be able to realize it. Then there is only one thing to do: have patience, wait, try again, wait again. In the subconscious, the work goes on. It matures, sometimes it dies. Unless I have the inner, incorruptible conviction: *this is the solution,* I do nothing. Not even if the whole Party tries to drive me into action.

Hitler knew how to wait in 1932, when his insistence on holding out until he could secure the Chancellorship appeared to court disaster. Foreign policy provides another instance. In 1939 he showed great patience while waiting for the situation to develop after direct negotiations with Poland had broken down and while the Western Powers were seeking to reach a settlement with Soviet Russia. Clear enough about his objectives, he contrived to keep his plans flexible. In the case of the annexation of Austria and of the occupation of Prague, he made the final decision on the spur of the moment.

Until he was convinced that the right moment had come Hitler would find a hundred excuses for procrastination. His hesitation in such cases was notorious: his refusal to make up his mind to stand as a

Presidential candidate in 1932, and his attempt to defer taking action against Röhm and the S.A. in 1934, are two obvious examples. Once he had made up his mind to move, however, he would act boldly, taking considerable risks, as in the reoccupation of the Rhineland in 1936, or the invasion of Norway and Denmark just before the major campaign in the west.

Surprise was a favourite gambit of Hitler's, in politics, diplomacy, and war: he gauged the psychological effect of sudden, unexpected hammer-blows in paralysing opposition. An illustration of his appreciation of the value of surprise and quick decision, even when on the defensive, is the second presidential campaign of 1932. It had taken Goebbels weeks to persuade Hitler to stand for the Presidency at all. The defeat in the first ballot brought Goebbels to despair; but Hitler, now that he had committed himself, with great presence of mind dictated the announcement that he would stand a second time and got it on to the streets almost before the country had learned of his defeat. In war the psychological effect of the *Blitzkrieg* was just as important in Hitler's eyes as the strategic: it gave the impression that the German military machine was more than life-size, that it possessed some virtue of invincibility against which ordinary men could not defend themselves.

No régime in history has ever paid such careful attention to psychological factors in politics. Hitler was a master of mass emotion. To attend one of his big meetings was to go through an emotional experience, not to listen to an argument or a programme. Yet nothing was left to chance on these occasions. Every device for heightening the emotional intensity, every trick of the theatre was used. The Nuremberg rallies held every year in September were masterpieces of theatrical art, with the most carefully devised effects. 'I had spent six years in St. Petersburg before the war in the best days of the old Russian ballet,' wrote Sir Nevile Henderson, 'but for grandiose beauty I have never seen a ballet to compare with it.' To see the films of the Nuremberg rallies even today is to be recaptured by the hypnotic effect of thousands of men marching in perfect order, the music of the massed bands, the forest of standards and flags, the vast perspectives of the stadium, the smoking torches, the dome of searchlights. The sense of power, of force and unity was irresistible, and all converged with a mounting crescendo of excitement on the supreme moment when the Führer himself made his entry. Paradoxically, the man who

was most affected by such spectacles was their originator, Hitler himself, and, as Rosenberg remarks in his memoirs, they played an indispensable part in the process of self-intoxication.

Hitler had grasped as no one before him what could be done with a
combination of propaganda and terrorism. For the complement to the
attractive power of the great spectacles was the compulsive power of
the Gestapo, the S.S., and the concentration camp, heightened once
again by skilful propaganda. Hitler was helped in this not only by his
own perception of the sources of power in a modern urbanized mass-
society, but also by possession of the technical means to manipulate
them. This was a point well made by Albert Speer, Hitler's highly intelligent Minister for Armaments and War Production, in the final
speech he made at his trial after the war.

Hitler's dictatorship [Speer told the court] differed in one fundamental
point from all its predecessors in history. His was the first dictatorship in
the present period of modern technical development, a dictatorship which
made complete use of all technical means for the domination of its own
country.

Through technical devices like the radio and the loud-speaker, eighty
million people were deprived of independent thought. It was thereby possible to subject them to the will of one man. . . .

Earlier dictators needed highly qualified assistants, even at the lowest
level, men who could think and act independently. The totalitarian system
in the period of modern technical development can dispense with them;
the means of communication alone make it possible to mechanize the
lower leadership. As a result of this there arises the new type of the uncritical recipient of orders. . . . Another result was the far-reaching supervision of the citizens of the State and the maintenance of a high degree of
secrecy for criminal acts.

The nightmare of many a man that one day nations could be dominated
by technical means was all but realized in Hitler's totalitarian system.

In making use of the formidable power which was thus placed in his
hands Hitler had one supreme, and fortunately rare, advantage: he
had neither scruples nor inhibitions. He was a man without roots, with
neither home nor family; a man who admitted no loyalties, was bound
by no traditions, and felt respect neither for God nor man. Throughout his career Hitler showed himself prepared to seize any advantage
that was to be gained by lying, cunning, treachery, and unscrupulousness. He demanded the sacrifice of millions of German lives for the
sacred cause of Germany, but in the last year of the war was ready to
destroy Germany rather than surrender his power or admit defeat.

Wary and secretive, he entertained a universal distrust. He admitted no one to his counsels. He never let down his guard, or gave himself away. 'He never,' Schacht wrote, 'let slip an unconsidered word. He never said what he did not intend to say and he never blurted out a secret. Everything was the result of cold calculation.'

While he was in Landsberg gaol, as long ago as 1924, Hitler had preserved his position in the Party by alowing rivalries to develop among the other leaders, and he continued to apply the same principle of 'divide and rule' after he became Chancellor. There was always more than one office operating in any field. A dozen different agencies quarrelled over the direction of propaganda, of economic policy, and the intelligence services. Before 1938 Hitler continually went behind the back of the Foreign Office to make use of Ribbentrop's special bureau or to get information through Party channels. The dualism of Party and State organizations, each with one or more divisions for the same function, was deliberate. In the end this reduced efficiency, but it strengthened Hitler's position by allowing him to play off one department against another. For the same reason Hitler put an end to regular cabinet meetings and insisted on dealing with ministers singly, so that they could not combine against him. 'I have an old principle,' he told Ludecke: 'only to say what must be said to him who must know it, and only when he must know it.' Only the Führer kept all the threads in his hand and saw the whole design. If ever a man exercised absolute power it was Adolf Hitler.

He had a particular and inveterate distrust of experts. He refused to be impressed by the complexity of problems, insisting until it became monotonous that if only the will was there any problem could be solved. Schacht, to whose advice he refused to listen and whose admiration was reluctant, says of him: 'Hitler often did find astonishingly simple solutions for problems which had seemed to others insoluble. He had a genius for invention. . . . His solutions were often brutal, but almost always effective.' In an interview with a French correspondent early in 1936 Hitler himself claimed this power of simplification as his greatest gift:

It has been said that I owe my success to the fact that I have created a *mystique* . . . or more simply that I have been lucky. Well, I will tell you what has carried me to the position I have reached. Our political problems appeared complicated. The German people could make nothing of them. In these circumstances they preferred to leave it to the professional politicians to get them out of this confused mess. I, on the other hand, simpli-

fied the problems and reduced them to the simplest terms. The masses
realized this and followed me.

The crudest of Hitler's simplifications was the most effective: in
almost any situation, he believed, force or the threat of force would
settle matters—and in an astonishingly large number of cases he
proved right.

III

In his Munich days Hitler always carried a heavy riding-whip, made
of hippopotamus hide. The impression he wanted to convey—and
every phrase and gesture in his speeches reflected the same purpose—
was one of force, decision, will. Yet Hitler had nothing of the easy,
assured toughness of a condottiere like Göring. His strength of personality, far from being natural to him, was the product of an exertion of
will: from this sprang a harsh, jerky and over-emphatic manner which
was very noticeable in his early days as a politician. No word was more
frequently on Hitler's lips than 'will', and his whole career from 1919
to 1945 is a remarkable achievement of will-power.

To say that Hitler was ambitious scarcely describes the intensity of
the lust for power and the craving to dominate which consumed him.
It was the will to power in its crudest and purest form, not identifying
itself with the triumph of a principle as with Lenin or Robespierre—
for the only principle of Nazism was power and domination for its
own sake—nor finding satisfaction in the fruits of power, for, by comparison with other Nazi leaders like Göring, Hitler lived an ascetic
life. For a long time Hitler succeeded in identifying his own power
with the recovery of Germany's old position in the world, and there
were many in the 1930s who spoke of him as a fanatical patriot. But
as soon as the interests of Germany began to diverge from his own,
from the beginning of 1943 onwards, his patriotism was seen at its
true value—Germany, like everything else in the world, was only a
means, a vehicle for his own power, which he would sacrifice with the
same indifference as the lives of those he sent to the Eastern Front. By
its nature this was an insatiable appetite, securing only a temporary
gratification by the exercise of power, then restlessly demanding an
ever further extension of it.

Although, looking backwards, it is possible to detect anticipations
of this monstrous will to power in Hitler's early years, it remained
latent until the end of the First World War and only began to appear
noticeably when he reached his thirties. From the account in *Mein*

Kampf it appears that the shock of defeat and the Revolution of November 1918 produced a crisis in which hitherto dormant faculties were awakened and directed towards the goal of becoming a politician and founding a new movement. Resentment is so marked in Hitler's attitude as to suggest that it was from the earlier experiences of his Vienna and Munich days, before the war, that there sprang a compelling urge to revenge himself upon a world which had slighted and ignored him. Hatred, touchiness, vanity are characteristics upon which those who spent any time in his company constantly remark. Hatred intoxicated Hitler. Many of his speeches are long diatribes of hate— against the Jews, against the Marxists, against the Czechs, the Poles, and the French. He had a particularly venomous contempt for the intellectuals and the educated middle-classes, 'the gentlemen with diplomas', who belonged to that comfortable bourgeois world which had once rejected him and which he was determined to shake out of its complacency and destroy in revenge.

No less striking was his constant need of praise. His vanity was inappeasable, and the most fulsome flattery was received as no more than his due. The atmosphere of adulation in which he lived seems to have deadened the critical faculties of all who came into it. The most banal platitudes and the most grotesque errors of taste and judgement, if uttered by the Führer, were accepted as the words of inspired genius. It is to the credit of Röhm and Gregor Strasser, who had known Hitler for a long time, that they were irritated and totally unimpressed by this Byzantine attitude towards the Führer, to which even the normally cynical Goebbels capitulated: no doubt, this was among the reasons why they were murdered.

A hundred years before Hitler became Chancellor, Hegel, in a famous course of lectures at the University of Berlin, had pointed to the role of 'World-historical individuals' as the agents by which 'the Will of the World Spirit', the plan of Providence, is carried out.

They may all be called Heroes, in as much as they have derived their purposes and their vocation, not from the calm regular course of things, sanctioned by the existing order; but from a concealed fount, from that inner Spirit, still hidden beneath the surface, which impinges on the outer world as on a shell and bursts it into pieces. (Such were Alexander, Caesar, Napoleon.) They were practical, political men. But at the same time they were thinking men, who had an insight into the requirements of the time— what was ripe for development. This was the very Truth for their age, for their world. . . . It was theirs to know this nascent principle, the necessary, directly sequent step in progress, which their world was to take; to make this their aim, and to expend their energy in promoting it. World-historical men—the Heroes of an epoch—must therefore be recognized as its clear-sighted ones: *their* deeds, *their* words are the best of their time.

To the objection that the activity of such individuals frequently flies in the face of morality, and involves great sufferings for others, Hegel replied:

World History occupies a higher ground than that on which morality has properly its position, which is personal character and the conscience of individuals. . . . Moral claims which are irrelevant must not be brought into collision with world-historical deeds and their accomplishment. The litany of private virtues—modesty, humility, philanthropy, and forbear-ance—must not be raised against them. So mighty a form [he adds else-where] must trample down many an innocent flower—crush to pieces many an object in its path.

Whether Hitler ever read Hegel or not, like so many other passages in nineteenth-century German literature—in Nietzsche, in Schopen-hauer, in Wagner—it finds an echo in Hitler's belief about himself. Cynical though he was, Hitler's cynicism stopped short of his own person: he came to believe that he was a man with a mission, marked out by Providence, and therefore exempt from the ordinary canons of human conduct.

Hitler probably held some such belief about himself from an early period. It was clear enough in the speech he made at his trial in 1924, and after he came out of prison those near him noticed that he began to hold aloof, to set a barrier between himself and his followers. After he came to power it became more noticeable. It was in March 1936, that he made the famous assertion already quoted: 'I go the way that Providence dictates with the assurance of a sleep-walker. In 1937 he told an audience at Würzburg:

However weak the individual may be when compared with the omnipo-tence and will of Providence, yet at the moment when he acts as Provi-dence would have him act he becomes immeasurably strong. Then there streams down upon him that force which has marked all greatness in the world's history. And when I look back only on the five years which lie behind us, then I feel that I am justified in saying: That has not been the work of man alone.

Just before the occupation of Austria, in February 1938, he declared in the Reichstag:

Above all, a man who feels it his duty at such an hour to assume the leadership of his people is not responsible to the laws of parliamentary usage or to a particular democratic conception, but solely to the mission placed upon him. And anyone who interferes with this misson is an enemy of the people.

It was in this sense of mission that Hitler, a man who believed neither in God nor in conscience ('a Jewish invention, a blemish like circumcision'), found both justification and absolution. He was the Siegfried come to reawaken Germany to greatness, for whom morality, suffering and 'the litany of private virtues' were irrelevant. It was by such dreams that he sustained the ruthlessness and determination of his will. So long as this sense of mission was balanced by the cynical calculations of the politician, it represented a source of strength, but success was fatal. When half Europe lay at his feet and all need of restraint was removed, Hitler abandoned himself entirely to megalomania. He became convinced of his own infallibility. But when he began to look to the image he had created to work miracles of its own accord—instead of exploiting it—his gifts deteriorated and his intuition deluded him. Ironically, failure sprang from the same capacity which brought him success, his power of self-dramatization, his ability to convince himself. His belief in his power to work miracles kept him going when the more sceptical Mussolini faltered. Hitler played out his 'world-historical' role to the bitter end. But it was this same belief which curtained him in illusion and blinded him to what was actually happening, leading him into that arrogant overestimate of his own genius which brought him to defeat. The sin which Hitler committed was that which the ancient Greeks called *hybris,* the sin of overweening pride, of believing himself to be more than a man. No man was ever more surely destroyed by the image he had created than Adolf Hitler.

IV

After he became Chancellor Hitler had to submit to a certain degree of routine. This was against his natural inclination. He hated systematic work, hated to submit to any discipline, even self-imposed. Administration bored him and he habitually left as much as he could to others, an important fact in explaining the power of men like Hess and Martin Bormann, who relieved him of much of his paper-work.

When he had a big speech to prepare he would put off beginning work on it until the last moment. Once he could bring himself to begin dictating he worked himself into a passion, rehearsing the whole performance and shouting so loudly that his voice echoed through the

neighbouring rooms. The speech composed, he was a man with a load
off his mind. He would invite his secretaries to lunch, praising and
flattering them, and often using his gifts as a mimic to amuse them.
He fussed about corrections, however, especially about his ability to
read them when delivering his speech, for Hitler wore spectacles in his
office, but refused to be seen wearing them in public. To overcome this
difficulty his speeches were typed on a special machine with characters
twelve millimetres high. Although his secretaries, like his personal
servants, tended to stay with him, he was not an easy man to work for,
incalculable in his moods and exacting in his demands.

Most North Germans regarded such *Schlamperei,* slovenliness, and
lack of discipline as a typical Austrian trait. In Hitler's eyes it was part
of his artist nature: he should have been a great painter or architect,
he complained, and not a statesman at all. On art he held the most
opinionated views and would tolerate no dissent. He passionately hated
all forms of modern art, a term in which he included most painting
since the Impressionists. When the House of German Art was to be
opened in 1937, Hitler dismissed the pictures chosen by the jury and
threatened to cancel the exhibition, finally agreeing to let Hoffmann,
his photographer, make a fresh choice subject to his own final approval. Hoffmann filled one room with more modern paintings, in the
hope of winning Hitler over, only to see the lot swept away with an
angry gesture. Hitler's taste was for the Classical models of Greece and
Rome, and for the Romantic: Gothic and Renaissance art were too
Christian for his liking. He had a particular fondness for nineteenth-
century painting of the more sentimental type, which he collected for a
great museum to be built in Linz, the town he regarded as his home.
He admired painstaking craftsmanship, and habitually kept a pile of
paper on his desk for sketching in idle moments.

Architecture appealed strongly to him—especially Baroque—and
he had grandiose plans for the rebuilding of Berlin, Munich, and
Nuremberg and the other big German cities. The qualities which attracted him were the monumental and the massive as in the new Reich
Chancellery: the architecture of the Third Reich, like the Pyramids,
was to reflect the power of its rulers. In Munich Hitler spent many
hours in the studio of Professor Troost, his favourite architect. After
Troost's death Albert Speer succeeded to his position. To the last days
of his life Hitler never tired of playing with architectural models and
drawings of the great cities that would one day rise from the bombed
shells of the old, especially Linz.

Hitler looked upon himself not only as a connoisseur of painting and an authority on architecture, but as highly musical. In fact, his liking for music did not extend very much further than Wagner, some of Beethoven, and Bruckner, light opera like *Die Fledermaus* and such operettas as Lehar's *The Merry Widow* and *La Fille du Régiment*. Hitler never missed a Wagner festival at Bayreuth and he claimed to have seen such operas as *Die Meistersinger* and *Götterdämmerung* more than a hundred times. He was equally fond of the cinema, and at the height of the political struggle in 1932 he and Goebbels would slip into a picture-house to see *Mädchen in Uniform,* or Greta Garbo. When the Chancellery was rebuilt he had projectors and a screen installed on which he frequently watched films in the evening, including many of the foreign films he had forbidden in Germany.

Hitler rebuilt both the Chancellery and his house on Obersalzberg after he came to power, the original Haus Wachenfeld becoming the famous Berghof. He had a passion for big rooms, thick carpets, and tapestries. A sense of space pleased him, and at the Berghof the Great Hall and the Loggia had magnificent views over the mountains. Apart from this delight in building and interior decoration, Hitler's tastes were simple and altered little after he came to power. Rauschning, who was frequently in Hitler's company in 1933, speaks of 'the familiar blend of *petit bourgeois* pleasures and revolutionary talk'. He liked to be driven fast in a powerful car; he liked cream cakes and sweets (specially supplied by a Berlin firm); he liked flowers in his rooms, and dogs; he liked the company of pretty—but not clever— women; he liked to be at home up in the Bavarian mountains.

It was in the evenings that Hitler's vitality rose. He hated to go to bed—for he found it hard to sleep—and after dinner he would gather his guests and his household, including the secretaries, round the big fireplace in the Great Hall at the Berghof, or in the drawing-room of the Chancellery. There he sat and talked about every subject under the sun until two or three o'clock in the morning, often later. For long periods the conversation would lapse into a monologue, but to yawn or whisper was to incur immediate disfavour. Next morning Hitler would not rise until eleven.

There was little ceremony about life at the Berghof. Hitler had no fondness for formality or for big social occasions, where he rarely felt at ease and which he avoided as far as possible. Although he lived in considerable luxury, he had few needs. He was indifferent to the clothes he wore, ate very little, never touched meat, and neither smoked nor drank. Hitler not only kept a special vegetarian cook to prepare his meals for him, but held strongly that eating meat or any cooked food was a pernicious habit which had led to the decay of past civilizations. 'There's one thing I can predict to eaters of meat, that the world of the future will be vegetarian.'

The chief reason for Hitler's abstinence seems to have been anxiety about his health. He lived an unhealthy life, with little exercise or fresh air; he took part in no sport, never rode or swam, and he suffered a good deal from stomach disorders as well as from insomnia. With this went a horror of catching a cold or any form of infection. He was depressed at the thought of dying early, before he had had time to complete his schemes, and he hoped to add years to his life by careful dieting and avoiding alcohol, coffee, tea, and tobacco. In the late-night sessions round the fireplace Hitler never touched stimulants, not even real tea. Instead he sipped peppermint-tea or some other herbal drink. He became a crank as well as a hypochondriac, and preached the virtues of vegetarianism to his guests at table with the same insistence as he showed in talking politics.

Hitler had been brought up as a Catholic and was impressed by the organization and power of the Church. Its hierarchical structure, its skill in dealing with human nature and the unalterable character of its Creed, were all features from which he claimed to have learned. For the Protestant clergy he felt only contempt: 'They are insignificant little people, submissive as dogs, and they sweat with embarrassment when you talk to them. They have neither a religion they can take seriously nor a great position to defend like Rome.' It was 'the great position' of the Church that he respected, the fact that it had lasted for so many centuries; towards its teaching he showed the sharpest hostility. In Hitler's eyes Christianity was a religion fit only for slaves; he detested its ethics in particular. Its teaching, he declared, was a rebellion against the natural law of selection by struggle and the survival of the fittest. 'Taken to its logical extreme, Christianity would mean the systematic cultivation of the human failure.' From political considerations he restrained his anti-clericalism, seeing clearly the dangers of strengthening the Church by persecution. For this reason he was more circumspect than some of his followers, like Rosenberg and Bormann, in attacking the Church publicly. But, once the war was over, he promised himself, he would root out and destroy the influence of the Christian Churches. 'The evil that is gnawing our vitals,' he remarked in February 1942, 'is our priests, of both creeds. I can't at present give them the answer they've been asking for but . . . it's all written down in my big book. The time will come when I'll settle my account with them. . . .They'll hear from me all right. I shan't let myself be hampered with judicial samples.'

Earnest efforts to establish self-conscious pagan rites roused Hitler's scorn: 'Nothing would be more foolish,' he declared, 'than to reestablish the worship of Wotan. Our old mythology had ceased to be viable when Christianity implanted itself. . . . I especially wouldn't want our movement to acquire a religious character and institute a form of worship. It would be appalling for me, if I were to end up in the skin of a Buddha.'

Nor is there any evidence to substantiate the once popular belief that he resorted to astrology. His secretary says categorically that he had nothing but contempt for such practices, although faith in the stars was certainly common among some of his followers like Himmler.

The truth is that, in matters of religion at least, Hitler was a rationalist and a materialist. 'The dogma of Christianity,' he declared in one of his wartime conversations,

gets worn away before the advances of science. . . . Gradually the myths crumble. All that is left is to prove that in nature there is no frontier between the organic and the inorganic. When understanding of the universe has become widespread, when the majority of men know that the stars are not sources of light, but worlds, perhaps inhabited worlds like ours, then the Christian doctrine will be convicted of absurdity. . . . The man who lives in communion with nature necessarily finds himself in opposition to the Churches, and that's why they're heading for ruin—for science is bound to win.

It was in keeping with this nineteenth-century faith in science replacing the superstitions of religion that Hitler's plans for the rebuilding of Linz included a great observatory and planetarium as its centrepiece.

Thousands of excursionists will make a pilgrimage there every Sunday. They'll have access to the greatness of our universe. The pediment will bear this motto: 'The heavens proclaim the glory of the everlasting.' It will be our way of giving men a religious spirit, of teaching them humility —but without the priests. For Ptolemy the earth was the centre of the world. That changed with Copernicus. Today we know that our solar system is merely a solar system amongst many others. What could we do better than allow the greatest possible number of people like us to become aware of these marvels? . . . Put a small telescope in a village and you destroy a world of superstitions.

Hitler's belief in his own destiny held him back from a thoroughgoing atheism. 'The Russians,' he remarked on one occasion, 'were entitled to attack their priests, but they had no right to assail the idea of a supreme force. It's a fact that we're feeble creatures and that a creative force exits.' On another occasion he answered his own question:

By what would you have me replace the Christians' picture of the Beyond? What comes naturally to mankind is the sense of eternity and that sense is at the bottom of every man. The soul and the mind migrate, just as the body returns to nature. Thus life is eternally reborn from life. As for the 'why' of all that, I feel no need to rack my brains on the subject. The soul is unplumbable.

What interested Hitler was power, and his belief in Providence or Destiny was only a projection of his own sense of power. He had no feeling or understanding for either the spiritual side of human life or its emotional, affective side. Emotion to him was the raw material of power. The pursuit of power cast its harsh shadow like a blight over the whole of his life. Everything was sacrificed to the 'world historical' image; hence the poverty of his private life and of his human relationships.

After his early days in Munich, Hitler made few, if any, friends. In a nostalgic mood he would talk regretfully of the *Kampfzeit,* the Years of the Struggle, and of the comradeship he had shared with the *Alte Kämpfer,* the Old Fighters. With almost no exceptions, Hitler's familiars belonged to the Nazi Old Guard: Goebbels, Ley, Hess, Martin Bormann; his two adjutants, Julius Schaub and Wilhelm Bruckner; his chauffeur, Julius Schreck; Max Amann, the Party publisher; Franz Xavier Schwarz, the Party treasurer; Hoffmann, the court photographer. It was in this intimate circle, talking over the old days, in the Berghof or in his flat in Munich, that Hitler was most at his ease. Even towards those like Julius Streicher or Christian Weber, who were too disreputable to be promoted to high office, Hitler showed considerable loyalty; when Streicher's notorious behaviour finally led to his removal from the position of Gauleiter of Franconia, he was still protected by Hitler and allowed to live in peace on his farm.

Apart from a handful of men like Ribbentrop and Speer, Hitler never lost his distrust of those who came from the bourgeois world. It was on the Old Guard alone that he believed he could rely, for they were dependent on him. More than that, he found such company, however rough, more congenial than that of the Schachts and Neuraths, the bankers and generals, high officials and diplomats, who were eager to serve the new régime once it had come to power. Their stiff manners and 'educated' talk roused all his old class resentment and the suspicion that they sneered at him behind his back—as they did. Dictatorship knows no equals, and with the Old Guard Hitler was sure of his ascendancy. Even Göring and Goebbels, who stood on more equal terms with Hitler than any other of the Nazi leaders, knew very well that there were limits beyond which they dared not go. 'When a decision has to be taken,' Göring once told Sir Nevile Henderson, 'none of us count more than the stones on which we are standing. It is the Führer alone who decides.'

Hitler enjoyed and was at home in the company of women. At the beginning of his political career he owed much to the encouragement of women like Frau Hélène Bechstein, Frau Carola Hoffmann, and Frau Winnifried Wagner. Many women were fascinated by his hypnotic powers; there are well-attested accounts of the hysteria which affected women at his big meetings, and Hitler himself attached much importance to the women's vote. If ladies were present at table he knew how to be attentive and charming, as long as they had no intellectual pretensions and did not try to argue with him. Gossip connected his name with that of a number of women in whose company he had been frequently seen, and speculated eagerly on his relations with them, from Henny Hoffmann, the daughter of his photographer, and Leni Riefenstahl, the director of the films of the Nuremberg Rallies, to Unity Mitford, the sister-in-law of Sir Oswald Mosley, who attempted to commit suicide at Munich.

Much has been written, on the flimsiest evidence, about Hitler's sex life. Amongst the mass of conjecture, two hypotheses are worth serious consideration. The first is that Hitler was affected by syphilis.

There are several passages in *Mein Kampf* in which Hitler speaks with surprising emphasis of 'the scourge of venereal disease' and its effects. 'The problem of fighting venereal disease', he declared, 'should be placed before the public—not as a task for the nation but as *the* main task.' According to reports which Hanfstängl, for example, repeats, Hitler contracted syphilis while he was a young man in Vienna. This may well be malicious gossip but it is worth adding that more than one medical specialist has suggested that Hitler's later symptoms —psychologial as well as physical—could be those of a man suffering from the tertiary stage of syphilis. Unless, however, a medical report on Hitler should some day come to light this must remain an open question.

A second hypothesis, which is not of course inconsistent with the first, is that Hitler was incapable of normal sexual intercourse. Putzi Hanfstängl, who knew Hitler well in his Bavarian days and later, says plainly that he was impotent. He adds:

The abounding nervous energy which found no normal release sought compensation first in the subjection of his entourage, then of his country, then of Europe. . . . In the sexual no man's land in which he lived, he only once nearly found the woman, and never even the man, who might have brought him relief.

The gallantry, the hand-kissing and flowers, were an expression of admiration but led to nothing more. 'We used to think that Jenny Haugg, his driver's sister, was his girl-friend. . . . Jenny would often be sitting in the back-seat waiting for him. They would drive off together, but I knew he was only going to a café to stay up talking half the night. A bit of petting may have gone on, but that, it became clear to me, was all that Hitler was capable of. My wife summed him up very quickly: "Putzi," she said, "I tell you he is a neuter." '

This too must remain a hypothesis, but Hanfstängl's belief (which others shared) is not inconsistent with what is known of Hitler's relations with the only two women in whom he showed more than a passing interest—his niece, Geli Raubal, and the woman he married on the day before he took his life, Eva Braun.

Geli and Friedl Raubal, the daughters of Hitler's widowed half-sister, Angela Raubal, accompanied their mother when she came to keep house for Hitler on the Obersalzberg in 1925. Geli was then seventeen, simple and attractive, with a pleasant voice which she wanted to have trained for singing. During the next six years she became Hitler's constant companion, and when her uncle acquired his flat on the Prinz-Regentenstrasse she spent much time with him in Munich as well as up at the Obersalzberg. This period in Munich Hitler later described as the happiest in his life; he idolized this girl, who was twenty years younger than himself, took her with him whenever he could—in short, he fell in love with her. Whether Geli was ever in love with him is uncertain. She was flattered and impressed by her now famous uncle, she enjoyed going about with him, but she suffered from his hypersensitive jealousy. Hitler refused to let her have any life of her own; he refused to let her go to Vienna to have her voice trained; he was beside himself with fury when he discovered that she had allowed Emil Maurice, his chauffeur, to make love to her, and forbade her to have anything to do with any other man. Geli resented and was made unhappy by Hitler's possessiveness and domestic tyranny.

On the morning of 17 September 1931, Hitler left Munich with Hoffmann, his photographer and friend, after saying good-bye to Geli. He was bound for Hamburg, but had only got beyond Nuremberg when he was called to the telephone by Hess and told that Geli was dead. She had shot herself in his flat shortly after his departure. Why?

Hoffmann, who knew both Hitler and the girl well, believed that she was in love with someone else and committed suicide because she could not endure her uncle's despotic treatment of her. Frau Winter, the housekeeper, believed that she was in love with Hitler, and that her suicide followed from disappointment or frustration.

Whatever the reason, Geli's death dealt Hitler a greater blow than any other event in his life. For days he was inconsolable and his friends feared that he would take his own life. According to some accounts, his refusal to touch meat dates from the crisis through which he passed at this time. For the rest of his life he never spoke of Geli without tears coming into his eyes; according to his own statement to a number of witnesses, she was the only woman he ever loved, and there is no reason to doubt this statement. Whether he would ever have married her is another matter. Her room at the Berghof was kept exactly as she had left it, and remained untouched when the original Haus Wachenfeld was rebuilt. Her photograph hung in his room in Munich and Berlin, and flowers were always placed before it on the anniversary of her birth and death. There are mysteries in everyone's personality, not least in that strange, contradictory, and distorted character which was Adolf Hitler, and it is best to leave it as a mystery.

Hitler's relations with Eva Braun were on a different level. As Speer later remarked, 'For all writers of history, Eva Braun is going to be a disappointment.'

Eva was the middle of the three daughters of Fritz Braun, a master craftsman from Simbach on the Inn. She was a pretty, empty-headed blonde, with a round face and blue eyes, who worked as a shop girl in Hoffmann's photographer's shop. Hitler met her there, paid her a few casual compliments, gave her flowers, and occasionally invited her to be one of his party on an outing. The initiative was all on Eva's side: she told her friends that Hitler was in love with her and that she would make him marry her.

In the summer of 1932 (less than a year after Geli's death) Eva Braun, then twenty-one, attempted to commit suicide. Hitler was understandably sensitive to such a threat at a time when he was anxious to avoid any scandal and, according to Hoffmann, 'it was in this manner that Eva Braun got her way and became Hitler's *chère amie'*.

Hoffmann's further comment is worth quoting in full:

At that time there was established no liaison between them in the accepted sense of the word. Eva moved into his house, became the constant companion of his leisure hours and, to the best of my knowledge, that was all there was to it. Indeed, I can think of no more apt simile than once more to liken Hitler to some ardent collector, who preferred to gloat over his latest treasure in the privacy of his own collection. . . .

That Eva became his mistress some time or other before the end is certain, but when—neither I nor anyone else can say. Not at any time was there any perceptible change in his attitude towards her which might have pointed to the assumption of more intimate relations between them; and the secrecy which surrounded the whole affair is emphasized by the profound astonishment of all of us in his most intimate circle when, at the bitter end, the marriage was announced.

Eva was kept very much in the background. She stayed at Hitler's Munich flat, where Hitler saw her as occasion offered, or went to the Berghof when he was in residence there. This led to strained relations with Hitler's half-sister, Frau Raubal, who still kept house at the Berghof after Geli's death and hated the upstart Eva. After a series of rows, Frau Raubal left for good in 1936, and thereafter Eva took her place as *Hausfrau* and sat on Hitler's left hand when he presided at lunch.

Hitler rarely allowed Eva Braun to come to Berlin or appear in public with him. When big receptions or dinners were given she had to stay upstairs in her room. Only after her sister, Gretl, married Fegelein, Himmler's personal representative with the Führer, during the war, was she allowed to appear more freely in public. She could then be introduced as Frau Fegelein's sister and the Führer's reputation preserved untarnished.

Eva made no pretensions to intellectual gifts or to any understanding of politics. Her interests in life were sport—she was an excellent skier and swimmer—animals, the cinema, sex, and clothes. Such ideas as she had were drawn from cheap novelettes and trashy films, the sole subject of which was 'love'. In return for her privileged position she had to submit to the same petty tyranny that Hitler had attempted to establish over Geli. She only dared to dance or smoke in secret, because the Führer disapproved of both; she lived in constant terror lest a chance photograph or remark should rouse Hitler's anger at her being in the company of other men, yet herself suffered agonies of jealousy at Hitler's interest in the women he met. Sometimes he did not come to see her for weeks at a time, and fear that he would leave her for someone else made her life a misery. Dissatisfied with her ambiguous status, she longed for the respectability of marriage.

After the beginning of the war Eva's position became more secure. Hitler cut himself off from all social life and was wholly absorbed in the war. She had no more rivals to fear, and the liaison had now lasted so long that Hitler accepted her as a matter of course. On the other hand, she saw much less of him. In the latter part of the war Hitler paid few visits to the Berghof and she was not allowed to move to the Führer's headquarters. At no time was she in a position to influence even the most trivial discussions.

None the less, in time, Hitler became genuinely fond of Eva. Her empty-headedness did not disturb him; on the contrary, he detested women with views of their own. It was her loyalty which won his affection and it was as a reward for her loyalty that, after more than twelve years of a relationship which was more domestic than erotic in character, Hitler finally gave way and on the last day of his life married her. Before that he had always refused to discuss marriage on the grounds that it would be a hindrance to his career. Explaining his action in his will, he spoke of 'many years of true friendship', and there is little reason to doubt that he was sincere in saying this. In Eva's company he was at ease and could cease to play a part. The nearest he came to being either human or happy in normal terms was during the hours he spent sprawling back in his chair beside her at tea-time, walking with her on the terrace at the Berghof, or going for a picnic with a few friends.

Egotism is a malignant as well as an ugly vice, and it may well be doubted whether Hitler, absorbed in the dream of his own greatness, ever had the capacity to love anyone deeply. At the best of times he was never an easy man to live with: his moods were too incalculable, his distrust too easily aroused. He was quick to imagine and slow to forget a slight; there was a strong strain of vindictiveness in him which often found expression in a mean and petty spite. Generosity was a virtue he did not recognize: he pursued his enmities unremittingly.

There is no doubt that Hitler, if he was in the right mood, could be an attractive, indeed a fascinating companion. On the outings in which he delighted he not only showed great capacity for enjoyment himself, but put others at their ease. He could talk well and he had the actor's gift of mimicry to amuse his companions. On the other hand, his sense

of humour was strongly tinged with *Schadenfreude,* a malicious plea-
sure in other people's misfortunes or stupidities. The treatment of the
Jews only roused his amusement, and he would laugh delightedly at
the description by Goebbels of the indignities the Jews had suffered at
the hands of the Berlin S.A. Indifferent towards the sufferings of
others, he lacked any feeling of sympathy, was intolerant and callous,
and filled with contempt for the common run of humanity. Pity and
mercy he regarded as humanitarian clap-trap and signs of weakness.
The only virtue was to be hard, and ruthlessness was the distinctive
mark of superiority. The more absorbed he became by the arrogant
belief in his mission and infallibility the more complete became his
loneliness, until in the last years of his life he was cut off from all
human contact and lost in a world of inhuman fantasy where the only
thing that was real or mattered was his own will.

V

'A man who has no sense of history,' Hitler declared, 'is like a
man who has no ears or eyes.' He himself claimed to have had a
passionate interest in history since his schooldays and he displayed
considerable familiarity with the course of European history. His conversation was studded with historical references and historical parallels. More than that: Hitler's whole cast of thought was historical, and
his sense of mission derived from his sense of history.

Like his contemporary Spengler, Hitler was fascinated by the rise
and fall of civilizations. 'I often wonder,' he remarks in his table talk,
'why the Ancient World collapsed.' Nor was this idle speculation. He
saw himself born at a similar critical moment in European history
when the liberal bourgeois world of the nineteenth century was disintegrating. What would take its place? The future lay with the 'Jewish–Bolshevik' ideology of the masses unless Europe could be saved
by the Nazi racist ideology of the élite. This was his mission and he
drew upon history to fortify him in it. Hence his interest in the Roman
Empire in which Christianity—the invention of the Jew, Saul of Tarsus
—had played the same disintegrative role as Bolshevism—the invention of the Jew, Marx—in the Europe of his own time.

To this view of history, this *Weltanschauung,* however repellent,
Hitler remained remarkably consistent. Once formed, it was rigid and
inflexible. Hitler's was a closed mind, violently rejecting any alternative view, refusing to criticize or allow others to criticize his assumptions. He read and listened, not to learn, but to acquire information

and find additional support for prejudices and opinions already fixed in his mind. Of historical study as a critical discipline, or of the rich fields of human history beside the quest for power, war, and the construction of empires, he was invincibly ignorant.

The hostility Hitler showed towards freedom of thought or discussion represented a personal dislike quite as much as a political expedient. On occasion he could be a good listener but he was intolerant of disagreement or even interruption once he had begun to speak himself. The habits of despotism extended from political to personal life, and he became accustomed to have his opinions on any subject accepted as the *ex cathedra* pronouncements of an oracle, no matter how ignorant and ill-founded they might be.

In fact, Hitler's views on every other topic besides politics were as dogmatic and intolerant—with this difference that in this case they were banal, narrow-minded, and totally unoriginal as well as harsh and brutal. What he had to say about marriage, women, education, religion, bore the indelible stamp of an innate vulgarity and coarseness of spirit. He was not only cut off from the richest experiences of ordinary human life—love, marriage, family, human sympathy, friendship —but the whole imaginative and speculative world of European literature was closed to him. His secretary recalls that his library contained not a single classic of literature, not a single book reflecting humane tastes. Everything that spoke of the human spirit and of the thousand forms in which it has flowered, from mysticism to science, was alien to him.

The basis of Hitler's political beliefs was a crude Darwinism. 'Man has become great through struggle. . . . Whatever goal man has reached is due to his originality plus his brutality. . . . All life is bound up in three theses: Struggle is the father of all things, virtue lies in blood, leadership is primary and decisive.' On another occasion he declared: 'The whole work of Nature is a mighty struggle between strength and weakness—an eternal victory of the strong over the weak. There would be nothing but decay in the whole of Nature if this were not so. States which offend against this elementary law fall into decay.' It followed from this that 'through all the centuries force and power are the determining factors. . . . Only force rules. Force is the first law.' Force was more than the decisive factor in any situation; it was force which alone created right. 'Always before God and the world, the stronger has the right to carry through what he wills. History proves: He who has not the strength—him the "right in itself" profits not a whit.'

The ability to seize and hold a decisive superiority in the struggle for existence Hitler expressed in the idea of race, the role of which is as central in Nazi mythology as that of class in Marxist. All that mankind has achieved, Hitler declared in *Mein Kampf,* has been the work of the Aryan race: 'It was the Aryan who laid the groundwork and erected the walls of every great structure in human culture.' But who were the Aryans?

Although Hitler frequently talked as if he regarded the whole German nation as of pure Aryan stock (whatever that may mean) his real view was rather different. It was only a part of any nation (even of the German nation) which could be regarded as Aryan. These constituted an élite within the nation (represented by the Nazi Party and especially by the S.S.) which stamped its ideas upon the development of the whole people, and by its leadership gave this racial agglomeration an Aryan character which in origin belonged only to a section. Thus Hitler's belief in race could be used to justify both the right of the German people to ride roughshod over such inferior peoples as the uncouth Slavs and the degenerate French, and the right of the Nazis, representing an élite, sifted and tested by the struggle for power, to rule over the German people. This explains why Hitler often referred to the Nazi capture of power in Germany as a racial revolution, since it represented the replacement of one ruling caste by another. As Hitler told Otto Strasser in May 1930: 'We want to make a selection from the new dominating caste which is not moved, as you are, by any ethic of pity, but is quite clear in its own mind that it has the right to dominate others because it represents a better race.'

In Hitler's and Himmler's plans for the S.S.—a racial élite selected with the most careful eye to Nazi eugenics—recruitment was to be open not only to Germans, but to Aryans of other nations as well.

The conception of the nation [Rauschning records Hitler saying] has become meaningless. We have to get rid of this false conception and set in its place the conception of race. The New Order cannot be conceived in terms of the national boundaries of the peoples with an historic past, but in terms of race that transcend these boundaries. . . . I know perfectly well that in the scientific sense there is no such thing as race. But you, as a farmer, cannot get your breeding right without the conception of race. And I, as a politician, need a conception which enables the order that has hitherto existed on an historic basis to be abolished, and an entirely new and anti-historic order enforced and given an intellectual basis. . . . And for this purpose the conception of race serves me well. . . . France carried her great Revolution beyond her borders with the conception of the nation. With the conception of race, National Socialism will carry its revolution abroad and recast the world.

I shall bring into operation throughout all Europe and the whole world this process of selection which we have carried out through National Socialism in Germany. . . . The active sections in nations, the militant, Nordic section, will rise again and become the ruling element over these shopkeepers and pacifists, these puritans and speculators and busybodies. . . . There will not be much left then of the clichés of nationalism, and precious little among us Germans. Instead there will be an understanding between the various language elements of the one good ruling race.

This is Hitler at his most flamboyant, and it is not to be taken too literally. Hitler was a master of nationalist appeal, and old-fashioned nationalism was very far from being played out in Europe. Hitler's foreign policy was nationalist in character, and nationalism, both that of the Occupied Countries and that of the Germans, cut across and wrecked the attempt to turn the Quislings and the S.S. into an international Nazi élite, just as it proved too strong for the Jacobins outside France in the 1790s. But it is also a passage characteristic of Hitler's way of talking: a straightforward claim to unlimited power was dressed up in the myth of a 'pure' race, just as on other occasions Hitler gave it a Wagnerian colouring and talked of founding a new Order of Knights.

What Hitler was seeking to express in his use of the word 'race' was his belief in inequality—both between peoples and individuals—as another of the iron laws of Nature. He had a passionate dislike of the egalitarian doctrines of democracy in every field, economic, political and international.

There are [he said in this speech to the Düsseldorf Industry Club] two closely related factors which we can time and time again trace in periods of national decline: one is that for the concepton of the value of personality there is substituted a levelling idea of the supremacy of mere numbers—democracy—and the other is the negation of the value of a people, the denial of any difference in the inborn capacity, the achievement of individual peoples. . . . Internationalism and democracy are inseparable conceptions.

Hitler rejected both in favour of the superior rights of the *Herrenvolk* in international affairs and of the Nazi élite in the government of the state.

Just as he opposed the concept of 'race' to the democratic belief in equality, so to the idea of personal liberty Hitler opposed the superior claims of the *Volk*.

National Socialism [Hitler declared] takes as the starting point of its views and its decisions neither the individual nor humanity. It puts consciously into the central point of its whole thinking the *Volk*. This *Volk* is for it a blood-conditioned entity in which it sees the God-willed building-stone of human society. The individual is transitory, the *Volk* is permanent. If the Liberal *Weltanschauung* in its deification of the single individual must lead to the destruction of the *Volk*, National Socialism, on the other hand, desires to safeguard the *Volk*, if necessary even at the expense of the individual. It is essential that the individual should slowly come to realize that his own ego is unimportant when compared with the existence of the whole people . . . above all he must realize that the freedom of the mind and will of a nation are to be valued more highly than the individual's freedom of mind and will.

In an interview with the *New York Times* Hitler summed up his view in the sentence: 'The underlying idea is to do away with egoism and to lead people into the sacred collective egoism which is the nation.'

The *Volk* not only gave meaning and purpose to the individual's life, it provided the standard by which all other institutions and claims were to be judged.

Party, State, Army, the economic structure, the administration of justice are of secondary importance, they are but a means to the preservation of the *Volk*. In so far as they fulfil this task, they are right and useful. When they prove unequal to this task they are harmful and must either be reformed or set aside or replaced by better means.

Here was the justification for the campaign of the Nazis and other Völkisch groups against the Weimar Republic: their loyalty had been, not to the Republican State, but to the *Volk*, for betraying the interests of which men like Rathenau and Erzberger had been assassinated. Justice, truth and the freedom to criticize must all be subordinated to the overriding claims of the *Volk* and its preservation.

The Strassers and the radical wing of the Party argued that if the same criterion were applied to the economic system it meant the socialist organization of the national economy in the interests of the *Volk*. Hitler's views about economics, however, were entirely opportunist. The truth is that he was not at all interested in economics. He preached the true doctrine of the totalitarian State—which the rulers of Soviet Russia also practised, but found it embarrassing to admit—the supremacy of politics over economics. It is not economics but power that is decisive. As early as 1923, at the time of the occupation of the Ruhr and the post-war inflation, Hitler kept on saying that Germany would not solve her problems 'until the German people understands that one can conduct politics only when one has the support of power—and again power. Only so is reconstruction possible. . . . It is not an economic question which now faces the German people, it is a political question—how shall the nation's determination be recovered?' During the Inflation and the Depression this was clever propaganda. He was able to cut through the technicalities of the economists, declaring that all that was needed was the united will of the German people to end their troubles—given that, the rest would follow. It also corresponded to Hitler's own practice when he came to power: faced with economic problems, you gave orders that they were to be solved; if the orders were not carried out, you shot people. It was on this basis that Hitler and Göring conducted the economic policy of the Third Reich, and left it to Dr Schacht and his successors to find the answers.

VI

As soon as Hitler began to think and talk about the organization of the State it is clear that the metaphor which dominated his mind was that of an army. He saw the State as an instrument of power in which the qualities to be valued were discipline, unity and sacrifice. It was from the Army that he took the *Führerprinzip,* the leadership principle, upon which first the Nazi Party, and later the National Socialist State, were built.

In Hitler's eyes the weakness of democracy was that it bred irresponsibility by leaving decisions always to anonymous majorities, and so putting a premium on the avoidance of difficult and unpopular decisions. At the same time, the Party system, freedom of discussion and freedom of the Press sapped the unity of the nation—he habitually described discussion as 'corrosive'. From this, he told the Hitler Youth, 'we have to learn our lesson: one will must dominate us, we must form a single unity; one discipline must weld us together; one obedience, one subordination must fill us all, for above us stands the nation.'

'Our Constitution,' wrote Nazi Germany's leading lawyer, Dr Hans Frank, 'is the will of the Führer.' This was in fact literally true. The Weimar Constitution was never replaced, it was simply suspended by the Enabling Law, which was renewed periodically and placed all power in Hitler's hands. Hitler thus enjoyed a more complete measure of power than Napoleon or Stalin or Mussolini, since he had been careful not to allow the growth of any institution which might in an emergency be used as a check on him.

Yet Hitler was equally careful to insist that his power was rooted in the people; his was a plebiscitary and popular dictatorship, a demo-cratic Caesarism. This distinguished the Third Reich from Imperial Germany: 'Then the leaders had no roots in the people: it was a class state.' After each of his early *coups* in foreign policy Hitler duly sub-mitted his action to the people for confirmation in a plebiscite. In the election campaign which followed the denunciation of the Locarno Pact and the reoccupation of the Rhineland, Hitler publicly declared:

In Germany bayonets do not terrorize a people. Here a government is supported by the confidence of the entire people. I care for the people. In fifteen years I have slowly worked my way up together with this move-ment. I have not been imposed by anyone upon this people. From the people I have grown up, in the people I have remained, to the people I return. My pride is that I know no statesman in the world who with greater right than I can say that he is the representative of his people.

Such statements may be taken for what they are worth, yet it is obvi-ous that Hitler felt—and not without justification—that his power, despite the Gestapo and the concentration camps, was founded on popular support to a degree which few people cared, or still care, to admit.

If the *Führerprinzip* corresponded to Hitler's belief in the role played in history by personality, the Nazi Party and particularly the S.S. exemplified the aristocratic principle, the role played by the élites. The first function of the Party was to recruit such an élite and from it to provide the leadership of the State. 'With the German Army as its model, the Party must see as its task the collection and advancement in its organization of those elements in the nation which are most capable of political leadership.'

Like all revolutionary movements, Nazism drew much of its strength from a new *carrière ouverte aux talents,* the formation of a new leader-ship drawn from other than the traditional classes.

The fundamental conception of this work [Hitler told the Party Rally in 1937] was to break with all traditional privileges, and in all spheres of life, especially in the political sphere, to place the leadership of the nation in the hands of hand-picked men, who should be sought and found with-out regard to descent, to birth, or to social and religious association—men chosen solely on the basis of their personal gifts and of their character.

The Party's fourteen years of struggle served as a process of natural selection—'just as the magnet draws to itself the steel splinters, so did our movement gather together from all classes and callings and walks of life the forces in the German people which can form and also maintain states.' In this way, even before coming to power, the Party created the cadres of leadership to take over the State. The difference between promise and practice will appear in the subsequent course of this history.

Once in power the Party remained the guarantor of the National Socialist character of the State. 'Our Government is supported by two organizations: politically by the community of the *Volk* organized in the National Socialist movement, and in the military sphere by the Army.' These, to use another phrase of Hitler's, were the two pillars of the State. The Party was a power held in reserve to act, if the State should fail to safeguard the interests of the *Volk*; it was the link between the Führer and his *Volk*; finally it was the agent for the education of the people in the Nazi *Weltanschauung*. Education is an ambiguous word in this context; on another occasion Hitler spoke of 'stamping the Nazi *Weltanschauung* on the German people'. For its highest duty was intolerance: 'it is only the harshest principles and an iron resolution which can unite the nation into a single body capable of resistance—and thereby able to be led successfully in politics.' 'The main plank in the Nationalist Socialist programme,' Hitler declared in 1937, 'is to abolish the liberalistic concept of the individual and the Marxist concept of humanity and to substitute for them the *Volk* community, rooted in the soil and bound together by the bond of its common blood.'

While Hitler's attitude towards liberalism was one of contempt, towards Marxism he showed an implacable hostility. The difference is significant. Liberalism he no longer regarded as a serious threat; its values had lost their attraction in the age of mass-politics, especially in Germany, where liberalism had never had deep roots, Marxism, however, whether represented by revisionist Social Democracy or revolutionary Communism, was a rival *Weltanschauung* able to exert a powerful attractive force over the masses comparable with that of Nazism. Ignoring the profound differences between Communism and Social Democracy in practice and the bitter hostility between the rival working-class parties, he saw in their common ideology the embodiment of all that he detested—mass democracy and a levelling egalitarianism as opposed to the authoritarian state and the rule of an élite; equality and friendship among peoples as opposed to racial inequality and the domination of the strong; class solidarity versus national unity; internationalism versus nationalism.

With Marxism there could be no compromise. 'When people cast in our teeth our intolerance we proudly acknowledge it—yes, we have formed the inexorable decision to destroy Marxism in Germany down to its very last root.' This was said in 1932, at a time when Hitler saw in the unbroken organization of the Social Democratic Party and the trade unions the most solid obstacle to his ambitions, and in the rival extremists of the German Communist Party, the only other German party whose votes mounted with his own.

Hitler regarded the Marxist conception of class war and of class solidarity cutting across frontiers as a particular threat to his own exaltation of national unity founded on the community of the *Volk*. The object of National Socialist policy was to create a truly classless society. 'The slogan, "The dictatorship of the bourgeoisie must make way for the dictatorship of the proletariat," is simply a question of a change from the dictatorship of one class to that of another, while we wish for the dictatorship of the nation, that is, the dictatorship of the whole community. Only then shall we be able to restore to the millions of our people the conviction that the State does not represent the interests of a single group or class, and that the Government is there to manage the concerns of the entire community.' This single-minded concept of the national interest was to be embodied in, and guaranteed by, the absolutism of the State, as it had been in the time of Frederick the Great and in the Prussian tradition of the State glorified by Hegel.

Just as Hitler ascribed to the 'Aryan' all the qualities and achievements which he admired, so all that he hated is embodied in another mythological figure, that of the Jew. There can be little doubt that Hitler believed what he said about the Jews; from first to last his anti-Semitism is one of the most consistent themes in his career, the master idea which embraces the whole span of his thought. In whatever direction one follows Hitler's train of thought, sooner or later one encounters the satanic figure of the Jew. The Jew is made the universal scapegoat. Democracy is Jewish—the secret domination of the Jew. Bolshevism and Social Democracy; capitalism and the 'interest-slavery' of the money-lender; parliamentarianism and the freedom of the Press; liberalism and internationalism; anti-militarism and the class war; Christianity; modernism in art (*Kultur-Bolschewismus*), prostitution and miscegenation—all are instruments devised by the Jew to subdue the Aryan peoples to his rule. One of Hitler's favourite phrases, which he claimed—very unfairly—to have taken from Mommsen, was: 'The Jew is the ferment of decomposition in peoples.' This points to the fundamental fact about the Jew in Hitler's eyes; unlike the Aryan, the Jew is incapable of founding a State and so incapable of anything creative. He can only imitate and steal—or destroy in the spirit of envy.

The Jew has never founded any civilization, though he has destroyed hundreds. He possesses nothing of his own creation to which he can point. Everything he has is stolen. Foreign peoples, foreign workmen build him his temples; it is foreigners who create and work for him; it is foreigners who shed their blood for him. He has no art of his own; bit by bit he has stolen it all from other peoples. He does not even know how to preserve the precious things others have created. . . . In the last resort it is the Aryan alone who can form States and set them on their path to future greatness. All this the Jew cannot do. And because he cannot do it, therefore all his revolutions must be international. They must spread as a pestilence spreads. Already he has destroyed Russia; now it is the turn of Germany, and with his envious instinct for destruction he seeks to disintegrate the national spirit of the Germans and to pollute their blood.

From this early speech of 1922, through the Nuremberg Laws of 1935 and the pogrom of November 1938 to the destruction of the Warsaw Ghetto and the death camps of Mauthausen and Auschwitz, Hitler's purpose was plain and unwavering. He meant to carry out the extermination of the Jewish race in Europe, using the word 'extermination' not in a metaphorical but in a precise and literal sense as the deliberate policy of the German State—and he very largely succeeded. On a conservative estimate, between four and four and a half million Jews perished in Europe under Hitler's rule—apart from the number driven from their homes who succeeded in finding refuge abroad. History records few, if any, crimes of such magnitude and of so cold-blooded a purpose.

VII

Stripped of their romantic trimmings, all Hitler's ideas can be reduced to a simple claim for power which recognizes only one relationship, that of domination, and only one argument, that of force. 'Civilization,' the Spanish philosopher, Ortega y Gasset, once wrote, 'consists in the attempt to reduce violence to the *ultima ratio,* the final argument. This is now becoming all too clear to us, for direct action reverses the order and proclaims violence as the *prima ratio*, or rather the *unica ratio*, the sole argument. It is the standard that dispenses with all others.'

Hitler was not original in this view. Every single one of his ideas —from the exaltation of the heroic leader, the racial myth, anti-Semitism, the community of the *Volk*, and the attack on the intellect, to the idea of a ruling élite, the subordination of the individual and the doctrine that might is right—is to be found in anti-rational and racist writers (not only in Germany but also in France and other European countries) during the hundred years which separate the Romantic movement from the foundation of the Third Reich. By 1914 they had become the commonplaces of radical, anti-Semitic and pan-German journalism in every city in Central Europe, including Vienna and Munich, where Hitler picked them up.

Hitler's originality lay not in his ideas, but in the terrifying literal way in which he set to work to translate these ideas into reality, and his unequalled grasp of the means by which to do this. To read Hitler's speeches and table talk is to be struck again and again by the lack of magnanimity or of any trace of moral greatness. His comments on everything except politics display a cocksure ignorance and an ineradicable vulgarity. Yet this vulgarity of mind, like the insignificance of his appearance, the badly fitting raincoat and the lock of hair plastered over his forehead of the early Hitler, was perfectly compatible with brilliant political gifts. Accustomed to associate such gifts with the qualities of intellect which Napoleon possessed, or with the strength of character of a Cromwell or a Lincoln, we are astonished and offended by this combination. Yet to underestimate Hitler as a politician, to dismiss him as an ignorant demagogue, is to make precisely the mistake that so many Germans made in the early 1930s.

It was not a mistake which those who worked closely with him made. Whatever they felt about the man, however much they disagreed with the rightness of this or that decision, they never underrated the ascendancy which he was able to establish over all who came into frequent contact with him. At Nuremberg, Admiral Dönitz, the Commander-in-Chief of the German Navy, admitted:

I purposely went very seldom to his headquarters, for I had the feeling that I would thus best preserve my power of initiative, and also because, after several days at headquarters, I always had the feeling that I had to disengage myself from his power of suggestion. I am telling you this because in this connexion I was doubtless more fortunate than his Staff, who were constantly exposed to his power and his personality.

Dönitz's experience can be matched a hundred times over. Generals who arrived at his headquarters determined to insist on the hopelessness of the situation not only failed to make any protest when they stood face to face with the Führer, but returned shaken in their judgement and half convinced that he was right after all.

On one occasion [Schacht records] I managed to persuade Göring to exercise his influence on Hitler to put on the brake in some economic matter or other only to learn afterwards that he had not dared raise the question after all. When I reproached him he replied: 'I often make up my mind to say something to him, but then when I come face to face with him my heart sinks into my boots.'

On another occasion when Schacht had demonstrated to the Minister of Defence, General von Blomberg, the hopelessness of finding any solution to a certain problem, Blomberg answered: 'I know you are right, but I have confidence in Hitler. He will be able to find some solution.'

The final test of this ascendancy belongs to the later stages of this history when, with the prestige of success destroyed, the German cities reduced to ruins, and the greater part of the country occupied, this figure, whom his people no longer saw or heard, was still able to prolong the war long past the stage of hopelessness until the enemy was in the streets of Berlin and he himself decided to break the spell. But the events of these earlier years cannot be understood unless it is recognized that, however much in retrospect Hitler may seem to fall short of the stature of greatness, in the years 1938 to 1941, at the height of his success, he had succeeded in persuading a great part of the German nation that in him they had found a ruler of more than human qualities, a man of genius raised up by Providence to lead them into the Promised Land.

Epilogue

Many attempts have been made to explain away the importance of Hitler, from Chaplin's brilliant caricature in *The Great Dictator* to the much less convincing picture of Hitler the pawn, a front man for German capitalism. Others have argued that Hitler was nothing in himself, only a symbol of the restless ambition of the German nation to dominate Europe; a creature flung to the top by the tides of revolutionary change, or the embodiment of the collective unconscious of a people obsessed with violence and death.

These arguments seem to me to be based upon a confusion of two different questions. Obviously, Nazism was a complex phenomenon to which many factors—social, economic, historical, psychological—contributed. But whatever the explanation of this episode in European history—and it can be no simple one—that does not answer the question with which this book has been concerned, what was the part played by Hitler. It may be true that a mass movement, strongly nationalist, anti-Semitic, and radical, would have sprung up in Germany without Hitler. But so far as what actually happened is concerned—not what might have happened—the evidence seems to me to leave no doubt that no other man played a role in the Nazi revolution or in the history of the Third Reich remotely comparable with that of Adolf Hitler.

The conception of the Nazi Party, the propaganda with which it must appeal to the German people, and the tactics by which it would come to power—these were unquestionably Hitler's. After 1934 there were no rivals left and by 1938 he had removed the last checks on his freedom of action. Thereafter, he exercised an arbitrary rule in Germany to a degree rarely, if ever, equalled in a modern industrialized state.

At the same time, from the re-militarization of the Rhineland to the invasion of Russia, he won a series of successes in diplomacy and war which established an hegemony over the continent of Europe comparable with that of Napoleon at the height of his fame. While these could not have been won without a people and an Army willing to serve him, it was Hitler who provided the indispensable leadership, the flair for grasping opportunities, the boldness in using them. In retrospect his mistakes appear obvious, and it is easy to be complacent about the inevitability of his defeat; but it took the combined efforts of the three most powerful nations in the world to break his hold on Europe.

Luck and the disunity of his opponents will account for much of Hitler's success—as it will of Napoleon's—but not for all. He began with few advantages, a man without a name and without support other than that which he acquired for himself, not even a citizen of the country he aspired to rule. To achieve what he did Hitler needed —and possessed—talents out of the ordinary which in sum amounted to political genius, however evil its fruits.

His abilities have been sufficiently described in the preceding pages: his mastery of the irrational factors in politics, his insight into the weaknesses of his opponents, his gift for simplification, his sense of timing, his willingness to take risks. An opportunist entirely without principle, he showed both consistency and an astonishing power of will in pursuing his aims. Cynical and calculating in the exploitation of his histrionic gifts, he retained an unshaken belief in his historic role and in himself as a creature of destiny.

The fact that his career ended in failure, and that his defeat was pre-eminently due to his own mistakes, does not by itself detract from Hitler's claim to greatness. The flaw lies deeper. For these remarkable powers were combined with an ugly and strident egotism, a moral and intellectual cretinism. The passions which ruled Hitler's mind were ignoble: hatred, resentment, the lust to dominate, and, where he could not dominate, to destroy. His career did not exalt but debased the human condition, and his twelve years' dictatorship was barren of all ideas save one—the further extension of his own power and that of the nation with which he had identified himself. Even power he conceived of in the crudest terms: an endless vista of military roads, S.S. garrisons, and concentration camps to sustain the rule of the Aryan 'master race' over the degraded subject peoples of his new empire in the east.

The great revolutions of the past, whatever their ultimate fate, have been identified with the release of certain powerful ideas: individual conscience, liberty, equality, national freedom, social justice. National Socialism produced nothing. Hitler constantly exalted force over the power of ideas and delighted to prove that men were governed by cupidity, fear, and their baser passions. The sole theme of the Nazi revolution was domination, dressed up as the doctrine of race, and, failing that, a vindictive destructiveness, Rauschning's *Revolution des Nihilismus*.

It is this emptiness, this lack of anything to justify the suffering he caused rather than his own monstrous and ungovernable will which makes Hitler both so repellent and so barren a figure. Hitler will have his place in history, but it will be alongside Attila the Hun, the barbarian king who was surnamed, not 'the Great', but 'the Scourge of God', and who boasted 'in a saying', Gibbon writes, 'worthy of his ferocious pride, that the grass never grew on the spot where his horse had stood'.

The view has often been expressed that Hitler could only have come to power in Germany, and it is true—without falling into the same error of racialism as the Nazis—that there were certain features of German historical development, quite apart from the effects of the

Defeat and the Depression, which favoured the rise of such a movement.

This is not to accuse the Germans of Original Sin, or to ignore the other sides of German life which were only grossly caricatured by the Nazis. But Nazism was not some terrible accident which fell upon the German people out of a blue sky. It was rooted in their history, and while it is true that a majority of the German people never voted for Hitler, it is also true that thirteen millions did. Both facts need to be remembered.

From this point of view Hitler's career may be described as a *reductio ad absurdum* of the most powerful political tradition in Germany since the Unification. This is what nationalism, militarism, authoritarianism, the worship of success and force, the exaltation of the State, and *Realpolitik* lead to, if they are projected to their logical conclusion.

There are Germans who reject such a view. They argue that what was wrong with Hitler was that he lacked the necessary skill, that he was a bungler. If only he had listened to the generals—or Schacht —or the career diplomats—if only he had not attacked Russia, and so on. There is some point, they feel, at which he went wrong. They refuse to see that it was the ends themselves, not simply the means, which were wrong: the pursuit of unlimited power, the scorn for justice or any restraint on power; the exaltation of will over reason and conscience; the assertion of an arrogant supremacy, the contempt for others' rights. As at least one German historian, Professor Meinecke, has recognized, the catastrophe to which Hitler led Germany points to the need to re-examine the aims as well as the methods of German policy as far back as Bismarck.

The Germans, however, were not the only people who preferred in the 1930s not to know what was happening and refused to call evil things by their true names. The British and French at Munich; the Italians, Germany's partners in the Pact of Steel; the Poles, who stabbed the Czechs in the back over Teschen; the Russians, who signed the Nazi-Soviet Pact to partition Poland, all thought they could buy Hitler off, or use him to their own selfish advantage. They did not succeed, any more than the German Right or the German Army. In the bitterness of war and occupation they were forced to learn the truth of the words of John Donne which Ernest Hemingway set at the beginning of his novel of the Spanish Civil War:

No man is an Iland, intire of it selfe; every man is a peece of the Con-

tinent, a part of the maine; If a clod bee washed away by the Sea, Europe
is the lesse, as well as if a Promontorie were, as well as if a Mannor of
thy friends or of thine own were; Any man's death diminishes me, because
I am involved in Mankinde; And therefore never send to know for whom
the bell tolls; It tolls for thee.

Hitler, indeed, was a European, no less than a German phenomenon. The conditions and the state of mind which he exploited, the
malaise of which he was the symptom, were not confined to one
country, although they were more strongly marked in Germany than
anywhere else. Hitler's idiom was German, but the thoughts and emotions to which he gave expression have a more universal currency.

Hitler recognized this relationship with Europe perfectly clearly.
He was in revolt against 'the System' not just in Germany but in
Europe, against the liberal bourgeois order, symbolized for him in
the Vienna which had once rejected him. To destroy this was his
mission, the mission in which he never ceased to believe; and in this,
the most deeply felt of his purposes, he did not fail. Europe may rise
again, but the old Europe of the years between 1789, the year of
the French Revolution, and 1939, the year of Hitler's War, has gone
for ever—and the last figure in its history is that of Adolf Hitler, the
architect of its ruin. *'Si monumentum requiris, circumspice'*—'If you
seek his monument, look around.'

IV. Poetry and Fascism: Spain and France

At first sight the bracketing of fascism in Spain and France, especially under an innocuous heading, seems to be an incongruity. In Spain, fascism allegedly triumphed in a vicious civil war with a boost from Hitler and Mussolini, and it presumably still rules with undiluted arrogance. In France, aside from the shabby wartime collaborationist régime of Marshal Pétain, fascism seems hardly to have existed. Moreover, there were many dissimilarities between the two countries in the early twentieth century: Spain was the heartland of religious obscurantism, military interference in politics, repressive government, social stagnation, economic backwardness, and she played only a peripheral role in European diplomacy; France was the mother of revolution, had achieved political democracy, social equilibrium, economic viability, was irreligious, and still figured among the world's great powers. Yet many similarities between the fascist movements in the two countries permit their discussion in a single section.

Fascism in Spain and France sprang from not dissimilar sources and shared many characteristics and desires. Neither "came to power" in the sense that Italian fascism and German National Socialism achieved state power. Spanish fascism, like the Republic it helped to topple, was a victim of the civil war. If the Falange emerged on the victorious side, it did so shorn of its vitality and its leader, who was executed early in the conflict and was honored by General Franco only after he was safely dead; it has survived as only one of the several pillars of Franco's government, providing ideological camouflage for what has been an essentially pragmatic régime. French fascism, on the other hand, was little more than a noisy nuisance, although its presence frightened politicians into taking more energetic counteraction than had been the case in either Italy or Germany. Both movements bore a heavy romantic flavor, appealed primarily to disenchanted nationalist intellectuals, seemed incapable of mobilizing a mass following, and, by themselves, were ineffective politically. Of the two, Spanish fascism was the more deeply nationalist; French fascists were fascinated by the international character of their movement, although they owed more than they cared to confess to French nationalism and conservatism. In one very significant regard, however, they differed greatly: French fascism was not identified with the personality of one man as was the Falange with José Antonio Primo de Rivera.

Spain is a land where the past weighs heavily upon the present. Permanent problems have done much to shape her history—e.g. the separatist character of regional demands for autonomy from Madrid or the persistence of extremist creeds—and these have been accentuated by a consciousness of decline since the sixteenth century, when Spain's greatness was legendary. Her modern history, from the era of the French Revolution through the civil war of 1936–1939, was a period of constant political turmoil interrupted by interludes of deceptive tranquility. Spain's transition to the modern world has been tortuous, painful, and turbulent. Spanish liberalism, lacking many of the requisites for a hardy flowering, became, by the beginning of this century, the private property of the privileged few. Her industrialization created great and untreated lacerations to her social fabric, and her semi-feudal agricultural economy contributed as well to the strength of anarchism, a creed that aimed at the annihilation of existing society. And Spain's army, accustomed by the politics of the nineteenth century to intervention in all state matters, stood by as the prideful guardian of the nation's interests. General Primo de Rivera, disgusted with the ways of politicians and fearful of social upheaval, proclaimed a dictatorship in 1923 with the blessing of the King, Alfonso XIII. This régime collapsed under the weight of its own

248 POETRY AND FASCISM: SPAIN AND FRANCE

ineptitude in 1930, and the dictator was followed into exile the next year by the King. Then in April 1931, a Republic was born: a spontaneous creation resulting from a manifestation of the lack of esteem that much of the nation, including the army, had for its King. Its founders, many of whom belonged to Spain's intellectual elite, assisted euphorically at its birth, confident that the establishment of genuine democratic institutions would solve the many problems of the Spanish inheritance. Such was not to be the case: by 1932, the Republic's leaders had squandered the fund of good will they had possessed only a year before, and they seemed incapable of coming to grips with real issues. It was in these circumstances that Spanish fascism made its appearance.

The only full-length account of the Falange has been written by a leading American student of Spanish history, Stanley G Payne of the University of California at Los Angeles. Excerpts from his book *Falange: A History of Spanish Fascism* are reprinted here. As in earlier selections, we are concerned primarily with the origins and development of the fascist movement and of its ideology. Payne deals in these pages with the Falange's leader, José Antonio Primo de Rivera, son of the dictator, tracing the highlights of his political career and examining his fascist philosophy. He demonstrates that José Antonio's fascism resembled its European counterparts: it preached revolution and disdained traditional conservatism even while it sought assistance from conservatives; it was anti-democratic, élitist, and imperialistic; it prescribed an end to class warfare, to be replaced by a "unity" imposed under the familiar banner of "authority, hierarchy, and order"; it had its romantic, idealistic qualities, which appealed so much to young intellectuals; and it demanded a total commitment to the nation as a "total unity." But there were exceptions to the usual fascist image. The Falange's chief disclaimed any role as a leader of the masses, and he cultivated, argues Payne, an "idealistic, poetic style of nationalism." A gentle, benign leader, and a "poetic" fascism? Perhaps. Payne reminds us, however, that Falangists were quite prepared, even eager, to demonstrate their virility by violence, and it was by this violence that the Falange contributed to the outbreak of the terrible civil war in 1936.

Since the Great Revolution that began in 1789, France has served as Europe's political laboratory. The varieties of liberalism and conservatism, republicanism and authoritarianism, flourished in nineteenth-century France, and she was among the first countries to produce, early in the twentieth century, a racist, anti-semitic, anti-democratic movement with a mass appeal—the Action Française. By 1934, however, on the eve of an allegedly fascist-led assault against Republican institutions, France seemed immune to the fascist infection. Her society was dominated by the middle classes; her working class was splintered by competing aspirants for its leadership and thus posed little threat to the established order. Her political system, created as a compromise in 1875, had weathered the siege of time and attacks from the Left and Right, and apparently commanded, if not the respect, the allegiance of the great mass of Frenchmen. Moreover, France had been a victorious power in the war, although at great human cost, and subsequently had played the role of policeman of Europe. But stability should not be mistaken for dynamism: France's foreign policy rested upon weakness; the nation seemed unable to pull herself out of the depression; and she was ruled by a middle-aged and elderly political class overly fond of inaction and ideological abstractions. In the new dynamic Europe of Nazi Germany, fascist Italy, and Soviet Russia, France's Republic began to appear old fashioned to many of her citizens, some of whom turned to fascism.

The final selection, "The Nature of Fascism in France" by Robert J. Soucy, originally appeared in the *Journal of Contemporary History*. Specialists have been puzzled by the apparently haphazard proliferation of fascist groupings in France in the 1930's, and have tended to emphasize their doctrinal diversity. Soucy, however, claims that these fascisms may be subsumed under a single broad rubric and that they were very much part of the French nationalist and conservative traditions. Most French fascists, he argues, were "nationalists first" and were caught up, at the time of Munich, in interlocking perplexities that made it impossible for one to be simultaneously a nationalist and an appeaser of Germany. Most striking for Soucy—and his observation applies in varying degrees to all of the fascisms we have examined—were the "spirit," the taste for adventure, the revolt against all that seemed inactive and stultifying in French life, that characterized French fascism. Here too was the preference for violence, even if it was circumscribed by a flow of words. But, like all the others, French fascism most likely perished in the violence that it had glorified.

1. The Falange

STANLEY G PAYNE

The far Right did not profit from the frustrations of Spanish liberalism in 1931–32. The conservative counterattack was being led by the moderate, semi-Republican, religiously oriented CEDA. Nonetheless, certain industrialists and financiers were becoming increasingly worried about the potentialities of the working-class movement. Intermittently, they discussed the possibility of creating some kind of nationalistic socialist front. Furthermore, the scattered partisans of General Primo de Rivera still harbored dreams of restoring political and economic stability to Spain by authoritarian means. Some of them looked to Mussolini for inspiration. However, these conservative desires and ambitions would never have found public expression in 1933 had it not been for a high-minded and resourceful young man, José Antonio Primo de Rivera, the eldest son of the late dictator. It was he who eventually brought together the divergent currents of Spanish fascism during the Republic.

José Antonio Primo de Rivera was born in 1903 into an upper-middle-class family with a strong military tradition. The Primo de Riveras were socially prominent in Andalusia, having intermarried with large landholders and merchants around Jerez de la Frontera. José Antonio's great-uncle, General Francisco Primo de Rivera, had been awarded the newly created title of Marqués de Estella for bringing the Second Carlist War to a close in 1878. When his father died in 1930, José Antonio became the third Marqués in that line.

José Antonio was very different from his father, who had been a jovial, sensual man, little troubled by intellectual problems. Like so many patrician Spaniards, José Antonio was educated in the law. He also received considerable instruction in literature and modern languages, and was an amateur poet. Although very popular and even something of a social charmer, he was known for his modesty

Source: *Falange: A History of Spanish Fascism* (Stanford, California: Stanford University Press, 1961), pp. 24–48; 74–80. Reprinted with the permission of the publishers. © 1961 by the Board of Trustees of the Leland Stanford Junior University.

and was never accused of presuming on his station as the dictator's son. He was first put to work at the age of sixteen in the business firm of a maternal uncle, where he handled a share of the English-language correspondence. He was a good student and did graduate work in law before completing his military service. He was basically a serious young man.

At the University of Madrid José Antonio took an interest in student politics, but despite his family background he spurned the backward Catholic students' organization and tended to favor the liberal faction in university affairs. He was careful never to identify himself with any sort of political activity during the seven-year dictatorship. Nonetheless, he was emotionally very much involved with his father's career, glorying in the dictator's successes and watching with dismay as his régime foundered. As the years drew on, José Antonio formed his own interpretation of the régime's mild but authoritarian policies. He later showed himself to have been strongly influenced by his father's scorn for all politicians and his faith in what he called "intuicismo" or "intuitionism." José Antonio came also to scorn the liberal intelligentsia which had attracted him as a student. The more they attacked and ridiculed his father, the more antagonistic he became toward their insistence on middle-class liberal democracy and parliamentary forms.

When the régime began to totter in 1928 and 1929, José Antonio put aside his literary pursuits and became seriously interested in public affairs. He began reading Spengler, Keyserling, Marx, Lenin, and Ortega, as well as the Spanish traditionalists. He speculated at length on the ambivalence of modern freedom, which enfranchised the masses but offered no shelter for cultural values; which vastly increased national wealth but so grossly maldistributed it that only a cataclysmic class revolution seemed able to remove the inequities. To him the liberal emphasis on abstract equality and internationalism seemed to obliterate the national, regional, and individual differences that had made European culture so rich.

By the end of 1929 the Spanish upper classes were ready and eager to let Primo de Rivera go. They had never supported his vague plans for reform, and they now feared that his continued presence as head of the government would only bring new and greater difficulties. The ailing dictator's resignation in January 1930 thus came as a relief to those who had profited most from his rule. He was bundled off to Paris, where he died within a few months.

José Antonio was deeply moved by his father's end and revolted by the hypocrisy of many erstwhile aristocratic supporters. Without hesitation, he undertook the political defense of the dictator. Primo de Rivera's most acute commentator has written that "in the main, the dictatorship fostered class cleavage and class particularism and made more difficult, almost impossible, the coexistence of the disparate elements of Spanish society." José Antonio was incapable of such an objective estimation of his father's record. He whitewashed the régime completely, and even tried to pretend that the disastrous financial policies of the dictatorship had helped stabilize the public treasury.

After Primo de Rivera fell, certain conservative forces which still favored his idea of a non-party directorship for the nation joined with the strongest supporters of the Monarchy to form the Unión Monárquica Nacional. This new organization was more than merely monarchist; it held to a certain vague conception of a monarchical government that would formulate, above the party system, national policies for preserving present institutions and effecting needed reforms. As the pressure from Leftists and Republicans grew stronger, most of the vested interests threw their support behind the Unión Monárquica, whose superficial interest in a few reforms offered them a convenient disguise.

José Antonio was asked to become Vice-Secretary General of the Unión Monárquica; he accepted the post on May 2, 1930, one month after the formation of the group. He declared that he looked upon this first venture into politics as an obligation, since all but two of the ministers who had served his late father were Unión members. José Antonio had no real concern with the Bourbon Monarchy, and Alfonso XIII's secretary had broken off personal relations with him after the fall of Don Miguel; but he was so accustomed to an aristocratic environment that he did not rebel against the unimaginative conservatism of the Unión Monárquica. His father had served the traditional institutions, and so would he, despite his personal bitterness against the leading Rightists for their undignified haste in helping get rid of Don Miguel. He announced that his only political aim was to defend his father's record and to continue his work, regardless of circumstances.

However, José Antonio's wide reading and energetic temperament were beginning to suggest to him that modern society and government could no longer be held together simply by the paternalistic defense of nineteenth-century institutions. Firmly believing that his father's ideas had been right, he began to realize that Don Miguel had pursued them in the wrong way. In February 1930, during a lecture at the Ateneo of Albacete on the juridical subject "What Is Just?," José Antonio had suggested that the just and fair could be ascertained only by considering the entire range of particular norms which might bear on a given problem. Taken in a political sense, this would seem to recommend a thoroughly open-minded, pragmatic approach. But no matter how tolerant José Antonio tried to be, he could hardly remain free of political prejudice when the very name Primo de Rivera was anathema to the liberals and the Left.

Not until several months after the fall of the Monarchy did José Antonio resolve to enter politics as a candidate for office. Unable to bear the attacks on his father's record that abounded in the Constituent Cortes, he decided to run for election to that body; he sought the support of the Right as a candidate from Madrid in the by-election of October 1931. He announced that he wanted to go to the Cortes solely

to defend the sacred memory of my father. But I do not present myself for personal vanity nor because of a taste for politics, which every instant attracts me less. . . . God well knows my vocation is amid my books, and that to separate myself from them to throw myself momentarily in the sharp vertigo of politics causes me real pain. But it would be cowardly or senseless if I dozed quietly while in the Cortes, before the people, accusations continue to be hurled against the sacred memory of my father.

During the campaign part of the Rightist press maintained a glacial tone, not wishing to compromise itself with any more Primo de Riveras. Despite this handicap José Antonio made a reasonable showing. His opponent, the revered liberal academician Bartolomé Manuel de Cossío, beat him by a margin of two to one, but that was better than many people had thought a Primo de Rivera could do in the Socialist Madrid of 1931.

After his electoral defeat, José Antonio returned to private life and devoted himself to building up a respectable private law practice. In his leisure hours he tried to sort out his political and social ideas, which were in a very confused state. At times he seemed very discouraged and sometimes spoke to friends about emigrating to America.

Meanwhile, he grew more and more antagonistic toward the old political and social régime in Spain, the régime his father had tried to save through mild reform but which had discarded his father and then collapsed before the liberal wave of 1930–31. Even when campaigning for the Unión Monárquica, José Antonio declared that one of his father's greatest achievements was overthrowing the rule of the political bosses who had dominated the Spanish provinces. He took a similar attitude toward the enormous social and economic abuses sanctioned by the Spanish Right. According to him, the only thing wrong with the late dictator's public development program and system of workers' representation was that, for lack of opportunity, they had not been carried far enough.

On the other hand, José Antonio could not tolerate the doctrinaire liberal theorists and intellectuals. This attitude, firmly rooted in family sentiment, was sometimes expressed in the bitterest terms. Defending his dead parent from their barbs, he had sneered, "Behold the ridiculous *intellectuals*, stuffed with pedantry. . . . How are they ever going to see—through their myopic eyeglasses—the solitary gleam of divine light?"

The incessant wrangling of the Republicans and the slowness of their approach to basic problems combined to complete José Antonio's alienation from political liberalism. He declared that intellectual positivism and political liberalism were in mortal crisis, and that the death of liberalism would be followed not by reaction but by revolution. Europe had entered the social age, in which traditional conservatism and old-guard liberalism were equally bankrupt.

If the Right was incompetent and the Center inadequate, the Left could not attract a man of José Antonio's aristocratic background. He considered revolution almost inevitable, especially for so backward a country as Spain. But radical change could take many directions, and José Antonio, as an esthete and an aristocrat, had no intention of becoming either a Marxist or an Anarchist. Instead, he wanted to take up his father's burden of national reform, on the same basis of authoritarianism and revolution-from-above at which Primo de Rivera had clumsily aimed. The difference was José Antonio's belief that the process of national authoritarian reconstruction must be made more radical and thoroughgoing in order to succeed.

Patriotic sentiment was familiar to José Antonio, who had grown up within the Spanish military hierarchy. Though his English literary training sometimes made him skeptical about the capabilities of the Spanish people, he accepted nationalism as the emotional lever necessary to engage popular enthusiasm for a non-Marxist program of revitalization. Furthermore, he was repelled to see his father's efforts to create national solidarity being undone by the regional autonomy statutes of the Republic Cortes.

José Antonio was an enthusiastic student of Ortega y Gasset and other theorists who advocated an elite. This belief in the role of what later came to be called the "creative minority" was consonant with the simplistic political notions on which his father's dictatorship had rested. A small group of national-minded reformers had swept away the political chaos of 1923 by authoritarian means. The same solution, he thought, could be imposed on the problems of 1933, except that it had to be more potent and supported by a real political movement.

By the beginning of 1933 José Antonio's political ideas coalesced in a plan for leading an audacious minority which would inaugurate radical political and economic reforms by authoritarian means, employing the ideological framework of nationalism to enlist the moral enthusiasm of the young. If successful, such a movement would not only save the political integrity of Spain but raise the country to a more prominent position in the new nationalist European order. For José Antonio, this was Spanish fascism.

Practical plans were slow to take shape in his mind. He hesitated for months trying to decide whether he should throw himself into the current of corporatist interest which had begun to run through sections of the Spanish Center and Right. His basic problem was to decide what kind of men he could best work with and what sort of cooperation he could expect from them. José Antonio was not bent on founding a new group of his own; indeed, he lacked the resources for such a task. He was drawn toward both the liberal leader Manuel Azaña and the conservative José María Gil Robles, but he decided that neither could provide the radically new initiative he wanted. The issues of *La Conquista del Estado* had aroused a certain interest, and when one of his law clerks joined the JONS José Antonio sent him to talk with Ledesma; but from his clerk's report the Jonsista leader seemed too brash and undisciplined, too cold and materialistic. José Antonio was searching for a political creed that would appeal to esthetic sentiment and the generous instincts—an idealistic, poetic style of nationalism.

Adolf Hitler's rise to power on January 30, 1933, quickened the interest of the Spanish Right in the nature and goals of fascistic nationalism. The first person to take advantage of the curiosity thus aroused had commercial rather than political ends in view. This individual was Manuel Delgado Barreto, a capable journalist then serving as editor of the Madrid daily *La Nación*, which had been founded in the twenties to serve as the mouthpiece for the Primo de Rivera régime and was still patronized by former leaders of the Unión Patriótica. Delgado decided to capitalize on the new wave of interest by establishing a weekly called *El Fascio*, which would be devoted to the discussion of things more or less fascist. He advertised this venture throughout the circles of the extreme Right and obtained enough advance subscriptions to assure the success of the paper. To supply copy he enlisted the services of Ledesma and his colleagues, who gladly accepted an opportunity to make free propaganda for themselves. Delgado also asked José Antonio Primo de Rivera and a few other nationalist writers, including Rafael Sánchez Mazas and Giménez Caballero, to contribute articles.

The first number of *El Fascio* was to appear on March 16, 1933. No one who wrote for it was greatly enthusiastic; most of the contributors realized that the paper was chiefly a middle-class business venture, and Ledesma even decried the mimicry of the title itself. José Antonio, partly against his better judgment, contributed a vague article about the nature of the nationalist state, which was supposed to establish some sort of permanent system that he never managed to explain clearly. The other articles ranged in style from the weird outpourings of Giménez Caballero to the rasping dialectic of Ramiro Ledesma. Some of the articles read almost like translations of the more abstract points of Nazi and Fascist doctrine.

El Fascio did not survive the day of its birth. With Germany just fallen into the hands of National Socialism and with fascist movements on the march in Austria and even in France, the liberals in power did not want to take chances in Spain. The entire first edition of *El Fascio* was confiscated, and further publication of the paper was banned by the government.

By this time it was well known that José Antonio was interested in fascism and entertained political ambitions in that direction. He now began to put out serious feelers of his own, seeking to unify some of the flutters of sympathy and interest aroused among the Right. When Juan Ignacio Luca de Tena, editor of the influential monarchist *ABC,* wrote a sympathetic criticism of *El Fascio,* José Antonio engaged in a friendly polemic with that newspaper. In his first letter he outlined an abstractly idealistic view of fascism:

Fascism is not a tactic—violence. It is an idea—unity.

Fascism was born to inspire a faith not of the Right (which at bottom aspires to conserve everything, even the unjust) or of the Left (which at bottom aspires to destroy everything, even the good), but a collective, integral, national faith. . . .

A fascist state is not created by the triumph of either the strongest or the most numerous party—which is not the right one for being the most numerous, though a stupid suffrage may say otherwise—but by the triumph of a principle of order common to all, the constant national sentiment, of which the state is the organ. . . .

If anything truly deserves to be called a workers' state, it is the fascist state. Therefore, in the fascist state—and the workers will come to realize this, no matter what—the workers' syndicates are directly elevated to the dignity of organs of the state. . . .

One achieves true human dignity only when one serves. Only he is great who subjects himself to taking part in the achievement of a great task.

Luca de Tena's reply was apt, if rather eulogistic. After defending *El Fascio's* right to exist, he pointed out that José Antonio's schema was excessively idealistic and not supported by political reality:

Only place "socialist" where you say "fascist," and the partisans of Marxism could subscribe to a very similar concept. . . .

What is born in the heart cannot be imported. And I suspect that your fascism has sprung from your great heart rather than from your brilliant intelligence.

During the spring of 1933 José Antonio corresponded with family friends, political associates of his father, representatives of the Spanish financial world, radical-minded monarchists, Jonsistas, and nationalistic ideologues of varying descriptions. Each group had its own ideas, often extremely vague, about the form a fascist movement should assume. Among the interested parties, José Antonio was taking the most definite stand, and he emerged as the most likely candidate to head an organized movement. García Valdecasa was too lukewarm and academic, Ledesma too unstable.

However, some of the businessmen who had expressed interest in helping finance a new nationalist movement showed little enthusiasm about backing another Primo de Rivera. They argued that a fascist leader must be a man of the people, like Mussolini, or a front-line soldier, like Hitler; if the workers were to be seduced, they must be seduced by one of their own kind.

A candidate whom Bilbao financiers had wanted to consider was the pragmatic, middle-of-the-road Socialist leader Indalecio Prieto. Having made his way up selling newspapers on the streets of Bilbao, Prieto fitted the working-class description they desired. As a practical politician, he had never lost contact with Vizcayan finance and industry, and within the Socialist Party he had tried to combat the irresponsible agitation of idealistic revolutionaries. In return, Bilbao

258 POETRY AND FASCISM: SPAIN AND FRANCE

capitalists had not been above sheltering him from police during the last days of the Monarchy. In 1932 they hoped he might become sufficiently disgusted with the wild talk and obstructionism of the Left wing of the Socialist Party to consider developing an alternative "national" socialism. But Prieto proved to be a dedicated working-class leader and a stout progressive. He refused to sponsor any variant of social fascism, although he later showed a certain personal interest in the national syndicalist movement.

Another possibility was Demetrio Carceller, the director of a petroleum company in the Canary Islands, who had risen from the proletariat to a significant position in the business world. Carceller was talented, possessed great drive and energy, and was not averse to entering politics. However, the total lack of concrete political preparation behind the ideas of the financiers eventually caused him to lose interest; besides, he was primarily interested in making money.

José Antonio was well aware of the suspicion with which he was viewed by business circles, and disclaimed any desire to make himself the *caudillo* of Spanish fascism. He told friends that he would like to help form a more authentic and popular kind of political movement, but not one purely of his own making. He declared that he had "too many intellectual preoccupations to be a leader of masses." "My intellectual vocation is one of the least suitable for the role of *caudillo*," he said.

On March 24, 1933, José Antonio authorized an old friend and distant relative, Sancho Dávila, to act as his representative in organizing those among the upper classes around Seville and Cádiz who were sympathetic to a nationalistic fascism. Dávila did not find the assignment easy. On April 2, José Antonio wrote to his cousin Julián Pemartín, who was helping Dávila:

It is true that the working out of this idea is something that will probably be reserved for a man of popular extraction. Being *caudillo* has something of the prophet about it, requiring a large dose of faith, health, enthusiasm, and anger that is not compatible with refinement. For my part, I would serve for anything better than for a fascist *caudillo*. The attitude of doubt and sense of irony, which never leaves those of us who have some degree of intellectual curiosity, incapacitates us for shouting the robust, unflinching cries that are required of the leaders of masses. Hence, if in Jerez, as in Madrid, there are friends whose liver suffers from the thought that I should want to make myself *Caudillo del Fascio*, you may reassure them with respect to me.

José Antonio had found a solid collaborator in Julio Ruiz de Alda, a famous aviator who had accompanied Ramón Franco on the first nonstop transatlantic flight to Buenos Aires in 1926. The Spanish Air Force had been a fertile breeding ground for radicalism in the twenties, but the Left had no appeal to Ruiz de Alda. A hearty, direct, military type, he had served as president of the National Aeronautic Federation, and had filled minor technical posts during the dictatorship. He was attracted by nationalist appeals and distrusted the established parties. After the founding of the Republic, he wrote to the Catalan politician Francesc Cambó, declaring that the republican system was entirely wrong and that a "totalitarian system" was needed. He made contact with Ledesma in 1931 and was briefly enrolled in Ledesma's group, but he never had anything to do with the later JONS.

Ruiz de Alda had helped set up the Spanish Company of Aerial Photogrammetric Works, which was to make an aerial survey of Spain in order to supply the data for a study of national water resources. This scheme fell through in 1932 when government aid was suspended, partly because of the radical Right-wing sentiments of Ruiz de Alda and his principal associates, the monarchist Ansaldo brothers. Embittered at this treatment, they established an "Aviation Armaments" group to lobby for nationalization of the virtually non-existent aircraft industry. By early 1933 various Right-wing figures had begun to sound out Ruiz de Alda on the subject of a national fascist party. As one of the obvious candidates for leadership in such a party, he was interviewed by Giménez Caballero for *El Fascio*.

In these circles Ruiz de Alda made the acquaintance of José Antonio. They considered themselves more sincere and idealistic than the opportunists and reactionaries around them, and discovered with mutual satisfaction that they could work together. They wanted to found a fascist movement, but on their own terms, not on those of the Bank of Bilbao.

Ruiz de Alda was level-headed and a good organizer. He was utterly inept as a public speaker, but his solid, methodical talents helped control José Antonio's sometimes unbridled rhetoric. The latter's grandiloquent concept of nationalism as *destino en lo universal* seemed too deterministic for Ruiz de Alda's simple activism. The aviator would have preferred to say "unity of mission," but his tongue was no match for José Antonio's.

It took the two several months to concert their efforts fully, and for some time they worked along separate but parallel lines. The first title José Antonio put forward for the proposed group was

Movimiento Español Sindical, a vague and abstract term. Ruiz de Alda wanted to label propaganda leaflets "F.E.," which might stand for either Fascismo Español or Falange Española (Spanish Phalanx). Rightist financiers soon placed adequate financial resources at the command of the two men, and by the early summer of 1933 they had begun to circulate around the capital a considerable number of tracts advertising their idealistic brand of national syndicalism.

This new activity, combined with the increasing energy of the Jonsistas in Madrid, frightened the Dirección General de Seguridad, which was being pressed by the Socialists not to take chances. Between July 19 and July 22, 1933, hundreds of suspected fascists were arrested all over Spain. Ruiz de Alda and José Antonio prudently removed themselves from circulation for a few days, but Ledesma was detained, along with a heterogeneous collection of Jonsistas, Anarchists, monarchists, Albiñanistas, retired officers, and ex-*upetistas* from the dictatorship. Ninety of the more important suspects were held for a week or two, until the police finally satisfied themselves that there was no "fascist plot" to worry about.

José Antonio and Ruiz de Alda resumed their organizational planning in August. They hoped to persuade García Valdecasas to dissolve his Frente Español and join hands with them. Valdecasas was definitely interested, but hesitated to become actively involved. At the end of the month the three had a conference with Ledesma in Bilbao, at which they explored the possibility of uniting forces with the JONS under a new name. Ledesma later admitted that he was "perhaps too intransigent" on this occasion. He proposed that José Antonio and Ruiz de Alda devote their efforts to expanding the JONS, which would then be directed by a new triumvirate headed by José Antonio. José Antonio, however, insisted on an entirely new party, one capable of attracting his late father's more conservative supporters as well as other elements which still disdained the JONS; he proposed that this party be called "Fascismo Español." Ledesma said that such second-hand titles and attitudes were out of the question and broke off the talks.

By late September José Antonio and Ruiz de Alda had completed their organizational work, and they decided to launch their movement at the next change in the national political weather. They had not long to wait. In October a caretaker government was ordered to adjourn the Cortes, and elections were scheduled for mid-November. The temporary limitations on political propaganda imposed earlier in the year were lifted, and full freedom of speech was to be allowed during the electoral campaign.

Favored for his family connections and his proven opposition to liberal idealogy in public life, José Antonio was offered a place on the Rightist lists in Madrid and in Cádiz. He rejected the offer from Madrid, since election there might have bound him to the cautious policy of the clerical CEDA. The Cádiz candidacy, which had been arranged with the help of his old oligarchical family friends, came with fewer strings attached. He accepted this proposal, since it offered a fairly certain seat in the Cortes and a platform for his own propaganda. He decided to announce his political candidacy and the organization of the new movement at the same time.

The Founding of the Falange

José Antonio's new national syndicalist movement was launched at a political meeting held at the Teatro Comedia of Madrid on Sunday afternoon, October 29, 1933. Free use of the theater had been offered by its owner, a friend of the Primo de Rivera family. National radio coverage had been arranged, and three speakers, José Antonio Primo de Rivera, Julio Ruiz de Alda, and Alfonso García Valdecasas, addressed the meeting. About two thousand people were present, most of them sympathetic Rightists; Ramiro Ledesma and a group of Jonsistas took seats near the front.

The highlight of the day, without question, was José Antonio's address. Its heavily rhetorical and tensely poetic style set the tone for the Falange's early appeals; and as the first official statement of the party's goals, it is worth quoting at length:

Finally, the liberal state came to offer us economic slavery, saying to the workers, with tragic sarcasm: "You are free to work as you wish; no one can compel you to accept specified conditions. Since we are the rich, we offer you the conditions that please us; as free citizens, you are not obliged to accept them if you do not want to; but as poor citizens, if you do not accept them you will die of hunger, surrounded of course by the utmost liberal dignity." . . .

Therefore socialism had to appear, and its coming was just (for we do not deny any evident truth). The workers had to defend themselves against a system that only promised them right and did not strive to give them a just life.

However, socialism, which was a legitimate reaction against liberal slavery, went astray because it resulted, first, in the materialist interpretation of life and history; second, in a sense of reprisal; and third, in the proclamation of the dogma of class struggle.

•   •   •   •   •

The *Patria* is a total unity, in which all individuals and classes are integrated; the *Patria* cannot be in the hands of the strongest class or of the best organized party. The *Patria* is a transcendent synthesis, an indivisible synthesis, with its own goals to fulfill; and we want this movement of today, and the state which it creates, to be an efficient, authoritarian instrument at the service of an indisputable unity, of that permanent unity, of that irrevocable unity that is the *Patria*.

And we already have the principle for our future acts and our present conduct, for we would be just another party if we came to announce a program of concrete solutions. Such programs have the advantage of never being fulfilled. On the other hand, when one has a permanent sense of life and history, that very sense gives solutions beyond the concrete, just as love may tell us when we ought to scold and when we ought to embrace, without true love having set up a minimum program of embraces and reproaches.

Here is what is required by our total sense of the *Patria* and the state which is to serve it:

That all the people of Spain, however diverse they may be, feel in harmony with an irrevocable unity of destiny.

That the political parties disappear. No one was ever born a member of a political party; on the other hand, we are all born members of a family; we are all neighbors in a municipality; we all labor in the exercise of a profession. . . .

We want less liberal word-mongering and more respect for the deeper liberty of man. For one only respects the liberty of man when he is esteemed, as we esteem him, the bearer of eternal values; when he is esteemed as the corporal substance of a soul capable of being damned and of being saved. Only when man is considered thus can it truly be said that his liberty is respected, and more especially if that liberty is joined, as we aspire to join it, to a system of authority, of hierarchy, and of order.

•   •   •   •   •

Finally, we desire that if on some occasion this must be achieved by violence, there be no shrinking from violence. Because who has said— while speaking of "everything save violence"—that the supreme value in the hierarchy of values is amiability? Who has said that when our sentiments are insulted we are obliged to be accommodating instead of reacting like men? It is very correct indeed that dialectic is the first instrument of communication. But no other dialectic is admissible save the dialectic of fists and pistols when justice or the *Patria* is offended.

•   •   •   •   •

But our movement would not be understood at all if it were believed to be only a manner of thinking. It is not a manner of thinking; it is a manner of being. We ought not merely to propose to ourselves a formal construction, a political architecture. Before life in its entirety, in each one of our acts, we must adopt a complete, profound, and human attitude. This attitude is the spirit of sacrifice and service, the ascetic and military sense of life. Henceforth let no one think that we recruit men in order to offer rewards; let no one imagine that we join together in the defense of privileges. I should like to have this microphone before me carry my voice into every last working-class home to say: Yes, we wear a tie; yes, you may say of us that we are *señoritos*. But we urge a spirit of struggle for things that cannot concern us as *señoritos;* we come to fight so that hard and just sacrifices may be imposed on many of our own class, and we come to struggle for a totalitarian state that can reach the humble as well as the powerful with its benefits. We are thus, for so always in our history have been the *señoritos* of Spain. In this manner they have achieved the true status of *señores,* because in distant lands, and in our very *Patria*, they have learned to suffer death and to carry out hard missions precisely for reasons in which, as *señoritos*, they had no interest at all.

I believe the banner is raised. Now we are going to defend it gaily, poetically. There are some who think that in order to unite men's wills against the march of the revolution it is proper to offer superficially gratifying solutions; they think it is necessary to hide everything in their propaganda which could awaken an emotion or signify energetic or extreme action. What equivocation! The peoples have never been moved by anyone save the poets, and woe to him who, before the poetry which destroys, does not know how to raise the poetry which promises!

In a poetic movement we shall raise this fervent feeling for Spain; we shall sacrifice ourselves; we shall renounce ourselves, and the triumph will be ours, a triumph—why need I say it?—that we are not going to win in the next elections. In those elections vote for whoever seems to you least undesirable. But our Spain will not emerge from [the Cortes], nor is our goal there. The atmosphere there is tired and murky, like a tavern at the end of a night of dissipation. That is not our place. Yes, I know that I am a candidate; but I am one without faith and without respect. I say this now, when it can mean that I lose votes. That matters not at all. We are not going to argue with habitués over the disordered remains of a dirty banquet. Our place is outside, though we may occasionally have to pass a few transient minutes within. Our place is in the fresh air, under the cloudless heavens, weapons in our hands, with the stars above us. Let the others go on with their merrymaking. We outside, in tense, fervent, and certain vigilance, already feel the dawn breaking in the joy of our hearts.

Although it was clear that the new movement would attract wider support than the JONS, it was not taken seriously by the political press. *El Sol*, the nation's leading liberal newspaper, aptly dismissed it as "A Poetic Movement," one largely concerned with style and outward forms: "We reject it in the first place for wanting to be fascist . . . and in the second, for not truly being it, for not being a deep and authentic fascism." Most of the Right concurred, although *Acción Española*, the clerical-corporatist-monarchist intellectual review, received the movement very favorably. An article by the Traditionalist leader Victor Pradera pointed out its similarities to Carlist corporatist antiparliamentarianism. Only the clerical reactionaries saw possibilities in the organization.

The Martínez Barrio government took an almost benevolent attitude toward the new movement. Police protection was provided for the Teatro Comedia meeting, which passed entirely without incident. José María Carretero, the leading pundit of the intransigent Right, wrote: "It seems a bit suspicious that the first public fascist meeting should end in an atmosphere of peaceful normality. On leaving the theater and stepping out into the clear, quiet street, I had the feeling of having attended a lovely literary tea at the Ateneo."

The movement did not receive a name until November 2, when the official organizational meeting took place. Either Ruiz de Alda or Sánchez Mazas suggested the ultimate choice, "Falange Española," a term which had been in the air for some time.

The Falange was the fifth party of the radical Right to be formed in Spain. Among the others, the Comunión Tradicionalista (the Carlists) maintained its customary isolation, and neither the JONS nor the *Albiñanistas* counted for anything. The leaders of the monarchist Renovación Española had no use for fascism, but because of the great dispersion of political forces in Spain they considered it more prudent to infiltrate the Falange from within than to ignore it. Hence a considerable number of monarchist zealots took up membership in the Falange during the winter and spring of 1934. They were tacitly led by Juan Antonio Ansaldo and his brother, both leading activists in Renovación Española, professional aviators, and personal friends of Julio Ruiz de Alda.

A fairly large number of people joined the movement during its first two or three months. Whereas the JONS claimed only a few hundred adult members in all Spain, the Falange soon signed up several thousand. This initial success was in large part due to the aura of conservative *primorriverismo* and paternal nationalism associated with José Antonio's name; a disproportionately large number of those who were first attracted to the party appeared to be disgruntled conservatives, retired Army men, and ex-*upetistas*. This conservative element was balanced only by a nucleus of students who were fascinated with José Antonio's rhetoric. An aura of vagueness surrounded the political program of the Falange; it was commonly supposed to be Spanish fascism, but each member had his own notion of what that meant.

At this stage the party leaders were hardly more enlightened. José Antonio had formulated no concrete goals, no day-by-day party program, and no general outline of party tactics; he continued to talk of a "poetic movement." Ruiz de Alda was no help with regard to ideology, and it proved impossible to obtain the cooperation of García Valdecasas. Within a fortnight after the organizational meeting Valdecasas married a marquesa and went off on a long honeymoon; he never returned to the party. Fearing that the movement would either fall apart or degenerate into street-gang violence, he had decided to have no part of it.

During the first months of the Falange José Antonio spent most of his time trying to spell out the theoretical premises of his political attitudes, although even among party members there were few who cared to listen to him. According to his philosophy, the individual achieved true significance only when occupied in some noble collective task: "Life is not worth the effort if it is not to be burnt up in the service of a great enterprise." Great enterprises were formed only by the free and enthusiastic union of individuals. Individuals bound together by historical tradition, material cooperation, and mutual destiny formed a nation.

A nation could guarantee the freedom of individuals because law and justice could arise only from its historical development and could be enforced only by its superior moral authority. Going one step further, the nation could fulfill its function and maintain the integrity of its institutions only by offering individual citizens a common destiny, to be achieved through a transcendent, national enterprise. That is, the nation was really possible only as Empire. When the nation lost its sense of a transcendent vocation and common destiny, when classes and regions pursued goals of their own, the ethical fabric of national life went to pieces. Social strife, economic misery, and political discord would end only when Spaniards once more forged a common destiny for themselves in the world.

The economic correlative of a common destiny was some form of

national coordination—a nationwide syndical system, for example—
which would guarantee economic justice and increase material production. At first, José Antonio's ideas on economic reconstruction
went little beyond this; in 1933–34 he was still preoccupied with
drawing up the outlines of his nationalist vision.

José Antonio's "destiny in the universal," which he had derived
from a concept of Ortega's, had few practical implications. He never
made it clear whether the phrase implied a restoration of Spanish
cultural dominance or a resuscitation of the Spanish Empire. Although dreams of empire were patently absurd considering Spain's
meager resources, José Antonio was not above dreaming. He was
apparently convinced that Europe was entering an area of conflict
that would bring great territorial realignments on the Continent and
in North Africa. Personally, José Antonio was a repressed Anglo-
phile and even admired Kipling. But as an intellectual, he had
absorbed all the antiliberal propaganda of his generation, and, like
Ledesma, he believed that the end of the Western liberal order was
at hand. If Spain could rejuvenate herself in time to follow the dynamic
new nationalist trend, she might greatly increase her territorial holdings and international influence. In private conversations José Antonio
later came to talk confidently of absorbing Portugal.

José Antonio wanted Spain to make a great historical leap, vaulting
feudal backwardness and liberal capitalism at the same time. Apparently he never imagined that it might be the possibilities and not the
impracticalities of liberalism that were exciting disturbance in Spain,
which had never known an honest system of liberal representation.
Rather than trying to help the nation resolve its differences, José
Antonio and his colleagues proposed to jam the mechanism of parliamentary government and replace it with an abstract system that few
people supported and even fewer understood. He thought that an elite
or "creative minority" could lead the nation to greatness. He forgot
that an elite can control a resistant majority only by the ruthless and
terroristic exercise of power.

José Antonio easily won a seat in the Cortes in the elections of
1933, placing second on the Rightist list at Cádiz. Alienated by the
corruption of Andalusian politics, he did not play an active role in
the new Cortes. Nevertheless, he took great care to make a good impression there, except when it came to the defense of his father's reputation or record, a matter on which he remained intransigent. He
prepared his infrequent speeches carefully, and was very pleased when
he could impress such leading orators of the Left as Prieto and Azaña.

His eloquence and personal charm won a number of friends for him in the national parliament. The clerical reactionary Ramiro de Maeztu remarked that in elegance of figure and gesture, the leader of the Falange reminded him more of the young Ramsay MacDonald than of Mussolini or Hitler. José Antonio's antagonistic comrade Juan Antonio Ansaldo used to tell him that he looked the perfect image of a proper president for the International Anti-Fascist League.

At the time the Falange was founded, the originators of national syndicalism in Spain, the JONS, were just beginning to prosper. According to Ramiro Ledesma, "The year 1933 was the real year of the JONS." An effort to form a student syndicate at the University of Madrid in the spring of that year was immensely successful; four hundred students joined immediately. A syndicate of taxi drivers was also set up, and one hundred young activists were organized into squads of four to do battle in the streets. Furthermore, a few elements of the moneyed Right came forward once more to provide a meager subsidy for Ledesma's radical agitation, and he was given enough money to begin publishing a new monthly review of JONS propaganda. By the summer of 1933 national syndicalist units were operating in eight cities of Spain. None of the groups had more than a few dozen members, but two of them (Valencia and Zaragoza) began to publish weekly reviews. Although he still had fewer than five hundred followers (apart from University students), Ledesma saw the future brighten for the first time.

The party's prospects were soon swept away, however, by the first wave of interest in the Falange, with its superior financial resources and propaganda facilities. As Ledesma later admitted, "The entry of new militants and the upward course of the JONS slackened most noticeably from the very beginning of FE."

Both parties suffered from the victory of the moderate Right in the elections of 1933. It became apparent that if Spanish conservatives could achieve their aims by parliamentary means, they would never support the authoritarian parties. After the fall of Azaña, both Ledesma and José Antonio had hoped to woo embittered liberals, but few of them had lost their faith. The largest group of all, the workers, grew more intransigent by the day. With so little potential support, two competing national syndicalist movements in Spain could hardly survive.

During the winter of 1933–34, there was considerable pressure on Ledesma to agree to a fusion of the JONS and the Falange. *Jonsismo's* main prop, its student following, had begun to fall away, seduced by José Antonio's rhetoric and the more lavish propaganda of the Falange. As incidents attending the sale of party papers in Madrid mounted, all available attention became focused on the Falange, and the prospects of the JONS were "paralyzed." The sources of financial support that had temporarily been opened to the JONS closed once more; the business world was prepared to sustain only one fascistic movement, and the Falange was the larger and safer party. At the same time, the leaders of the Falange were having difficulty maintaining discipline, and José Antonio thought that fusion with the JONS would make it easier to control the amorphous reactionaries in the Falange. For his part, Ledesma finally decided that

the enormous defects of the FE were, perhaps, of a transitory character, and could be overcome. As for that alluvial mass (the Falange), it lacked vigor and a unified historical consciousness, so that it should not have been difficult to displace it from the areas of control. On the other hand, the JONS, utilizing the resonant platform of the FE, could popularize its ideas with relative ease.

Ledesma thought that Ruiz de Alda's military mentality and quasi-totalitarian aspirations were very favorable to *Jonsismo,* and would tilt the balance of internal power.

On February 11, 1934, the National Council of the JONS, representing the nine local Jonsista groups then in existence, met in Madrid to consider a merger with the Falange. A majority of the fifteen-member Council voted to consider terms of unification, while condemning certain "grave errors" in the Falange which they proposed to rectify. Since José Antonio and Ruiz de Alda were also anxious for union, there was very little difficulty in arriving at terms. It was agreed that the new movement would henceforth be called Falange Española de las Juntas de Ofensiva Nacional-Sindicalista, or, in moments of fatigue, F.E. de las J.O.N.S. All the Jonsista slogans and emblems (the yoked arrows, the red and black flag) were officially adopted by the new organization. The unified movement would be directed by a triumvirate composed of José Antonio Primo de Rivera, Ramiro Ledesma Ramos, and Julio Ruiz de Alda. José Antonio insisted that Ledesma take membership card No. 1 in the Falange, because of his seniority. José Antonio became No. 2, Redondo No. 3, Ruiz de Alda No. 4, and so on. Each local unit of the Falange was to be called a *Jons.*

In a general sense, the two groups had been very similar, and the union worked well, although the monarchists and conservatives who had signed up to work for "Spanish fascism" were not enthusiastic about the revolutionary dialectic of the JONS. The only member to desert Ledesma's small following was Santiago Montero Díaz, a history teacher and ex-leader of Communist youth who headed the JONS group at the University of Santiago de Compostela. In announcing his resignation in a letter to Ledesma, he declared that national syndicalism could thrive only on the basis of "revolutionary rivalry" with Marxism. The "Rightist limitations" of the Falange would be mortal, he said. "Despite all the merely verbal declarations to the contrary, the membership, content, and political tactics of the Falange are in open opposition to the national revolution."

Although the personality differences between Ledesma, the intellectual proletarian, and José Antonio, the aristocratic esthete, were never overcome, the Jonsistas strengthened the Falange a great deal. Ledesma was correct in believing that the revolutionary rhetoric of the JONS would eventually prevail over the monarchist-*upetista* sentiment in the Falange. In the first month after the merger Falange propaganda began to adopt a tone and content characteristic of Ledesma and Redondo; this helped fill the gap between the verbal incompetence of Ruiz de Alda and the fine spiritual tension of José Antonio's talk. Falange ideology henceforth took its esthetic tone from José Antonio and much of its practical content from Ramiro Ledesma.

Forced to compete with Ledesma for internal leadership, José Antonio began to place increasing emphasis on revolutionary aims. He was pushed still further in this direction by the hesitations of the older conservative supporters of the Falange. Although their money was vital, José Antonio began to realize in 1934 that he would have to work himself free of them; if he did not, they would eventually cripple his party and abandon him, just as they had his father. But the break did not occur immediately, for the party was just entering a year of internal crisis.

The Party of José Antonio

José Antonio came into his own as a political leader in 1935. He had eliminated his opponents, and the Falange was his own instrument. If he sometimes spoke of the trials and humiliations of a political chief, he also spoke of the exhilaration of public leadership. Although he could never be a *Duce* or a *Führer,* José Antonio was the *Jefe,* and the hero of his young men. Even his political enemies privately acknowledged his charm and sincerity. His only personal regret was that he was unable to shake off completely the *señorito* label attached to his background and family name.

José Antonio was now in a position to express his liberal "elitist" attitudes in directing the party. Shortly after founding the Falange he had said:

Until now fascism has been supported by the lower middle class. The workers will be convinced afterward. The comfortable classes must bring their historic prestige to the support of fascism. They will have to recover their lost status by means of sacrifice and effort.

If we triumph, you may be sure that the *señoritos* will not triumph with us. They must find worthy employment for their talents, regaining the worthy position they squandered in idleness.

During 1935 José Antonio refined this elitist theory. In a major speech at Valladolid in March, he sharply distinguished the Falange's aims from the "romantic" Nazi method of "racial instinct" in a superdemocracy. According to José Antonio, Spain needed a strong state dominated by a revolutionary elite because she was incapable of generating a natural middle-class elite on the liberal French or English pattern. A militant minority would guide the revolutionary movement over its entire route: "In order to realize this goal [the national revolution], it is necessary not to organize masses, but to select minorities —not many, but few, though ardent and convinced; for so everything in the world has been done." The minority would reform the economic structure, elevate the lower classes, and abolish artificial privilege; the superior, not the popular, voice was to command.

It was doubtful that José Antonio had the temperament of a fascist, in the conventional sense of the term. He continued to dine, albeit secretly, with liberal friends; he was too willing to admit that the opposition was human, too friendly in personal relations, to fit the pattern.

His more intemperate followers could say, "Neither Unamuno nor Ortega nor all our intellectuals together are worth one rabid twenty-year-old, fanatical with Spanish passion," but José Antonio merely joked, "We want a happy, short-skirted Spain." Party activists thought up elaborate plots for assassinating Prieto and Largo Caballero, but José Antonio would not countenance them. At one demonstration he threw his arms around a young Leftist who got in the way, to protect him from his own Falange following. He would not permit irresponsible talkers like Giménez Caballero to speak at Falange meetings, nor

would he allow anyone to shout "Down with ——" or "Die ——"
during party rallies:

The anti-somethings, no matter what their something may be, seem to be
imbued with residues of Spanish *señoritismo*, which is actively, yet un-
reflectively, opposed to anything its subject does not participate in. I am
not even anti-Marxist, or anti-Communist, or . . . anti-anything. The
"antis" are banished from my lexicon, like all other barriers to ideas.

Counselors like Francisco Bravo had to keep telling him to be
"fascist," to be more stern and distant. It was the firm opinion of
Madrid liberals that "José Antonio, as he is known to intimates, is a
fascist *malgré lui.* . . . He is a parliamentarian unknown to himself."
In the words of the Reuters correspondent, "tall, thirty, soft-voiced,
courteous, José Antonio was one of the nicest people in Madrid."
"He looked very unreal in his role of a Fascist leader."

Ramiro Ledesma offered one of the most acute analyses of the *Jefe,*
which defined his seemingly impossible contradictions as a political
leader:

It is characteristic of Primo de Rivera that he operates on a series of
insolvable contradictions traceable to his intellectual formation and the
politico-social background from which he emerged. His goals are firmly
held, and he is moved by a sincere desire to realize them. The drama or
the difficulties are born when he perceives that these are not the aims in
life which truly fit him, that he is the victim of his own contradictions, and
that by virtue of them he is capable of devouring his own work and—what
is worse—that of his collaborators. Behold him organizing a fascist movement, that is, a task born of faith in the virtues of impetus, of an
enthusiasm sometimes blind, of the most fanatical and aggressive national
patriotic sense, of profound anguish for the social totality of the people.
Behold him, I repeat, with his cult of the rational, . . . with his flair for
soft, skeptical modes, with his tendency to adopt the most timid forms of
patriotism, with a proclivity to renounce whatever supposes the call of
emotion or the exclusive impulse of voluntarism. All this, with his courteous temperament and his juristic education, would logically lead him to
political forms of a liberal, parliamentary type. Nonetheless, circumstances
hindered such a development. To be the son of a dictator and live tied to
the social world of the highest bourgeoisie are things of sufficient vigor to
influence one's destiny. They swayed José Antonio in that they forced
him to twist his own sentiments and search for a politico-social attitude
that might resolve his contradictions. He searched for such an attitude by
intellectual means, and found it in fascism. Since the day of this discovery
he has been in sharp conflict within himself, forcing himself to believe

that this attitude of his is true and profound. At bottom he suspects that it is something that has come to him in an artificial, transient way, without roots. That explains his vacillation and mode of action. It was these vacillations which made him at times prefer the system of a triumvirate, curbing his aspiration to the *jefatura única*. Only when, because of the internal crisis, he saw his pre-eminence in danger did he determine to take it over. It is strange and even dramatic to watch a man not lacking in talent struggle valiantly against his own limitations. In reality, only after overcoming these limitations can he hope one day to achieve victory.

There is no evidence the Falange had any official contact with the Nazi or Fascist parties before 1936. On the one hand, the Spanish movement was somewhat embarrassed by the derivative nature of its ideology, and on the other, the Germans and Italians could find little reason to pay it any heed.

Il Popolo d'Italia had greeted Delgado Barreto's *El Fascio* with a scornful article about cheap, third-class imitations of foreign ideologies. This blast was unsigned, but Guariglia, the Italian envoy in Madrid, feared it might have been written by the Duce himself. During the next months Guariglia labored to dissipate the antagonism created by such statements. Just before the founding of the Falange, he managed to get José Antonio a thirty-minute interview with Mussolini during the future *Jefe*'s brief vacation in Italy. Although José Antonio wrote a prologue to the Spanish translation of Mussolini's *Il Fascismo* and hung an autographed photo of the Duce beneath his own father's portrait in his office, he had no real personal respect for the Italian leader. He told his intimates that Mussolini had neither created a new juridical system nor effected a revolution, but had merely constructed a myth that the Spanish movement might exploit to its own profit.

José Antonio's only contact with the Nazis, or, for that matter, with German civilization, was made during the spring of 1934 when he visited Berlin while en route to England for a vacation. On that occasion, only minimum notice was accorded him as a foreign fascist leader. He neither attempted to obtain, nor was offered, an audience with Hitler. He was received by a few minor Nazi dignitaries, but no more. In Germany José Antonio was pleased neither by the language, the people, nor the Nazi party. He found the Nazis to be a depressing group, rancorous and divided. He returned to Spain with his once high estimation of National Socialism badly damaged.

He now fully realized that the Falange would profit little by any association with other fascistic parties, whatever their relative sincerity or efficiency; it was up to the Spanish leaders to develop a uniquely

Spanish fascist movement, and thus differentiate themselves in the mind of their native public. Most party luminaries felt the same way. One of Ledesma's principal complaints against José Antonio had been the unfair one of mimicking foreign movements. As the Falange leader most closely connected with traditionalist Catholic sentiment, Redondo was constantly preoccupied with this problem. Ruiz de Alda joined the Jonsista leaders in rejecting foreign ideology as authoritative.

At the big party rally in Valladolid, José Antonio had emphasized that every nation had a different way of realizing its aspirations. Stating this by analogy, he referred to certain verse forms in the poetry of the sixteenth century that had originated in Italy but were later developed even more fully in an authentically Spanish style. The comparison may have suggested more than he meant, but it illustrated what he had in mind. José Antonio later declared that "Fascism is a universal attitude of return to one's [national] essence," and insisted that every nation had its own native style of political expression.

The 1934 visit to Berlin was José Antonio's first and last formal meeting with any foreign political groups. Since fascistic movements were nationalist by definition, he declared there could be no such thing as a "fascist international." When one was actually formed a year later in Montreux, Switzerland, he refused to attend it or to acknowledge it publicly. He did not change his position even under the wheedling of Italian Fascist agents.

Party propaganda soon ceased to call the party "fascist," and José Antonio began to lean over backward to distinguish the Falange from other movements. In the Cortes, he declared: "It happens that fascism has a series of interchangeable external characteristics, which we by no means want to adopt." On December 19, 1934, he announced in *ABC*, "What is more, Falange Española de las J.O.N.S. is not a fascist movement." This was nothing less than a complete reverse of terminology.

José Antonio publicly admitted that a fascist-style movement might become merely outward show. He explained that the Falange sometimes made great use of emblems and ceremony only to stimulate the sluggish nationalist sentiment in the country. Although the Falangists staunchly defended Italian policy from the beginning to the end of the Abyssinian adventure, they refused to accept Mussolini's label. Their own fervid nationalism was, in fact, the only consistently sustained point in the party program.

The more self-sufficient the Falange became, the more it stressed far-reaching economic reform, which it called "revolution." The *Jefe* admitted in private discussion that there was little difference between his economic views and those of moderate Socialists like Indalecio Prieto. However, he explained:

When we speak of capitalism, . . . we are not talking about property. Private property is the opposite of capitalism: property is the direct projection of man on his possessions; it is an essential human attribute. Capitalism has been substituting for this human property the technical instrument of economic domination.

The only really radical point in the Falange's economic program was a proposal to nationalize credit, an operation which José Antonio thought could be accomplished in fifteen days. He thought it would "humanize finance."

The Falange Chief was particularly well informed on agrarian problems, and his suggestions were commended even by acknowledged experts. José Antonio tried to collect information on agricultural affairs in every province of Spain. He understood that poor land required large units of cultivation, while fertile soil might be more widely distributed. He believed that large holdings forming natural units of cultivation should be protected, while excessively small peasant strips should be consolidated; some sections, he thought, would have to be taken out of production altogether. The state would encourage the growth of new industries to absorb the resulting transfer of excess population.

In a big meeting at Salamanca on February 10, 1935, and again before Madrid's "Círculo Mercantil," on April 19, 1935, he stressed that national syndicalism did not propose a socialized economy but only a certain amount of state socialism for vitally needed reforms. He repeated his earlier statement that Mussolini's corporatism represented no more for Spain than a point of departure.

The nationalist content in the Falange's propaganda was in large part conditioned by the reaction against the Catalan and Basque autonomy statutes provided by the Republic. The regionalist problem was one of the principal dilemmas in Spain. Because of their bitterness against the central government, Catalan nationalists had participated with the Left in the 1934 rebellion.

Although the Falange condemned regional separatism, it did not reject regional differences. José Antonio went out of his way to commend the unique qualities of Catalonia, Galicia, and the Basque Provinces. The Falange did not oppose limited local administrative autonomy, but it denounced the separation of an entire region from the national sovereignty.

Unlike most of his followers, José Antonio was no blind nationalist. He had been educated in the Anglophilia of the liberal aristocracy and admired much of the Anglo-Saxon world, especially the British Empire. Ruiz de Alda mentioned Gibraltar in every second speech, but José Antonio was not primarily concerned with that kind of nationalism. He knew that Spaniards would have enough trouble ordering their lives at home, and once remarked to the Reuters representative, "You see, Mr. Buckley, there are a group of typical Spaniards talking, talking eternally. It is very difficult indeed to organize our race for constructive work."

I say to you that there is no fruitful patriotism, which does not arrive through criticism. And I must tell you that our patriotism has also arrived by the path of criticism. We are not moved in any way by that operetta-style patriotism which sports itself with the current mediocrity and pettiness of Spain and with turgid interpretations of the past. We love Spain because it does not please us. Those who love their *patria* because it pleases them love it with a will to touch, love it physically, sensually. We love it with a will to perfection. We do not love this wreck, this decadent physical Spain of today. We love the eternal and immovable metaphysic of Spain.

2. The Nature of Fascism in France

ROBERT J. SOUCY

In 1961 Maurice Bardèche, a French writer who had been a fascist before the war, published a provocative new work entitled *Qu'est-ce que le Fascisme?*. Bardèche boldly reaffirmed his commitment to fascism and argued that it is an ideology, especially in its French version, that has been badly misunderstood, unfairly maligned, and wrongly given up for dead. True fascism, he contended, is no more brutal than the democratic or Marxist philosophies that condemn it; German atrocities committed against Frenchmen during the Occupa-

Source: *The Journal of Contemporary History*, No. 1, *International Fascism, 1920–1945*, pp. 27–55. Copyright © 1966 The Institute for Advanced Studies in Contemporary History, with permission of Harper and Row, Publishers.

tion derived largely from wartime conditions and the need to deal with guerrilla warfare, atrocities duplicated in any case by Allied soldiers against German civilians. Nor should true fascism be confused with Nazi racist and extermination policies—aspects of German national-socialism which were 'deviations' from the basic creed. Because of confusion in the public mind as to what fascism really is, said Bardèche, there has been a failure to acknowledge that fascism is rapidly being reborn today in many parts of the world, including France, although, because the word itself has fallen under a cloud, the phenomenon itself now exists under new labels. Consequently, neo-fascists like Nasser in Egypt and young technocrats in France, men working to fuse nationalism and socialism together once again, are seldom associated with an ideology that is discredited in theory if not in practice. Thus, there are thousands of young men in the world today who are fascists without knowing it.

Whatever the shortcomings or insights in Bardèche's analysis, it once again raises a basic problem faced by historians of modern France: what exactly was the nature of French fascism both before and during the Second World War; what exactly were its fundamental or predominant characteristics? Bardèche himself points out one of the very real difficulties in dealing with the subject: the very diversity and complexity of the movement. This is perhaps much more the case with fascism in France than in other countries, because it never had a single, unified, centralized party. Instead of one fascist party, there were several, running all the way from Georges Valois' *Faisceau* founded in 1925 to Jacques Doriot's *Parti Populaire Français* established in 1936. Even if the historian limits himself to discussing the two largest French fascist movements of the 1930s, Doriot's PPF and Marcel Déat's *Rassemblement Nationale Populaire* (RNP), or to the ideas advanced by one of France's leading fascist newspapers, *Je suis partout,* or by prominent French fascist intellectuals like Robert Brasillach and Pierre Drieu La Rochelle, a great deal of variety, contradiction, and sheer ideological confusion remains. Nevertheless, patterns and common denominators do exist which permit generalizations about even a phenomenon as protean as French fascism.

The few historical studies to date that have attempted to characterize fascism in France before the war have raised a series of important questions in approaching the matter. Was French fascism rooted in native French political traditions or was it simply an ideology imported from abroad? Why was it a relatively weak force on the French political scene before, and even during, the Second World War—

because it was not an indigenous philosophy? Was it closely related to traditional French conservatism (or, as some prefer, conservatisms), or was it an altogether separate entity? Were its goals primarily nationalistic or European? Did it differ markedly from German national-socialism, and if it did, why did many French fascists collaborate with the Germans during the war? And finally, did French fascism even possess an ideology, a clearly defined set of political, social, and economic goals, or was it, as some have said, a sort of fever, an emotional indulgence lacking doctrinal respectability? Several scholars have suggested, in this regard, that it was essentially a kind of romanticism, one which relied upon a vague 'aesthetic' approach to politics, an approach wanting in both reason and realism, and that consequently French fascism can hardly be viewed as a serious ideology at all.

Certainly, of all these questions, the problem of the origins of French fascism is one of the most difficult. According to René Rémond's *La Droite en France,* fascism was a phenomenon quite alien to French political traditions. Most of the so-called fascist leagues of the 1920s and 30s were not really fascist at all but Bonapartist and Boulangist in character and inspiration, connected with past nationalistic movements rather than with 'contemporary foreign experiences'. The riots of 6 February 1934, which led many at the time to talk of a fascist peril, actually resembled more a 'Boulangist agitation than the March on Rome'. There were, Rémond concedes, a few organizations which did copy—in a dull and unimaginative way—Italian or German fascism, movements like *Francisme,* the *Solidarité Française,* and the *Parti Populaire Français,* but by their very failure, by their inability to win any mass public support, they demonstrated just how foreign was fascism to French political thinking. Only Doriot's *Parti Populaire Français,* founded in 1936, was able to win any significant political following and even it remained relatively feeble. 'Thus, before 1936, nothing justifies the legend of French fascism,' concludes Rémond.

This kind of analysis has several drawbacks. First of all, it totally discounts various statements made by leading French fascist writers acknowledging their ideological debt to thinkers like Sorel, Péguy, Barrès, Proudhon, La Tour du Pin, and Maurras. As one French national-socialist declared: 'Our doctrine has its roots in the soil of France.' On the other hand, French fascists like Marcel Déat freely admitted that there was a 'European' side to their fascism, that it was part of a general revolution which crossed frontiers, and that some imitation did occur. True as this may be, it by no means rules out the many intellectual antecedents which fascism had in French thought well before the 1920s. As Eugen Weber has pointed out, national-socialist and fascist ideas in France have a lengthy history; they can be found in the political campaigns of Maurice Barrès at the turn of the century and even in the Jacobinism of the French Revolution. Certainly, in terms of intellectual history, there was little that was un-French about a great many of the ideas associated with fascism. Anti-Semitism, surely, was nothing new to a nation that had lived through the Dreyfus Affair, nor were such things as anti-parliamentarianism, anti-intellectualism, authoritarianism, hero-worship, and justifications of political violence. Simply because these ideas were rooted in Bonapartism or Boulangism or some other political heritage makes them no less proto-fascist, for not only were these movements events unto themselves but they sowed the seeds for later movements, and some of these were fascist. If French fascism was influenced by other fascisms, it also had a national past of its own; consequently, in many instances developments abroad merely served to fortify a set of pre-existing attitudes at home. Moreover the fact that fascism failed to achieve mass public backing in France hardly demonstrates that it was an ideology non-indigenous to that country. A political party need not win popular support to be rooted in several of its country's political traditions. Were this not so it might be said that Hitler's Nazi party was 'un-German' because it lacked mass public support before the onset of the depression.

If it was not because of the lack of a native intellectual ancestry, why then did fascism fail to capture a wide public following in France? Why was it that even France's largest fascist party, the PPF, never attracted more than 250,000 adherents? Economic and social factors were undoubtedly important. France not only escaped the economic consequences of the devastating inflation which plagued Germany in the early 1920s, but she was spared the political and social consequences as well; the threat that the lower middle classes might be proletarianized was never as serious in France as it was in Germany, and thus the pressure on this segment of French society to support the cause of fascism was considerably less. Moreover, the depression itself never hit France as catastrophically as it did her neighbour across the Rhine; partly because of the balance, partly because of the relative stagnation, of her economy. Less industrially developed than Germany and more agricultural, France, although far from untroubled during this period, never suffered the same degree of widespread economic hardship and mass discontent which gave such a boost to the Nazi

Revolution. Bardèche makes the point, for example, and quite co-gently, that fascism is a doctrine which lacks a natural clientele among the electorate; only during times of crisis does it find one among the petty bourgeoisie, a class which, feeling threatened from above and below, responds emotionally to 'heroic' leadership. Consequently, 'when there are no occasions for heroism', fascism declines.

Another major weakness of French fascism was its failure to coalesce behind a single individual or a single party. Fascism in France was a movement of sects which never overcame their differences, often largely personality differences. Even during the Nazi Occupation, Doriot's PPF and Déat's RNP failed to merge; the reasons are still vague, but the personal animosity and distrust between the leaders of the two formations was at times almost comic. There were also bitter conflicts, both personal and political, within the PPF, conflicts which eventually tore the party apart. Sometimes feelings were rooted in old literary feuds, as was primarily the case with Brasillach and Drieu La Rochelle. But the most devastating division of all involved important matters of policy. In October 1938, just after the Munich settlement, several leading members of the PPF resigned in protest over Doriot's position on foreign policy; they now denounced the policy of pacifism and appeasement towards Germany they had accepted until then, and called for a rapid build-up of France's military strength and for a firm stand against Hitler. Among those who defected were important party ideologues like Drieu La Rochelle, Bertrand de Jouvenel, and Paul Marion. The issue of foreign policy was not their only reason for leaving. Doriot's quest for financial support from French business in-terests helped disillusion individuals like Drieu who took the party's avowed 'socialism' somewhat more seriously. As he later complained, Doriot was no different from the Radical politicians he had so long despised: both in domestic and foreign policy, Doriot had behaved 'like a vulgar La Rocque'.

In effect, both Doriot and Déat failed to build a lasting political bridge to either the Right or the Left. According to Brasillach, French businessmen eventually concluded that it suited their interests more to subsidize the Radical Party than the fascists, while, at the same time, the PPF and the RNP were unable to overcome the image the working classes had of them, that they were simply agents of capi-talism, an image abetted by newspaper accounts of fascists killing workers in the Spanish Civil War. 'Fascism, Hitlerism, [and] totalitari-anism for twenty years have succeeded each other in the naïve abomi-nation of the mob,' Déat wrote bitterly in 1942. 'Simply because, very astutely, they have been made synonyms for social and political reaction.' After the fall of France in 1940, of course, fascism for most Frenchmen also became associated with the hated invader, but it had begun to decline as a domestic political force as early as 1938, having failed miserably in its attempt to become a mass movement.

In this regard, it is necessary to make a distinction between fascism and conservatism in France before and during the Second World War; millions of Frenchmen were conservatives, but only a small minority were ever fascists. The Vichy regime was chiefly a regime of conservatives, not fascists, at least until the very last months of the war when French fascists, with the help of the Germans, were finally given several key governmental positions. The differences between conservatism and fascism in France have been underlined repeatedly by students of the French Right since the war, by René Rémond, Eugen Weber, Peter Viereck, and others. Not only were French fascists often critics of 'social-reactionaries' and 'bourgeois' values during the 1920s and 30s, but their editorials attacked Vichy policies time and time again during the war years. In 1942, for example, Doriot accused the men of Vichy of having led France down the road to decadence and defeat before 1940 by opposing social change at home and war against bolshevism abroad, adding that France would suffer further setbacks if Vichy insisted upon continuing a policy of conservative *attentisme.* Weber has shown how French fascists were often at loggerheads even with the *Action Française,* how Maurras broke with Georges Valois, for instance, in 1925, when Valois founded the *Faisceau,* and later with Brasillach, another former disciple, when Brasillach took the leap to fascism and then to complete collaborationism.

Understandably, perhaps, post-war scholarship has tended to emphasize the various areas of disagreement between men like Maurras and Brasillach. Conservative historians especially have concentrated their efforts on showing the doctrinal incompatibility between the fascist Right and the conservative Right (denying at times that fascism even belongs to the 'Right'). Scholars have argued that Maurras and his followers, as well as most French conservatives, were fundamentally different from fascists in several respects: they were enemies of 'Jacobin' centralization, *étatisme,* and the authoritarian state; they were devoted to the restoration of decentralized government and local freedoms; they were hostile to theories of popular sovereignty (which submerged the *pays réel* beneath the *pays légal*); and they were believers in social stability and a rational approach to politics rather than in revolutionary turmoil and fascist romanticism. 'Fascism dreams only of upheaval,' says Rémond. 'The Right wants to be reassured and aspires after stability.' Above all, it has been emphasized, conservatism in France was a philosophy of the bourgeoisie, of the socially-reactionary bourgeoisie, and as such it was clearly at odds with the 'social' programme put forward by French fascists, men who failed to view social justice with the same 'horror' as conservatives. Finally, some scholars have held that fascism and conservatism in France also differed radically in their respective loyalties to nationalism. Whereas conservatism was a highly nationalistic faith in the 1930s, grounded as it was in the thought of anti-German patriots like Barrès and Maurras, it was the European, non-nationalistic orientation of French fascism which led many of its adherents to collaborate with the Nazis during the Occupation. Because of all these differences then, it is a mistake to regard fascism and conservatism as one: 'The two notions are, in fact, irreducible.' Indeed, Paul Sérant has even gone so far as to declare: 'to pretend to establish a kinship between fascism and traditional [conservative] doctrines would be in vain. . . .'

The difficulty with this view of the relationship or lack of relationship between fascism and conservatism in France is that many of the lines that have been drawn dividing the two were never as distinct and tidy as has been suggested, and furthermore, that the two philosophies shared many common denominators which were often far more important in determining their political behaviour than the elements which separated them. Ideologically, certainly, there were many ties. Respected conservative thinkers like Barrès and Maurras had long preached many of the doctrines which fascists like Brasillach and Drieu adhered to, from a glorification of power, 'realism', and authoritarian leadership to a hatred of parliamentarianism, politicians, and humanitarian liberalism. Moreover, those who emphasize Maurras' commitment to decentralized government and local freedoms fail to mention, at least in this regard, his willingness to condone and even praise authoritarian and *étatiste* measures when they were taken by the Vichy regime. There was nothing surprising about this, however, for, as Professor Rémond himself once observed, the principles of the *Action Française* had long been, in effect, a 'melange of authority and indiscipline, tradition and insubordination'. Hence, while condemning 'Jacobin' centralization, Maurras acknowledged that when a monarchist state came to power again it might have to institute a temporary dictatorship in order to impose a proper state of affairs. In this, Rémond notes, Maurras was not unlike totalitarian Marxists. Nor, one might add, was he unlike totalitarian fascists.

As for the contention that conservatives differed from fascists in their coolness towards theories of popular sovereignty (although Barrès, for one, advocated during his lifetime a kind of authoritarian democracy based on his notion of *la terre et les morts*), this coolness, in fact, was much more of a common trait with French fascism than an uncommon one, for French fascism generally was more elitist in doctrine than German national-socialism. More true is the observation that French fascists tended to glorify revolutionary, direct-action tactics far more than conservatives, although even here one can cite the violent activities of the *Camelots du Roi,* the activist wing of the *Action Française,* to show that resort to force was not foreign to 'conservatives'. Nevertheless, on balance, fascists did *talk* revolution more than conservatives, especially more than the sort of conservative who dominated the Radical Party throughout most of the 1920s and 30s. Still, the lines between fascism and conservatism in France were often blurred.

What the two camps had most in common, of course, was their anti-communism. It was this above all which made them political bed-fellows on so many occasions, uncomfortable ones no doubt but still bedfellows. Indeed, French fascist writings sometimes leave the impression that all else was secondary to one primary goal: to mobilize France against communism at home and abroad. 'Our policy is simple; we seek the union of Frenchmen against Marxism,' declared Doriot in 1938. 'We want to clear France of agents of Moscow.' Or, as Bardèche said of fascism after the war: 'Its mission of defending the West remains in one's memory, and it is still the principal meaning of the fascist idea.' It was this fixation, among others, which led many French fascists to favour Germany during the Munich crisis of 1938 and to collaborate with the Nazis after 1940: Germany presented a check against Soviet penetration into Europe. This notion, too, contributed mightily to the often remarkable, or perhaps not so remarkable, editorial agreement between the conservative press and the fascist press in France during the late 1930s, this and the growing disenchantment with a Third Republic which among other things could allow Léon Blum's Popular Front to come to power. Consequently, as Professor Rémond puts it, the conservative press in France after 1936 displayed 'a more and more marked inclination for fascism' as it happened that 'a part of the classical Rights let themselves be won over by the vocabulary and circumvented by the propaganda of fascism'. Actually, it is probably more correct to say that instead of being 'won over' and 'circumvented' by fascist notions, French conservatives simply found that many of these notions coincided with their own. A conservative traditionalist, for example, would not have had to change thinking caps to have accepted Brasillach's contention that one's identity is rooted in the soil and heritage of one's country (an idea that Brasillach himself received from Barrès and Maurras), or to have approved Doriot's statement that 'a nationalism understands itself only if it looks for its sources in the old traditions of the French provinces'.

Too often historians of the French Right have made the mistake of rigidly divorcing conservatism from fascism in theory when in practice, that is historically, these movements interpenetrated one another in a very disconcerting way—disconcerting at least if one expects intellectual and political phenomena to be nicely compartmentalized and self-contained. Scholars like Sérant, Plumyène, and Lasierra, it is true, have acknowledged that fascism in France did take some of its elements from the conservative Right, but then they contend that, once formed, fascism acted *against* the Right. As has been shown, this simply was not always the case. The beliefs which fascism and conservatism had in common drew them together on more than one occasion, especially when communism or Soviet Russia was at issue. That they disagreed on some questions does not mean that they did not agree on others. The most that can be said is that while French conservatives, to be sure, were *not* fascists, they often behaved as if they were, and while fascists were not conservatives they often shared many conservative positions.

Perhaps the best way to see how blurred and untidy were the lines which separated them is to examine their respective positions on the question of socialism. It is this measurement which many historians of the French Right have selected as the primary criterion for dividing the two camps, despite the fact that socialism was only one of many elements in fascist ideology—and not necessarily the most important element at that. Eugen Weber, for example, has argued in his study of the *Action Française* that Maurras cannot be called a fascist because he was opposed to socialism and in any case always regarded economic questions as secondary. *'Politique d'abord'*, not economic reform, was Maurras' principal concern. Weber's definition of fascism at this point becomes quite important. By focussing on the economic issue, his definition *excludes* the conservative Right; yet had he concentrated on other Maurrasian and conservative doctrines, he might just as well have *included* it. Moreover, if one assigns so much weight to the matter of socialism in defining fascism, one might wonder whether Hitler

was a fascist or a conservative; after all, in purging the socialist wing
of the Nazi party in 1934, Hitler, too, followed a policy of *politique
d'abord*. The same can be said of Mussolini's much publicized corporatism, a 'social' programme which, once in operation, benefited
Italian employers more than Italian workers. Finally, if one closely
examines the economic programmes advocated by France's two largest fascist parties in the 1930s, one can question whether these movements, too, were not less concerned with a fundamental economic
transformation of society than with other matters.

To be sure, French fascist speeches and tracts were filled with attacks upon 'plutocratic' capitalism and expressions of devotion to
'fascist socialism'. Typical was Drieu's proud comment in *Socialisme
fasciste* (1934): 'Fascism is a reformist socialism, but a reformist
socialism which has, it seems, more fire in its belly than the old classical parties.' Yet when one examines the exact content of the socialism
which was espoused, the gap between their social-economic programme and that of many conservatives is not nearly as wide as expected. This is particularly striking in regard to the position which
Doriot and the PPF took vis-à-vis the middle classes. In *Refaire la
France* (1938), for example, Doriot lamented the 'ruin' of the middle
classes and the 'frightful' crisis they faced as a result of the devaluation
of the franc and the fiscal burdens they had to bear. He noted sympa-
thetically that not only did their situation differ from that of the
proletariat but that they represented 'a state of soul quite distinct from
the proletarian state of soul'. The real enemy, he emphasized, was not
the bourgeoisie as a whole but rather big business, monopolies, the
great financial trusts. In fact, one of the major sins of the Popular
Front was that it favoured these large institutions at the expense of
small and middle-sized businesses. The solution was not to nationalize
industry (which was to confuse socialism with 'the bureaucratization
of production' and 'super-protected industry'), but to suppress the
protected sector of the economy, the web of monopolies, and to
strengthen the free sector, the sector of small private enterprise. Under
fascism, political representation would be based upon new criteria,
upon professional rather than geographical lines, but economic life
would operate according to traditional capitalist principles, especially
according to the principle that 'Individual profit remains the motor of
production'. There would be a ceiling, however, on the profits of big
business (the surplus falling into a social welfare fund), and corporations which used their capital without social responsibility would be
challenged; but the principal economic task of government would be

to protect the free sector from the protected sector by taking measures to decentralize industry and democratize capital.

The economic programme which Déat presented in his book *Le Parti Unique* (1942) was much the same. Like Doriot, Déat paid his respects to the petty and middle bourgeoisie as 'guardians of precious traditions' and declared that their position in French society had to be safeguarded if they were not to be wiped out by the larger industrial and commercial enterprises. A corporate state would help small businessmen band together in employer organizations which would enable them to overcome their weakness vis-à-vis big business. Fascist socialism, consequently, was far from hostile to the great bulk of the middle classes; in fact it would be their saviour:

> The necessary rescue of our middle classes will be one of the happiest effects, one of the most essential objectives of the National Revolution. And that is what socialism should mean to them. At this point, we are a long way from any Marxist nonsense about the automatic concentration of our large enterprises and about the inevitable elimination of our small producers, people whom Marxists would discard, throwing them into the wage-earning class.

Déat made it quite clear also that fascist socialism was not an enemy of private property. 'All property is legitimate to the degree that it is not harmful to the common interest, even more so if it serves it.' Industry, he insisted, should be controlled and regulated but not nationalized. Nationalization indicated distrust of industry on the part of the State and failed to make wage-earners any less wage-earners. A fascist economy would be a planned economy to the extent that no factory would be allowed to manufacture 'no matter what at no matter what price and pay no matter what salaries', but private management, which had the competence and the staff, would look after the 'details'. Fascist socialism would excommunicate no one; services rendered would alone count. The industrialist who was intelligent and efficient would prosper, although he would no longer be driven solely by the profit motive, for he would be a leader in the full sense of the word, one who would continue to know the 'joys of command' but who would also know the joys of responsibility towards his workers. Finally, unlike Marxism, fascist socialism would not be abstract, doctrinaire, and monolithic, a system run by a centralized bureaucracy; instead it would be 'realistic and concrete', empirical and dynamic, leaving each employer to take his chances, with a great deal of freedom to operate his business as he saw fit.

Both Déat and Doriot agreed, therefore, that a 'brutal transfer of property' was unnecessary and unwise and that there was no need for the workers to become 'co-proprietors' of the factories. Once the power of big business was broken, small businessmen could be counted upon to meet their social responsibilities. 'Our personal working-class experience has taught us,' said ex-worker Doriot, 'that small employers easily come to agreement with their workers against the Marxists in order to insure social justice and to protect themselves against the enemies of production and prosperity.' Fascism, therefore, would end class struggle and inaugurate class cooperation. Indeed, wrote Déat, this was the very meaning of totalitarianism: 'Totalitarianism is conciliation, a reconciliation.'

Stripped of its rhetoric, what Doriot and Déat's socialism amounted to was a programme designed more to suit the small and middle bourgeoisie than the proletariat. Highly significant in this regard was Déat's statement in 1942 that the socialism he advocated was not simply a programme for the working class but a programme for all classes, for, he said (and here his candour was exceeded only by his opportunism), France was not a country of large industrial enterprises nor was it even primarily an industrial country, and thus if fascism addressed itself to only one part of the nation it would lack '*élan*'.

No doubt this was one reason why French fascist party programmes were as attentive to the grievances of the peasantry as they were to those of the lower bourgeoisie. Doriot and Déat both expressed their regret at falling agricultural prices and the growing exodus from the farms. Déat called for a rigorously equal exchange of products and services between the countryside and the cities, and condemned what he said was a situation in which the city-dwellers 'duped' the peasantry. Doriot emphasized that fascism, unlike Marxism, had no intention of making the peasant a 'diminished citizen'; it wanted to put an end to the migration from the farms because it abhorred 'the frightful concentration of large cities generating misery, unemployment, and social troubles'. Instead of liquidating or collectivizing the peasantry, fascism would work to preserve the small private farm by creating new credit facilities, by helping the peasants to specialize in products of quality, and by expanding the domestic market for their products by diverting the agricultural output of France's colonies elsewhere. Such measures had to be taken because 'the peasant is the essential support of a society such as ours', and 'represents the best virtues of our people'. Déat agreed. He, too, insisted that France must maintain a strong peasantry, 'physically robust and healthy, morally solid and balanced'. Indeed, so much did he agree with Doriot's glorification of the peasantry and its virtues that he announced that the cultivation of these virtues was a major goal of fascist socialism. 'Peasant socialism has no other aim and no other meaning,' he said. 'And it is indeed socialism since here again it is a question of integrating the mass of the peasantry, in accordance with its proper rank and place, into the community.'

As a matter of fact, fascist socialism seemed to have something for everybody. At the same time, for example, that the PPF called for less *étatisme* and fewer bureaucrats, it stated that 'dignity commanded' that lower functionaries be paid better salaries and that higher functionaries be treated in a manner 'worthy of their functions'—especially in regard to pensions. The dignity and rights of women were also identified as special concerns of the PPF; subsidies should be granted to mothers with many children and jobs easy for women to fill should be made available to them. The 1936 platform of the PPF also made provision for the material needs of the liberal professions, the intelligentsia, and the artisan class. 'In short,' it said '[the PPF] will defend the interests of all those whose activity constitutes a traditional element of social equilibrium in France.'

If this was socialism, it was hardly a socialism far removed from a great deal of traditional French conservatism. In the middle-class and peasant orientation of its party platforms, at least, it was certainly much closer to French conservative thought than to Marxian socialism. If French fascism offered a 'third way' between communism and liberalism, as its proponents argued, it was a third way which nudged the Right far more than the Left. To point to the socialism advocated by French fascists as the major factor distinguishing their ideology from conservatism before and during the Second World War is to misjudge the character of that socialism. This is not to discount entirely, of course, the French fascist criticism of the evils of capitalism, especially big capitalism, nor its commitment to a certain amount of government economic regulation and planning. This kind of socialism *was* part of their creed, but it was simply not as revolutionary nor as divorced from conservatism as many scholars have suggested.

Some French fascists, it is true, did take the avowed socialism and anti-capitalism of fascist ideology more seriously than others, especially literary intellectuals like Drieu, Brasillach, and Bardèche, men who were violently opposed—emotionally, intellectually and morally—to bourgeois society and bourgeois values. Indeed, one must always keep in mind the temperamental differences between *literati* like these and party organizers like Doriot and Déat; the latter, constantly faced with the practical problem of trying to enrol large sections of the public, often a bourgeois public, behind their banners, were more apt to dilute the movement's socialism than were some of their followers (a phenomenon likewise present in German national-socialism). One reason which Drieu later gave for his break with Doriot in 1938, it will be recalled, was his disenchantment with Doriot's dealings with conservative financial backers.

Yet even in the fascism of someone like Drieu, a concern for socialism or economic reform was not the primary motive force. Like many French fascists, Drieu was more concerned with advancing a 'spiritual' revolution than a material one. As a result, his conception of socialism was almost ascetic at times, equating as he did materialism and creature comforts with moral decadence and physical weakness, and rejecting Marxian socialism because of what he felt was its too great emphasis on material and scientific goals. Moreover his contempt for those who hungered after the goods of this world was not restricted to the bourgeoisie, for, as he once scornfully remarked, the workers in this regard 'were more bourgeois than the bourgeois'. Yet his brand of socialism was sufficiently different from Hitler's to cause him, on several occasions during the 1930s, to condemn Hitler's professions of socialism as sheer hypocrisy. After visiting Germany in 1934, for instance, he expressed his disappointment at the fact that Nazi economic policies remained quite conservative and that German capitalists continued to profit handsomely; in 1936 he dismissed Hitler and Mussolini as nothing more than 'armed guards of capitalists'; and in 1939 he agreed with Hermann Rauschning that the Nazi Revolution was, for this reason, essentially a revolution of nihilism. Consequently, it is highly questionable that Drieu decided to collaborate with the Germans in 1940 primarily out of a commitment to socialism. Nor did men like Doriot and Déat have any more reason than Drieu to believe that the Nazis would bring economic reforms in their wake. Before Hitler came to power in Germany this might have been the case, but by 1940 his economic record was there for all to see.

Why then did many French fascists become collaborators? If the 'socialism' of the Nazis was not the major reason, then what was? Was it because they shared with their German counterparts a belief in racism, a mystical faith in the masses, a devotion to the *Führerprinzip,* because they were Nazi sympathizers in all things? Or was it because they were Europeans first and nationalists second? Or finally, was their anti-communism the most important factor? Of all these possible reasons, only the last seems to have played a major role, and even it was not the most important motive for some French fascists.

Paul Sérant indicates in his *Le Romantisme fasciste* that anti-semitism and racism were not central to French fascism until rather late in the day. He gives 1936 as the turning point, the year Blum's Popular Front came to power in France. It was only then that the fascist press in France made anti-semitism a cardinal issue, for at least two reasons, neither of which had much to do at first with racial theory: Blum's Popular Front government, the major threat to French fascism at that time, was particularly vulnerable to such a campaign (Blum himself and several of the members of his government were Jews); and the charge could also be made that it was the Jews in France who, because of their hatred of Hitler, were trying to drag France into a war with Germany. That this campaign was more a matter of expediency than conviction is seen from the fact that even after 1936 most spokesmen for French fascism equivocated agonizingly on the question of race, not becoming full-fledged racists until the German Occupation.

Drieu La Rochelle is a good example of this development. In 1931 he heaped scorn upon the Nazi idea of a biologically distinct German race, ridiculing it as a delusion held by 'nostalgic petty bourgeois' who ignored the migrations of history. In 1934, after his visit to Germany, he took issue with the 'eugenic conservatism' of the Nazis and what he called their tendency to divide humanity into castes on the basis of blood. After 1936, however, his writings reflected a definite turn towards anti-semitism, yet of a sort which still condemned Hitler's brand as excessive and which was notably ambiguous as to whether Jewishness was 'an irreducible biological fact' or a matter of cultural conditioning. At one point in 1938, for example, he was tortuously on both sides of the question when he concluded that there *was* a biological difference which *'en gros'* differentiated Europeans from Jews, but at the same time refused to dismiss the possibility that *certain* Jews could be modified by education and assimilated into French society. (Even as late as 1942, Marcel Déat distinguished between the Jew who was harmful to the French community and who should be deported, and the Jew who fought and shed his blood for France and who should be accepted as 'an honourable and honoured ally'.) It was not until after the fall of France that Drieu began to talk about 'the very simple laws by which the life of peoples is based upon the fecundity of soil and blood', and even then he felt it necessary to justify his new position by equating racism with Aryanism and Aryanism with Europeanism. 'From this point of view, Germanism is simply the advanced guard of Europeanism,' he wrote.

Does this suggest then that French fascism was more European in orientation than nationalist? Not necessarily. Here again the gap between conservatism and fascism in France was not so wide as might be expected. It is true that after 1940 Drieu and many of his colleagues tended to emphasize the European aspect of fascism, presenting Hitlerism as a means of creating a third force between communist Russia and the democratic capitalist powers. In Drieu's case, Europeanism had been a major tenet of faith as far back as 1931, when he wrote a tract entitled *Europe contre les patries*. However, by the late 1930s, after his conversion to fascism, he was like most French fascists a nationalist first and a European second. Indeed, so prominent was his nationalism during these years that he presented French fascism as an important means of strengthening France *against* Nazi Germany and fascist Italy, believing as he did that it was 'the only method capable of barring and turning aside the expansion of [other] fascist countries'. French national security came first, he said, and it counted far more than ideology when it came to making alliances. Thus he urged France to bolster its diplomatic ties with liberal-democratic England against national-socialist Germany. 'Systems change, but countries remain,' he declared. He vehemently condemned the idea of allowing France to be invaded by foreign troops, even fascist troops. In retrospect, a passage he wrote in 1937 is both ironic and tragic:

> It is all very nice to shout: 'Long live the Soviets' or 'Bravo Hitler' when one is tranquilly at home, among Frenchmen, comfortably settled. It might not be so pretty when there are thousands of Stalinist or Hitlerian mercenaries tramping their boots across our soil, singing their own songs, swearing in their own languages and looking at our women. . . . Why do you expect Russians or Germans trained by dictatorships to conduct themselves better than French soldiers during the Revolution, men thought to have been made tender by utopian speeches? Foreign troops can be nothing but humiliating.

This kind of nationalism, however, did not prevent Drieu and other spokesmen for French fascism favouring the appeasement of Hitler during the Munich crisis of 1938, although not without misgivings. They did this not so much because they were pro-German as because they were anti-Russian, and also, even more important, because they felt that France had no chance of winning a war against Germany in

1938—a position, it should not be forgotten, that was generally shared by the French conservative press—a nationalistic press—at that time. Nor should it be forgotten that shortly after Munich, Drieu and several others quit the PPF in protest against Doriot's continued pacifism towards Germany—and that, not long afterward, Doriot himself adopted an ultranationalist, anti-German posture. Indeed, the reasons for this split within the PPF are still obscure. It may well have resulted more from a dispute over tactics than from any fundamental differences over ideological issues like nationalism. After all, Doriot himself had left the PCF in 1936 in order to establish a party of *national* socialism, free from Russian dictation. The doctrine of the PPF was one of 'intransigent nationalism', Doriot said; 'Our credo is *la patrie*'. Later, in less happy circumstances, he collaborated with the invader—for the same reason many conservatives did: to serve the interests of France (as he conceived them). In 1942 he insisted that French fascism must retain a certain identity and autonomy of its own within the New Order—the pathetic plea of a hard-pressed nationalist.

Finally, the notion that French fascists before the war were sympathetic to Germany in all things and therefore collaboration was temperamentally a natural path for them to take after the fall of France is one that can easily be disputed. Not only were most French fascists quite nationalistic before 1940 and committed to a distinctively *French* brand of fascism, but most of the leading intellectuals of the movement looked more to Latin fascisms for inspiration—to Italy, Spain, and Portugal—than to German nazism. Drieu's disenchantment with many aspects of Hitler's Germany from the mid-1930s onward has already been mentioned. When Drieu wrote what was perhaps the most popular French fascist novel of the pre-war period, *Gilles* (1939), it was among the fascists of Spain not those of Germany that his hero sought fulfilment. Brasillach, also, was much more an admirer of Spanish fascism than German. The ideas of its founder, José Antonio de Rivera, were a major source of his early attraction to fascism, while Spain itself was for Brasillach the place of 'all audacities, all grandeurs, all hopes'. On the other hand, when he crossed the Rhine and attended the Nuremberg rallies in 1937, he failed to respond with equal enthusiasm. Although some recent commentators on Brasillach's career have made a great deal of his descriptions of these rallies, suggesting that they were wholly sympathetic accounts, what Brasillach actually emphasized a great deal of the time was the *strangeness* with which these rites struck him. To him, he said, Germany was 'prodigiously and profoundly and eternally a *foreign* country'. He did admire the emotion and vitality which these rallies generated in their German audiences, and he admired their emphasis on youth, but many of the ideas and symbols which characterized them, and which he found particularly German, struck him at times as almost ridiculous. When he wrote in his death cell in 1945 that throughout most of his life he had not been intellectually in touch with Germany, he was being perfectly honest.

The differences between French and German fascism, certainly, were many and great. Not only was racism much less important in the French version, but (perhaps as a consequence of this difference) neither was there such an emphasis on *Massendemokratie,* on totalitarian democracy, on the *Volk* as the ultimate source of political sovereignty and national greatness. Despite the provisions in its party programmes aimed at winning a broad mass following, French fascism was generally a much more elitist ideology than its German counterpart. In part, it may have been forced to exaggerate its elitist side because of its failure to become a mass movement. But there was also a genuine ideological distaste on the part of many of the intellectuals of the movement for any doctrine which glorified the masses rather than small groups of exceptional men. After all, the major criticism which French fascists made of their country was that it was decadent —and by implication that most of their countrymen were decadent too. Men like Drieu and Brasillach were especially critical of what they felt was the lack of vitality and will displayed by the French people in comparison with other peoples, and consequently they called for an authoritarian elite to pull the nation out of its slothful habits. Even the politicians of French fascism, men like Doriot and Déat, sensitive as they were to public opinion, made it clear that, in the last analysis, the government they had in mind would be a government much more for the people than by the people. Despite their talk of political representation through syndicalist corporations, ultimate political power, under fascism, was to reside in the hands of a single party and a single elite. The membership of this elite, it is true, was to be recruited from all classes of the population and from all regions of France. This was an important difference between fascist thought and a great deal of conservative thought, for fascist theoreticians insisted that those who governed should not be drawn from *just* the traditional hierarchies and authorities but from the lower classes as well, from wherever exceptional ability manifested itself. Thus, while both camps shared a common distaste for notions of popular sovereignty, they disagreed, although only in part, as to who would compose the ruling elite.

Fascists, in this respect at least, were more democratic than many conservatives. However, their attitude towards the broad body of the masses remained quite as undemocratic.

Indeed, one of the major differences between French and German fascism was that Nazi ideology conceived of the Leader as a figure who derived his powers from the *Volk* and whose will was therefore law even unto the ruling elite, whereas French fascism with its far less exalted notion of the masses never subscribed to the *Führerprinzip* with the same degree of zeal. Drieu, for example, insisted that members of a true elite were partners not servants of their leader, and that their voices carried great weight in the decisions that were made. In fact, in *Socialisme fasciste,* he denounced all dictators, contemptuously remarking that they arose only when men were at their weakest. He concluded that while the masses, being 'a little female', were prone to abandon themselves to these 'living gods', a truly virile elite would always resist this kind of subservience. As he had declared a year earlier in his play *Le Chef*: 'There is an appalling weakness in men who give themselves to another man. When there is a dictator, there is no longer an elite; it means that the elite is no longer doing its duty.'

This elitist side of French fascism cannot be emphasized too much. It was one of the major attractions which fascism held for sensitive, intelligent *literati* like Drieu, Brasillach, Bardèche, and others. They were especially seduced by the notion of being part of a tightly-knit group of young, loyal, virile comrades—of being part of a *team*. Fascism was first of all a spirit, Brasillach once said, and 'it is the spirit of the team above all else'. At times the fascism of these men seemed little more than a schoolboy dream, a cult of masculine friendship, a notion of camaraderie—but there was more than this involved: there was the sense of enhanced personal power which comes from being part of a dynamic company of men, and, perhaps most of all, there was an end to the feeling of isolation and alienation which plagued people like Drieu. No longer, said Drieu shortly after his conversion to fascism, did one have to be like thousands of individuals in the modern world who tremble with cold in their little rooms in the great cities and who feel the need to rush together to keep warm. By joining the PPF, the 'paralysis' of individualism is overcome and men relearn *'la vie de groupe'*. 'There, one no longer lives alone, one lives together,' Drieu wrote in *Avec Doriot* (1936). 'There, one does not die each in his corner, . . . there one lives.' Freedom becomes no longer a matter of individual autonomy but of personal force, and the greatest personal force comes from being in and living through a group. Hence

Drieu defined liberty as 'the power a man receives from being bound to other men'. Much the same sensation was described by Brasillach in his *Notre Avant-Guerre* (1941) when he told how he and many of his fascist comrades were exhilarated by 'living together' in mass meetings 'in which the rhythmic movements of armies and crowds seemed like the pulsations of a vast heart'.

Drieu underlined, however, that not just *any* group would do; it had to be a truly elite group, its members young, militant and courageous. It was these qualities, he argued, which particularly distinguished fascists from their political opponents, especially from the great bulk of communists and socialists, and herein, he said, lay one of fascism's greatest appeals and sources of strength. In fact there were moments when Drieu put so much emphasis on personal qualities, activist qualities—aggressiveness, courage, vitality, force—that his fascism seemed little more than a mystique of action for action's sake—as when he declared in 1937, for example, that it was not the programme of the PPF which counted so much as its spirit, its spirit of combat and action. Perhaps the most striking example of this aspect of his fascism occurs in his novel *Gilles,* during the episode in which the hero, after witnessing the February 1934 riots in Paris, proposes a remarkable plan of action to the leader of one political organization:

> Open an office immediately to recruit combat sections. No manifestos, no programme, no new party. Only combat sections, which will be called combat sections. With the first section that is formed, do no matter what. Attack Daladier or defend him, but with acts that are completely concrete. Invade, one after another, a newspaper of the Right and a newspaper of the Left. Have this person or that person beaten up at his home. At all costs, break with the routine of the old parties, of manifestos, of meetings, of articles and speeches.

A revolution of nihilism? Not necessarily. The fact that Drieu was inclined to downgrade certain ideological questions at certain moments does not mean that he lacked an ideology or that he was unconcerned with doctrine. His cult of action and force was itself a doctrine and the source in turn of other doctrines. It was precisely because fascists like Drieu glorified power and energy and vitality, and condemned French society for its decadence, for its lack of these qualities, that they demanded a radical transformation and a spiritual regeneration of that society. Not only was this critique the inspiration for a variety of doctrines and programmes, but more than anything else, perhaps it separated fascists in France from conservatives and traditionalists.

For what preoccupied one French fascist writer after another—and what was one of the most distinctive features of their ideology—was their overwhelming sense of national decadence, their feeling that France was debilitated and weak, that it was sunk in torpor and somnolence. The underlying premise of so much of their thought was that France had declined drastically since her former days of glory and that this was largely due to the moral and physical degeneration of her people. Part of the blame was placed on 'plutocratic capitalism', and thus a brand of national 'socialism' was advocated to enhance the economic power of France vis-à-vis other nations, but on the whole French fascists viewed French decadence as primarily a moral problem (which is one reason, perhaps, why the economic programmes they devised seem mild by Marxian standards). Like Drieu, most French fascists conceived their revolution to be essentially a spiritual revolution. They argued that France suffered from a declining birthrate, from egoism and individualism and materialism, from a lack of vitality and force, not so much because of economic conditions (French fascist thinkers unanimously rejected a strictly economic or materialistic explanation of history and society), but because of certain philosophical conceptions, especially democratic and liberal philosophical conceptions, which had misled the French people. Once these conceptions were replaced by superior conceptions, French society would be regenerated.

For someone like Brasillach fascism was also, in no small measure, a revolt of youth against its elders, a revolt of a young, healthy, idealistic generation against an old, sick, rotten one. It was not a point of view likely to endear itself to middle-aged conservatives. No doubt, too, most Frenchmen were less interested in being regenerated than in eating well, less concerned with youthful asceticism than with the material comforts of life. Here again there was a distinct difference between fascists and many conservatives, especially well-established, comfortable conservatives. Like Drieu, Brasillach and his friends at *Je suis partout* despised the materialistic values of the bourgeoisie and their debilitating attachment to creature comforts, and, like him, they dreamed of a new generation of Frenchmen, strong in body, comradely in spirit, and 'scornful of the thick possessions of this world'. One result was that there was often a good deal of primitivism involved in their revolt. 'In truth,' Bardèche tells us, 'man, such as he is conceived of by fascists, is a young savage who believes only in those qualities which one needs in the bush or in the arctic; he denounces civilization, for he sees in it only hypocrisy and imposture.'

But there was a great deal more to the fascist concept of man than that. Indeed to a large extent the central vision of French fascism was its vision of ideal manhood, its concept of the *homo fascista,* its notion of the 'new man' that a fascist society would produce. The aim of fascism, said Déat, was to create the 'total man', or, as Bardèche later said, 'to form men according to a certain model'. And they were sure that the model was there before them. Brasillach declared proudly in 1941:

   . . . during the last twenty years we have seen the birth of a new human type—as distinct and as surprising as the Cartesian hero, as the sensitive encyclopedist of the eighteenth century, as the Jacobin 'patriot'—we have seen the birth of fascist man. In fact, as science distinguishes the *homo faber* from the *homo sapiens,* we should perhaps present to classifiers and to amateurs at this sort of thing this *homo fascista.*

Again and again, spokesmen for French fascism emphasized that it was 'this new image of man' that was the most essential part of their movement and which more than anything else set them apart from their rivals.

   What is the portrait of the *homo fascista* which emerges from their writings? He is a man of energy, virility, and force—above all of force. He views life in Darwinian terms, as a struggle for survival in which the strong triumph over the weak. He believes that the only justice there is in this world, as Brasillach expressed it, is 'that which reigns by force'. Hence he does not avoid fighting and bloodshed but welcomes it, for only in combat does he fully become a man. His physical courage is fortified by a strong body. In times of peace he is an athlete hardened by sport. He is no egocentric individualist, however, because he realizes that he finds personal fulfilment only through the group, and consequently he respects cohesion, discipline, and authority. He is a man of action, will, and character; he is, in short, a *hero,* one who determines history rather than being determined by it.

   Thus, said the defenders of Fascist man, he contrasts sharply with Marxist man or Democratic man. Men are born neither naturally good nor naturally equal. There is no inevitable progress in history nor is history determined solely by economic conditions. The fundamental error of Marxism is to believe that mankind is simply the product of material forces and that man himself is nothing more than 'a certain number of kilos of organic materials'. Unlike Marxism, fascism does not ignore the 'human factor' in history and the role of dynamic individuals. 'Fascism,' said Drieu, '. . . surpasses socialism by its sense of man.' Or as Bardèche puts it:

Fascism does not furnish as does communism an explanation of the history of the world; it does not propose a key with which anyone can decipher reality. It does not believe in fate; on the contrary it denies fate, opposing it instead with the will of men and believing that man forges his own destiny. . . . Fascism judges events and men in relation to a certain idea of man which is its own.

This certain idea of man, it was emphasized, has little in common with what democracies try to make of man. Democratic theory produces human beings who can read but have no morality, who seek comfort and security rather than the heroic life, who are petty individualists concerned solely with their own self-interest rather than members of a community devoted to something greater than themselves. Fascism wants to break the 'shell of [this] egoism', wrote Paul Marion in his *Programme du Parti Populaire Français* (1938), and revive 'the taste for risk, the confidence in self, the sense of the group, the taste for collective *élans* and the memory of those unanimous faiths which made possible the cathedrals and the miracles of France'. Democracies lack this *beau idéal,* and consequently they fail to produce the heroes fascist societies do. Nor do most conservatives, even those of the royalist *Action Française,* often approach this ideal, bogged down as they are in material self-interest and bourgeois decadence, lacking dynamism and—according to Drieu La Rochelle at least—a certain necessary brutality: 'A monarchist is never a true fascist, because a monarchist is never a modern: he has not the brutality, the barbaric simplicity of the modern.'

It was this striking vision of man, perhaps more than anything else, which attracted figures like Drieu and Brasillach to fascism in the 1930s and was responsible for their eventual conversion. Certainly it was one of their most powerful motives for collaborating with the Germans after 1940. It was something which they did have in common with the Nazis, something which weighed more heavily in the scales of decision than the differences which separated them. Sickened by France's easy defeat, convinced that their countrymen had proven their decadence in that defeat, they looked to the Germans to provide Frenchmen with a new ideal to pattern themselves after, and they felt that the Germans presented such an ideal in what Drieu called the 'Hitlerian man', the new kind of conquering German forged by the Third Reich. As Bardèche said later, not only did nazism appear to him and his friends as the best agency available at the time for combatting communism and liberalism in Europe, but if the Germans lost the war there would be no chance at all of implementing 'the new idea

of man' which the Nazis embodied. Men like Bardèche collaborated
not so much because they agreed with each and every doctrine the
Germans espoused, but because they were enamoured of many of the
personal qualities of the invader, their vitality, their force, their capacity for struggle. Indeed, even at the end, in 1945, when all was lost
and nazism lay under a cloud of war crimes, Brasillach, writing in
prison while awaiting execution, would, partly to justify the cause
which had been his undoing, call attention to the last-ditch stand the
Germans had made against the Allies:

In these years when she had been hard on others, Germany showed
that she accepted, with the same hardness, the blows she received from
others. She proved, superabundantly, her vitality, her genius for adaptation, her courage, her heroism. Throughout her cities burned by phos-
phorous bombs, a whole people stiffened, and in the conquered countries
from which American and Russian power finally expelled him, the
German soldier, besieged as he was, fought with the energy of the outlaw
that some used to admire when their souls were loyal. . . . It is impossible
that all these virtues will be lost forever. They are part of the common
treasure of our civilization.

A final question remains. Was French fascism an ideology at all?
Was it, as some scholars have concluded, primarily a 'fever', a movement lacking clear-cut goals and doctrinal seriousness, a movement, to
quote Professor Weber, in which 'the ends of action count less than
action itself', a movement lacking 'an anterior plan or series of plans
inspired by the original doctrine'? Was it, as these scholars suggest,
essentially a romantic adventure, a kind of sentimental, emotional
fling whose participants were 'more interested in gestures than in doctrine', more concerned with style than substance, more apt to be irrational, subjective, and aesthetic in their approach to politics than
realistic, objective, and tough-minded? The trouble with descriptive
adjectives of this kind, of course, is that they have a way of rebound-
ing. In the first place, all ideologies no doubt have a certain emotional
content that affects their doctrines if it does not inspire them. There is
nothing very remarkable about French fascism in this respect. 'To treat
[political] ideas as the offspring of pure reason would be to assign them
a parentage about as mythological as that of Pallas Athene,' Sir Lewis
Namier once said. 'What matters most is the underlying emotions, the
music, to which ideas are a mere libretto, often of a very inferior
quality.' Secondly, most ideologies have what could be called a subjective vision of the good society (all value-systems, surely, are subjec-

tive in this sense), and most ideologies, certainly, are accompanied by a definite aesthetic of their own. To be sure, a man like Brasillach did speak of fascism as a 'poetry' and was fascinated by 'poetic' images, images of young men camping around fires at night, of mass meetings, of heroic exploits of the past—but then Marxism, too, has its conception of life in the classless society, and conservatives their idylls of the hallowed past. An image-laden vision of the good society—which few ideologies equate with the present society, with present objective reality —is hardly unique to French fascism and cannot be dismissed as mere 'subjectivism' or 'aestheticism'. Finally, French fascism was certainly as notable for its glorification of realism and pragmatism as for its expressions of 'romanticism'. Its belief that the strong triumph over the weak and that might makes right, its scorn for ivory-tower intellectuals divorced from concrete reality, its emphasis upon confronting the harsh 'facts' of life, its equation of violence with virility, its contempt for 'Romantics' who refuse to dirty their hands in political action— were all fundamental aspects of fascist 'realism'.

As to whether French fascists, realists or romantics, were seriously committed to a definite ideology or not, the evidence is mixed. Literary intellectuals like Drieu and Brasillach did often emphasize the spirit of fascism more than its programmes, and even Doriot, on one occasion at least, admitted that the doctrines of the PPF were 'insufficient and flabby' compared to the energy and force of its members. (Indeed, this emphasis upon spirit instead of doctrine made it that much easier for French fascism to penetrate the conservative Right during the 1920s and 30s, and for conservative attitudes to penetrate it.) Still, it would be wrong to conclude that French fascism was only a 'fever'. Its party programmes took quite explicit positions on the major issues of domestic and foreign policy, and even if some of its doctrines may be labelled romantic they were still doctrines. As suggested earlier, French fascism's disgust with all that was decadent and its cult of energy and force had important doctrinal consequences. Not only did France, the nation-state, have to be made strong again, but a new society had to be created to produce a new kind of man. In this, French fascists were just as doctrinaire as Lycurgus when he set out to legislate a new Spartan man into existence. Besides corporatism and an authoritarian state, French fascist writers called for 'a revolution of the body', a multiplication of athletic teams, scouting groups, hiking associations, youth hostels, sport stadiums, and above all, the eventual replacement of France's largest cities by colonies scattered through the countryside connected by ultrarapid means of communication. Only when the bodies of Frenchmen were freed from the dehumanizing effects of a purely urban existence, wrote Drieu La Rochelle, would they overcome the spiritual decadence that engulfed them. 'Thanks to us,' said Paul Marion of the PPF, 'the France of camping, of sports, of dances, of voyages, of collective hiking will sweep away the France of aperitifs, of tobacco dens, of party congresses and of long digestions.' According to Drieu, all the other reforms of fascism should be subordinated to the reform of the body, to what he called physical reform:

. . . the physical reform of man must be our immediate enterprise, inasmuch as it is the most urgent task before us, and it must be instituted concurrently with the reform of the economy; in fact, the reform of the economy must take its lead from the necessities of physical reform (which is the essential programme of the fascist revolution).

Not only did French fascism have a definite ideology, as should be clear by now, but it was a highly moralistic, highly serious-minded one. Indeed, despite its glorification of realism and force, perhaps the most striking thing about this ideology was its *moralism,* its righteous indignation at all it deemed decadent and its zealous determination to root out sinfulness (e.g. weakness) wherever it was found. Bardèche remarks in *Qu'est-ce que le Fascisme?,* for instance, that no regime is more concerned with the 'moral health' of a society than a fascist regime, and this is why fascism devotes itself to 'the systematic elimination of all that discourages, dirties, or disgusts'. Democracies, on the other hand, are known for their moral laxity:

[Democracies] allow all aspects of life to be open to all sorts of inundations, to all sorts of miasma, to all sorts of fetid winds, building as they do no dikes against decadence, expropriation, and especially mediocrity. They have us live on a steppe where anyone can invade us. There is only one purely negative password: to defend liberty. . . . The monsters who make their nest on this steppe, the rats, the toads, the snakes, they transform it into a cesspool. . . . As for mediocrity, it takes over like an insidious poison in peoples whom democracies cram with education without ever giving them a goal and an ideal; it is the leper of the souls of our time.

It was this kind of moralism which led many French fascists to risk public animosity and even death in behalf of their cause—and which also led them to condone some of the most authoritarian and ugly political acts of their times.

Suggested Additional Readings

I. ORIGINS AND DEFINITIONS OF FASCISM

Arendt, Hannah. *The Origins of Totalitarianism.* Cleveland, Ohio: Meridian Books, Inc., 1958.

Fromm, Erich. *Escape From Freedom.* New York: Avon Books, 1965.

Pulzer, Peter G. L. *The Rise of Political Anti-Semitism in Germany and Austria.* New York: John Wiley & Sons, Inc., 1964.

Rogger, Hans, and Weber, Eugen (eds.). *The European Right: A Historical Profile.* Berkeley, California: University of California Press, 1965.

Weber, Eugen. *Varieties of Fascism.* Princeton, New Jersey: Anvil Books, 1964.

Weiss, John. *The Fascist Tradition.* New York: Harper & Row, Publishers, 1967.

II. THE ITALIAN EXAMPLE

Chabod, Federico. *A History of Italian Fascism.* London: Weidenfeld & Nicolson Ltd., 1963.

Deakin, F. W. *The Brutal Friendship: Mussolini, Hitler, and the Fall of Italian Fascism.* New York: Harper & Row, Publishers, 1962.

Fermi, Laura. *Mussolini.* Chicago: University of Chicago Press, 1961.

Finer, Herman. *Mussolini's Italy.* Hamden, Connecticut: Archon Books, 1964.

Germino, Dante L. *The Italian Fascist Party in Power.* Minneapolis, Minnesota: University of Minnesota, 1959.

Hughes, H. Stuart. *The United States and Italy,* rev. ed. Cambridge: Harvard University Press, 1965.

Kirkpatrick, Ivonne. *Mussolini: A Study in Power.* New York: Hawthorn Books, Inc., 1964.

Mussolini, Benito. *My Autobiography.* New York: Charles Scribner's Sons, 1928.

Salvemini, Gaetano. *The Fascist Dictatorship in Italy.* New York: Howard Fertig, Inc., 1966.

Wiskemann, Elizabeth. *The Rome-Berlin Axis.* New York: Oxford University Press, Inc., 1949.

III. HITLER AND NATIONAL SOCIALISM

Allen, William Sheridan. *The Nazi Seizure of Power.* Chicago: Quadrangle Books, Inc., 1965.

Davidson, Eugene. *The Trial of the Germans: Nuremberg, 1945–1946.* New York: The Macmillan Company, 1966.

Eyck, Erich. *A History of the Weimar Republic,* 2 vols. Cambridge: Harvard University Press, 1963.

Halperin, S. William. *Germany Tried Democracy.* New York: W. W. Norton & Company, Inc., 1965.

Heiden, Konrad. *Der Führer.* Boston: Houghton Mifflin Company, 1944.

Hitler, Adolf. *Mein Kampf.* Boston: Sentry Editions, n.d.

Mayer, Milton. *They Thought They Were Free: The Germans, 1933–1945.* Chicago: Phoenix Books, 1965.

Mosse, George L. *The Crisis of German Ideology: Intellectual Origins of the Third Reich.* New York: Universal Library, 1964.

————. *Nazi Culture.* New York: Grosset & Dunlap, Inc., 1966.

Neumann, Franz. *Behemoth: The Structure and Practice of National Socialism.* New York: Harper & Row, Publishers, 1966.

Taylor, A. J. P. *The Course of German History.* New York: G. P. Putnam Sons, 1962.

Trevor-Roper, Hugh. *The Last Days of Hitler.* New York: The Macmillan Company, 1947.

IV. POETRY AND FASCISM: SPAIN AND FRANCE

Carr, Raymond. *Spain, 1808–1939.* New York: Oxford University Press, Inc., 1966.

Jackson, Gabriel. *The Spanish Republic and Civil War, 1931–1939.* Princeton, New Jersey: Princeton University Press, 1965.

Ramirez, Luis. *Francisco Franco.* Paris: Français Maspero, 1965.

de la Souchère, Elena. *An Explanation of Spain.* New York: Random House, 1964.

Micaud, Charles A. *The French Right and Nazi Germany.* New York: Octagon Books, Inc., 1964.

Plumyène, Jean, and Lasierra, Raymond. *Les Fascismes français, 1923–1963.* Paris: Editions Du Seuil, 1963.

Rémond, René. *The Right Wing in France from 1815 to de Gaulle.* Philadelphia: University of Pennsylvania Press, 1966.

Werth, Alexander. *The Twilight of France, 1933–1940.* New York: Howard Fertig, Inc., 1966.